LIFE IS WITH PEOPLE

LIFE IS WITH PEOPLE

The Culture of the Shtetl

MARK ZBOROWSKI AND ELIZABETH HERZOG

FOREWORD BY MARGARET MEAD

Schocken Books • New York

First SCHOCKEN PAPERBACK *edition 1962*

Second printing, 1964
Third printing, 1965

This edition is published by arrangement with
International Universities Press, Inc.

To

RUTH BENEDICT

Library of Congress Catalog Card No. 62-13141
Manufactured in the United States of America

CONTENTS

Part III

. . . INTO GOOD DEEDS . . .

Part IV

. . . INTO MARRIAGE . . .

Part V

AS THE SHTETL SEES THE WORLD

FOREWORD

Human cultures are the most distinctive creations of human beings, drawing as they do not only upon the special contributions of the singularly gifted, but upon the imagination, explicit and implicit, of every man, woman and child who live within them, and through them, and who, each generation, remodel the traditions which they have received from their cultural ancestors. But although human cultures are the most distinctive creations of the human, they are also the most fragile, for they live primarily in the habituated beings of living persons. Like a dance, for which the music and the choreography have never been written down, a great part of any human culture is lost to humanity when the group which has carried it, devotedly, in every word and gesture, is dispersed, or destroyed, or forsakes the traditional ways for ways which are new. Patient historical and archaeological work—once a culture has vanished—may bring us back fragments of drama, dance positions copied from a vase, epitaphs and inscriptions; we may try to reconstruct the stuff of comedy from a row of gargoyles on a medieval cathedral, or the ecstasies of the worshipers of Dionysus from a few lines of verse— the very cadence of which is not certain. From such historical studies, something is saved to become part of the rich inheritance of all future men and women—often enough is saved to fire the imagination and evoke the nostalgia of the gifted in many succeeding generations. But much is lost.

Anthropology has been, by the very nature of its original subject matter, the study of those peoples who by accidents of geography have remained outside the main currents of history, living their lives in special and unfamiliar ways—the science which has been devoted to catching the essence of a culture just as it was changing forever into something new and strange—sometimes after almost all the human beings who had once participated in its highly stylized rituals and joys, had themselves suffered a sea change, forgotten their mother tongue, put on the clothes and the habits of an emigrant or an immigrant group. This experience, gained from piecing together the memories of old warriors, the tones which linger on in a grandmother's voice, and the gay little games of children which still carry the form, although they have lost the content of the past, is part of what an anthropologist brings to the study of any culture—a capacity to listen to the broken accents of the present, and reconstitute the whole which was the immediate past. Anthropologists do not work primarily with documents—and when they do they work differently—nor with potshards, except as they draw on the help of archaeologists. We work with living materials, although sometimes the eyes which look backward are already failing with age, and the hand that demonstrates to us how a gesture should be made, or a tool shaped, is tremulous and uncertain.

This book is an anthropological study of a culture which no longer exists, except in the memories, and in the partial and altered behavior of its members, now scattered over the world, rearing their children in new ways, to be Americans or Israelis, as members of collective farms in the changed lands of Eastern Europe. Within another generation this culture of Eastern European Jews, who lived in the small towns and enclaves within the area stretching from the eastern borders of Germany to the western regions of Tzarist Russia (embracing Poland, Galicia, Lithuania, White Russia, the Ukraine, Bessarabia, Slovakia, and the northeastern regions of Hungary) will no longer be represented perfectly in any single human being. There will be rich historical records, stories and plays and folklore, learned commentaries and exhaustive compilations of data, but the people will be gone, their children will be making their lives of new stuff. With the traditional capacity of the Jews to preserve the past, while transmuting it into a breathing relationship to the present, much of the faith and hope which lived in the shtetl will inform the lives of the descendants of the shtetl in other lands. But the laughter will change, has changed already in Iowa or Israel or Queensland. Perhaps not soon again will there be Jewish communities of which a personal God is so much a living reality that people can say, with the smile one has for the very cherished, "If God lived in the shtetl, He'd have His windows broken."

This book is an attempt to bring our anthropological discipline to the task of preserving something of the form and the content, the texture and beauty, of the small-town life of Eastern European Jews, as it was lived before World War I, in some places up to World War II, as it still lives in the memories of those who were reared in the shtetl, and in the memories of Jews in other lands, who can remember the stories their grandparents told, the tremendous happy worrying bustle with which the holidays were prepared for, the unrelenting eagerness with which a grandfather tested his grandson for signs of intellectual worth. It lives on, more than a little, in the memories of those who, themselves without any Jewish birthright, nevertheless have at some point warmed their hands by a shtetl fire, or sharpened their wits against the many-faceted polishing stone of talmudic reasoning. As the people of Eastern Europe have emigrated over the world, the first generation immigrants have carried to the countries of the west, something of this way of life, which could in turn be incorporated in some slight part, by the immigrants from other countries who lived in the new street, by the rural descendants of earlier comers, who loitered and wondered—as I did as a child—in some shop where a craftsman mended shoes, with patient hands, and spoke the while in many tongues, until my own daydream of somehow learning many languages, became informed with the possibility.

To understand what has been attempted in this book, it is necessary to go back a decade, to the particular interests which some of us who worked with Ruth Benedict began to develop during World War II, when, unable to go into the field to study the primitive peoples of the world, and spurred by the threat of a totalitarianism which threatened irrevocably to destroy much of what men had made to live by, we considered how our anthropological training could be applied to practical wartime problems of understanding what was happening in Europe and in Asia. My first interest in the possibility of studying Eastern European Jewish culture came in a conversation with Erich Fromm, as the intricate integrity of a traditional ritual came to life in his voice as he talked of one of the Eastern European Jewish religious movements. Anthropologists work with contrast, and I glimpsed for a moment what one might learn, if one followed Jews, who had themselves a cultural tradition as distinct as this, as they also adapted to and absorbed the cultures of other countries, Poland, Russia, Austria, Hungary, Roumania. At the same time Ruth Benedict began working on European cultures, working at a distance, trying to piece together from the accounts of exiles and the evidence of history and literature, something of the culture of Roumania and Poland, Hungary and Holland and Italy, to provide some guidance to our wartime efforts, as we attempted to nourish the resistance movements in these inaccessible countries. Among her informants, there were always many Jews, who found the sort of questions which she asked stimulating and interesting, matching her disciplined anthropological comparativeness with their experience of having lived in a world which included always at least two cultures, that of Jews and that of the particular nation among whom they lived. As she listened and questioned and recorded, she began to wonder if it would be possible to study systematically what was consistently the Jewish cultural element which distinguished the perception of a Hungarian or Polish Jew from a Hungarian or a Pole, whose antecedents were Christian.

When the war was over an opportunity to develop further our wartime methods was given us in the project which Ruth Benedict inaugurated, Columbia University Research in Contemporary Cultures, under a grant from the Office of Naval Research. Here, without the pressures for immediate application to the practical problems of writing propaganda leaflets or briefing men who were to be parachuted down behind the Nazi lines, we were free to experiment with the methods we had developed, to test and refine the requirements of working on cultures at a distance, whether that distance was provided by time, so that we worked with cultures which no longer existed as organized societies, but only in the minds of individuals, and the interrelations of individual families—like that of pre-Soviet Russia and of the shtetl; or distance provided by man-made barriers in the present, as in present-day Czechoslovakia, or China. As we planned which cultures we would study, we decided together to undertake a study of the Jews in each of the cultures in which we were interested. So as originally planned we would have had a study of Czech Jews, Russian Jews, Polish Jews, to parallel our general studies of Czech, Russian and Polish cultures. In spite of the glimpse we had both had of the cultural distinctiveness of Eastern European Jewish behavior, we still thought of a Polish Jew primarily as a Pole who was Jewish, by religion and upbringing and habits of intermarrying within his own group, just as we thought of Jewish Americans as Americans with special traditional religious and social practices of their own. Words like the ghetto still meant for us unwilling segregation of a people who had every wish to be simply part of a wider community. When we read Kurt Lewin's famous little essay on the greater security of the Jewish inhabitant of an all-Jewish, semiclosed community—this still had no vivid cultural meaning for us.

So the project started, with a group of workers assigned to gathering materials on Jews in different parts of Europe, and Ruth Benedict asked Professor Conrad Arensberg of Columbia University to act as convener of the group, who though himself non-Jewish was in accord with her about the importance to anthropology of direct comparison of European cultures and the need for a study of Jewish backgrounds in the terms of cultural anthropology, for themselves and for an understanding of American society. In the Columbia project, we have learned to work in groups, so that workers of both sexes, different types of background, and training may bring their combined insight to bear on the material which is gathered and prepared for the group by each one. We also have tried to make it a rule to include in each working group, members of the culture which we are studying as well as members of other cultures, to ensure the type of understanding which comes from combining deep personal participation in a culture with the insights that come from contrast, and from disciplined anthropological methods. As the seminar studying Jews began to work, it became clearer and clearer, to the anthropologists among them, that we were not merely dealing with differences among Poles or among Ukrainians which could be referred to a difference in religious faith, in occupational opportunity, or traditional social position in the society, but with a living whole, that the Eastern European Jews had in fact a living culture, which was essentially all of a piece whether they paid their taxes and marketed in Polish or Ukrainian or Hungarian, or were ruled by Czar or Emperor. We realized this with growing excitement for while all anthropologists have the experience of working out the essential form of the cultures which they study, we seldom have the experience of discovering the existence of a whole at which we had not guessed.

The record of what this discovery meant to us is different, as we differed in our past experience; for Ruth Benedict and myself it tied together all the half-understood glimpses which we had had, as we had listened to the comments of Jews from various Eastern European backgrounds, integrating the mass of unrelated individual experiences with Eastern European Jews which we had had through the years, the gift that had somehow been unexpected and out of context, the sudden withdrawal of assent in the face of some remark which had seemed quite usual. For Conrad Arensberg, the Jewish shtetl community merged against his field study of the Irish countryman and his wide sociological acquaintance with traditional rural and peasant cultures in Europe, America and Asia. For him, thus, the structural connections between such a community and its culture evoked many parallels and raised many problems for community study and the analysis of social structure. Against the traditional peasant values of Eastern Europe the Jewish values contrasted sharply; their parallels to those of congregational communities elsewhere, as in early New England and the Levant, made them fruitful subjects for further study still to come. For those in the group who were of East European Jewish background, the half-understood tones in their parents' voices became newly meaningful, for those with an East European orthodox past, the sharp contrasts between the old culture and the new were redrawn.

The crucial person in our seminar group was Mark Zborowski, who combined in one person the living experience of shtetl culture in the Ukraine and Poland and the disciplines of history and anthropology through which to interpret his memories and readings, and the new materials which members of the project collected from interviews and written materials. For him, this book is the realization of a plan cherished for many years and discussed with Dr. Benedict at the beginning of the project. Elizabeth Herzog brought a social science background and varied experience in social research, especially in the area of opinion and attitude analysis, combined with her skill as a writer. Together, using the work of the group as a basis, they have developed the analysis and presentation offered in this book.

Natalie F. Joffe, anthropologist, brought the fruit of many years' experience in the study of special aspects of immigrant cultures in the United States; long association with Ruth Benedict and with me; unusually extensive reading; and close contact with her parents' knowledge of the Yiddish language, literature, and shtetl life. Naomi Chaitman, in addition to her outstanding skill as an interviewer, brought her anthropological training and a living experience with Eastern European Jewish culture, gained in the learned environment of her parents' home and through wide contacts with the Jewish community in Montreal and in New York. Sula Benet brought her own Russian and Polish background and her many years' study of the culture of the Polish peasantry; Theodore Bienenstok his familiarity with his native Polish Jewish culture and training in the fields of law and sociology; Irene Rozeney an anthropological training which assisted her in interpreting her dual cultural experience of living first in Poland and then in France.

Toward the end of the project the group was joined by three members of the Department of Scientific Research of the American Jewish Committee: Ruth Landes contributed her broad and rich anthropological experience and her second generation acquaintance with the culture. Fay Stollman and Harold Mendelsohn brought sociological training and acquaintance with the culture through their families.

At different times, others contributed to the work of the group: Elsa Bernaut, Denise Freudmann, Paul Garvin, Louise Giventer, Fela Gibel, Thelma Goldberg, Ruth Hallo, Hsien Chin Hu, Norman Miller, Sidney Mintz, Marion Marcovitz, Joan Nicklin, Julius Rabin, Vera Rubin, Rosemary Spiro, Rose Wolfson.

Of great value in the analysis were documents prepared by May Edel describing the Brownsville community of New York; and by Celia Stopnicka Rosenthal in the seminar conducted by Ruth Benedict, describing in detail the life of her native town in Poland.

Our method was a combination of interviewing Eastern European Jews, observing life in Eastern European Jewish households, and analyzing history and literature, drama and pictorial records, analysis of films. These materials were shared by the research group, who together, working and talking in the very rhythms of the culture about which they were learning, developed a conceptual understanding. In traditional anthropology, a disciplined member of western anthropology has gone into the field to use all five senses, and every ounce of intellectual energy that could be mustered for the task, to understand the complexities of an alien culture. In this new kind of anthropology, members of different disciplines, from different modern cultures, work together, using the senses, the memories, the perceptions and insights, the organizational skills and capacity to develop and test hypotheses, of the different members of the group, as a delicate and unique research tool. There were long sessions in which the protest of women educated in the west was mixed with the zeal of the anthropologists in search of the cultural truth, as we battled over the question as to whether women had really been conceived as having souls—in the shtetl—however fair the promise that the good wife of a good man might sit at his feet in "the World to Come," and listen to the endless learned conversations in which he would spend the future life. In the sharpness of the discussion, the attitude of the men, who "just didn't talk about women's souls" became clearer; more interviewing was recognized as necessary, and we re-examined together an interview with a shtetl-born woman who summed the question up aptly, "Women have the real souls, but men have the *recognized* souls." So, for the interplay which is provided by village life in an ongoing society, we substituted the microcosm of the seminar, which mirrored the dialectics of the shtetl.

In working out this portrait of the shtetl, for it is a portrait rather than a series of photographs, a composite picture of a way

of life, not the factual record of a single village, there was reflected all the special problems of writing about Jewish culture,
as well as the more general ones of writing about any modern
literate culture. One of the special characteristics of Jewish culture is that it is the culture of a people who have lived as communities within a larger society, who themselves did not constitute a nation, and who therefore had always to include in any
picture of themselves the picture which their neighbors, who belonged within the same state but had a different culture, had of
them. In every society any group which is highly differentiated
culturally from other groups has the task of dealing with an
image of themselves which includes all the ways in which they
separate themselves from the others, both self-approving and
self-deprecatory, but also the ways in which the others separate
themselves from them. So we find between men and women, in
most societies, a series of beliefs about themselves and about
each other, some of which are highly flattering, some derogatory.
This is true also as between country people and city dwellers, between those who work with their hands and those who work with
words, between the young and the old. Each group proclaims its
superiority in some respects and admits openly or covertly, inferiority in others. So the Jews of Eastern Europe, living side by
side with Poles and Ukrainians and Hungarians, have maintained
strong positive images of themselves, but attended also to the
negative images held by their neighbors, the while they elaborated
negative images of their neighbors, openly, and positive images
covertly. The very self-definition of the Jews as God's Chosen
People, the People who were willing to accept the onerous
burden of His Covenant, includes in it the concept of the un-
chosen, who must somehow be reckoned with. And side by side
was the traditional Christian world, with its self-images set
against the contrasting image of the Jewish community. As the
non-Jewish serving maid learned to enforce the dietary laws by
which her employers lived, so in the schools of Poland little Jewish boys, committed by their culture to value learning and piety
above physical prowess, read the stories of Polish heroes, with
admiration as well as with the required disapproval, and that
covert admiration has perhaps played a part in the new Israeli

patriotism. In working out a picture of East European Jewish culture, the research group which contained both Jews and Gentiles, both those who stemmed from Eastern Europe and those who did not, the double images of the self and of the other, had to be brought to the light, and examined with scrupulous care. That this was done by a group who, regardless of origin, took delight in the culture of the shtetl, is not so much a statement of bias, as a statement of the kind of emotional atmosphere in which cultures, like the character of individuals, are safe. We looked closely at the negative images, as well as the positive. We looked at the uncompromising orthodoxy which denied to the worshipers of images a living faith. And we looked at the neighbors who could so split their hearts and consciences that, while they protected Jews whom they knew as individuals from harm, they could take part in pogroms against other Jews. The ambivalence remains, part of the self-picture and the picture drawn from the outside, which is inevitable when culture and larger group membership are not identical, when one lives and speaks as a member of a distinct culture within a larger social group, and yet cherishes his historic identity.

This book has been designed to present as a whole the culture of Eastern European Jews, giving the common core which was shared by all of them, however great the local difference. We have kept the number of ethnographic details low, partly so as to keep the central themes uncluttered, partly because details do vary from locality to locality, and small differences will destroy for the reader familiar with one area a sense of the overriding regularities which distinguish this culture as a whole. This monograph can be regarded as a primary source on Eastern European Jewish culture, based as all primary sources are in anthropology on first-hand observation of and listening to living human beings.

As our understanding grows of the way in which human beings have created cultures for themselves, within which and through which they can live, so also our recognition of the value of each culture has grown. Where the past often offered to men membership in the culture to which their parents had belonged, and only curious spectatorship of every other culture, the findings of history and anthropology make available, to all literate peo-

ple, not only the records of their own past but also the cultures
of other peoples, to be learned, and cherished, as the great works
of art and the musical themes of different civilizations become
part of the common treasure of all cultivated human beings. This
book, this record of a whole way of life, has been written from
the inside, where the mother's tears of mingled joy and sorrow
glistened through her fingers as she lit the Sabbath candles. It has
been written from the inside, purposely, for only so can the
inner meaning be lighted up, to be shared by the literate world.
But the inside picture has also been seen with a perspective drawn
from outside, a perspective gained not only through the eyes of
other cultures but also through the disciplines represented in the
group. The shtetl life, as described here, has disappeared, partly
as a result of the Bolshevik Revolution but largely through the
violence of the Nazi occupation. Many of its values will survive
among those with shtetl ancestry now living in other countries,
where other kinds of thread draw gossamer distinctions different
from the Sabbath thread which walled off symbolically, the
shtetl from the outer world. An organized systematic knowledge
of the culture from which they came, in addition to a scientific
account of a culture, should contribute to a new understanding
of these values. But this book has further implications for Americans of all kinds, all beliefs, every origin, from Africa, China or
Europe, who as they have learned ways in which diverse peoples
may live together, also have as their cultural birthright a share
in the traditions of each.

MARGARET MEAD

American Museum of Natural History
New York City, May, 1951

PREFACE

The purpose of this book is to present a study of a culture: the culture of the shtetl, the small-town Jewish community of Eastern Europe. It is an attempt to show the special ways in which these people have met the problems common to all mankind.

It is a culture that is not remote. On the contrary, it is one with which many have had direct or indirect contact, through its representatives or their descendants. Therefore the bringing together and interrelating of its features and details—those that are familiar, those that have been dimly sensed, those that were unknown—may have a special significance for many people. Brought together so that main culture themes and patterns can be perceived, these heretofore scattered items permit an understanding that for many feels fresh and new. This has been so for the authors themselves and for those who have read or heard about the material presented here.

"Now I understand—" is a very frequent response to this material. It may be an understanding of one's own parents, of one's friends and neighbors. Or it may be an understanding of the ways of a people known only through literary or historical appreciation, through casual or second-hand contacts, or through stereotypes. The aim has not been an understanding of individuals, but since the individual is the carrier of the culture an integrated portrayal of the culture may also illuminate the individuals who, directly or indirectly, have been affected by it.

For its inhabitants, the shtetl is less the physical town than the people who live in it. "My shtetl" means my community, and community means the Jewish community. Traditionally, the human rather than the physical environment has always been given primary importance. Emphasis on the Jewish portion of the community was inevitable, for historical developments had excluded it from membership in the larger community. Socially and legally it was an entity in itself, subject to special laws and responsible—within strict limits—for regulating and conducting itself.

It must be emphasized that this is a portrait of a culture and not a photograph or a diagram. Its subject matter is not ethnographic minutiae but rather prevailing patterns. It is, moreover, a composite portrait. Despite countless local variations, the Jews of Eastern Europe had one culture, possessing the characteristics that mark a culture: a language, a religion, a set of values, a specific constellation of social mechanisms and institutions, and the feeling of its members that they belong to one group. The effort has been to capture the core of continuity running through the Jewish culture of Eastern Europe rather than the details in which localities and regions differed. Where forms are described, the most representative one has been selected; or only the basic features have been reported, minimizing the details that vary from place to place.

The culture portrayed is that of the shtetl and not that of all Jews. Much that is reported would not be true for Jews in large cities of Eastern Europe during the period covered by this study, and certainly not for German Jews or those in other countries. At the same time, certain values and certain patterns have their counterparts in any Jewish culture. All trace their descent back to the same historical root and share the same biblical tradition. The extent to which certain values or observances are common to all groups would be a subject for further research, as would the striking congeniality between certain characteristics and values of the shtetl and of the United States. In some respects the two cultures show remarkable parallels, while in others the contrast is equally striking.

Because the core culture is the subject of study, no effort has been made to cover all the shades and levels of acculturation as expressed during the twentieth century in such developments as secularized schools, modifications of dress, political and labor activities, and generally increased participation in the life of the larger society. Nor has there been an attempt to rehearse historical events in sequence. The effort is to portray the living culture rather than to trace the origin of its manifestations. The emphasis is on interrelations rather than on initial causes.

The present tense is used, but it is the historical present. Basically the picture is pre-World War I, although for some areas it held true up to the beginning of World War II. The life described here no longer exists. People and culture have been destroyed, and soon it will be too late to find the models for a living picture. Yet, despite destruction and transplantation, something of the culture endures in new places and in modified forms; just as some essence of the tradition has always survived death and destruction.

The methods employed are those worked out in the Columbia University Research in Contemporary Cultures and described in its official statement: "The project employs some standard procedures of anthropology . . . and has developed some additional lines of research. The interviewing techniques of field anthropology . . . are checked and augmented by . . . intensive analysis of selective written materials, films, photographs, and other data. Interview data are analyzed with a view to building up a systematic picture of main regularities . . . within the culture. These regularities are viewed in their relation to the institutions of the societies that produced them.

"Cultural anthropology provides the methods used to check the findings, drawn from intensive interviewing, against the formal patterns of a culture and also furnishes methods for analyzing folklore, social organization, ritual behavior, and similar problems. . . . During the last ten years these methods have been used effectively in the United States for study of contemporary cultures which were inaccessible to field study because of wartime conditions.

"The methods described are necessarily inappropriate for the establishment of statistical frequencies of any sort. They are concerned with main regularities . . . not with establishing to what degree some particular facet of these regularities is manifested in any given group, or at any particular time."

The present study is drawn primarily from life, although literature, drama, films, graphic materials and other sources have been used to check and to supplement the findings of interview-

ing and observation. Direct quotations used in the book are taken
from intensive and in many cases frequently repeated interviews
with 128 informants who had migrated to New York from the
shtetl and with ten more whose parents had come from there.
These direct interviews have been reinforced by a great deal of
less formal and concentrated interviewing.

In addition to oral interviews, about fifty extensive life his-
tories were available from the collection of the Yiddish Scientific
Institute—Yivo. All of this material was enriched by the experience of those members of the group who had first-hand acquaintance with the culture.

Literary sources have been subsidiary to material obtained
from informants, but have been of indispensable help in getting
both confirmation and perspective—that is, in checking the existence, the dimensions and the incidence of the patterns and
features described by the informants.

The chief religious and academic references are given in
the bibliography, but it would be impossible to list all the Yiddish and Hebrew literary and autobiographical works that have
contributed as background to this study. Yet the works of such
writers as Sholem Aleichem, Mendele Mocher Sforim, Perez, Ash,
and others, have probably contributed more than the academic
discussions. It is feasible only to acknowledge in general terms a
debt to all the many writers, living and dead, whose names are
not mentioned here.

All quotations from informants are given verbatim, without
change of tense or grammatical construction. We felt that the
culture could speak most clearly through their own unedited
words. Apparently many of the informants sensed the nature of
the interviewing. One of them protested when a fellow informant
tried to introduce secondary sources: "You are telling her what
you read in books and what you heard. Books she can read herself, she doesn't have to ask you. She wants to know what I saw
. . . so let me tell it my way."

In order to differentiate them from the many others that are
used, all quotations from informants are followed by the typo-
graphical sign°.

Sayings and proverbs are quoted freely, as are prayers and

those phrases or passages from Bible or Talmud that have become part of shtetl idiom. With minor changes, the translations of the prayers are those of Rabbi Hertz.* Folk songs follow the versions given in Ausubel's *Treasury of Jewish Folklore.** Legends are based on the translations in Ginzberg's *Legends of the Jews.** For permission to use this material, we thank the authors and the publishers: Bloch Publishing Co., New York; Crown Publishers, Inc., New York; Jewish Publication Society, Philadelphia.

That the transliteration of Yiddish words offers a difficult problem is suggested by the existence of several conflicting methods. True to the spirit of the shtetl, the authors have not followed any one of these entirely. Basically we have tried to adhere as much as possible to the system adopted by the Yiddish Scientific Institute. Modifications have been made, however, in order to represent the words in the way most likely to be pronounced correctly by an American reader not familiar with scholarly phonetic symbols. This aim is almost impossible to fulfill, and the results represent the fruit of long and earnest struggle. Two major changes have been incorporated: doubling of a consonant in order to encourage correct pronunciation of the preceding vowel, and adding an "h" after a final "e" in order to prevent its being interpreted as silent. A few words such as Bar Mitzvah and Torah are familiar in English and for these the most common spelling has been retained, even when it conflicted with the system generally followed and with the shtetl pronunciation. Differences in grammatical form and number are indicated in the Glossary, where the Hebrew derivation is also shown.

The number of Yiddish words and phrases used was a shock to the authors when the Glossary was compiled. It can only be said that this is about half as many as the first version boasted. It is perhaps characteristic of the culture that for one who knows Yiddish—and for many who do not—the Yiddish words are so rich in flavor and in color that no translation seems satisfactory. Yiddish words are italicized the first time, and only the first time, they appear.

This book is a continuation of work done by a group, and

*See Bibliography, pp. 431–32

the authors are indebted to each member for his share. Two people contributed most directly. Each chapter was discussed with Natalie Joffe and Naomi Chaitman. This consultation was in addition to the initial contribution of each—the magnificent interviewing done by Naomi Chaitman and the investigation of background sources by Natalie Joffe, as well as her discussion of some basic aspects of the culture. (See Bibliography.)

The book is dedicated to the late Ruth Benedict. No words are attempted in this dedication because no words are adequate to express the feelings evoked by that name, in those who knew her well and who worked closely with her: the appreciation of intellectual giving, guiding and inciting to growth; the sense of grandeur that was of the mind and of the spirit; the simple, glowing affection for her as a human being. For the authors there is a special sense of loss in the fact that she did not read this book which grew out of work with her.

To Margaret Mead we owe a threefold appreciation. It was she on whom the leadership of the project rested after Dr. Benedict's death, and who sustained the continuity of the work and eventually brought about the writing of the book. Her chairmanship brought stimulation to the group discussions and provoked an atmosphere of lively question and exchange of ideas in which new light was thrown on specific aspects of the culture. We are grateful also for the complete freedom accorded, once the group sessions had ended and the writing of the book began—freedom to analyze and to integrate the material collected. This freedom is the more appreciated since she took time to read and comment on the book as it progressed.

We are indebted to Conrad Arensberg for his contribution as convener of the group and the perspective added by his experience in community studies, which helped greatly in working out the interrelations of various features of the culture, as well as in viewing it in comparison to other cultures.

From the outset, the problems of production were greatly eased by the interested and understanding help of Leila Lee, the Office Manager of the project.

In all stages of progress we have received constant help from

Regina Zborowski, who served as informant, as critic, as discussant and often as moral support.

For generously putting at our disposal its rich collections of personal documents, of books and of graphic materials, and for frequent consultation with members of its staff, we are deeply indebted to the Yiddish Scientific Institute—Yivo.

All the examination and all the analysis that went into this book would have been impossible without the informants who supplied the chief nucleus of the data. The readiness with which they gave their information, the quality of what they gave, their acceptance of the interviewers who questioned them, are expressions of the culture itself as well as of their feeling for it. The only adequate return for their help would be an adequate picture of their shtetl, and we hope it has been given.

E. Herzog

M. Zborowski

Prologue

THE ROAD TO THE SHTETL

The small-town Jewish community of Eastern Europe—the *shtetl*—traces its line of march directly back to Creation. The Exodus from Egypt, the giving of the Law on Mount Sinai, are seen as steps along the way, historical events no less real than the Spanish Inquisition or the Russian Revolution.

For the world at large, the record is more obscure. In the oldest inscriptions of the Egyptian and Babylonian kings, no mention is made of the Hebrews who, among other Semitic and non-Semitic tribes, guided their flocks from oasis to oasis in the area between Mesopotamia and the Jordan. No scribe registered their entrance into Egypt under the scourge of famine, and none recorded their dramatic departure under the leadership of Moses. Among the bloody battles between the Egyptian armies and the invaders of Syria and Asia Minor, the conquests of Joshua passed unheeded.

Even the unification of the clans under the warrior-king David failed to impress the ancient chroniclers. The name of Solomon, great builder of the Temple, is known only through the records of his own people. The history of the kingdoms of Judah and Israel, until their destruction in the eighth and sixth centuries B.C., had meaning chiefly for the scribes of the Bible.

This small and insignificant people has been, for most of its long history, a people without dominion. The road from Mount Sinai to the shtetl was over three thousand years long and during only a few centuries of that time was Israel an independent nation. Its actual independence ended when the Babylonian invaders destroyed the Temple of Solomon and exiled the population of Jerusalem in the sixth century B.C.

Although the Babylonian exile was brief and the Temple was restored, the Jews did not regain full sovereignty. Along with

29

other Asiatic kingdoms, they were subjected successively to the authority of Persia, Greece and Rome. The daring revolt of the Maccabees against the successors of Alexander the Great did create an illusion of independence, but it was lost less than two hundred years later, when Palestine became a Roman province. The Jews tried to repeat the exploit of the Maccabees, this time against the Roman Emperors, but after several years of desperate struggle the legions of Titus broke their resistance. When the Second Temple was destroyed and the city of Jerusalem was burned in 70 A.D. the Jewish nation ceased to exist as a political entity. For the next twenty centuries the Children of Israel lived in the Diaspora, in Exile, the dispersion among the nations. Jerusalem remained a symbol of the glorious past and of the eternal hope for the future.

When they went into exile, they left behind few tangible traces of their culture—far too few shards and structures to satisfy archeologists of a later day. They took with them the key expressions of their existence as a sovereign people—the Presence of their God, the Law He had handed down to them upon Mount Sinai, and their faith in His Covenant. According to the shtetl, the Children of Israel have survived solely because of the Covenant made with God in accepting His Law. Some outsiders, who question the historicity of the event, nevertheless hold that the idea of the Covenant is responsible for the survival of a folk whose material culture had all but disappeared from the land that was their home, leaving the Wailing Wall as the traditional concrete evidence of their sway.

It is the Covenant with God, says the shtetl, that has enabled a weak and homeless people to survive the great empires of Egypt and Babylon, Greece and Rome, Byzantium and Islam, and has caused their sacred books to enter into the Holy Writ of half the world.

The legend tells that before God gave His Law to Israel He went among all the nations of the earth, asking of each, "Will you accept my Torah, my Law?" All refused it, saying, "We do not want Thy Torah!" Upon this, the legend says, He came to Israel and spoke to them: "Will ye accept the Torah?" They said to Him, "What is written therein?" He answered, "Six hundred and thirteen commandments." They said, "All that the Lord has spoken we will do and we will hear."

Under the Covenant, the people of Israel are bound to accept God as their only God. They are bound also to fulfill all His commandments, the six hundred and thirteen precepts included in the original Law as handed down on Mount Sinai. The Eternal One, on the other hand, agreed in the Covenant to cherish Israel as His Chosen People among all the nations. It is His privilege to punish any failure to live up to the pact, and it is their right to reap the promised rewards if they fulfill their part of the agreement.

This was the Law that the Jews took with them into exile, at a time when political and military misfortune had enhanced its importance. In the last century before the destruction of the Temple and of their political unity, national leadership had shifted little by little from the presiding potentates and priests to the teachers and scholars whose primary function was the interpretation and elaboration of the Law. When the nation received its final military blow in the destruction of the Temple, the sanctity of the place of worship and the unity of a common realm were vested in the Books of the Law, the Torah. The same year that the Temple was burned to ashes, the rabbinical academy at Yavneh was founded.

The wanderings of the Diaspora have been marked by a series of new centers for studying the Law, shifting from one country to another as circumstances changed. The exiles spread into all parts of Europe and the East, but where conditions were most favorable, a center of learning would blossom and Jews from less favored places would flock to build up a prosperous community. This, then, would be the center of Jewish culture until invaders from without or persecution from within the country would enforce a move. A new culture center would develop and many from less favored places would seek it out. The migrations during the Diaspora were never a total movement out of one place into another. Rather, they were a greater concentration shifting to one spot where a few had lived earlier, and away from another where many had been before and a few would still remain.

After Palestine, Babylonia of the Sassanians harbored the great rabbinical academies for several centuries. Under the generally tolerant rule of the Babylonians, the scholars completed the ordering of the monumental body of the Law's interpretation, the Babylonian Talmud. Here, too, they built the fundamentals of their social and cultural existence in the Diaspora. Here they set the patterns of community structuring for a culture within a culture, a perennial minority adapting itself successively to a series of hosts.

With the rise and expansion of Islam, the Near Eastern Jews began to develop their communities in Spain. Under the fluctuating favor of the Moslem leaders they built up their Spanish, or Sephardic, communities so solidly that when the Babylonian center began to decline under Mongolian invasions, Spanish Jewry could take over the cultural leadership of Israel.

Until their destruction by the Inquisition, and the expulsion of the Jews in the year that Columbus discovered the New World, the Sephardic communities evolved their specific form of Judaism. It was an eclectic form, combining the truth of the Bible and Talmud with the wisdom of Aristotle and Plato, the liturgical poetry of the prayer books with the style of the Arabian divans. The Sephardic heritage became a colorful mosaic of mysticism and rationalism, philosophy and talmudism, poetry and science.

Meanwhile, within their ghetto walls, the Jewish communities of Italy, France and Germany had been evolving the Ashkenasi pattern of Judaism. *Ashkenaz* is the Hebrew name for Germany, where the most populous communities were located. Unlike the Sephardic Jews, the Ashkenazim were isolated from their neighbors, by edict and also by preference. In their centers of learning, traditional talmudism remained "uncontaminated" by non-Jewish culture. There was no place in their writings for worldly poetry and philosophy, but only for heavy volumes of rabbinical commentary and discussion. All life was oriented toward rigorous fulfillment of the commandments, reported in the Torah and expounded in the Talmud. No detail was too trivial to have a root in some religious prescription; the word of God resounded through every act of daily life.

In Spain, the Jewish scholars were free to compose their

works—secular or religious—in either their traditional language or the language of the country. The Ashkenazim banished all foreign languages from their literature, which was written only in Hebrew, the language of the Bible. For everyday use, Yiddish became their language, and it has remained theirs through years of migration and change.

It has become also a symbol of continuity maintained in spite of—perhaps because of—modification. The basis of the Yiddish language was a medieval German dialect with which Hebrew elements were combined. During the centuries it developed its own structure and style. In each new setting elements from local vernaculars have been absorbed, modified to suit the Yiddish idiom. Whoever knows Yiddish can understand the Yiddish of anyone else, even though some of the words may be incomprehensible. Yet each region has its own accent and idioms, which can be recognized and identified.

Western Europe never fully replaced Spain as the outstanding center of Jewish culture. The unremitting succession of restrictions, expulsions and massacres left no opportunity for that. The history of the Ashkenasi communities is one of intermittent flight and destruction. When governments frowned and violence grew frequent, there would be a new exodus to a new country, where a new rabbinical academy would be established and would flourish, until the next wave of destruction.

When the Crusaders began to exterminate local "infidels" on their way to the Holy Land, the Jews of Western Europe began to look to the East for haven. An old legend tells how, in the days of the Black Death, a group of exhausted refugees came to an unknown country east of Germany. As they beheld it, a voice from Heaven announced in Hebrew, *"Polin!"*—here thou shalt rest! The name of the country was Poland.

Here they stayed, and more of the Ashkenazim came to join them, spreading through Eastern Europe. In Poland and beyond, in Russia, they found old Jewish communities dating back to the times of Greek colonization, or founded by refugees from the Byzantine Empire. Two streams of the Diaspora became united in Eastern Europe. One descended from refugees who had entered directly from Near Eastern Asia through the Black Sea. The later stream flowed in from Western Europe, in flight from France, Germany or Bohemia.

The Polish rulers, eager to develop their backward provinces, welcomed the immigrants from the West, experienced in commerce and industry. They granted them privileges and liberties, religious freedom and communal autonomy. Here the Ashkenazim found a haven where they could continue their way of life. And here evolved the most populous, the most cohesive and culturally the most homogeneous Jewish communities in Europe. For centuries to come, Eastern Europe would be the Jewish culture center.

The themes which had characterized the Ashkenasi community of Western Europe continued to develop: isolation from the non-Jewish world and complete penetration of religious precept and practice into every detail of daily life. By the time restrictions and pogroms caught up with them, as they did very shortly, the patterns laid down in Babylon and modified in Western Europe had further strengthened and crystallized.

The small town, the shtetl, was the stronghold of this culture. Whether among Poles or Russians, Lithuanians or Hungarians, the Jews retained their ways and their language—responding to the environment, assimilating much of it, integrating it into their way of life, yet keeping the core of their own tradition intact. They spoke Yiddish, wrote and read Hebrew, bargained in broken Polish or Ukrainian. In large cities, as time went on, more and more of them rebelled against the sole authority of the Torah. The shtetl, also touched by waves from without, felt the impact less violently and resisted more sturdily. Only the wars and revolutions of the twentieth century, with the final destruction of six million lives, put an end to its role as the current home of the tradition.

How and why it survived so long is a question that has been much debated and will not be simply answered. A large part of whatever answer there is lies in the shtetl itself, its way of life and most of all its way of thought.

Part One

Remember the Sabbath

I

SABBATH EVE

It is told that God said to Israel, "If you accept my Torah and observe my Laws, I will give you for all eternity the most precious thing that I have in my possession."

"And what," asked Israel, "is that precious thing Thou wilt give us if we obey Thy Torah?"

God: "The future world."

Israel: "But even in this world should we have a foretaste of that other?"

God: "The Sabbath will give you this foretaste."

. . . . .

Sabbath brings the joy of the future life into the shtetl. This is the climax of the week, "a different world, no worry, no work."°* One lives from Sabbath to Sabbath, working all week to earn for it. The days of the week fall into place around the Sabbath. Wednesday, Thursday and Friday are "before Sabbath," and they draw holiness from the Sabbath that is coming. Sunday, Monday and Tuesday are "after Sabbath," and they draw holiness from the Sabbath that is past. Any delicacy that one finds during the week should be bought and kept, if possible, "for Sabbath."

The Sabbath is a day of rest, joy and devotion to God. None must work, none must mourn, none must worry, none must hunger on that day. Any Jew who lacks a Sabbath meal should be helped by those who have more than he. But of course one hopes not to need help, for no matter how poor a man may be he counts

---

*As noted in the Preface, direct quotations from interviews are followed by a °. For other quotations the usual marks are used.

on the Lord to provide for the Sabbath meal. Some stroke of luck, some sudden opportunity to earn the price of a fish and a fowl will surely turn up at the last moment—if only one goes after it hard enough. Many stories and legends describe miracles by which God at the last moment provided Sabbath fare for a devout Jew who lacked means to "make Sabbath."

Sabbath is a Queen and a Bride; and on the Sabbath, "every Jew is a king."

Perhaps not every Sabbath in every shtetl was alike for all the Jews of Eastern Europe. Perhaps everyone did not always enjoy a happy Sabbath. Yet the memories that live through the years have a glowing uniformity. On no point is there more unanimity than on the significance and the feeling of Sabbath in the shtetl. It is remembered as a time of ecstasy—father in a silken caftan and velvet skullcap, mother in black silk and pearls; the glow of candles, the waves of peace and joy, the glad sense that it is good to be a Jew, the distant pity for those who have been denied this foretaste of heaven.

Friday is the day of the eve of Sabbath, *Erev Shabbes*. It is set apart from other days because, although it is not a holiday, it is the day on which one makes ready to greet the Sabbath. The shtetl housewife wakes up earlier than usual with the thought, "Today is Erev Shabbes—I must hurry!" Even if she usually works at the shop or market, on this day she will try to stay home to prepare for the reception of the Queen Sabbath. First of all she pours over her hands the "fingernail water"—the water that stood by her bed overnight in a glass or a cup to be at hand for the ritual ablution that must start each day, and says the short morning prayer with which each day must begin. Then she puts on her oldest dress, her work apron, ties a kerchief over her head, and rolls up her sleeves.

Before the others are awake she "fires the oven" with logs so that it will be ready for use. She feeds the family as they appear, as quickly as possible, and bundles the boys off to school. Meanwhile she inspects the dough that she set to rise last night for the Sabbath loaf, the *hallah*. She begins to clean the chicken that she bought yesterday, watching anxiously—"it shouldn't happen!"—for any forbidden flecks of blood, blister on the gizzard or other calamity that would raise doubts whether her chicken was *kosher*—ritually fit to eat.

If it did happen, someone would have to hurry to the rabbi asking breathlessly, "Is it kosher?" and waiting in painful suspense until the rabbi, after studying the chicken and the relevant laws, declared, "Kosher!"

The fish, also purchased on Thursday, must be cleaned, chopped, seasoned, prepared for cooking. "Without fish," the saying goes, "there is no Sabbath." All the rest of the Sabbath food must be prepared as well, for after sundown no fire may be lit, no work may be done. There will be noodles, that the housewife kneads and flattens out, rolling the thin sheet into a long floury coil, slicing it and spreading the fine slivers to dry on a clean cloth.

Next she braids the dough into "twists" ready for baking. Before the loaves are placed on the hot bricks she throws a bit of dough into the fire saying, "Blessed be Thou, Oh Lord our God, King of the Universe, who hast hallowed us by His commandments and commanded to take of the hallah."

This is one of the three rituals known as the "womanly" duties. Without this offering, hallah would not be fit for its part in the Sabbath feast. If by mischance she forgets it, however, she can "take hallah" when she removes the loaves from the oven.

From sunrise to sunset the day is a race with time. The whole house must be cleaned, the floors swept and sanded, the woodwork washed, the kitchen tables and benches scrubbed, the towels changed. The housewife darts from broom to oven and back again, peering, stirring, prodding, dusting, giving commands to her daughters and ordering all màles to keep from underfoot.

The day whirls on; the hallah has been lifted out with a long-handled shovel, and glazed with white of egg. The loaves are high and light—God has answered the prayer whispered while she was kneading the dough, and she will not be ashamed before her husband, her family and the neighbors.

To fit each task in with all the others requires a high order of domestic engineering, especially since the boys come home from school at noon on Friday and must be disposed of with a snack—perhaps with a smack. Of a woman who has trouble coping with the domestic routine and runs a confused house, it is said scornfully, "For her every day is Erev Shabbes."

Meanwhile the beggars make the rounds of houses and stores, for in most places Friday is the beggars' day. Each beggar has his regular beat and each household has its pile of coins ready, probably presided over by one of the children. Each beggar is known, and in turn knows the amount he may expect from each household. If he is given two kopeks where three are the rule, there will be no end to his rage and complaints. Sometimes food will be given instead of money, and a privileged beggar may be given both.

Each Friday the same duties are done in the same order and each Friday brings the same anxiety that Sabbath may arrive before all is ready. A woman knows the tasks and their order from long experience, reaching back to childhood in her mother's house; and from her mother's house she also knows the Friday fear that the sun may set too soon. The fear is sharpest when the whole routine must be fitted into the "short Friday" of midwinter.

After the house is cleaned she turns to the children, who must be washed from the tops of their crowns to the tips of their toes, and dressed in clean clothes from inside out. Their heads must be doused, soaped and finally rinsed with kerosene and the odor of their cleanliness is an aura about them. After they are dressed they are stiff with the command to keep their clothes clean for the Sabbath.

A pile of clean clothes must be prepared for each of the men and older boys. Carefully folded on top of the bundle is the *talis koton* that they must always wear, and wear in such a way that it is visible. It is a large square of white wool with black stripes along two edges and with a hole in the middle so that it can be slipped over the head. At each corner are knotted fringes, and the knots must be the correct kind and number. It is also called "four corners," *arba kanfos.*

A male Jew wears it from the time he begins to walk, and is forbidden to move about without the talis koton. A child cannot wear it before he is trained to be "clean," however, for there would be danger that it might be defiled. Some men wear it even in bed. A blessing must always be said when it is put on and although almost no women wear it, the regulations stipulate that a woman who does so must say the blessing.

When the men return from their shops and market stalls, or from their journeying, the bundles will be ready for them. Wherever one is, he will try to reach home in time to greet the Sabbath with his own family. The peddler traveling from village to village, the itinerant tailor, shoemaker, cobbler, the merchant off on a trip, all will plan, push, hurry, trying to reach home before sunset on Friday evening.

As they press homeward the *shammes* calls through the streets of the shtetl, "Jews to the bathhouse!" A functionary of the synagogue, the shammes is a combination of sexton and beadle. He speaks with an authority more than his own, for when he calls "Jews to the bathhouse" he is summoning them to a commandment.

All who can, respond. The women are usually so caught in the tangle of their preparations that they must perform their ablutions at home. But the men and boys seize their clean clothing and from all the streets they bear down on the bathhouse, their bundles under their arms. There they will be cleansed in the bath and purified by three ceremonial immersions in the pool of "living water" known as the *mikva*. Meanwhile, they will be entertained by the conversation of their peers. The bath is like a Turkish bath and those who are prosperous enough to stop work early can plan to linger chatting in the steam, slapping themselves with "brooms" made of supple twigs, and basking. For the others the ceremony must be brisk, since Sabbath is almost here.

Coming home from the bathhouse, dressed in their clean clothes, they put away the soiled garments and cover themselves with the carefully cherished Sabbath caftan, tying in its fullness with a silken girdle. The Sabbath caftan is usually of "silk." It may be sateen if the man is very poor, and the black fabric, whatever it is, may be green with age, frayed and mended. But the Sabbath caftan is made of "silk" and is a very special garment, stored away during the week with the rest of the Sabbath and holiday clothes. There is a Sabbath cap too, also of a precious fabric—satin or velvet perhaps for the opulent. The coat pockets must be emptied of all money, since none may be touched or carried on the Sabbath. If by any chance the coat is put on after sundown, children will happily perform the duty of emptying father's pockets, rewarded by the privilege of keeping for themselves any stray coins they may find.

The boys, down to the very smallest, are dressed like their fathers in long black caftan and black cap or hat. The very little ones may have short trousers underneath, and childish socks peeking out from under the hem of the dignified coat.

At last the housewife, with house and family furbished for the taste of heaven on earth, turns to preparing herself. By the time she is ready the men have returned from the bathhouse, still racing against time—for they must be at the synagogue by sundown. They depart quickly while she puts the last touches on her own costume. The kerchief is replaced by the wig or sheytl that covers her cropped hair, and her splashed and rumpled cotton dress is replaced by the Sabbath dress of black silk, enriched with whatever jewelry she has to mark her dignity as a wife and mother.

For many women a Sabbath without jewelry would be almost like a Sabbath without chicken or fish. The ideal Sabbath jewel is a necklace of pearls. It is said that even if hard times forced one to pawn her pearls, she might hope to have them back for the Sabbath. "On Monday morning, mother returned her pearls (to the pawnbroker) and then on Friday night he would bring them to her again."°

As the sun sets, Queen Sabbath enters the shtetl, to be greeted by the men and boys at the synagogue, by the women and girls at home. The precise moment when each Sabbath begins is noted on the official calendar and is announced by the shammes. Then the mother in her sheytl, her Sabbath dress and pearls, performs the ritual of lighting the candles. No household will have less than two and those that can afford it will have one for each living member of the home family, in a five or seven branch candlestick of silver or brass—with additional holders if they are needed. Probably the candlestick is a family heirloom handed down from mother to daughter through the generations. There are few heirlooms in the shtetl, but most households have their treasured Sabbath candlesticks. If a family should have to leave "God forbid," whatever else may be abandoned, the candlestick will be kept.

The woman of the house lights the candles, praying as she does so, "Blessed art Thou, oh Lord our God, King of the Universe, who hast hallowed us by His Commandments and commanded us to kindle the Sabbath light!" She says the prayer in Hebrew, which she may or may not understand, for Hebrew is the language of religion. Her prayer is almost inaudible to earthly ears. Men say some prayers aloud but a woman usually moves her lips and barely murmurs the words. Having lighted the candles she moves her arms over them in a gesture of embrace, drawing to her the holiness that rises from their flames. She draws the holiness to herself, but not for herself only, for she represents her household.

In the glow of the flames and of their sanctity she covers her eyes with her hands, and now she says her own prayer, dictated by her heart. This prayer is not in the language of ritual but in Yiddish, her own vernacular. She is free to pray as she will, but she will probably repeat one of the familiar forms that have been used through the years, begging for the welfare of each member of her household, adding only the few special phrases and pleas that mark the prayer as her own.

Often she weeps as she prays and it would be hard to say to what extent the tears themselves are part of the ritual. For so many generations women have wept as they prayed over the Sabbath candles, tears of grief or of gratitude, of hope or of fear, tears for themselves, for their families, for their people. Through the years little girls have seen their mothers standing rapt and the tears between their fingers shining in the candle light, seeming to be part of the prayer.

Lighting the candles is another of the three commandments special to women. The third is the ritual purification at the mikva after menstruation. If a woman performs her three commandments without fail, she may feel secure about her future life.

Once the candles have been lighted, Sabbath is within the home. All is ready. The race is won, anxiety vanishes, the breathless rush of the day changes to slow serenity which will continue until the new week begins. The table is prepared, with its white cloth, two Sabbath loaves set out on it and covered with a napkin—if possible, an embroidered one. The housewife herself is dressed and ready, no work need be done nor is any permitted. Therefore on Friday evening in the first peace of Sabbath she may sit at ease with no sense of guilt for idleness, and open her book. This is the special prayer book for women, containing the prayers women need to know, with Yiddish translations of the ones that are in Hebrew. In the book also are legends, sermons and homilies to help her fulfill her duties as a Jewish wife and mother. So she may sit quietly reading—if she knows how to read—until the men return from the synagogue.

She will not have long to wait, for the Friday evening service at the synagogue is short. Its main feature is the welcoming by the Chosen People of the Sabbath, their Bride. "Come, oh Cherished One, and meet the Bride! Let us welcome the face of Sabbath! . . ."

There is little time for musing and reading before the men return, the head of the household and his sons, and perhaps the *oyrekh*, the guest for the Sabbath meal. If the household can afford it there will surely be an oyrekh, for without a guest no Sabbath is truly complete. He may be a stranger from some other community who was unable to get home for the Sabbath. He may be a delegate, traveling to collect funds for some educational institution. He may be, poor fellow, a Jewish conscript posted in town. Or he may be a rabbinical student studying day and night, and fed by different households in turn so that in a sense his board constitutes a community fellowship.

Whoever he is, any stranger in need will come to the synagogue on Friday evening and at the end of the service he will expect to be invited to some home. First rights of hospitality usually go to the more prosperous. The shammes may bustle up to a rich man and tell him, "I have a guest." Or the rich man may ask the shammes, "Anyone for the Sabbath?"

There is a legend that every Sabbath God sends the prophet Elijah, dressed as a needy stranger, to visit the Jews and observe the way they are fulfilling His Commandments. Accordingly the stranger one brings home may be the prophet. No legend is required, however, to stimulate Sabbath hospitality. Prophet or beggar, to feed the hungry is a "good deed," especially if the stranger is a Jew who can eat only kosher food. Therefore it is a privilege to share the Sabbath feast, even if by ill luck it is a meager one.

The first words as the men and boys enter are *"Gut Shabbes,"* the weekly greeting exchanged with all the holiday zest of an annual Happy New Year. The man of the house recites his greeting to the Sabbath Angels, "Peace be unto you, ye ministering Angels, messengers of the most High . . ." He does not murmur as did his wife, but speaks audibly, slowly pacing the room as he prays, with his head bent slightly and his hands behind his back. Little boys imitate their father's words, his posture, his gait, and the oyrekh joins them. When the small boy becomes a father and his little sister a housewife, the words of the prayers, the gestures, the intonations will already have become part of them.

The father says a second prayer, the chapter "in praise of the virtuous wife" from the Proverbs of Solomon. "A woman of worth—who can find her? For her price is far above rubies. The heart of her husband trusteth in her . . ."

Now the head of the family fills the ceremonial goblet with wine, takes it into his hands, and chants the *kiddush*—the prayer consecrating the Sabbath—and the blessing over wine. He fills the cup to the brim, symbolizing abundance, and all stand while he "makes kiddush."

When the father finishes he takes a sip from the goblet and hands it to his wife. The wife, daughters and younger children say the blessing over wine, but not the kiddush, and each takes a sip. The older boys and the oyrekh say kiddush after the father, also over a full cup of wine. If a very honored guest is present— a grandfather or a learned man—he is given the privilege of saying kiddush first. The word kiddush means consecration. The ritual establishes the presence of the Queen Sabbath in the family and the participation of all its members in the Sabbath holiness.

The Sabbath meal, like every meal, is preceded by the ceremonial washing of the hands, pouring water over them three times as the blessing is said. Before sitting down the father re-

moves the hat in which he returned from the synagogue and almost with the same gesture substitutes a skullcap from his pocket,
since it is commanded that his head be covered at all times. Then
at last the family gather around the table set with the best linen
and the best dishes. During the week, meals may be hurried and
irregular, eaten in snatches and in solitude, whenever one has
time or feels hungry. During the week the mother may never find
time to sit at the table. But on Sabbath all sit down together, men
and boys on one side, women and girls on the other. The father
sits at the head, the mother at his right. The festive table is set in
the best room—if they have one—which during the week is little
used except as a retreat in which the father can study.

The lengthy meal begins with the blessing of the hallah. The
father silently and deliberately removes the napkin, lifts the two
loaves, holding them together, then sets them down again. He
passes the knife over one of them, then cuts the other in half and
gives each person a slice. Each one breaks a bit from his slice, dips
it in salt, and "makes the blessing" for bread. All blessings are
in Hebrew and while they are being pronounced no word of a
profane language must be spoken. Therefore during the ritual
prologue of the meal the only words uttered are in Hebrew, and
—except for the kiddush—are murmured rather than spoken
aloud.

The rule against breaking into the sacred language with the
vernacular may lead to embarrassment. If the father suddenly
finds there is no towel to wipe his hands after the hand washing,
or no knife for the blessing of the hallah, or no salt for it, he cannot ask in Yiddish for the missing article, and even if he knows
the word in Hebrew his wife may not. Therefore he must resort
to dumb show, gesticulation and inarticulate grunts to announce
the emergency.

When the ritual prologue is finished, the mother brings in
the fish, spiced and perhaps sweetened, and gives each one a piece.
The father receives the head in deference to his family status and
he may then present it to his wife in token of her excellence and
his esteem. The fish is followed by chicken broth "clear like
amber" with the finely cut noodles, after which comes boiled beef
or chicken, or both.

The delicacies of Sabbath are enjoyed slowly, with time to appreciate each mouthful, and with pauses between each course. The mother's hard work is rewarded by admiring comments about her skill—the flavor of the fish gravy, the golden color of the fat on the soup, the tenderness of the fowl—"it falls apart in your mouth." This is the time when she receives her weekly recompense of praise.

The waits between courses give time for learned conversation between father and sons, for comments on community affairs, or for plying the oyrekh with questions about his own shtetl, and about what he has seen and heard on his travels. As the men converse the girls and women listen eagerly, their eyes active and their tongues still.

At the end of the meal all pour a few drops of water on their hands. Knives, symbolic of bloody weapons, are covered or taken away and *zmiros* are sung—a series of songs praising God and celebrating good cheer. The placid zmiros melodies, associated with the happy, peaceful afterglow of the Sabbath meal, are among the favorite Jewish tunes and the ones most apt to be hummed during hours of work or meditation.

The Sabbath candles burn lower as the meal comes to an end. No member of the family may blow them out or move the candle holders because on the Sabbath a Jew must avoid all contact with fire or with anything related to it. Therefore at bedtime all lights will be extinguished and all fires taken care of by someone who is not subject to the severe Sabbath regulations. Often some non-Jew, a *shabbes goy*, is paid by the community for this service. As he goes from house to house, he may also be rewarded by the individual families with a piece of hallah, different in appearance and taste from the dark bread of his everyday menu.

As the family go to bed, they know that every other Jewish household in the shtetl has enjoyed the prescribed observances in the same way. They know too that all are enjoying release from care. Not only weekday acts but even weekday thoughts are forbidden on the Sabbath. One must put aside all concern about business, money, family problems, and think only of God and His Law; for Sabbath is a foretaste of the future life in which there will be no worry, but only happiness and the pleasure of studying the Holy Words.

Even the soul is different, for on Sabbath an additional soul, *nshomeh yeseyreh,* is joined to it. All week this soul is with God but on the Sabbath nshomeh yeseyreh is added to each man, woman and child; and while it is present no cares or worries can spoil the joy that is a foretaste of the future.

Not only does each Jew know that all those in the shtetl are sharing his Sabbath experience. He feels, beyond that, a community with Jews who are celebrating the Sabbath all over the world. This is a major strand in the Sabbath feeling—a sense of proud and joyous identification with the tradition, the past, the ancestors, with all the Jewish world living or gone. On the Sabbath the shtetl feels most strongly and most gladly that "it is good to be a Jew."

II

SABBATH DAY

According to tradition, the synagogue is a House of Study, a House of Prayer and a House of Assembly. On Sabbath morning it is chiefly a House of Prayer.

After the morning rituals—the "fingernail water," the blessings,—and perhaps a glass of sweetened tea, the Jews of the shtetl move in family groups to attend the Sabbath services. All are wearing their Sabbath best, although it appears uniform and somber as compared to the brilliance and variety of the Sunday best the neighboring peasants will wear to church the next day for their Sabbath.

The father comes first in the family group. Men usually wear a black caftan reaching at least to the knees but in some regions to the ankles, and girdled for prayer with a black silk cord knotted around the waist—to separate the godly part of the body, the mind and the heart, from the lower part. Most of the men wear beards and the pious have earlocks, for both the beard and the locks growing over their ears should be left untouched by scissors or by blade from infancy. The men must have their heads covered at all times, with a hat or the small skullcap called *yarmelkeh.* On the way to the synagogue, the Sabbath yarmelkeh is replaced or covered by a hat, perhaps one with a fur brim around which are set small fur tails.

The women, walking a little behind their husbands, are also dressed in black or dark colors, brightened by their best jewelry and perhaps a lace scarf thrown over the matron's wig. If their daughters were with them the pastel blues and pinks of the girls' dresses would brighten the Sabbath parade to the synagogue, but young girls usually stay at home to sleep or play or gossip or tend the babies while the grownups and the boys are at the Sabbath services.

The family groups moving toward the synagogue proceed at a Sabbath pace—slow, measured, dignified, in contrast to the weekday rush. The sons clustering around their parents look like small beardless editions of the father. Some of the little boys may proudly carry the mother's prayer book, perhaps decorated with silver clasps and velvet covers, probably handed down from her own mother. And one of them may carry the father's praying shawl, his *talis*, folded in the case his wife embroidered for him as a wedding gift. The white talis, striped in black and fringed at the corners, is the garment that clothes the man in the folds of his faith. It enfolds him while he prays, perhaps even while he studies the Holy Law, and it is wrapped about him when he is buried. His father's talis was wrapped about him when as a tiny child he was carried to school for the first time, and when for the first time he was "called to the Torah"; and he wraps his talis about his own son for the same occasions. Each morning before his first prayers, he must examine the fringes of his talis to make sure that they are kosher—that is, ritually fit for use—that all the knots are in order and none of the tassels is torn.

If a child does not carry the father's talis, the man will wear it over his shoulders, for on Sabbath it is forbidden to carry anything outside one's own home. For the same reason, a handkerchief will be tied around the wrist or tucked into the belt rather than carried in the pocket. A little boy is less strictly governed by this prohibition, although he also must observe the Sabbath regulations within appropriate limits.

Only under one condition may a pious man carry his own talis or prayer book on Sabbath. If a "fence" has been constructed around a group of houses, the area enclosed may be regarded as one's home, and objects may be carried in it. The "fence," *eyruv*, is a cord or a wire, stretched around the shtetl, under the supervision of the rabbi, who concludes the ritual by declaring that "this is no longer a public domain, but the domain of an individual." There is always the danger, however, that—despite the weekly inspection—the "fence" may have been broken at some point, in which case carrying would no longer be permissible.

Therefore it is safer not to carry even the ritual objects. Moreover, full observance of the Sabbath prohibitions is more in keeping with the well-beloved and much enjoyed feeling of the Sabbath, the feeling that it is another world, another life, another set of customs.

The family may attend services at the main synagogue, the *shul*, open only on Sabbath or holidays. Or they may go to the *besmedresh* which, unlike the shul, is open always for prayer and study. If the shtetl is very small indeed, the shul and the besmedresh may be one. As a rule, however, a shtetl will be more rich in congregations than the size of its population would suggest. If it is big enough it may have a number of guild synagogues—one for tailors, one for shoemakers, one for butchers. If the family belong to the *Hassidim* they will go to the services of their chosen Hassidic congregation.

It would be possible, though not usual, to go to no synagogue, but to join a *minyan* or quorum of ten adult male Jews. Any room can serve as a place for prayer, provided it holds the Holy Scrolls and has on its doorpost a *mezuzah*. The mezuzah is a small box or tube in which is sealed a piece of parchment bearing stipulated passages from the Bible written in twenty-two lines. Its presence on the doorpost makes a room or a house Jewish, for it has been commanded, "Thou shalt bind the words of the Law for a sign . . . upon thy door." The mezuzah is "kissed" on entering and on leaving the house.

The main synagogue, the real shul, is more elaborate than the other houses of worship in the shtetl, yet it lacks the splendor associated with a church. The exterior conforms to whatever style of architecture prevails in the locality. The interior is apt to be comparatively nondescript. Long benches, facing the East, support wooden racks that serve as "reading desks" for the bench behind. In the center is a railed-off platform, the *bimah,* on which stands a table where the scrolls are unrolled for reading. From the bimah, also, sermons are preached, important community announcements are made, funds for community services are raised, and individual grievances are expressed.

Only at one point is there elaborate decoration. At the center of the Eastern Wall, the *mizrakh,* is the Ark of the Torah, a cabinet of wood ornamented with carving. Before its carved doors is hung a rich curtain of velvet or satin, heavily embroidered. Each of the Holy Scrolls within the Ark contains the full text of the Torah—the five books of the Pentateuch. The scrolls are encased in sumptuous covers of satin or velvet—white, red, bright blue, yellow—embroidered with gold or silver, perhaps with spangles. The six-pointed star of David is usually a prominent part of the design. Other favorite themes are lions of Judah, the tablets of the ten commandments, and the doves that symbolize peace.

The Holy Scroll is wound on two handsome wooden rollers and covered with its splendid cloak, which is often replaced by a special holiday mantle for great occasions. It is further adorned with a crown of wrought silver in which are set bells that tinkle when it is carried from the Ark where it reposes to the bimah where it is read. In the drab surroundings, the richness of the Torah's setting is as pronounced an oasis as is the brightness of Sabbath itself against the humdrum weekday round. There may be numerous scrolls in the Ark, for to present a Torah to the shul is a favorite and mandatory form of visible piety.

When the family enters the synagogue, the women and men separate. The women go to *ezras noshim*, the women's section—a separate upstairs room, with windows through which they can hear the service and see a little of it. The men pass through an outer room or lobby to the main assembly room. At the entrance is a basin and a pitcher from which they pour water over their hands three times, repeating the blessing that always accompanies this act. Before praying or eating, the hands must be wet three times with "living"—that is, not stagnant—water, and the correct blessing must be "made."

Then the man proceeds to the seat he has bought or inherited from his father. If he is a man of high status, a leader in the community, it will be at the Eastern Wall, the mizrakh, toward which all faces are turned when prayers are said. A man of somewhat less exalted standing will sit in the front row—"the mirror"—facing the mizrakh, while behind him are the common people, and at the very rear, around a large bare table near the entrance, are seated the beggars and the strangers. The rabbi and his assistant, as the most honored members of the community, are nearest to the Ark on the Eastern Wall.

Before beginning his Sabbath prayers the man covers his head with his talis, so that he is completely enveloped by the great white shawl which falls down to his ankles on all sides, but under no circumstances must be allowed to drag on the floor or to be stepped on. As he puts it on, he pronounces the blessing for the talis. Like all the ritual blessings it begins with the words, "Blessed art Thou, oh Lord our God, King of the Universe. . . ." A minimum of one hundred blessings should be said each day. They are uttered whenever a ritual garment is put on, before eating or drinking, on seeing a learned man, in connection with any strange or unusual event and also with such life activities as going to bed, putting on new clothes, bodily elimination. The blessing for putting on the talis ends, ". . . and who hast commanded us to enwrap ourselves in the fringed garment."

Having pronounced the blessing, one puts the talis around his shoulders and is ready to begin his Sabbath morning prayers. They are a composite of paeans to God, blessings, thanksgivings and pleas, drawn from Bible chapters or psalms and from prayers composed in different periods of Jewish history. Their order is fixed, and though most men know most of the prayers, each one keeps his prayer book open throughout, to avoid error. The ignorant have to follow the text word by word and although many of them understand the Hebrew, a few—and most of the women— do not.

Prayers are accompanied by a rocking movement of the body, from the waist or from the toes. The motion varies from an almost imperceptible swaying through the more pronounced rocking of the very orthodox, to the violent movements of the Hassidim. Some prayers are chanted with a special melody, some are said aloud and slowly, some are murmured at great speed. Some are said in sitting position, some standing. Some are read, chanted or sung by the cantor who stands behind a pulpit near the Ark, and the congregation repeats or responds.

When one comes in late, as some do, he must go through the prayers in their proper order until he catches up with the cantor and the congregation, which is done with incredible speed. The whole room is a swaying mass of black and white, filled with a tangle of murmur and low chantings, above which the vibrant voice of the cantor rises and falls, implores and exults, elaborating the traditional melodies with repetitions and modulations that are his own. The congregation prays as one, while within that unity each man as an individual speaks directly to God.

The most important prayer of all—on Sabbath as on week-days—is the silent prayer, the Eighteen Blessings, which must be read silently, not swaying but standing still, facing the East. No word may be said and no interruption allowed during the Eighteen Blessings.

The women upstairs are also going through the Sabbath prayers. Like the men, they are seated in order of descending status from front to rear. There is rustling of Sabbath silks and silent comparing of Sabbath jewels, as they repeat the prayers after the *zogerkeh*—a woman who, unlike most of them, is able to read and understand Hebrew. She reads the prayer and they repeat it after her, following each syllable and intonation. When she says, "women, now you must weep," the women weep. Her service is rewarded, not by money, but by the gratification of performing a "good deed."

At a certain point the cantor interrupts the prayers for the reading of the Torah—the five books of the Pentateuch. The entire text is divided into weekly sections so that in the course of one year the whole of the Torah will be read. Every weekly section is followed by the reading of a small portion from the Prophets, called Haftorah.

The Holy Scroll is carried with jingling bells and due ceremony, from the Ark to the bimah, where it is carefully unrolled to the proper passage and placed on the table. Each week several members of the congregation are honored by the *aliyah,* that is by being "called to the reading" of part of the section for that day. The one who is called does not actually pronounce the sacred words, since that would entail too great a risk for himself and the community. If he should make a single slip some misfortune might fall upon the shtetl. Therefore it is necessary to have a professional "Master of reading" who has been trained to chant the text without an error. This expert, moreover, must read each syllable and not depend on his memory for it, even though he undoubtedly knows it well. He points out word by word, with a decorated pointer of ivory or lacquered wood, shaped like a hand with a pointing index finger—since the holy text must not be touched with the "naked hand." The pointer must not be made of metal, for metal is used in weapons that shed blood.

As he reads, the man who has been called stands at his right, silently moving his lips. But at the end, as at the beginning, he pronounces a blessing in a sure, ringing voice, each time kissing the edge of his talis with which he has touched the holy text. Then he moves to the left side, where he stands during the following section, at the end of which he returns to his seat and is succeeded by the one who was called after him.

To be called at all is an honor, but certain passages are more honorific than others and are cherished rewards of service to the community. One of these is the enumeration of the blessings given by Moses to the Jews before his death. But most choice of all is the first chapter of Genesis, and the privilege of "reading" this section is auctioned off each year, the proceeds going to the community services through which the shtetl protects the welfare of its members. The weekly prize is to be *maftir*, that is to be called to the reading of the Haftorah.

All readings are marked by some donation to the community. When a man is "called up" he will whisper into the ear of the *gabai*, or manager of the synagogue, the amount he plans to give, and this will be announced to the congregation. Each man gives in accordance with his means, and if he is too poor to give at all he will offer a token donation of a penny. If, on the other hand, a man of substance has lagged in his contributions to the community welfare, one way of prompting him to open his pocket is to call him to the reading of the Torah. No one can refuse a call to the Torah which is really a call by the Torah; on the contrary, he must rise quickly and come with swift steps. If, however, he is infirm with age or illness, it is permissible for him to move slowly, leaning on a cane if need be—despite the Sabbath proscription against carrying—or assisted by some other person.

Seven men are called to read each week. The first two must always be members of the two known surviving tribes of Israel: the Kohanim, or priests; and the Levites. A bridegroom is called both before and after his wedding. A new father is called "even if the baby is a female," a boy is called when he "becomes a man" at the age of thirteen. One who wishes to thank God for escape from danger, one who leaves or returns to the community, one who presents a Torah to the synagogue, is given the opportunity to celebrate the occasion by "reading" the Law and by making a contribution to the welfare of the shtetl. If two men have equal rights to be called for a certain reading, the more learned of the two has first claim; and if the two are equal in learning, they cast lots for the privilege.

The reading is a lengthy process and few stay through the whole of it. Children swarm out when it begins, to play or to listen to their elders. Knots of men gather in the outer room to debate points of the Law or current events, leaning forward attentively with a hand cupped over one ear to catch the fine points of the discussion. Often a little boy will be seen at the edge of such a group, his hand at his ear, straining forward in exact imitation of his father's stance. Meanwhile, the women also talk among themselves and some may go home to set the Sabbath table.

The coming and going, the murmur of voices from outside, are not felt as disrespect to the Law. As long as the minyan, ten adult male Jews, is present for the beginning of the reading and six are there at the end, the requirements have been satisfied. The synagogue is literally the Home of Prayer, and one moves freely there as in the home of his Father.

When the Torah has been restored to the Ark with a jingling of bells and a reverent kiss, the second half of the prayers is said. At the end, all exchange greetings, "Gut Shabbes." The men fold up their prayer shawls or drape them about their shoulders again and all go out, pausing for more talk in the outer room or the yard of the synagogue—all with the deliberate, leisurely pace that marks the Sabbath. If any oyrekh remains to be cared for, some householder will hale him home, but usually the Friday night oyrekh enjoys the hospitality of his host throughout the Sabbath.

As the family groups return through the unpaved shtetl streets, they see about them the other members of the community, the non-Jews, *goyim,* going about their business as usual, the children running barefoot through the mud. And as they see, they pity the barefoot goyim, deprived of the Covenant, the Law, and the joy of Sabbath. True, they will have their own kind of Sabbath on the following day. But it is a different kind, "something else again." Moreover, for the devout members of the shtetl, Sunday is part of the week and no true Sabbath at all. "We thought they were very unfortunate. They had no enjoyment . . . no Sabbath . . . no holidays . . . no fun . . ."° "They'd drink a lot and you couldn't blame them, their lives were so miserable."°

The Saturday meal is eaten at once so that the "delight of Sabbath," *oneg Shabbes,* which follows the meal, may be as long as possible. The *cholent* is taken from the oven where it has been kept since the day before. It is a hearty dish that may contain a variety of ingredients in addition to fat and potatoes or groats, eaten with the cold remains of last night's chicken and with draughts of vodka or brandy for the men. There will be *kugel* also, a baked pudding made of noodles, brown and sweet, with raisins and cinnamon.

Now the real Sabbath peace, *menukhas Shabbes,* descends. After the long, arduous week comes the Sabbath rest. Quiet falls over the shtetl, as in every house the father sleeps, perhaps with a handkerchief over his face to keep off the flies, and the mother who never rests all week lies sleeping while the sun shines. Throughout the shtetl, all obey the command to banish thoughts of daily problems, to enjoy and to rest. It is commanded to forget all cares and therefore one is at peace. The children, who soon have enough of resting, play quietly so that their sleeping elders will not be disturbed.

They awaken to a new phase of Sabbath. On Saturday afternoon, after the nap and a reviving glass of tea—brewed from the kettle that has been kept hot since yesterday—the Sabbath "hearings" are in order. In all the more literate households, the fathers test their sons to discover what progress is being made at school. The boy's teacher is likely to drop in for this exercise, sitting tensely with his glass of tea, for his reputation and his income hang on his pupil's performance. From time to time he may try to prompt the boy. The mother sits by quietly, in pained suspense if things go badly, beaming if the performance is good. She may not understand the Hebrew words and the fine shades of meaning, but she comprehends fully the frown or the smile on her husband's face.

If the boy does badly he will endure the consequences at school tomorrow. If he does well he will be rewarded with fruits or cookies—not with money, for that is untouchable in the Sabbath world.

As the afternoon continues, neighbors, relatives, friends, drop in to sip a glass of sweetened tea, to nibble a cookie or a piece of cake or to enjoy some "Sabbath fruit," and to talk, the women apart discussing their affairs, the men conversing about points of the Law, the rabbi's latest sermon—but not about business for all thoughts of business are in exile.

Before sundown another light meal will be eaten—for there must be three on the Sabbath. The "third meal" is preceded by a short afternoon service at the synagogue, and followed by the evening service there.

When the men return from evening prayers, the Sabbath is almost over, and it is time for the *havdolah,* the ritual of the separation which marks its end. The father says a prayer over a goblet of wine, full to overflowing, then takes a silver box, treasured like the candlesticks as a family heirloom, and filled with aromatic spices. A daughter holds the special havdolah candle made of braided wax. He looks into the wine, then drinks of it, leaving only enough to quench the candle. The sons, too, "make havdolah" but if a girl should drink of the sanctified wine she would grow whiskers. The father looks at his fingernails, dips his fingers in the remaining drops of wine, passes them lightly over his eyes and behind his ears, then quenches the candle with the wine.

He ends the havdolah with a greeting to all, "A *gute vokh,*" a good week. The mother with downcast face silently moves her lips in a prayer for protection during the week to come—the prayer of women, "God of Abraham":

God of Abraham, Isaac and Jacob
The Holy Sabbath passes away;
May the new week come to us
For health, life and all good;
May it bring us sustenance, good tidings,
Deliverance and consolations, Amen.

Like her greeting to the Sabbath this farewell is in Yiddish, but more than that prayer, it is filled with concern for the daily problems of making a living. Like the father, at the end of her prayer she wishes to all "a gute vokh."

With the melancholy words "gute vokh" the charm of Sabbath is broken. The Queen-Bride, who transformed every Jew into a King for a day, is leaving the shtetl. Children lend her a symbolic escort by going far out to the edge of the village with her, sorrowfully watching her depart.

Some Hassidic Jews try to retain her late into the night, through the *mlaveh malkeh,* "escorting the Queen." As long as the candles are not lit, they maintain, the Sabbath has not ended, and sometimes they will sit in darkness—sometimes until midnight—holding off its departure. Gathered at their meeting place or at the home of some prominent Hassid, they eat hallah, symbol of Sabbath, and herring, symbol of the weekday world. They drink deep of cheering liquor, praying, singing, dancing in praise of God. To prolong Sabbath is a boon not only for themselves, for as long as it lasts the souls in hell can rest and only when the week begins must they return to their tortures.

For the rest of the shtetl, Sabbath has ended. The family moves from the "better" room back into the kitchen. The silver candlesticks, spice box, and wine goblet are back in the cupboard, the embroidered napkin is taken off the table, the Sabbath clothes laid away until next week. The business man turns from the Holy Books to his bookkeeping and the artisan goes back to his tools, to use the last few hours before sleep. With a deep sigh the women, the men, the children begin the "vokh"—the week.

The word vokh with its adjective *vokhendik,* to describe everything connected with everyday life, means to the shtetl much more than "week." This word has the meaning of earthly as opposed to heavenly, sadness as opposed to joy, humiliation as opposed to pride. The symbol of Sabbath is the white, "beautiful hallah," the symbol of the vokh is the dark heavy rye bread of every day. The skilfully seasoned, costly fish is the main Sabbath dish, a piece of salt herring is the everyday food. The content of Sabbath is rest, devotion to God and one's fellow man—the content of vokh is hard work and the breathless "chase after *parnosseh*," a livelihood. Vokh means for the shtetl the return from the high citadel of faith to the world where one is misunderstood, despised, and often hated.

The Sabbath duties are hard. The countless regulations, prohibitions and commandments reduce to a minimum the freedom of movement and activity. The Sabbath rest is a prescribed duty and to violate it is an unforgivable sin. "One who does not fulfill the commandments of Sabbath, sins against the entire Law." But the gratification of Sabbath, the opportunity to escape the "vokh," to devote a full day to the family, to the community, and to the most beloved activity, study of the Law, exalts the devout Jew of the shtetl. It fills his heart with joy and pride, and also with pity for his neighbor, the peasant, who—free from the anxious burden of Sabbath prohibitions—is also deprived of enjoying the blessed contrast between Sabbath and vokh.

III

AFTER SABBATH

The chief focus of the Sabbath world is within the four walls of the home. The focus of the vokh is the shtetl itself, the shtetl of the teeming market place, the unpaved streets, the shabby wooden buildings. In summer the dust piles in thick layers which the rain changes to mud so deep that wagon wheels stick fast and must be pried loose by the sweating driver, with the assistance of helpful bystanders. After a rain, streams and puddles of muddy water invite the children to splashing and wading from which they emerge streaked and smeared. When the mud gets too bad, boards are put down over the black slush so that people can cross the street.

The thirsty dust is further moistened by the dishwasher and other liquid refuse of the shtetl which is emptied out in the streets. "By the smell of the street water," it is said, "you can tell what day of the week it is."

The main street of a large shtetl may be paved with jagged stones, set in as they are found, with no attempt to shape or smooth them. The pointed stones are called "cat's heads" and when a cart drives over them the bang and clatter of its wheels shout aloud the news of its passage.

The houses of the rich are in the center of the town, around the market place. A few buildings may have two stories, the others will be shabby, unadorned, one-story structures, some with a yard and perhaps a small vegetable garden surrounded by a fence, often broken down.

There is no "Jewish" architecture. The characteristic features of the buildings are their age and their shabbiness. Comparison of their state with the better grooming of the peasant houses is a reminder of the usual contrast between urban and rural dwellings in poverty-stricken areas of Eastern Europe. The poorest peasant spends his spare time puttering about his home, repairing the door, the fence, the whitewashed walls. The impoverished city dweller accepts the condition of his house as part of the state of things, beyond his jurisdiction.

The general appearance of neglect declares in addition the fact that the house is viewed as a temporary shell. "My shtetl" is the people who live in it, not the place or the buildings or the street. "My home" is the family and the family activities, not the walls or the yard or the broken-down fence. A shtetl family that has lived in the same house for generations would detest and resist the idea of moving away. Yet, essentially, the house remains a temporary dwelling, inhabited for a brief moment of history. It is not part of the family entity, to be cherished and tended. Doctrine teaches that only the mind and the spirit endure—"life is a hallway to heaven"—and even the least soulful Jews of the shtetl, through force of circumstance if not of conviction, treat their physical dwelling places in accordance with this teaching.

A long history of exile and eviction strengthens the tendency to regard the dwelling place as a husk. True, it is not unheard of or even uncommon for a shtetl family to inhabit the same house for a hundred years. Yet at any moment the fatal decree may strike, and they may be tossed from the homestead into the deep dust of the road. Daily activities are pursued as if today's condition would continue forever; but the setting in which they are placed is slighted as if it would be snatched away tomorrow.

In a small shtetl the Jews and the peasants may be close neighbors. In a large one, most of the Jews live in the center and the peasants on the outskirts, near their fields. The other inhabitants are the animals who share the streets, the yards, and on occasion the houses. Many families have chickens, geese, perhaps a goat or even a cow. The peasants in addition have numbers of highly domesticated pigs which roam the streets, enjoying the "kosher" garbage of the Jews to whom the pig is a forbidden animal, wandering into a yard through a broken fence and rooting about there until the children chase them out. A large, dignified sow, followed by her trotting piglets, can find good hunting in a shtetl and will wander happily until her master calls her by name and she dutifully waddles home, with her little ones trailing after through the congenial mire of the unpaved streets.

No shtetl is complete without a cemetery, a House of Prayer —or at least a minyan, and a mikva. A few very small ones are not complete, however, and severe effort is required to compensate for the deficiencies. If there is no cemetery, a funeral means carrying the body to another shtetl, perhaps a walk of miles—with the shrouded, black-palled corpse on the shoulders of the bearers, followed by the funeral procession, the wailing women bringing up the rear.

If the community is so very small that there is no shul, the whole population must move to a larger shtetl for the great holidays known as the Days of Awe. Food, holiday clothing and other necessaries are prepared in advance, loaded onto carts and wagons with the people, and trundled over sharp stones or deep mud for the exciting eight-day period of prayer and festivity. The visitors thoroughly enjoy the brief period in a "real" town, while their hosts are entertained by the awkward rustic behavior of their guests.

If the community is too small to support a rabbi, it is necessary to go to a neighboring shtetl for judgment on matters of ritual propriety, civil right, or personal dispute. The rabbi or his assistant, the *dayan,* must be accessible at any time to any Jew, for at any time a crisis may arise that requires immediate decision.

The heart of the weekday shtetl is the large open market place, surrounded by the "better" houses—many with stores in them. The stores of the large shtetl are often specialized, while in the smaller ones are found the "general" stores crammed with a medley of merchandise calculated to appeal to the taste and needs of the peasant customer. The whole contents of many of these "stores" could be bought for "a bit of cash." On market day the stores come to life. The owner stands in front of his door calling in and, if need be, pulling potential customers in by their coat sleeves—for this may be the one day when he can earn what he needs for the week and for Sabbath. He may even hire a boy to stand in the street and persuade customers, by words re-enforced with a persuasive hand on the elbow, to come in and see how much better and cheaper his employer's wares are than any others.

Market day is the antithesis of Sabbath in many respects, including its tempo. Even the morning prayers are said at top speed, though none of the required observances is actually skipped over. First of all on awakening, for every man, woman and child, comes the "fingernail water," because one must not walk four steps in the morning before pouring it over the hands and saying the blessing.

Every morning except Sabbath, men and boys over thirteen bind on the phylacteries, *tefillim*, containing small pieces of parchment on which are written pertinent passages from the Torah. One of the small leather cases is bound on the forehead —"they shall be for frontlets between thine eyes"—and one on the left arm, which does less work than the right—"thou shalt bind them for a sign upon thy hand." A left-handed man would bind the phylactery on his right arm. It must be done in standing position and no interruption by word or by act is permitted while the long, narrow black straps are adjusted and the blessing is being said. The phylacteries must be handled with extreme care, for anyone who allowed them to fall on the floor would have to fast during the entire day.

They are worn, with the talis, while the series of morning prayers is said. An extremely pious Jew wears his tefillim, as well as his talis, while he studies the books of the Law, carefully removing them when he must put his book aside for some less lofty activity, and pronouncing the blessing each time he puts them on again.

A man about to rush to market hurries through his morning prayers as quickly as possible, then puts the phylacteries away in an embroidered case, as handsome as his circumstances permit. In doing so he must make sure that they lie next to—not on top of—each other, with the head phylactery at the right in tribute to its superior position.

Breakfast is likely to be only a piece of black bread with an onion, finished quickly so that he may be on his way to market, where those who come first fare best.

The large open market place is divided into sections where different commodities or services are offered for sale, and each section has its characteristic odor that mingles with the prevailing blend of people and of animals. In the dairy section the vendors have their sweet butter wrapped in cool leaves, well covered over, their sour cream in earthenware pots, their vats of milk and buttermilk. Whatever one sells in the shtetl is measured out carefully and then a bit added "for a good measure." In the fish section, live fish swim about in tubs while the "sleeping fish" are laid out in boxes with ice and salt, waiting for customers.

Here each salesman acts as his own barker, crying aloud the special virtues of his wares. Groups of women crowd around the peasants who have brought their farm produce for sale, jostling each other in the attempt to get first choice. Bargaining is raised to a fine art. For Jew and peasant alike, to pay the price asked or to refuse to modify the first price named would be contrary to custom. If it is an important negotiation between men, like the sale of a cow or a horse, the ceremonial of transaction involves the stretching out and withdrawing of hands, the seller striking his palm against the palm of the buyer, the buyer pulling away until agreement is reached when they shake hands and thus seal the bargain.

When the buyer or seller is a woman, which is often the case, the procedure is more verbal and much more vivacious. The acquisition of a Sabbath fish may take on all the suspense of a pitched battle, with onlookers cheering and participants thoroughly enjoying the mutual barrage of insults and exhortations. Points are scored through technique and finesse, and the process of bargaining has as much interest and zest as the final result.

In the early morning the market place with its stalls and clearings is comparatively quiet. The best bargains can be found then, before the prices for the day are set. There are late bargains too, when everyone is eager to get rid of his merchandise and go home. The middle of the day is the time of "the real scream and noise."°

All sales are for money, there is no barter in kind; and there is a turnover not only in goods but also in role. The seller of the morning becomes the buyer of the afternoon. Having disposed of his farm and dairy produce, the peasant uses his receipts to stock up on the more urban products offered by the Jew.

The crowds in the market place are predominantly women— those who come to buy and those who come to sell. All are dressed in their weekday clothes, drab mended dresses, a shawl over the shoulders, and each one carries a basket on her arm. Some will have a purse but more often a woman will keep her coins in a corner of her large handkerchief, tied in a knot, *knippl*. For protection against pickpockets, the knippl is carried in a pocket of her petticoat and in order to reach it or to put it back she hauls up her outer skirt and digs deep into the pocket.

There are a good number of men also, peasants who bring their produce, merchants and peddlers from the neighborhood, artisans with their tools, selling their wares or making repairs in the market place, and receiving orders for work outside.

The uniformity of the men's Sabbath day dress is broken by the addition of such practical features as high boots, like those the peasants wear. Some of them even lay aside their long black caftans for strenuous labor, but the talis koton is always retained. Their weekday gait is quick, the expression of their faces is tense, for during the vokh one is always "chasing after parnosseh," a livelihood.

The market represents the chief contact between the Jew and the non-Jew, who for the shtetl is primarily the peasant. Aside from the market and scattered business negotiations, they inhabit different worlds. And in the dealings that bring them together they represent different aspects of the economy. The non-Jew, the goy, is a farmer. The Jew, officially proscribed from owning farmland, is urban.

The seeds of all their relations are in this market-place contact. They need each other, as customer and as source of supply. They are able to do business with each other, for the most part in friendly fashion. The peasant will have his special peddler for small purchases, his special customer for eggs or potatoes. He will give first preference to this Jew, loyally repulsing other offers. The Jew will try to buy his grain regularly of one peasant. A sturdy business relationship is built up between them.

At the same time, each distrusts and fears the other. It is not that each knows the other will try to cheat him in bargaining, for this is merely a part of the market game, a game that belongs to Eastern Europe and is as native to the peasant as to the Jew. "The Polish or Ukrainian peasant wouldn't like to buy without bargaining with the customer. The peasant has to feel that he got a bargain. So the storekeeper asks twice as much because he knows he will bargain the price down. The customer may leave the store five times, and come back, and bargain and bargain."°

There is beyond this surface dealing, however, an underlying sense of difference and danger. Secretly each feels superior to the other, the Jew in intellect and spirit, the "goy" in physical force—his own and that of his group. By the same token each feels at a disadvantage opposite the other, the peasant uneasy at the intellectuality he attributes to the Jew, the Jew oppressed by the physical power he attributes to the goy.

It is no rare occurrence for the market day to end with violence. The peasant, having sold his wares, will celebrate his profits—and perhaps drink them all away—at a Jewish inn. When he can no longer pay for liquor and still insists on more, he will be thrown out, whereupon if he is already inflamed by drinking he sets up a cry, "The Jew has cheated me!" If a group of comrades who have shared the activities of the day should join him, a token riot may follow. The pattern is familiar to Jew and to peasant and it exists behind their consciousness through the friendliest of dealings.

As the economic center of the shtetl, the scene of buying, selling and mingling, the market place epitomizes the interdependence, the reciprocity, the ambivalence that exist between Jew and Gentile. The tensions produced by their relations and mutual attitudes result in a working equilibrium which prevails until some accident upsets it. The area directly affected by this equilibrium is limited to the area of contact between the two groups, and each withdraws from it to lead his own separate life. When the equilibrium is upset, however, the consequences may invade any home in the shtetl.

As much as possible, the shtetl of the vokh is thrust outside the Sabbath world. Yet in the world of the market place the values of the Sabbath world persist, and the structure of the synagogue has set its imprint. The structure of the community is, in fact, the structure of the synagogue.

This is not because the secular order is carried into the synagogue, but because it would be impossible to separate the religious from the secular—they are fused into one whole. Every act of the weekday world falls within the jurisdiction of divine Law and none is too trifling to be considered in relation to the Law. Every Jewish boy who plays among the market stalls has been consecrated to the Law, and its commandments are upon him every hour of every day. During the week, as on the Sabbath, his activities are conditioned by the solemn dedication with which, as an infant, he was inducted into the Jewish community: "May he enter into Torah, into marriage and into good deeds."

Part Two

May He Enter Into Torah . . .

I

THE EASTERN WALL

A Jewish community without a center of learning is unthinkable, and a shtetl of any size will have several varieties of school: a *kheyder*, where the youngest children study, a besmedresh for both prayers and study, a *talmud toyreh* for those whose parents cannot pay tuition, a *yeshiva* for higher studies. Study is the duty and joy of a man reared in the shtetl tradition. As a duty it is twice prescribed. In order to be a good Jew one must obey the commandments of the Scripture. In order to obey, one must know them. In order to know them, one must study. Moreover, to study is a *mitsva*, a deed commanded by God.

The 613 mitsvos define the essential obligations of the devout Jew. Among the first is the mitsva of learning: "Thou shalt teach them [God's commandments] diligently unto thy children, and shalt talk of them when thou sittest in thy house, and when thou walkest by the way, when thou liest down and when thou risest up."

Not all, or nearly all, of the mitsvos are observed even by orthodox Jews. Some are impossible because they presuppose the conditions that existed in biblical times. Some may be neglected because they are too difficult for even the most devout. But those which constitute the main base of Jewish behavior—ethical rules, social duties, religious beliefs, dietary regulations—remain in force. Among these the mitsva of learning has never lost its strong position. On the contrary, during the long centuries of exile its importance increased, especially for Jews of Eastern Europe.

To share one's learning is also a mitsva. Those who know the Law are under obligation to explain it to those who are less learned, and the unlearned depend upon the erudite for general instruction as well as for specific advice in the countless questions of interpretation that arise during the course of daily life.

The joy, like the duty of study, is twofold. There is pleasure in the exercise itself, which history has made the most cherished recreation of the shtetl. Moreover, the pursuit of learning offers to the scholar of the shtetl a means of escape from dark reality, from home troubles, from persecution, into a joyous identification with his past and with his people.

In any community that adheres strictly to the tradition, some men are always engaged in fulfilling the divinely decreed obligation of study. If his occupation does not permit a Jew to devote himself entirely to learning, he may study in the morning before work, or in the evening, or devote at least one day a week —the Sabbath—to study. Not all of them do so; but those who do are recognized as living up to the traditional pattern.

Even the "ignorant" man is usually able to spell out, with whatever difficulty, the prayers in his prayer book. He does not know Hebrew, the language of ritual and of learning; but he knows the alphabet that serves both for Hebrew and for Yiddish, and he is able to pronounce words that may be incomprehensible to him. The women, who are not supposed to study the Law, often—though not always—are taught to read Yiddish, and their familiarity with the Hebrew letters enables them to read some of the prayers they cannot understand. Complete inability to read is almost unknown. "In villages where only one peasant knows how to read, you'll hardly find one Jew who can't,"° it is said; and, "no matter how 'common' a Jew was he could still read his prayers."°

Rules of behavior and translations of prayers are published in Yiddish for those unable to read Hebrew, and Yiddish is the language of profane literature. An orthodox man, of course, would be above reading a Yiddish book, and if a school boy did so in secret he would be ashamed and afraid to be found out.

The Yiddish language is rich in terms for referring to a learned man: *lerner,* or studious one; *ben Toyreh,* son of the Law; *baal Toyreh,* master of the Law; *lamdn,* erudite one; *talmid khokhem,* wise scholar, erudite one; *masmid,* one who is always bending over his books; *kharif,* the acute; *iluy,* genius, superior or accomplished person; *oker horim,* "uprooter of mountains," one who excels in competitive scholarly pyrotechnics; *gaon,* genius. These are only a few of the terms used in everyday speech. Many more refined and complicated references are employed in writing, to describe the amount and character of the knowledge attained by a learned Jew.

Learning gives prestige, respect, authority, and status. In the synagogue, the men who sit along the Eastern Wall, the mizrakh, are pre-eminently the learned and the rabbi, as the most learned of all, has the most honored seat of all—next to the Ark where the Torah is kept. These men are sometimes referred to as "the mizrakh," sometimes as "the Faces," *pney,* of the community. Those at the rear, near the Western Wall, are the most ignorant.

Conversely, it is the unlearned who throng the market place, the women and the untutored workers. If a learned man appears, he walks among the stalls like a visitor from another land and is greeted with deference by those he meets there. He passes by, hardly aware of the piled-up merchandise over which they haggle, for he inhabits a world of the mind. His Sabbath clothes differ from his weekday costume only in the elegance of the fabric, just as his weekday thoughts and pursuits retain the form set by the Sabbath world.

The men who sit along the Eastern Wall and who live aloof from the market place are known by a variety of names. They may be called the *fayneh yidn,* the fine Jews; the *eydeleh,* the noble; the *erlikheh,* the honest and pious. The *balebatisheh,* the burghers, are almost but not quite in this top category.

Perhaps the most generally used term for the upper social register is the *sheyneh yidn,* the fine—or literally, the beautiful Jews. They are also called *sheyneh layt,* the beautiful people. This use of the word beautiful to connote other than physical qualities is characteristic of a people for whom intangibles have a concrete reality. One speaks of a beautiful deed or a beautiful event. To call a house "sheyn" means, not that its outward aspect is pleasing, but that the household is orderly, dignified, harmonious. Those who offer wholehearted generosity are sometimes said to "beautify" the orphan and the pauper. Obscene language, on the other hand, is referred to as "ugly words."

Those who sit at the rear of the synagogue are known as the *prosteh yidn*, the "common Jews," and this term has far wider currency than any of the words used to designate the sheyneh. It is striking that if one asks a former member of the shtetl about the terms applied to its two main social categories, a wide array of synonyms for sheyneh will be given, but a comparatively limited range of definition. The term prosteh, on the other hand, is almost universally used, alternating only now and then with *hamoyn*, plebs, the crowd. The definitions of prosteh, however, show far more variation.

Any definition of either term will refer, directly or indirectly, to at least one of the three basic criteria of status. These three, of which the third is really the product of the first two, are: learning, wealth, and an almost indefinable concept, *yikhus*, that describes family background with respect to learning and wealth.

The social spectrum of the shtetl shows at each end a vivid, unalloyed, unmistakable stratum, while between these extremes lie innumerable layers, clearly perceptible yet merging in such a way that no sharp boundary line can be drawn between them. One end, the completely sheyneh, is marked by possession of all the high status criteria; the other, the completely prosteh, by possession of none. In between, the various layers combine in varying proportions the three basic criteria of status.

The people in the shtetl are keenly aware of each individual's position on the social spectrum. Expectations with regard to social, economic and ethical behavior and role are explicitly linked to it. In determining the position, a larger amount of one value may compensate for a defiicit in another. Moreover, the position is not necessarily permanent, for all status except sex and age is achievable through acquiring or augmenting one of the basic values.

Historically, traditionally, ideally, learning has been and is regarded as the primary value and wealth as subsidiary or complementary. Economic pressures and outside influences have made of wealth a constant contender for first place in the value hierarchy. Both the force of the external pressures and the force of the tradition are demonstrated by the extent to which wealth

as a status criterion is translatable into a substitute for, or
equivalent of, learning.

Ideally the sheyneh yidn possess both learning and wealth,
"learning and substance in one place." The typical mother's daydream, as expressed in folksong, is that her son shall become "a
learned student and also a clever businessman." A man of great
learning belongs automatically to the sheyneh, however, no
matter how poor he is. A man of great wealth but slight learning is rated as sheyn if he uses his money in accordance with the
Law that is the sole subject of study, and if he moves and acts in
a manner consonant with its teaching.

Thus, even though a wealthy man has failed to fulfill wholly
the mitsva of learning, by scrupulous observance of many other
mitsvos he can enjoy the status of the sheyneh. The man of great
wealth who exhibits the approved behavior is known as a *nogid,*
a man of honor and substance, a leader in the community. If he
is rich but heedless of the Law in his deportment and the use of
his wealth, he is "a parvenu pig." Money, then, is most acceptably
a status criterion when it serves as handmaiden to the primary
criterion, study.

The approved behavior which marks a man as sheyn embraces both externals and intangibles. His manner shows decorum and restraint. He is a man of honor and integrity, "his
word is as good as a bank."° More than this, he is a man of social
conscience, fulfilling his responsibility to the community by
service to the group and its individuals. His accepted obligation
is to succor and protect those who are less wealthy, less privileged
than he. He "sees to it that the poor people have something to
'make the Sabbath' and that there is order in the community."°
It is his obligation also to advise and instruct. "And the sheyneh
yidn would see to it that quarrels were straightened out. And
they did all this of their own free will. They were never paid
wages for it. Something else they used to do was to study where
the prosteh yidn would hear and maybe learn something. For example between afternoon and evening prayers there is some
time. Nobody went home then. They would sit around in shul
and study. The sheyneh yidn used to study out loud and the
prosteh would listen to them and ask questions. The sheyneh

yidn must answer all these questions. In fact they used to inspire the prosteh yidn to ask questions and sometimes over one paragraph in the Talmud they would spend hours. This was the role of the sheyneh yidn."°

Moreover, they are under constant obligation to conform to the correct traditional pattern of manhood, evolved through the generations from devout study of the Law. "My father was a conscientious and honest person . . . dressed nicely, had a long beard like sheyneh yidn are supposed to have, belonged to societies to help the poor and needy, helped the yeshiva boys, and was a good and religious Jew."°

The man who is prost lacks both learning and the attributes regularly associated with it. He is further described as one uncouth, unmannered, given to unseemly language and at times to "un-Jewish" behavior—that is, to behavior at odds with the ideal set up by the learned tradition. To brand a person un-Jewish in the shtetl carries the same kind of rebuke as the term "un-American." It means not only divergence from the group pattern, but also a falling away from the values and standards considered noblest and best.

A few characterize the prosteh as those who "work for others and are not their own masters."° A good many, in other ways, relate the status to occupation. "The prosteh are the butchers . . . they are the shoemakers, the tailors . . . they are the ones who do the real dirty work."° Occupation, however, is associated with status through its relation to education and not in itself. A man who works with his hands is not necessarily prost, if he has the manners and the learning to entitle him to a different rating. On the other hand, he cannot be completely sheyn for that requires a life devoted to learning or to its social equivalents, and such a life is incompatible with manual labor. Symbolically, therefore, the "rough" occupations have come to be identified with the prosteh.

Yikhus, the third in the trilogy of elements that contribute to high status, is ultimately a derivative of the other two. It relates to family background and position, but cannot be called pedigree since it can be acquired currently as well as by inheritance, and does not necessarily require transmission "by blood." Essentially it is a product of learning plus wealth, of learning without wealth, or of wealth so used as to be translatable into the highest common denominator—the fulfillment of divine command.

Yikhus achieved through inheritance is proportionate to the number of learned, eminent or notably charitable men in the family. A person describes his own yikhus or that of another by listing the scholars and philanthropists on his family tree. This ancestor yikhus, known as *yikhus ovos,* cannot be retained merely by right of inheritance. If it is not constantly validated through activities of the individual himself, then his yikhus dwindles. Moreover, a man whose family lacks yikhus may attain it for himself. The status differentiation, symbolized in the arrangement of the synagogue seats, exists in conjunction with a strong emphasis on individual equality. The "common man" seated on the wooden bench at the rear of the synagogue can aspire to a seat on the East Wall, if not for himself then for his son. The son may become sheyn by outstanding scholarship, by great business success combined with "sheyn" use of his profits, or by the right kind of marriage.

If the learned son of prosteh parents achieves marriage with the daughter of a man who has great yikhus, his parents acquire yikhus by the alliance; similarly, they gain yikhus from a son who attains learning or wealth through his own efforts. If a man becomes a *baal yikhus,* "Master of yikhus," through his own success in study or in business, it is called *yikhus atsmo,* "by oneself," as differentiated from the kind that is derived through others.

The varieties, degrees, and definitions of yikhus are infinite, and provide scope for infinite discussion. It is a subject one can argue endlessly, safe in the knowledge that nobody is ever persuaded to change his mind about it, because convictions regarding it are based far more on social and family identification than on observable fact. People outside of the family sometimes fail to see or refuse to acknowledge the basis of its claims to yikhus. If it is the best kind, however, handed down through generations of learned ancestors, it can remain untarnished through any amount of dusty squalor.

There are a haughty few who refuse to recognize yikhus "by oneself" and who would resist any relative's marriage to a person whose yikhus did not extend back for seven or eight generations. There are those who deny that "money yikhus" is really yikhus at all. "There were two kinds of sheyneh yidn, those who came from yikhus and those who were learned. Of course if you had money it helped a little."° On the other hand, some cynics— usually prost—claim that yikhus is basically a matter of money, or at least that money can gain for anyone the equivalent of yikhus. "The rich people, and those with yikhus, had their matsos baked first, the poor later . . ."° and again, "the poorer people or those with less yikhus sat at the end of the table according to rank."°

Whatever standard they recognize, the family with yikhus will strive to maintain it, to keep its purity unsullied, and if possible to augment it. Many a girl has been forced to renounce her beloved because to marry beneath her yikhus would "put a spot on the family name."° For a man who "comes from yikhus" to engage in manual labor, even under stress of economic necessity, is a calamity for manual labor has come to symbolize the antithesis of the social ideal—a life devoted entirely to study. "My cousin was disgraced because he became a locksmith . . . his brothers and sisters, even while supported by him, referred to him as 'the *prostak*' despite the fact that he had been well-educated in his youth."°

However it may be defined, analyzed and weighted, yikhus is the badge and the measure of aristocracy. At the same time, to the extent that it is accessible to all and must be validated by the efforts of the individual, it bears witness to the principle that potentially all men are equal. The assumption of equality is as important as the fact of class differentiation in the social structuring of the shtetl.

Within a community the yikhus of every member is generally known to the last detail, and to recite one's yikhus to new acquaintances is an integral part of an introduction.

The cover of a rabbinical treatise frequently carries the full yikhus of its author. His name is often lost among the names and relationships of his illustrious ancestors, his and their honorific titles and claims to fame, and the titles of his and their published works. A serious bibliographer may find a time-consuming problem in the attempt to discover which of the many individuals

named on the cover actually wrote the volume in his hand. Thus
the more famous the author, the less of this apparatus is employed. Maimonides, for example, "is his own yikhus," and his
name would appear upon the cover without ancestral embellishment.

Everyone in the community knows also whether a person
is more or less prost, more or less sheyn—that is, his precise status
as defined by his combination of the three variables. "There were
different grades of prosteh yidn . . . some of them were very
prost, they were practically illiterate. Others could learn a little
bit so they were less prost, but still belonged to the prosteh."°
The gradation may be extremely subtle: "The ones who make the
soles on the shoes are considered low prost. Those who make the
upper parts of the shoes are already higher."°

The more the individual is divorced from the ideal picture
of the learned man, the more prost he is; the closer he comes to
that ideal, the more sheyn. "If he can learn a *little,* knows a *little*
more Torah, and has a *little* money, why then he's not quite so
prost."°

The community will remember, too, what one's original
status was, no matter how much it may change. The "parvenu
pig" is "one who has come up," an *oyfgekummener.* Even if he
donates much and ostentatiously to charity, if he is ignorant and
ill-mannered and given to dressing "loudly" he will be despised,
scorned, perhaps even feared. His children will be known as the
offspring of a parvenu and therefore as dubious assets.

If one of the "real sheyneh" with a "big yikhus" and a
creditable history loses his money, he becomes an object of pity
and delicate charity. Such a person is an *opgekummener,* "one
who has come down." When he enters a house he will still be
treated as sheyn, even though he has become an honorable
pauper. Money will be conveyed to him anonymously and secretly,
in order to spare his feelings. On the other hand, an opgekummener who has lost his fortune through acting prost—drinking
and carousing, violating the traditional pattern—rouses no pity.
Sympathy is showered on his parents and family but for him
there is only scorn, and the memory of his former position merely
accentuates the depth to which he has sunk.

A Jew without learning is incomplete. He is an ignoramus, an *amorets;* and an ignoramus is the most despised member of the community. There is a saying in the Talmud, "Better a learned bastard than an ignorant priest."

The rank order of Jews with regard to their quality as Jews would approximate their rank order in learning. The most complete of all is the profoundly learned man. A woman is not supposed to have learning, and to the extent that she achieves it her Jewishness may be impaired. The most perfect woman with regard to fulfillment of the Law is still less complete a Jew than the learned man—in her complete form she remains partial, as an entity in herself. She is not viewed as a separate entity, however, but as a member of a unit in which the parts are complementary.

The amorets, the ignorant man, is less adequate a Jew than the woman, for he has been commanded to have much learning and in fact he has little or none. The non-Jew, by his original rejection of the Covenant, placed himself outside the hierarchy, like a star that exists beyond the solar system, and therefore he has no status with regard to learning. He is an essential part of the great universe, but within the strictly Jewish order, which is an order determined by degree of learning and which defines study only as study of the Law, the non-Jew has no role and no status.

The man of outstanding learning enjoys top honors in the community. He "is his own yikhus." He fulfills the prime requisite of the "beautiful Jew." Besides having a seat at the Eastern Wall, he is called more often than others to the reading of the Torah, and receives the passages that are valued most. At social gatherings he is accorded the best place; if he is very learned, the host will insist on giving him the head of the table at family feasts, and he will be served first. At a circumcision ceremony, he will often be given the honor of holding and presenting the child.

When he speaks he will be heard with deference, and not interrupted. In shul during the period between prayers, he will be surrounded by a group respectfully listening to his comments on some passage in the Talmud, or on events in the life of the community, or even on political problems. His advice will be sought on matters of moment for individuals and for the community. He will be the trusted recipient of secrets that must be kept, money or jewels that must be deposited. He is the preferred arbiter in business disputes, although his knowledge of the subtleties of business transactions may be limited. He is not even expected to know the value of money, but it is taken for granted that the keenness of his mind, sharpened by lifelong study, will allow him to penetrate the most complicated business.

A talmid khokhem, a wise scholar, is easily recognizable in the streets of the shtetl. He walks slowly, sedately, absorbed in his thoughts. His speech is calm, rich in quotations from the Bible or the Talmud, allusive and laconic—his words "are counted like pearls." He is greeted first by other members of the community, in deference to his high position. Not only the poor but also the wealthy greet him first, if they are less learned than he. His response will reflect the status of the other person. If the salutation comes from an ignoramus, there will be just a barely perceptible wink, and sometimes even that is omitted. If the other person merits it, there will be an inclination of the head.

A learned man seldom laughs aloud. Excessive laughter, like any sort of excess, is considered the mark of an amorets. He will react to a joke or a witty saying by a smile or a very short and restrained laugh. The talmid khokhem must indicate his dignity and sophistication by his behavior and his appearance.

The shtetl ideal of male beauty again reflects the high value set on learning. A man with *hadras ponim,* a distinguished, beautiful face, ideally has a long beard—symbol of age and therefore of wisdom. His forehead is high, indicating well-developed mentality; his complexion is pale, revealing long hours spent over books. Thick eyebrows showing penetration jut out over deep-set, semiclosed eyes, indicating weariness from constant poring over texts—eyes that shine and sparkle as soon as an intellectual problem is discussed. Very important are the pale, delicate hands, evidence that the owner has devoted his life to exercise of the mind rather than of the body.

If a man cannot achieve for himself or for his son the status of talmid khokhem, the next best move is to achieve contact with a scholar. Parents dream of marrying their daughter to a learned youth or their son to the daughter of a learned father. The match-maker, who is a very important institution in the shtetl, has in his notebook a list of all the eligible boys and girls within range. Under each name is a detailed account of his yikhus, in which the most important item is the number of learned men in the family, past and present. The greater the background of learning, the better the match. The sages have said, "A man should sell all he has in order to get for his son a bride who is the daughter of a scholar."

The dowry of a girl is proportional to the scholarship of the prospective bridegroom. Very rich fathers used to go to the yeshiva and ask the director for the best student, whom they would then seek as a son-in-law. An outstanding student would receive not only a rich dowry, but also a given number of years of *kest*—that is, of board at the home of his parents-in-law while he continues his studies. In this way the son of a prost family may marry into a family with yikhus; and in this way learning serves as a potent instrument of social mobility—perhaps the most potent in the shtetl society.

"Torah is the best of wares," is a popular saying among Eastern European Jews. The father will support his son, the sisters their brother, the father-in-law his son-in-law, in order to give opportunity for study. Moreover, it is correct for the wife of a gifted scholar to earn a livelihood for the family while he remains with his books, and for the whole community to subsidize the poor student. If a man were not devoting himself to study, he would be scorned as a ne'er-do-well for letting his wife support him, and he would be despised as a beggar if he lived on the community; but as a scholar he enjoys both support and prestige.

Parents seek a learned son-in-law or the daughter of a learned father, not only because of a desire to augment the yikhus of the family and a genuine admiration for intellectual prowess. In addition, learning is viewed as a guarantee of high moral and social standards. An amorets, an ignoramus, is not merely un-schooled. He is also suspected of being a man who does not know how to behave socially, one with low ethical principles, who will treat his wife without due respect and may even beat her. And above all, he is a man who would not know how to bring up his children. If he proves himself better than the habitual expectation he may evoke surprised and approving comments.

It is assumed that a learned man will be a good husband and father. One of the basic principles of Jewish education is that the mere fact of learning the rules of behavior, which are the commandments of God, causes one to behave in accordance with them. The assumption implies a native desire to know the will of God and a native inclination to obey it. All that is required is the opportunity to discover, through pious and unceasing study, the true import of the commandments.

The wife of the learned man will be treated according to the rules for conjugal relations which are in the Holy Books. The children will grow up to be scholars. A girl who comes from a family of learned men will be a good wife and a good mother. She will be modest and well behaved, and—most important of all —she will put her husband's studying above everything else because she understands the value of learning.

If one has a daughter there is still another advantage in seeking for her a learned spouse. Learning assures the future life, the *Olam Habo*. A woman does not study—learning is for men only. If she is a good wife, however, especially if she facilitates her husband's studies by earning a living as well as running the house, she will be rewarded by a share of her husband's eternal happiness. All these considerations stimulate parents to dream of a son-in-law who will be a talmid khokhem, a dream expressed in a popular lullaby for baby girls:

> Under Gitteleh's cradle
> Stands a snow-white kid
> The kid went off to trade
> With raisins and almonds
> But what is the best trade?
> Gitteleh's bridegroom will study
> Torah he will study
> Holy books will he write
> And good and pious
> Shall Gitteleh remain.

The prestige that is linked with learning erases the all-important difference in age. As a rule there is a definite separation according to years, and seniority commands deference. A small child is an incomplete member of society, and as such commands little respect from the male adult. His presence is required at synagogue because the atmosphere is essential to his education. But a child is "only a child."

A boy's position changes, however, when he begins to study, and his prestige increases in proportion to the progress he makes at school. The first real mark of respect he receives is when he passes his primary studies and enters the second stage. When he advances to study of the Talmud he is considered almost an adult, especially if he shows special aptitude. He may participate in debates of adults, and his opinion carries equal weight. A bearded man will not be ashamed to bring some difficult talmudic question to a young boy of thirteen or fourteen who is known as a future talmid khokhem. A boy who is known as a genius, iluy, will be shown the same deference as a learned adult. A child of eight who was precocious enough to know by heart all the prayers and half of the Pentateuch, with the accompanying commentary of Rashi, was treated with more respect than many adults.

The persistence and antiquity of this pattern is suggested by an episode in the life of Christ, described by the Evangelist Luke (Luke 2, 41–52). The twelve-year-old Jesus was found in the temple discussing the Law and confounding bearded scholars by his profound and penetrating questions. The situation—depicted in well-known paintings by Dürer, Van Dyck, Botticelli, and others—bears striking similarity to the treatment and behavior of a precocious student in the Eastern European shtetl.

"A rabbi's son, who was known as an iluy, a scholar, used to come to play chess with my father. He would be invited into the best room, treated with all respect. He was only a couple of years older than I was . . . but for me he wasn't a boy."°

In view of the advantages attached to scholarship—status, prestige, a rich wife, the joy of study itself—it is natural that to be a scholar is considered the most desirable career of all. The student is the pride of his family, and more. He brings them honor and joy, sheds on them the reflected glory of his yikhus. Every

male infant is potentially a source of honor for his family.
Potentially he represents fulfillment of the pattern of the ideal
Jew. He represents also the possibility of social achievement.
From his birth there lies on his shoulders not only the warm
weight of their love but also the sum of their hopes and expectations. This is part of the security he finds in his home. It is also
part of his *ol*, his yoke or burden.

From infancy the boy is guided and prodded toward scholarship. In the cradle he will listen to his mother's lullabies:

> Sleep soundly at night and learn Torah by day
> And thou'lt be a Rabbi when I have grown grey.

or

> My Yankeleh shall study the Law
> The Law shall baby learn
> Great books shall my Yankeleh write
> Much money shall he earn.

or

> A boy who'll study the Gemara
> The father will listen with happiness and joy
> A boy who grows to be a talmid khokhem . . .

The whole family, mother, aunts, sisters, everyone who is in
close contact with the baby, will watch for anything in his behavior that could be interpreted as a sign of intellectual precocity.
A smile, an unexpected gesture, an imitation of an adult's expression, will be considered a *khokhmeh,* expression of exceptional intelligence—and parents and neighbors will exclaim about
the little prodigy.

As soon as the baby starts to talk, his mother teaches him religious blessings. More important, however, the child is steeped
in the atmosphere and the spirit of learning. For the most part
the father participates little in the life and activities of a very
small son. If he is a learned man, however, most of his time at
home will be spent over his books, and while he studies he will
take the little boy on his lap. Even before the child is able to talk,
he becomes familiar with the "little black points," the letters on
the pages. He becomes used to the melody of learning—the chant

always uttered as the scholar reads, to the father's continual rocking back and forth as he studies, to the general aspect of a book.

The father does not object if the child turns the page, or even if he closes or opens the book; but one thing is strictly prohibited—to damage it or throw it on the floor. From the very beginning a book is held up as a subject of awe, and the whole process of learning is surrounded by an aura of veneration. When father is studying, all must be quiet. No noisy games are allowed. The child sees his mother and the other members of the family avoid the least noise because "the father studies," "the father is looking into a book."

When a learned relative or guest comes into the house, the child sees the respect that is showered upon him, and a mother will never forget to tell her son, "When you grow up you must be a talmid khokhem, like him." A boy is usually named after a deceased grandfather or an ancestor, and preference is given to the learned. The namesake will be reminded constantly to follow his example and become a lamdn, a ben toyreh. Thus, learning is a frequent topic of family conversation, of mother's lullabies, of blessings, of wishes and of exhortations that the child receives from day to day.

Once he starts to school, the boy is the "jewel" of the family. Every Saturday, when the father holds his weekly "hearing," while the teacher sits by, the mother feels her fate too is involved. If he does well she will be proud because she is "bringing up a good Jew." She is rewarded not only by her feelings as a mother, but also by the realization that in training her son to fulfill the mitsva of learning she is adding to her own prospects of enjoying Olam Habo.

Each new step in the curriculum is an occasion for family celebration, at home and in the synagogue. At such celebrations the boy must show his intellectual mettle and his progress by some original interpretation of a sentence from the Torah.

If he shows ability and enthusiasm, the family is happy and the parents radiate their pride. If he is indifferent or incompetent, they will reproach him, painting his future in appalling colors: "What will become of you? What will you be? A tailor? A shoemaker? An amorets!" The father will try to stimulate his intellect by threats, by punishments, by beating. A boy who plays hookey may expect the worst, and it is a pious father who declares between strokes of the cat-o'-nine-tails, "You'll become a talmid khokhem if I have to kill you!"°

Nothing must interfere with school. "I remember that I didn't have any high boots and the mud came up very high that year. So mother used to carry me on her back to kheyder, but I had to go to kheyder."°

The most important item in the family budget is the tuition fee that must be paid each term to the teacher of the younger boys' school. "Parents will bend the sky to educate their son."° The mother, who has charge of household accounts, will cut the family food costs to the limit if necessary, in order to pay for her sons' schooling. If the worst comes to the worst, she will pawn her cherished pearls in order to pay for the school term. The boy must study, the boy must become a good Jew—for her, the two are synonymous.

II

FROM THE KHEYDER TO THE GRAVE

Every region, every social or economic group, every intellectual or religious faction has its own special features with regard to education. Yet in the educational pattern as in the others, variations are less striking than the unbroken identity, the core of continuity reaching across Eastern Europe and through the multiple strata of shtetl society.

"Learning" has a beginning but no end for, "The Torah has no bottom." Formal education begins between the ages of three and five when the boy is first taken to the *dardeki kheyder*, the small children's school.

Entrance into the kheyder is a painful experience for the mere baby who is taken away from his mother's familiar presence to spend ten or twelve hours a day at study. The child cries, the mother may be tearful, but wrapped in his father's prayer shawl the boy is carried out of babyhood, out of the home circle, beyond the enveloping warmth of feminine protection. And though the mother may weep, she would never oppose the commandment to teach Torah to a "big boy who is already three years old."°

To stimulate his interest at the first lesson, candies or coins are thrown from above him onto the open prayer book from which he is learning his first letters—the letters that spell the Hebrew words for "Eternal" and "Truth"—*Shaday*, and *Emess*. His father will carry him to school for the very first day, will sit with him during the first lesson, and then celebrate his son's new status by distributing cakes and candies to all his schoolmates.

Now he is "a kheyder boy," the center of attention and admiration—provided he gives a good account of himself. Proudly he will announce to relatives and neighbors, "Today I finished

learning all the letters of the alphabet." But by the same token
he is no longer free to run and play, except during the brief hours
when he is not at school. From eight to six, five days a week, and
half a day on Friday he sits in the teacher's home, in a small and
poorly furnished room, crowded with fifteen or twenty children
of assorted ages, and lays the foundation for a life of study.

To ease the entry into the adult, masculine realm of study,
a special assistant of the teacher will carry the child to and from
school every day, until he is ready and able to go by himself. The
assistant, the *belfer,* is usually rough with his charges and often
manages to collect from them as bribes the sweets and pennies
given to them by their mothers. Each day the belfer escorts five
or six children to the school, carrying the very smallest in his arms
where often enough they cry loudly and beat with their fists
against him. The others cling tightly to his caftan or to each
others' hands, so that the whole cavalcade is safely joined together for the journey. The townspeople are accustomed to its
passage, and to the unwilling wails.

The teacher, the *melamed,* is more formidable than the
belfer, daily collecting from his small charges a toll for his own
misery. He barely manages to live on the meager tuition fees he
receives from their parents, so that he and his family are chroni-
cally underfed. There are tales of how the melamed's wife or
daughters manage to spirit away the bread and butter given to
the child by his mother for the noon-day meal and then explain,
"the cat stole it."°

To add to the melamed's troubles, he is looked down upon
by the whole community. To share a wealth of knowledge is
among the most "beautiful" of deeds; to sell a meager stock of it
is unworthy. . . . "One should not make an axe of the Torah," it
is said.

The *dardeki melamed,* who lives by selling what should be
given, is not even a learned person. If he were, he would be a
rabbi or a teacher of advanced students. It is generally assumed
that a man who teaches little children has fallen into his profession because he failed elsewhere. "One who can't even tie a
cat's tail becomes a melamed."

Almost every Jew in the shtetl knows enough to teach little

children the first elements. But almost any of the slightly schooled would prefer to carry his own studies further and make his living at some other occupation. Even the rabbi in the shtetl does not receive direct payment for dispensing his knowledge of the Law; other means, sometimes roundabout, are found for enabling him to make a living.

The dardeki melamed, goaded by economic pressure and public scorn, seldom has any pedagogical ability or interest, is always gloomy and angry because of his "poor and miserable life,"° and never misses a chance to vent his spleen by severe, often sadistic punishments. "The cat-o'-nine-tails seldom hung useless and idle."°

Memories of childhood often include accounts of the melamed's punishments—a field in which he usually showed more energy and enterprise than in the field of letters. "When the melamed started to beat us, he forgot all limits and no cries or screams would stop him . . . people gathered at the windows of the kheyder and someone would run to tell the mother of the victim."° Sometimes afterwards, if a boy's face were too badly pinched or scratched, "the melamed's wife would take the butter from our lunch-time rolls and smear it on to make it heal, so it wouldn't look too bad at home."°

"The worst day was Thursday when the melamed's wife started to nag him about money for Sabbath provisions."° Another reason for Thursday beatings is the Sabbath "hearings," for if a boy makes a bad showing the melamed might lose a pupil. Sunday is the best day because the melamed is relaxed and rested after the peace of Shabbes.

To complain at home about the melamed's methods is of no avail. The teacher is right. This is the way the father was taught, this is the way one opens, painfully and laboriously, the portals to eternal truth and wisdom. There is no support from home. The mother may peer through the windows, weeping in agony as her child is beaten for failing to know his lesson, for speaking while another was reciting, for laughing when he should have been deep in the Holy Writ. But she will not raise a finger or say a word of protest.

Despite the long hours of work punctuated by the lash, the

kheyder experience is not one of unmixed gloom and hardship. Experience is seldom perceived as unmixed, for the shtetl is not given to absolute and categorical contrasts—things are seldom all black or all white. Reality is accepted as a composite of many elements, some of which may appear to be contradictory. Going to kheyder is a painful privilege, but to be a member of the Chosen People is itself a privilege that is painful as well as precious.

There are pleasant hours at the kheyder also, especially the hour of twilight. Each afternoon the melamed goes to shul for afternoon and evening prayers, lingering between the two short services to chat with the men he meets there, so that in all he is away about an hour. In winter, the school is dark by this time and candles are too expensive to waste during the melamed's absence. The children sit in the darkness, close together on the benches at the table where they study, or huddled near the oven for warmth. They may nibble a bit saved from the lunch each brings to school, perhaps some bread and jam, or even by luck a piece of bread spread with goose fat. One will exchange with the other, in the companionable quiet of the melamed's absence.

Above all, this is the hour for stories. Crowding together against the winter cold and the fear of the wonders they are describing, they tell each other tales in which themes carried over from pagan myths jostle with folklore rooted in the Talmud. In the melamed's absence the strict program of Hebrew erudition is broken into by a medley that mingles biblical miracles with the spirits and demons shared by all the folk, Jews and peasants alike. The boys tell each other in turn about the spirits who throng the shul after midnight, and the tricks they play on anyone who has to sleep there—so that a beggar would rather sleep on the floor of the humblest house than enjoy the honor of a bench in the shul. They tell about the devils who haunt the woods at night, the *sheydim,* and how some of them even get into the shtetl streets when it is very dark. They tell about the *dybbuk* who enters the soul of a person so that he becomes possessed and speaks with a voice not his own, uttering blasphemies that would be far from his true mind. They tell of Lilith, Adam's first wife, who steals children; and of children kidnapped from their parents by gypsies, or by wicked men who deliver them into Army service.

Children of Hassidim will repeat tales their fathers bring from the Rebbeh's court, about the miracles wrought by "wonder man."

When the melamed returns, all are glad to light the candles they have brought from home. For an hour or two they continue to study, sitting quietly side by side, each with his candle before him. Then at last they go out into the cold night where the shtetl is quite dark except for the lights that shine faintly through the house windows. Each boy carries his lantern, and all, even the bigger ones, hold hands. Still under the spell of the stories, they are afraid of the bad spirits. They fear also the Gentile boys who sometimes attack them on the way home. As they move down the dark street, gripping their lanterns and each other's hands, now and then a child drops away to enter his home. The band grows smaller, and their speed increases until the last one, left alone, breaks into a run and continues with all speed to his own door.

The teaching methods of the kheyder demand tremendous intellectual effort of a child who is almost a baby. The candies thrown on his first lesson book sweeten only the first hour of learning. From then on there is no attempt to sugar-coat the subject matter. No textbooks with pictures, no storytelling, no educational games are used. The only guides to lead him into "the Gates of Torah" are dingy, tattered prayer books with incomprehensible letters and words, and old Bibles used over and over again. The process of learning is the endless repetition of unfamiliar Hebrew words, memorizing each letter, each syllable, the rote meaning of each word, translated separately without reference to grammar or derivation.

Real understanding of the text is left for later. Sometimes even the true meaning of the word is neglected, especially when some botanical or zoological name occurs. In these cases, instead of translating the word exactly, the melamed—who himself does not always know the meaning—will say, "a kind of fish," "a kind of beast," "a kind of tree."

Swaying as one reads, and chanting the words in a fixed melody, *nign,* are considered necessary for successful study. Like praying, reading a sacred text is accompanied always by incessant rocking forward and back, forward and back; and the words are read aloud in a low-voiced chant that rises and falls. "It's easier to remember what you study when you rock."° The crowded room in the melamed's house, where the children study from early morning until nightfall, is filled always with a buzzing and humming, above which rises the shrill voice of the child who is reciting, or the sudden boom of the melamed as he pounces on some transgressor. The sound of study "as noisy as a market"° can be heard in the street outside, as one approaches the house.

The swaying and the chanting become automatic. Later, the students will acquire also the appropriate gestures with the index finger and the thumb, sweeping the thumb through an upward arc of inquiry and nailing down the point of the answer with a thrust of the index finger. Study is not passive but active, involving constant motor and vocal activity.

Above all, the students are trained to be attentive to the words of the melamed and ready to repeat the reading or the translation of a word the moment he indicates it with his fateful pointer. Inattention and absentmindedness are severely punished and very often sleeping interest is wakened by the lash. The melamed has great opportunity to descend on the inattentive, since the pupils are at different points in their studies and each proceeds at his own pace. While one individual or group is reciting, the others are supposed to give their full attention to their assignments, but the dignity of being "kheyder boys" does not prevent them from being little children. There are secret signals and messages, bursts of playing if the melamed leaves the room for a moment—usually paid for in full when he returns.

Yet little by little, the child does learn to read and to translate. In the small, ill-lit, ill-ventilated room he lays the foundation for the next steps, steps that may lead him at last into "the world of Torah."

In this first and most elementary kheyder, the pupils learn the elements of reading, and the prayers. Within a few months a child has mastered *ivreh*, the mechanics of reading, as differentiated from *ivreh taytsh*, reading with translation.

Then he is ready to begin studying the Pentateuch, or *khumesh*, an event celebrated at his home by a ceremony that follows extensive preparation. It is a double celebration, really, for the parents invite their friends to the ceremony and later the kheyder boys are entertained.

In the center of a table spread with pastries, nuts, and wine, stands the boy, now about five or six years old. He is dressed in his holiday clothes and occasionally even hung with as many watches and pieces of jewelry as the family can assemble or borrow. Next to him, their hands on his head, stand three "blessers," boys who know khumesh and have been taught the special blessings required by the occasion. All four boys are covered with a talis. The father and his friends sit around the table, the father at the right of the melamed. Since this is a ceremony for men, the boy's mother and her friends enjoy the performance from a distance.*

> An elaborate dialogue takes place between the teacher and
>   the children:
> Teacher: "Little boy, little boy, what are your father and
>   mother doing now?"
> Boy: "My father and my mother are having a beautiful cele-
>   bration."
> Teacher: "Is it because you are beginning to study khumesh
>   that your father and mother are making such a beauti-
>   ful celebration?"
> Boy: "Yes, Teacher, you guessed right."
> Teacher: "Perhaps you would like to 'say some Torah'?"
> Boy: "Of course! That is what I was created for. Although
>   I am not yet worthy to 'say Torah' before you, yet I will
>   say a few words. My teachers and friends . . ." (The
>   boy gives an explanation of the first sentences of Gene-
>   sis.)
> The First Blesser: "Bow down your head and I will bless you.
>   You shall have a wife with twelve curls, and each curl
>   shall have in it the holiness of each of the Tribes."

*The ceremony, including the dialogue, is fairly standard throughout the Eastern European area. The version given here is from a monograph; Yekhiel Shtern, "A Kheyder in Tyszowce (Tishevitz)," *Yivo Annual of Jewish Social Science,* Vol. 5, pp. 159 ff. Yiddish Scientific Institute—Yivo, New York, 1950.

Second Blesser: ". . . May our blessings be fulfilled and as
you wear the watches on your heart and as our hands
are on your head, so shall these blessings come true."

Third Blesser: "I wish you that the blessings which have
been said by the two Blessers shall be fulfilled, but I will
add still another one: may your life and the life of your
family be as sweet as the fine fruits of a tree that grow
near a spring."

All of the guests who up to now have been silent, say: "Congratulations!"

At this point the women shower candy and nuts on the
children. The khumesh beginner sits next to his teacher, before
an open book, and a second dialogue begins:

Teacher: "What are you studying, little boy?"
Boy: "Khumesh, my Teacher."
Teacher: "What does khumesh mean?"
Boy: "Five."
Teacher: "Five what?"
Boy: "Five books in the Holy Torah."
Teacher: "What are their names?"
(Boy enumerates the books.)
Teacher: "Which book are you studying, little boy?"
Boy: "I am studying the Third Book."
Teacher: "What is its name?"
Boy: "*Vayikro.*" (Leviticus.)
Teacher: "What does Vayikro mean?"
Boy: "He called."
Teacher: "Who called? The rooster on top of the stove?"
Boy: "No. The Lord called Moses to tell him the Laws of
sacrifice."
(The dialogue continues, with a discussion of the Law of
sacrifice.)

After the ceremony, the guests enjoy the refreshments, above
all the cookies the mother has prepared especially for the celebration. The boy is now launched in the second kheyder, and entitled to be known as a "khumesh boy."

The khumesh boy does not begin his study of the Pentateuch

with the first book Genesis, and its delightful stories, but with
Leviticus, the dull and difficult theory of sacrifices. At first he
continues to learn each word separately, but gradually he advances to translation of whole sentences. This is ivreh taytsh,
reading with translation. When he has reached this point, he begins to memorize some elementary commentaries. The most
popular commentator of the Torah and the Talmud, and the
one most studied in khumesh kheyder, is Rashi, who lived in the
eleventh century A.D. It is not enough for the young student to
understand and to translate the text of the Pentateuch. This is
child's play, beneath the dignity of a khumesh boy. In addition,
there must be comment and interpretation. The words and sentences have a special significance above and beyond their simple,
direct meaning, and in order to understand them truly it is necessary to pore over the commentary of Rashi. For example, the
Bible says: "When Sarah died her age was a hundred and twenty
and seven years." Rashi asks, "Why the repetition of the 'and'?"
The answer he offers is that not only was she a hundred and
twenty seven years old at her death, but also at this age she
looked as beautiful and young as at the age of twenty; and that
at the age of twenty she looked as beautiful and young as at the
age of seven. From his study in the khumesh kheyder the child
becomes acquainted not only with direct explanation of direct
statements, but also with involved interpretation and the search
for hidden meanings.

Khumesh and Rashi represent merely the elementary phases
of study, in which pupils are taught directly by the melamed, as
befits small children and beginners. In the highest kheyder, the
gemoreh kheyder, that sort of instruction is gradually replaced
by the principle of independent study under the guidance of the
teacher. This melamed is of a different order from the scorned
teacher of the dardeki kheyder. The intellectual caliber and the
status of the teacher rise with the level of the school.

The gemoreh kheyder is devoted chiefly to study of the
Talmud, which covers an infinite variety of aspects and problems, ancient and contemporary, religious and secular. Talmudic
studies consist of continuous discussion, commentary and interpretation, with the help of innumerable commentators and in-

terpreters. With equal concentration the child of eight or nine must study the holiday ritual in the Temple of Solomon, the ethics of man-to-man dealings, the laws of divorce, or the rules governing connubial behavior during menstruation.

It is with the talmudic studies that the true joy of learning is born. In the dardeki kheyder and the khumesh kheyder the work was routine, mechanical, boring, repetitious, depending on memory rather than on understanding. Talmudic studies open the way to exercise of individual capacities and imagination.

The beginning of this phase is not celebrated as spectacularly as the beginning of the khumesh. Yet the gemoreh kheyder, where the boy of ten or eleven begins to study the main code of Jewish wisdom, is a crucial phase of his education. Here he begins to display the real quality of his memory, and his power to spend long hours over a difficult problem, using the countless commentaries and interpretations with aptness and insight. Here he shows whether he has the caliber of the true talmid khokhem.

His teacher's opinion is not enough. The father may take him from time to time, on a Sabbath, to be examined by some member of the family who is known as a lamdn—an erudite one —or to any famous scholar in the community, and the verdict will be awaited anxiously. When a learned guest from out of town visits the household, the father will provoke a scholarly discussion in order to find out what the visitor thinks about his son's endowment. The whole family listens to the conversation, especially the mother, because the opinion of a learned man means a great deal for the future of her son. The great question is: does he have the talent for a life of study, or should he interrupt his education and go into trade or business?

If the boy is judged capable of becoming a talmid khokhem, he is sent from the gemoreh kheyder to the highest institution of learning—the yeshiva, the rabbinical academy. There, among hundreds of boys from different towns and provinces, under the guidance of eminent scholars, he will devote all his days and a great part of his nights to study. A "yeshiva boy" customarily sleeps no more than four or five hours a night, rising at daybreak or earlier and sitting over his books until long past midnight.

The general principle of the yeshiva is independence and

self-reliance. The program of study allows for infinite variation. The basic study is exhaustive analysis of the Talmud and its commentators. In addition, each student is privileged to spend a large share of his time on the part of Jewish wisdom that appeals to him most. If he is attracted by mystical problems, he will study the *kabala;* if philosophy is his field, he will delve into the works of the philosophers; if he is interested in legal questions, he will concentrate on the Talmud and its commentators. In all cases the approach is the same; commentary, interpretation, referring of the different texts to the biblical quotation that is their ultimate source.

Talmudic study is often called *pilpul,* meaning pepper, and it is as sharp, as spicy, as stimulating as its name implies. It involves comparison of different interpretations, analysis of all possible and impossible aspects of the given problem, and— through an ingenious intellectual combination—the final solution of an apparently insoluble problem.

Penetration, scholarship, imagination, memory, logic, wit, subtlety—all are called into play for solving a talmudic question. The ideal solution is the *khiddush,* an original synthesis that has never before been offered. This mental activity is a delight both to the performer and to his audience. Both enjoy the vigor of the exercise and the adroitness of the accomplishment. And at the same time, both relish demonstrating their ability to perform on so lofty and esoteric a level. When two accomplished scholars engage in pilpul, they will be surrounded by an admiring group that follows each sally in eager silence, and later will discuss the fine points with each other—possibly working up a new argument about which scholar carried the day.

The yeshiva teacher enjoys a status close to that of rabbi, for it requires infinite learning and capacity to lead the most advanced students. If he has some other source of income, he is recompensed only by the rewards inherent in fulfilling the mitsva of sharing his wisdom with others. If he must accept money, he is not paid by the individual parents, like the small children's melamed, but receives an impersonal stipend from the institution.

The honored teacher of the yeshiva is strictly a guide. He

will give an assignment from the Talmud, usually some complex, paradoxical problem which the students have to work out—drawing on a vast array of commentators and analyzing the topic among themselves by way of rehearsal for classwork. During the recitation period the problem will be discussed by the students and teachers, an exercise in which teacher as well as students will strain to excel. Such assignments are apart from the individual study projects of each student.

Many yeshivos do not have regular classrooms, but use the besmedresh with the bimah in the middle. Even in a formal classroom, however, the students often jump up on the benches in their excitement, or leave their seats in order to crowd around the teacher. Their great reverence for him is no deterrent to the vehemence of the arguments they hurl against each other and against him. A good teacher presides over the verbal battles with dignity and strength, preferring the active students to the ones who are passive and silent.

In order to be able to devote his life to study, the *yeshiva bokher,* "yeshiva boy," has to be assured of material subsistence. *"Im eyn kemakh, eyn Torah,"* says the proverb—"If there is no bread there is no study." Very few of the students have parents who can support them, however. The solution of this problem demonstrates once more the importance attached to study of the Law—the community takes over the burden of supporting, not only the yeshiva itself, but each individual student.

Deputies travel in cities and towns of Eastern Europe raising money to support the yeshiva. Such deputies are honored guests in the towns through which they pass. Moreover, members of the community where a yeshiva is established board the individual students. At the beginning of the term, each householder offers "days" according to his economic status; that is, promises to feed a student for one or more days each week. A rich man offers several days to several students, a poor man only a scanty meal one day each week, for one student. Some, who for one reason or another are unable to feed the student at home, replace the meal by coins to buy food—not always enough. In some way everyone must fulfill the obligation to support the study of the Law among the people of Israel.

The great majority of the students subsist by thus "eating days" with different members of the community, and it is said that the dream of a yeshiva bokher is, "a house seven floors high; on each floor lives a nogid; and with each nogid, I'll have a 'day.' " Innumerable stories are told about the exploits and the hardships of the yeshiva bokher in the course of "eating days."

It is relatively few who attend the yeshiva, a special elite drawn from the outstanding students of the gemoreh kheyder. The number of advanced students is further limited by the distance of many towns and cities from the centers where the yeshivos are located.

For those unable to continue their studies in the yeshiva, the place for advanced study is the besmedresh, the House of Study. It is usually a local synagogue, for the synagogue is as much a house of study as a house of prayer. In the besmedresh, between the prayer services, students old and young study the same subjects pursued in the yeshiva, under the same independent and individualized curriculum. One of the learned men in the community adopts the role of teacher, helping the students in their work. He serves without pay as a matter of course, for his tutelage is a mitsva. Since the teacher's role is minimal in advanced studies, however, the work does not lag or suffer even when none is available.

In the besmedresh, as in the yeshiva, poor students of ability are supported by the community through "eating days." The students in the besmedresh, however, include some not found in the yeshiva. One group is composed of men who have interrupted their yeshiva studies because of marriage. Supported by their fathers-in-law, they continue their studies in the local besmedresh. To this group belong also men who are devoting their time to study while their wives earn the living for the family.

Another group of students consists of workmen, businessmen, tradesmen, who, after their daily work, still strive toward learning, even though they do not belong to the really erudite. These nonscholarly students, who are not qualified to study independently, are grouped in associations or teams called *khevros*. Each khevreh studies a definite segment of Jewish lore, appropriate to the background and training of the members, and such associations are named for the subject studied. There will be a *khevreh mishnayes,* which studies only the Mishna, or Code of Law without the talmudic commentary; a khevreh *Shulkhan Arukh,* which studies only the popular compendium of Jewish laws, etc. The members of the khevreh frequently hire a melamed who helps them through the difficulties encountered in their studies. Sometimes the melamed will be a young boy who is famous for his knowledge and learning, and who gains honor and prestige through sharing his erudition.

Whether a man is a great savant or one who spells out his words, syllable by syllable, in the khevreh the amount of knowledge amassed by his study is not officially labeled. There is no degree marking the completion of a certain phase of study, for completion does not exist—"the Torah has no bottom." The diploma the student receives after a few years in the yeshiva indicates only that he has the right to exercise the function of rabbi. He does not receive with it a special scholarly degree with an appended title.

On the contrary, every Jew from the tailor who studies a chapter of the Pentateuch weekly to the intellectual "uprooter of mountains" dazzling the yeshiva with his pilpul, is called *Reb,* "my Teacher." This form of address has become the shtetl equivalent of "Mister" and is used as a matter of course. When scholars use other forms of address, they describe the level and quality of intellectual excellence, and not the officially accredited amount of knowledge. The title *Rov,* or Rabbi, is functional rather than academic, and is acquired only when a man begins to serve in that capacity.

Each student goes at his own pace, concentrating on the area most congenial to him. Each is equally proud of the fact that he is studying. Each, when he has completed a reading of the Talmud, or of some self-imposed assignment, will celebrate the achievement, whether his work is quite elementary or highly advanced. The whole congregation participates in such a celebration, which is called *siyum,* meaning completion.

The man will proudly announce after the Sabbath reading of the Torah that he is "making a siyum," and invites the con-

gregation to celebrate it with him. After the services, all stay to
enjoy cakes and brandy brought by the servant of the synagogue,
the shammes. The shammes of the besmedresh always has such
provisions on hand for the numerous celebrations that are held.
If the man is very important, his siyum is announced by the
shammes, and if an association has been reading together, the
celebration will be announced and held in the name of the whole
khevreh. One who has celebrated reading a portion of the Talmud
proceeds to assign himself a new section. One who has celebrated
a reading of the whole, begins all over again.

The study of the Holy Books may be interrupted or may
diminish in intensity, but it never stops. No matter how long
a man lives, he can continue to explore new wonders in the
limitless intricacies and vistas of the Law. During middle age,
unless he is one of the scholarly elite, he must spend at least part
of his time making a living. But after retirement the very devout
man will once more devote to study all his waking hours except
those that are spent in prayer. And the waking hours will be
many. He will rise before daybreak and study before his morning
prayers, hurry to the synagogue, returning for breakfast before
plunging again into study. His day of study will be broken by
two more trips to the synagogue, by meals, and by occasional
learned discussions. Only after midnight will he stop for sleep,
in order to be up again in the early morning for the daily round
of study and prayer. Of such a man it is said that he is always
"over the Torah and over his services."

Not every Jew in the shtetl is a scholar or even a learned
man, but intellectual achievement is the universally accepted
goal. There are few Jews from Eastern Europe who have not attended the kheyder at least for a short time. Even those who have
almost completely abandoned the traditional observances speak
with pride about their childhood studies. And the traditional
expectation for a boy born in the shtetl is that from the kheyder
to the grave he will devote some portion of his time to study.

Among the exceptions whose earliest education was not received at the kheyder are the boys who attend the Talmud
Toyreh. It is almost axiomatic that no Jewish boy in the shtetl
should be wholly deprived of schooling, and any shtetl of sub-

stantial size will have a Talmud Toyreh, supported by the community, for children whose families cannot afford the kheyder
tuition. These children are orphans, for the most part, since
parents and relatives would strain to the breaking point and beyond to avoid the necessity—and the humiliation—of sending a
child to the Talmud Toyreh. Everything about the institution is
undesirable from the shtetl viewpoint. The curriculum regularly
includes only the most elementary Hebrew and religious studies,
and the quality even of this teaching is suspect. In addition, the
language of the country is taught there and more arithmetic than
is required in the study of the Law—for even the most orthodox
kheyder usually does offer the bare rudiments of arithmetic, without which even the ideal scholar cannot conduct his life. The
curriculum of the Talmud Toyreh also, as befits the humble life
prospects of those who attend it, sometimes includes instruction
in a trade.

Since most of the pupils are orphans, the children in the
Talmud Toyreh are fed and clothed—and sometimes housed—at
the expense of the community. Their clothes are even more drab
and their heads cropped even more closely than those of the
other boys—always, of course, with due regard for the cherished
earlock which bobs at each side of the small, shaven skull.

The "Talmud Toyreh boy," in his stiff, heavy uniform, is
easily recognizable at sight. He feels keenly his position and the
hostility on both sides occasionally leads to fights between the
kheyder boys and the pupils of the Talmud Toyreh, fights in
which epithets, blows and yells are freely exchanged.

To be a yeshiva boy is a proud role, even though, like the
Talmud Toyreh child, he is hungry and shabby, fed and clothed
by the community. The yeshiva boy is potentially one of the
sheyneh, and has won this opportunity through his intellectual
ability, aided and supported by his doting family or by the community. One day he will be a rabbi, or a great scholar, and perhaps will marry the daughter of a wealthy man.

The lot of the Talmud Toyreh child is a heavy one, during
the experience and in retrospect. He is an orphan, the most
pitiable of human beings, or a son of parents who either cannot
or will not pay for giving him the education required for a digni-

fied life in the shtetl. His future is blocked. He will be apprenticed to a trade, will learn only the bare essentials of Hebrew lore and will never have the opportunity to fulfill the ideal pattern.

Men who studied at the Talmud Toyreh when they were children usually prefer not to mention it and not to be reminded of it. The whole society appears to be reticent about the plight of the Talmud Toyreh child. In the literature and in the talk of informants, there is far more reference to donations for support of the institution than to the experience of those who attended it. Uneasiness seems to be associated with the Talmud Toyreh which, although it fulfills the shtetl standard of helping the needy, nevertheless countenances a merging of sacred and worldly teaching that violates the traditional spirit of study.

The program of book learning, from the kheyder to the grave, has been for centuries the traditional pattern of the shtetl. Through the centuries it has been tested but never broken by infiltration and bombardment from without. It remained the dominant force of the culture despite the fact that a bridge to the outer world existed, in the artisans and workers, in the women, in the antiorthodox groups, in the forces engendered by the Enlightenment.

III

SEALED ON MOUNT SINAI

The importance, the prestige, the glamor attached to study flow from Mount Sinai. Here, according to the shtetl, were forged the values by which the people live and the social structure through which those values are expressed. For it was here that Israel entered into the Covenant, which defines man's relations with God and sets a pattern for his relations with his fellow man.

This eternal pact, *Bris*—made with Abraham, renewed with Isaac and with Jacob—was finally sealed with all Jews for all time by the giving of the Law on Mount Sinai. It is by definition a twofold agreement. On the one hand, the Jews accept God as their only God, accept the "yoke of the Law"—refused by all other nations on earth—and undertake to fulfill all His commandments. The Lord, on the other hand, promises to cherish Israel as His Chosen People, carriers of the Truth, and to reward them in the end if they live up to their obligations.

Not only the generation of the Exodus from Egypt agreed to fulfill the divine commandments, the mitsvos. Even the generations to come were present at Mount Sinai when, amid lightning and thunder, the Lord transmitted to Moses the tablets of the Law. Each member of the shtetl was there, and each is committed as explicitly as was Moses himself to the Covenant.

The 613 commandments or mitsvos enumerate specific duties which relate to three major obligations. One is the obligation to study constantly the word of God, in order to gain ever greater knowledge of the commandments and to approach the Truth that lies in the Holy Books. Equally important is the obligation to establish a family, in order to preserve and increase the number of those dedicated to the service of the true God. The third major obligation is observance of the myriad social, economic, and ritual activities directed toward fulfillment of the commandments that regulate the relationship between man and God, between man and his fellow man, between man and himself. All of the mitsvos are directed toward one or more of these fundamental obligations.

In return, the people who devote themselves to fulfillment of the mitsvos count on three specific privileges based on the Covenant. It gives them the right to ask for health and livelihood, *gezunt un parnosseh,* with the hope that if the commandments are fulfilled this request will be granted. Health and comfortable living, taken together, are called *Olam Hazeh,* This World. Moreover, they count on Olam Habo, the World to Come. Finally, they look forward to the coming of Messiah and the return of the Jews to the Promised Land. The coming of Messiah will end the sufferings of the Diaspora, the exile, inflicted as punishment for past violations of the pact.

Inherent in the pact is the idea of reward and punishment. Every day the pious Jew repeats, among the thirteen articles of faith: "I believe with perfect faith that the Creator, blessed be His name, rewards those who keep His commandments and punishes those who transgress them."

The words of the Prophets, the sermons of the Preachers, the precepts of the Moral Books, all repeat the concept of the pact with its attendant rewards and penalties: if you do thus you will be rewarded, but if you do not you will be punished. Both the punishments and the rewards are described in detail.

In their daily prayers, on the other hand, the Jews respectfully and repeatedly remind God of the pact, of their efforts to fulfill it, and of their consequent claims upon Him.

"We are Thy people, the children of Thy covenant . . ."
"Have mercy upon us for the sake of Thy covenant . . ."
". . . remember unto us the covenant of our fathers, and the testimony we bear every day that the Lord is One. Look upon our afflictions, for many are our griefs and the sorrows of our hearth. Have pity upon us, Oh Lord, in the land of our captivity, and pour not out Thy wrath upon us for we are Thy people, the children of the covenant! . . ." "Oh Lord God of Truth vouchsafe blessing and prosperity upon all the work of my hands, for I

trust in Thee that Thou wilt so bless me through my occupations and callings that I may be enabled to support myself and the members of my household with ease and not with pain, by lawful and not by forbidden means unto life and peace. In me also let the scripture be fulfilled: Cast thy burden upon the Lord and He shall sustain thee. Amen."*

The Covenant solemnized on Mount Sinai became binding on each Jew for all time. It is renewed, however, with the birth of each male Jew, through the act of circumcision. The ritual is named for the pact, *bris mila,* or covenant by circumcision, and makes the newborn Jew subject to all the privileges and all the obligations of the Jewish people. The significance of the ceremony is expressed in the ritual blessing which accompanies the act of circumcision: dedicating the child to Torah (study of the Law), to *khupa* (marriage), and to *maasim tovim* (good deeds).

There is no excuse for conscious violation of the commandments, nor is ignorance of the Law an excuse, for the pact enjoins upon every male Jew the mitsva of study. The original commandments make some allowance for human frailty, but their exemptions are subject to specific rules and conditions, which one must know in order to be sure that his behavior is not an invitation to punishment in this world or the next. Since every rule has its exemptions and every exemption has its limitations, continuous study of the commandments, prohibitions, and regulations becomes imperative to the correct observance of the pact.

Ignorance of immediate circumstances is not equated with ignorance of the Law, for God is not conceived as a rigid dogmatist. He is believed to understand that humanity has human limitations. Accordingly, if a person violates a commandment because he has been deceived or misled, he does not bear the guilt of the violation, but the person who deceived him does. If a woman buys a piece of meat from a shop that carries the familiar sign "kosher," meaning that it sells only meat which is ritually fit to eat, and if the seller dishonestly gives her meat that is ritually unfit, the sin is not hers but his. A prosperous shtetl family discovered that for months their servant had been giving them "nonkosher" meat because it was cheaper, and pocketing

*From the morning prayers.

the difference herself. They purified all the dishes and utensils that had been defiled, but—after consultation with the rabbi—they were not troubled by a feeling that they had done wrong or that God would hold it against them. Nevertheless, a good housewife, no matter how wealthy she is, feels it her duty to exercise constant supervision and may "spend most of her time in the kitchen just to make sure the servant did everything right."°

The entire body of the Law in its original, categoric form is contained in the first five books of the Pentateuch, known as the Torah. These five books, often referred to as khumesh, "five," are inscribed on scrolls and read in the synagogue over and over again. Hence the Holy Scrolls kept in the Ark of the synagogue are also referred to as the Torah.

Torah may also be used, however, to refer to the entire Bible of the shtetl—the Pentateuch, the Prophets, and the Hagiographa. The meaning of the Torah has been expanded still further. The commandments in their primary form, as set forth in the Pentateuch, are not always clear in their application to all specific aspects and situations. The danger of transgressing them is so direct and the consequences can be so harmful to the community as well as to the individual, that the Sages during the centuries before the destruction of the Temple and the three centuries after its destruction, continually worked to clarify them by explanations and interpretations. They also constructed a "fence"—*syag* or *geder*—around the original Law, consisting of supplementary regulations and prohibitions. This "fence" sets up a margin of error, so that one who observes the "fence" regulations is insured against any possibility of violating the original commandments. The "fence" regulations have come to be as binding as the original commandments, and in practice the shtetl makes no difference between them. In erudite discussion, however, and sometimes in critical situations, the learned man recognizes a distinction and may lower the "fence" while preserving intact the original core.

The body of the interpretations, clarifications, and additional "fence" commandments worked out by the Sages is the Talmud. Although in written form, it is regarded as the "oral Law" to differentiate it from the "written Law," the original Torah, dictated to Moses on Mount Sinai.

The Talmud represents the oral interpretations of the Torah, not written as they were expounded but reconstructed later by students of the Sages who gave them. The students depended wholly on their memories, for it is considered a disrespect to the Sacred Writings to take notes while they are being discussed. The habit of memorizing rather than writing has persisted, even in the kheyder where pupils inscribe the words of the melamed, not in their notebooks, but in their minds. The reconstruction itself is in the form of notations rather than full-flowing prose, so that the Talmud and its earlier commentaries are in a laconic and at times almost cryptic style. This style set a pattern for centuries to come, and affected spoken discourse as well as the written word.

The "oral Law" is as sacred and as much cherished as the "written Law" and "Torah" came to embrace the Talmud as well as the original five books of the Pentateuch. Moreover, since the completion of the Talmud, generation after generation of scholars have continued to study the original commandments and their later exposition, interpreting the interpretations of the Sages, commenting on the commentaries of the successive interpreters. Their works and writings in turn became sacred literature. The scholar's version of the Torah or the Talmud came to resemble graphological goldsmithery, the jewel of the text set in a surrounding expanse of commentary.

The standard edition of the Talmud states as the central text a regulation from the Mishna, which is the original elaboration of the commandments given in the Pentateuch. This brief text from the Mishna is followed by a long discussion and commentary, known as the Gemara and handed down by later sages. The texts of the Mishna and Gemara, which are the essence of the Talmud, are framed by a column of commentary on each side. On the inner margin appears the commentary of Rashi, whose name is inseparable from the basic Jewish texts, on the opposite margin are additional comments of later scholars, the *Tosfos*. Bordering these columns of commentary are scattered notations—*khiddushim* or *novellae*—by still later authorities, in a form so condensed and abbreviated as to amount almost to a learned code.

Each regulation from the Mishna is presented separately, with an attendant body of discussion, including references from the Pentateuch. The pattern of central text and surrounding commentary is repeated in other basic works, such as the Mishna itself, the works of Maimonides and the Shulkhan Arukh. These standard editions are points of reference for the countless thousands of scholarly volumes that have been written through the centuries and are still being produced. Some scholars devote themselves entirely to study of one text, and such a man is known as the "squire" or weapon bearer of that work. The work as well as the man is called the "squire," for an author is known by the title of his major book, which is used as if it were his name.

It is the name of an author's work and not his personal name that identifies him, even to literate people. A man will be called the grandson of *Arba Turim,* "The Four Mountains," and not of Jacob ben Asher who wrote that well-known work. The author of a major treatise on ethics is known as *Menoras Ha-Maor,* "The Menorah of Light," and most of those who have studied the book do not know that his own name was Isaac Aboav. It will be said that So-and-So was married to a descendant of *Khofetz Khayim,* "One Who Wants Life." The author is important, not as an individual, but as the instrumentality of the book. His personality and personal life are irrelevant. Authors who wish— as many do—to immortalize their names, contrive to incorporate them into the title itself. *Mogen Abraham,* "The Shield of Abraham," was written by Rabbi Abraham Abale; *Pney Yehoshua,* "The Face of Joshua," was written by Rabbi Jakob Yehoshua. Thus the irrepressible urge for personal immortality is reconciled with the tendency of the culture to place the work before the individual.

Often, however, authors are referred to by initials—either their own or those of their major works. It is possible to make the initials identical. For example, *The Words of a Priest* was written by Rabbi Shabtai Ben Mayer Ha-Cohen and the initials commonly used for both author and book are SHaKH. On the other hand, Rabbi Yehoshua Mellekh Ben Alexander Cohen is known only as SMEh—the initials of his major work, *Seyfer Meyiras Eynaim,* "The Book of the Light of the Eyes."

Ultimately, the entire Jewish religious literature, all the wisdom contained in the centuries of scholastic commentary, came to be known as the Torah. Hence, to "study Torah" means not only study of the original five books but also the study of thousands upon thousands of volumes published during the long centuries of Jewish history. It is as important to study the books of recent authors as the writings of the ancients, because new light may be thrown on a traditional mitsva as changing conditions create new situations. Any besmedresh or yeshiva has libraries containing the basic works and as many additional volumes as can be assembled through the efforts of the young boys who go about soliciting funds for books. It is an essential activity, for the basic works are worn and torn by constant use.

Eventually Torah came to mean the whole of Jewish lore, which embraces the whole of Jewish life. The Truth it contains is the only possible and acceptable truth for the shtetl.

The attitude toward the Truth is expressed in the physical treatment of the Torah which contains and symbolizes the essence of the Law. It is not a dead doctrine to be embalmed in books and stored away on shelves, but is a living thing, and accordingly, the Holy Scroll of the Torah is treated almost as a live being. It occupies the most honored "seat" of all, on the East Wall of the synagogue. If there is a fire in the synagogue—and fires are frequent in the shtetl—young and old will plunge into the flames to save the Torah from "death." A Torah that has been destroyed by flames, or desecrated during a pogrom—trampled in the mud, mauled by profane hands—is given burial in the cemetery, enveloped in a talis as if it were the corpse of a pious man. It will be mourned with tears and outcries, fasting and prayers, and finally memorialized by recitation of the kaddish. In times of rejoicing, too, the Torah is treated as a human being, and will be embraced and whirled as a partner in the dance. The man who is called to the reading of the last section of the Torah is called "bridegroom of the Torah," and the one who begins the annual cycle of reading is called "bridegroom of In-the-beginning."

The sacred literature called Torah provides the texts that the boy begins to study in kheyder and continues to study until the end of his days. It is more than a code of law, for it is also

a code of ethics and a handbook of daily behavior. Every detail
—social, religious, economic, moral—is examined and discussed,
and a definite rule is set for it, with exceptions, limitations, and
implications fully defined. It may be a primary prohibition, forbidding him to eat pork, or a "fence" prohibition forbidding him
to talk to women in order to avoid all possibility of adultery. It
may be a primary command not to commit murder, or a "fence"
command not to study without wearing a girdle which will
separate the upper or sacred part of the body from the lower or
profane part. It may be an injunction to succor the orphan, or an
injunction against thinking about a business deal on the Sabbath.
No subject is too large and none is too small to be included in
the all-embracing attention of the scholars.

A large part of this monumental literature is devoted to
human relations. Situations that cannot be governed by decree
are discussed in the Talmud and its commentaries—situations involving honesty, love, the ties between man and wife, parent and
child, conduct at table or at public assemblies. All of Jewish culture is the subject of Jewish learning. Each detail of life supplies
an opportunity to fulfill God's command, and at the same time
is loaded with the danger of violating some rule set down in the
pact.

The Covenant which God concluded with Israel is a mutual
welfare pact, and is so interpreted. Its purpose is not only to insure to the Almighty recognition and obedience, but also to insure to mortal man enjoyment of this world, Olam Hazeh, and
happiness in the world to come, Olam Habo. Its authority is
absolute, its spirit humane and rational. "The Law is given for
Man and not Man for the Law," is a constant refrain; "the Law
is to live with and not to die with." There is a blanket dispensa-
tion that, with three exceptions, one may do anything at all to
preserve his life if there is "mortal danger," *pekuakh nefesh*. The
three things that are forbidden even on pain of death are: "conversion, bloodshed, and immorality."

On these three points the ethics of the shtetl are rigid. Aside
from them, the Torah is viewed as a code that is absolutely binding yet at the same time subject to interpretation and adjustment. As the course of history introduces changes in social, eco-

nomic and geographical conditions, the Law must be adapted to meet them, so that man will not be put in the impossible position of having to choose between the Law and life itself.

The learned man is the arbiter in the problem of adjustment which history has made a constant and crucial problem for the Jews. It is his task to translate historic obligation into current fulfillment by an appropriate interpretation of eternal law in the light of ephemeral conditions. If the interpretation is ingenious enough it can eliminate hardship for all concerned, and at the same time remain true to the spirit.

Such ingenuity can go to great lengths without involving any disrespect to the Law, for to help humanity is an absolute good. This human editing of divine precept often appears paradoxical to a mind not schooled in the tradition. On the one hand there is a legalistic preoccupation with the letter of the Law, a verbalistic exercise that reaches extremes of virtuosity until often it seems to be pursued largely for its own sake. On the other hand, there is an underlying concern for the spirit of the Law as expressed in the Holy Books.

Whatever the subject of discussion may be—the receiving of mail on Sabbath, a business dispute, the correct form of the text folded inside the phylacteries—the ultimate reference will be to a quotation from the Pentateuch. No matter how intricate the reasoning, how far-flung and far-fetched the allusions, citations and syllogisms, all revert finally to the basic belief that the divine will is actuated by intelligence and reasonableness and that under extreme exigency the letter of the Law must yield to the spirit which dictates always the preservation of human life and the fostering of human welfare.

The rigidity of the original prescription is often softened by a "but-if" formula which opens the door for adjusting a sweeping commandment to a particular human case, or to universal human limitations. For example, observance of the Sabbath is the most important mitsva—*but if* one is in jail or on a desert island, he may merely count the days and observe every sixth one, until release or rescue permits him to return to the rhythm of the true calendar.

The Torah must be read in shul by an adult with a beard—

but if no literate bearded adult is present, it may be read by a boy of thirteen. On the Sabbath one must not carry anything outside the "pale of Sabbath"—*but if* the eyruv, or ritual cord, is placed around the village with due ceremony and prayer, the whole shtetl may be considered as lying within that "pale." The wife must light and bless the Sabbath candles—*but if* a man has no wife he performs the ritual. If the wife is blind, the husband must light the Sabbath candles—*but if* a blind woman is a widow, she performs the mitsva. Cooking is prohibited on the Sabbath—*but if* a person's health requires a freshly cooked meal, special exemption is permitted. In fact, within certain limits, one may eat whenever and whatever the doctor prescribes. The health clause is not a blanket exemption, however, for illness has different stages and degrees, and the specific rulings must be studied for each case. Even aside from health considerations, the dietary rules involve boundless erudition and endless "but-ifs." An orthodox rabbi is called upon daily to reconcile strict observance of law with human needs and limitations. One of them undertook to explain the principle on which he decided questions connected with dietary laws:

"When a person brings me a chicken which he bought for Sabbath, and has doubts whether it is kosher or not, I examine it. There is always a possibility of declaring it kosher or *treyf* (unfit). You will always find in the Books an authority you can refer to in order to take your decision in either way. So your duty is to take into consideration the person who came to you. If it is a poor man who spent his last money to buy a chicken for Sabbath, or it is too late to buy another chicken and the person will be deprived of a chicken for the Sabbath, you will try to find in the books an opinion which will give you the possibility of declaring the chicken kosher. If, however, the person is rich, and would not be very much hurt, you may declare it treyf. That is why there is no possibility to appeal from the decision of a local rabbi to a rabbi in some other locality. The other rabbi presumes that the local rabbi knows the Law as well as he does, and if the local rabbi rendered a specific decision he took into consideration not only the Law, but some specific reasons."°

In order to protect human life it is necessary to safeguard the means by which human life is maintained. Therefore it is correct to interpret the Law in such a way that a man's livelihood is not jeopardized. A yearly problem, for example, is posed for the grain dealer, the grocer, and others by the rule that forbids a Jew to have any grain or grain product in his possession on Passover. According to the Law, he must sell such products before the holiday begins. In practice, as a result of ingenious interpretation, it is accepted usage for him to "sell" his goods to a non-Jew for a token sum, and to "buy it back" for the same sum after Passover has ended. The "sale" is made official by a written contract, signed in the presence of the rabbi.

A large part of the literature consists of digests and compilations of rules and interpretations providing for a vast array of contingencies. The basic handbook of such material is the *Shulkhan Arukh*, "The Set Table"—one commentary on which is *The Table Cloth*. Only the most erudite can cope with the original Shulkhan Arukh, in four weighty tomes, and its numerous "squires." For less profound students there are abridged editions with less text and less commentary. As the intellectual level of the reader descends, the versions become less and less heavy, in form and in content, until for the women and the prosteh there are slim manuals, written in Yiddish and devoid of commentary, but interwoven with edifying maxims and exhortations.

One of the most popular of these handbooks is Joseph Danzig's "Life of a Man," *Khayey Odom,* which has gone through numerous editions since its first publication in the eighteenth century. It is apt to be "Life of a Man" that the pious artisan will read of a Sabbath afternoon—and if he should be asked who wrote it he would probably answer, "Why, Khayey Odom, of course!"

The attitude toward permitted relaxations or modifications of the rules is highly varied. Some will use them as an excuse for bending the original commandment to their own convenience. On the anniversary of a death, one is supposed to study a chapter of the Mishna in memory of the deceased, or at least to read over a few psalms. *But if* one is unable to study, it is permissible to hire someone else to do it. Some people who actually are able to study, nevertheless hire another person to save themselves the trouble.

On the other hand, a truly devout Jew often resists the leniency that friends and relatives advise. An ailing old man may reject food and even medicine on Yom Kippur, although the rabbi himself urges that he eat to sustain his life and points out to him the very place in the book where "it stands written" that he ought to preserve his health.

Nazi records of the Polish occupation tell of "stubborn" Jews who said they would rather die than transgress the Sabbath—even though they knew that God would pardon them the violation of His mitsva in the face of mortal danger. There are tales of Jews who wore their white prayer shawls and prayed openly in public, even though many of them were deported for it. Always it was for "the Holiness of the Name," *Kiddush Hashem,* with a fervor that swept aside the blanket permission to sacrifice religious observance rather than one's life in the face of mortal danger.

Since no realm of life is divorced from the Law embodied in the Holy Books, the shtetl draws no line between the religious and the secular. Strictly speaking, there are no secular elements, since all life is one fused whole and all truth is embodied in the sacred writings. For the shtetl, the opposition is not so much between secular and nonsecular, as between Jewish and non-Jewish.

The sacred writings stem directly from Mount Sinai, from God, and nothing can be learned which was not stated or implied long, long ago in the basic works or the commentaries of the Sages. "It is a shame that so many Jews study other subjects to find the answers, when actually everything is in the Torah. The Holy Books cover every detail of life."°

Rigid distinctions of time are blurred and blended in the tradition of Jewish learning. The constant reference to ancient texts for contemporary problems and to modern texts for illumination of antiquity, has forged an unbreakable chain uniting the past with the present, and the works of each separate scholar form a lasting link in this chain. The discussion between two talmudists of the second century about which parts of a sacrificed lamb should go to the High Priest in the Temple have not lost their actuality even though the Temple, the sacrifices, the Priests no longer exist. A clever student from the shtetl will throw new light upon the problem, drawing upon the brilliant interpretation of a medieval scholar. The zealous yeshiva boy participates in discussions between Rabbi Hillel and Rabbi Shamai who both lived in the first century A.D., analyzes the arguments of a seventeenth-century Rabbi which support one against the other, and arrives at his own original conclusions. The *Responsa* of the medieval rabbis furnish answers to questions about contemporary business transactions.

Not only the past and the present are interwoven in the learning continuum. In the days to come, when Messiah brings together all the Jews and rebuilds the Temple, the learned ones will study Torah together and the Lord himself will discuss the problems that could not be mastered and were left pending "until the coming of Messiah." This continuum from Moses to Messiah links together Rabbi Akiba, the scholar tortured to death by Roman legionnaires, Don Isaac Abarbanel who led the exiled Jews from Spain the year the New World was discovered, and the famished yeshiva boy studying and starving under Nazi rule in Poland. There are no dates in Jewish learning. In order to locate in time a famous Jewish scholar, the modern historian has to reconstruct the chronology on the basis of allusive discussion of a religious ruling with reference to a calamity that overtook the Jewish nation during the reign of a known king or emperor.

The continuum overrides limits of space as well as of time. A page of the Talmud looks the same now as two hundred years ago, and the same in Vilna as in Shanghai. All over the world, students are poring over the same Torah, the same Talmud, the same commentary of Rashi; and with the same melody little children are piping the same text as they begin their study of Mishna: "Two have grasped a garment. . . ." No matter where he wanders, the shtetl scholar, if he finds a traditional community at all, will find the same studies being pursued, the same problems debated, with the same zeal and zest.

Moreover, problems that arise from the conditions of Jewish life in one country are debated by scholars in another. Historians discovered a great deal about the economic and social life of Jews in medieval Europe from the *Responsa* of the masters who conducted yeshivas in Persia. A rabbi in Germany will consult his colleague from Poland on a difficult question sent in by a student in France.

The learned tradition, then, not only serves to transmit the culture but is also a cohesive force, maintaining unity and continuity in time and in space. Deprived of common territory and common national history since the beginning of the Diaspora, the Jews have maintained a stable realm in the domain of the intellect. When a scholar takes a sacred book into his hands, he immerses himself in the tradition that reaches out of the far past into the living present. Through study he finds the joy of identification with his God, his tradition and his group, for "Torah, God and Israel are One."

The unperturbed disregard of western time and space limitations assumes that the unity of the tradition is stronger than any break in physical or temporal continuity. This assumption helps to explain why the talmudic scholar regards his discipline as practical and realistic while to the outsider it appears abstract and theoretical. Every discussion is geared to a concrete situation, one that may be imaginary but is never impossible. In order to facilitate understanding of a given problem, an example, a parable, a legend will be used to lend concreteness. To the true talmudic scholar, it must be remembered, such a problem as correct carving of the sacrificial lamb is no abstraction but a concrete situation that has occurred and may occur again when the Temple is rebuilt.

Such a scholar classes his studies as applied science—the science of applying divine commandments to daily life. He has scant regard for pure science, pure literature, pure poetry. He can see in such studies no direct goal or purpose, or, as he would say, no *takhlis*. Everything must have takhlis, or else it has no reason to exist. "What is the takhlis?" will be the first response to what the hearer regards as a foolish question, and to say with a shrug "there's no takhlis in it" is to dismiss the subject from all consideration.

It is immaterial whether you apply your findings now or in the days to come, in actual dealings with people or in analyzing the behavior of a hypothetical ancestor performing an imaginary act, but they must be applied. There is no pure philosophy, pure esthetics, pure mathematics in the learning tradition of the shtetl. Mathematics is studied in connection with biblical problems in agriculture or architecture, esthetics in connection with the decoration of the Temple, philosophy in conjunction with ethics or with understanding the nature of God.

Similarly, a piece of fiction must have a moral. It must be told or written in order to teach. Poetry is not just an esthetic arrangement of words and sentences, but a beautifully phrased expression of praise for the Lord, or of some moral idea. The Song of Songs is not regarded as a love poem but as an allegorical presentation of the relationship between the Lord and His people, Israel. As a mere paean of love, the Song of Songs would have no takhlis and no moral.

The character of traditional learning, and the emphasis placed upon it, contribute to a paradoxical attitude toward the authorities that are constantly being cited. On the one hand, constant reference to the dicta of the Sages is the backbone and the measure of scholarly technique; a man is judged by the scope of his acquaintance with the authorities, and his adroitness in drawing upon them to build his argument. On the other hand, there is incessant checking and revising of their statements against one's own judgment.

Truth, as perceived by the imperfect but always searching mind, is never simple and single. It is never *the* Truth and is always subject to interpretation. The absolute Truth represented by the divine Law is inaccessible in full even to the most powerful human intellect. Each word in the Torah has, according to esoteric tradition, four kinds of meanings: the direct, the interpreted, the allusive, the secret. No mortal intellect can master and hold all four levels for all conceivable subjects.

Since final Truth is with God, final authority lies only in Him and no man can claim to have mastered the whole of wisdom. All men share the ability to perceive some portion of Truth, large or small, and all share the inability to perceive the ultimate whole. Therefore, the decision of the highest authority on earth remains to some degree provisional and relative. At the same time, everyone who studies is able to approach nearer and nearer to understanding, to edit and interpret divine commandments in the light of temporal needs and so through his own efforts to become a relative authority. On the one hand, then, there is an elaborate rank order of scholarship, and on the other the master scholar, however dazzling his achievements, is in a sense only *primus inter pares.*

No matter how wise a scholar may be, his words will be weighed, examined and questioned, not only by his peers but also by those who admit that his learning far outshines their own. The humblest will follow and criticize the discussions of the erudite, and will dispute with each other about the fine points—which one cited the most convincing authorities, where both were wrong. Moreover, no authority is taken as final, for someone else may see an aspect not yet revealed. Therefore any answer is subject to further checking and revision.

The individual, then, relies on his own judgment in the acceptance and manipulation of what the authorities say, rather than depending on the authorities for a final dictum to be accepted without reservation. "Even God will be discussed, and you can see that after so many centuries they still discuss the Holy Books, they still argue, for the Lord does not want man to be blind."° Moreover, the people of the shtetl feel confident that the reasoning process applied to divine law is adequate for coping with any human, worldly problem. Scholars in the besmedresh, accordingly, discourse freely on diplomatic relations between nations, the military strategy of famous generals, or the competence and worth of eminent statesmen, testing the behavior of all against their own judgment, sharpened by talmudic discipline.

The spirit of the talmudic training is the spirit of the shtetl itself. The same elements are present in the attitudes toward scholastic authority and in the attitudes toward social status. In any area, recognition of a clearly defined and minutely graded hierarchy is combined with an equally clear assumption that potentially all men are equal. The man at the top of the social or economic scale is subject to question and disapproval on the part of the poor and humble. The deeds and words of any leader are subject to criticism and discussion, if not openly then secretly, at home or in the besmedresh. For every individual the final appeal must be to his own judgment; if the subject matter itself is beyond him, then he must debate with himself the reliability of conflicting authorities.

The attitudes and thought habits characteristic of the learning tradition are as evident in the street and market place as in the yeshiva. The popular picture of the Jew in Eastern Europe, held by Jew and Gentile alike, is true to the talmudic tradition. The picture includes the tendency to examine, analyze and re-analyze, to seek for meanings behind meanings, and for implications and secondary consequences. It includes also a dependence on deductive logic as a basis for practical conclusions and actions.

A situation is never simple. The Poles maintain that if you ask a Jew how to get to a certain place he will give you a discourse on all the ways you should not go, and why, before coming out with the answer. They have a saying, "this is as difficult as getting a Jew to tell you the way." On the other hand, they claim that a Jew who wants to get to a certain place will inquire about every least detail of the route, and not satisfied with one clear answer will check and recheck along the road, asking of each person, "Is this really the way to the shop of——?" and "Is there a better or shorter way to go?" So, to one who is very inquisitive they will say, "You act like a Jew asking how to get somewhere."

In life, as in the Torah, it is assumed that everything has deeper and secondary meanings, which must be probed. All subjects have implications and ramifications. Moreover, the person who makes a statement must have a reason, and this too must be probed. Often a comment will evoke an answer to the assumed reason behind it or to the meaning believed to lie beneath it, or to the remote consequences to which it leads. The process that produces such a response—often with lightning speed—is a modest reproduction of the pilpul process. A woman running in to ask her neighbor for the loan of a pot used to cook meat will receive the warm response, "Congratulations, *mazltov!* When will the wedding be?" Amazed, she asks, "But how did you know?"

"Nu, why shouldn't I know? You have a meat pot of your own so if you borrow mine you must plan to cook a lot of meat. But you never eat meat except on Shabbes and holidays, and this is the middle of the week, so you must have something to celebrate. Now what could you have to celebrate? Here you are with a sick husband and two sons out of work. But you also have a daughter, may the evil eye not fall on her, and she is of an age to marry. Therefore that must be it, and mazltov, may she live in good health with her bridegroom, and may you have much joy from them and many fine grandchildren."° And so it was.

A similar lightning process of applied pilpul logic accounted for the reaction to a notice that by decree of the local official, every house in a certain shtetl must be freshly painted. At once men started buying farm produce and merchandise and setting up stores, while in the besmedresh the scholars debated deep into the night, with abstruse citations from remote antiquity down through the ages, "Will the war be with Turkey or with Germany?"

The reasoning was: Why must the houses be painted? Obviously, because some important government official is coming to this shtetl. But why should an important government official come to a place like this? Obviously, only one thing would bring him—military maneuvers. But why would military exercises be carried on here of all places? Obviously that would only happen under threat of real war. But with whom would such a war be? Obviously it would be with Turkey or with Germany. But with which country? This was the question, and the only question that remained. Obviously too, if soldiers are to be quartered here, there will be buying, and the shtetl prepared feverishly to receive new customers. The year was 1914.

In politics and in business the deliberations of co-workers or of partners show considerable resemblance to the discussion of a problem in the yeshiva. Business partnership in the shtetl presents a pattern of constant discussion, often involving reproaches for failure to apply logic, to assess correctly the meanings behind the appearance, and to act accordingly.

Linked with the analytic approach of the shtetl are a proverbial reluctance to indulge in easy generalizations, and a relativistic rather than a positivistic view. Since Truth has so many aspects and so many levels, each situation must be analyzed in its own terms. By using repeated if's, but's and but-if's, all possible pro's and con's must be weighed before an answer is accepted.

The aversion to generalization, and the preference for the concrete over the abstract are evident in answers to direct questions. "Will everyone have an equal share in Olam Habo?" "I don't know, I was never there."° The relativistic and provisional view discourages the classic opposition between "yes" and "no," for everything contains elements of both. It is proverbial in Eastern Europe that a Jew will avoid answering a question by a simple yes or no. According to his tradition it is the business of the thinker to recognize and to reconcile incompatibles or opposites, in the realm of the spirit and in the practical world—realms which themselves are inseparable. Moreover, overtones and undertones of implication or assumption are a proper part of the question and the response.

Countless anecdotes, told by and about the Jews of Eastern Europe, are based on the ingrained assumption that in any situation "there are always two possibilities." If the worst one comes to pass, there are still two possibilities; and if the more evil of those eventuates, there are two possibilities in that—and so on, ad infinitum. One never forgets that "every stick has two ends."

In keeping with his own conception of contradictory reality, the man of the shtetl is noted both for volubility and for laconic, allusive speech. Both pictures are true, and both are characteristic of the yeshiva as well as the market place. When the scholar converses with his intellectual peers, incomplete sentences, a hint, a gesture, may replace a whole paragraph. The listener is expected to understand the full meaning on the basis of a word or even a sound. It is assumed that a truly learned man is familiar not only with quotations from Torah and Talmud, but also with the trend that comment or interpretation would be apt to take. Accordingly, in speaking or writing, a scholar may pronounce only the first words of a sentence, expecting his hearer to complete it in his mind. Such a conversation, prolonged and animated, may be as incomprehensible to the uninitiated as if the excited discussants were talking in tongues. The same verbal economy may be found in domestic or business circles.

The scholar in his ivory tower, remote from the market place and protected from the impact of its crass concerns, is still both the hub and the model of the community. In his retreat he shares the attitudes and mental mechanisms of his more mundane fellows. The same Covenant that dominates all his deeds and all his thoughts exerts its influence on their behavior, from the prayer with which they greet the day to the prayer with which they sink into sleep.

IV

THE WOMAN'S SHARE

"Man and woman created He them."

The Torah gives two stories of creation, both of which are reflected in the shtetl. According to the first, as elaborated in the Talmud, the original human being was male and female in one. But God separated the two elements and from then on they were distinct entities, neither of which is complete without the other and each of which is constantly seeking the other in order to attain completion. Just as truth is made up of positive and negative elements, so reality is composed of contrasting parts, each of which is indispensable.

The complete Jew is an adult with a mate and offspring. No man is complete without a wife; no woman is complete without a husband. For each individual the ideal center of gravity is not in himself, but in the whole of which he is an essential part.

The man's area is the shul, as House of Study, as House of Prayer, and as House of Assembly. Here he rules supreme. The woman's area is the home and here she is relative if not absolute ruler. The balance of mitsvos expresses and defines the allotment of areas. The mitsva of learning, one of the most important for men, is not for women. On the contrary, "a Jewish woman who is Talmud-trained is not a good commodity."

A girl goes to a girls' kheyder, where she learns how to read and write a little Yiddish. She also learns to read some Hebrew, for which the same characters are used, but the reading is mechanical and uncomprehending, like the first reading of the boys. "If a girl can read a little, pray a little, then she's a real 'intellectual.' "°

Most of the prayers have been translated into Yiddish for

her, if she wishes to consult them. Usually, however, she repeats
the Hebrew text without understanding, spelling it out for herself when she is alone and at shul following the lead of the zogerkeh, the woman who leads the services. For those who are not
equal to the most elementary requirement, the saying provides
that "when a Jewish woman cannot pray she at least counts the
windows in the synagogue."

Her education has a somewhat desultory character. Sometimes the girls study in the same room with the boys, sometimes
in a separate room. They may have the same melamed or a different one, possibly the wife of the boys' melamed. Their daily
sessions are much shorter than the boys', often not more than
two hours, for they must run home to help their mothers about
the house and to take care of the children. For them, study is
marginal to their primary activities, while for the boys it is the
major occupation and goal.

The average woman does learn to write a letter, with some
difficulty, and to read a Yiddish novel with great pleasure. Two
parallel literatures exist in the shtetl. For the learned there are
the sacred Hebrew writings. For the women and the prosteh men
there is the vast Yiddish literature that came into being for their
benefit. It includes both religious and nonreligious books, all
written with a simplicity and clarity beneath the dignity of a
real scholar.

The most popular Yiddish book, found in every shtetl household, is the Yiddish version of the Pentateuch, divided into
weekly sections exactly like the real Torah in the shul. The Yiddish version is called *Tse'eno u-Re'eno,* "Go Out and See!" It
invites the soul into the great expanse of true belief where all
the sages dwell, to behold the joys of living in that realm. The
sections from the Torah proper are interwoven with legends and
homilies, and through careful study of this household Torah
women learn a great deal about the legendary—though not about
the legal—part of the Pentateuch. A pious woman can follow in
her home the weekly readings at shul. She may be able to quote
passages and cite authorities. She will know, for example, why
it is so great a mitsva to kill a spider that seventy-seven sins will
be forgiven in exchange. And she knows how the great Hillel,

too poor to pay for his yeshiva studies, listened through a window in the roof until he was covered over with snow and was barely saved from freezing.

Many older women read a great deal, and the *Tse'eno u-Re'eno* of any household is tattered through use. The pages are tear-stained, too, for tears are a correct accompaniment of feminine reading, almost as rocking back and forth is of masculine study. You weep when you read about the destruction of the Temple and the other calamities that befell the children of Israel. A woman, too, expands and identifies as she reads. The tribulations of the Israelites are identified with her own personal troubles, her *tsores;* the griefs of the Diaspora are merged in the problems of her own hearth. And the identification brings solace, for "trouble shared by many is half a consolation."

A woman weeps even more when she reads the *Tkhinnos,* the prose poems written in Yiddish for women, by rabbis who graciously condescend to the vernacular in order to impart edifying thoughts for holidays, Sabbath and other special occasions.

These are only one part of the books brought in by the book peddler, *moykher sforim,* on his way from shtetl to shtetl. As he approaches the market place, with his skinny, dejected nag and tumble-down cart loaded with books and ritual wares, the girls come running, shoving and crowding to get first chance as he cries: "Books for women and sacred books for men." The "books" are in Yiddish and the "sacred books" in Hebrew. He will certainly have a version of the *Maasseh Bukh,* "The Story Book," and tales of the adventures of Prince Bovo. He will also have translations from foreign folk tales, or semireligious and semi-folk narratives about the miraculous lives of seers and wonder men. But the girls and women will be even more eager for the romantic novels of Shomer and Isaac Mayer Dik.

Until the nineteenth century the available fiction diet was of a character and quality that appalled the few serious readers who sampled it. The Yiddish literature that became familiar in Western Europe and the United States began as a reaction against the tawdry fiction offered to Yiddish readers, and an attempt to bring them something better.

One of the well-known Yiddish authors of the nineteenth

century, Mendele Mokher Sforim, took his pseudonym from the book peddler. Like Sholem Aleichem, he wrote Yiddish under a pen name in order to preserve his status among intellectuals, while writing under his real name in Hebrew for serious magazines and newspapers, addressed to a male audience. Despite the precaution, these men were proud of their mission in writing good books for those deprived of "real learning." This was writing with a purpose, a takhlis, though perhaps the chief function it performed was beyond the original aim. For it was these novels that first brought knowledge of the shtetl into the modern West. Sholem Aleichem's epitaph, which he himself wrote and which can be seen on his grave in New York, sums up his own purpose and the social cleavage that gave it significance:

> Here lies a Jew, a simple one,
> He wrote in Yiddish for women
> And for the prosteh folk he was
> A humorist, a writer.

No less popular than the story books are the peddler's dream books, telling the significance of any dream you have. And among the best sellers of all is the *brifshteller,* the "letter-composer," with model letters to fit any occasion. Hundreds of women in hundreds of towns will write to their husbands identical letters, copied out of some brifshteller, each telling her man about her special affection and esteem for him and about the health of their children. Those who are not literate enough to copy a letter from a book will employ the local letter writer to do it for them. When the answer comes, many a woman is unable to read it herself, but must get some man to tell her what news it brings from her husband in America or her son in the service. She will beg him to go over it again and again until she knows every word. Then she will "read" it to her friends and neighbors, turning the page at the right place and pointing out, "See, where he says he misses his mammeh."

When the book peddler has satisfied the women and the prosteh men, he will move to the yard of the shul, where the learned men are to be found. Here he will sell his Hebrew vol-

umes and his ritual objects—praying shawls, phylacteries, mezu-
zos, the many small items essential to piety.

His move brings home the difference in center of the two
worlds. The woman's world lies outside of the kheyder and the
besmedresh. For the most part women are barely literate in Yiddish and cannot understand the Hebrew they read. Nevertheless
many girls do learn Hebrew, as witness the fact that the shul
seldom lacks a zogerkeh to read the services. "Everybody wants
to go to kheyder,"° and some girls achieve it at least for a short
time. If there is no son in the family to be a kheyder boy, to be
examined on a Sabbath afternoon, to shed luster and inflame
pride by his recitations, a father may so yearn for an intellectual
heir that he will try to build up his daughter into one. Some
girls, too, are so eager to study that they win their point. Some
are able to listen to the lessons of their brothers, in prosperous
families where a tutor is employed. Therefore a few women are
schooled in the traditional lore.

Moreover, the world of nontalmudic study is far more accessible to girls than to their brothers. Because they are excluded
from the mitsva of studying divine Law they may also escape the
proscription on studies that are *treyf possl*—unfit and forbidden.
While the son of a wealthy home is in kheyder, his sisters may learn
music and languages, and in recent years they have been more
free than he to attend concerts and theaters. Comparatively few
may be in a position to profit by this license, but many daughters
of the rich have made the most of their opportunities. Girls succeeded earlier than boys in going to secular schools. A girl who
was able to study at all had more freedom of choice because her
intellectual development mattered so much less—"she's only a
girl," and "a girl is something else."

Up to a point, education enhances a girl's value as a bride,
but that point is set by her functions as helpmeet to the learned
man. Too much learning is unfeminine and the shtetl prefers to
have woman stay in her own area. If she is too "strong-minded"
it says with respect but still with disapprobation, that "she has a
man's head."

Since study of divine Law, the primary status criterion, is

not for women, they are automatically excluded from top honors in the community. A woman's formal status is indirect. It relates, not to herself as an individual, but to her position as wife and mother. For men there is the title "Reb," but for the woman there is no corresponding generalized title. She may be referred to as the wife of her husband, "Isaac's Sara," and addressed by her name without a title, or as "Housewife," *Balebosteh*.

To be a spinster is a dreadful fate which fortunately occurs far more in the anxious forebodings of girls and their parents than in fact. The shtetl does not provide a place for an *"alteh moyd."*

What happens to an old maid in the world to come is a question answered so diversely and with such bemused hesitation as to demonstrate how little attention it has claimed. Olam Habo, the world to come, is pictured traditionally in masculine terms, as a glorified, eternalized yeshiva. The dutiful wife sits at her husband's feet and enjoys eternal bliss through him. What she does while he spends eternity in ecstatic pilpul is not clearly defined. Presumably for her, as for the prosteh, paradise will offer different and more appropriate activity. Even on this earth, however, women listen in rapt silence to the scholarly disputes of the men in their homes, and it may be that the role of eternal audience is considered their best reward. The vagueness of the shtetl public on this subject, and the lack of concern evinced by the women themselves, are more impressive than the variety of the paradises described on request. The fact of future bliss, the mechanisms by which it may be won or lost, are specific and command consensus if not unanimity. That a woman's husband is somehow the cup from which she sips her heavenly reward is also agreed. But the precise content of heavenly enjoyment is both vague and variable.

What the future life holds for an unmarried girl is a question for the learned, as is the problem of the second wife, if the widower of a good woman remarries. Nobody is quite sure and nobody seems to care very much. On one point, however, all are confident: if the woman has been a good Jew, she will be made happy in Olam Habo, and there is no danger that she will suffer because of a technicality. Some just and comfortable arrange-

ment will be made for her, but these are details that one entrusts
to the erudite and to a God who is both just and merciful. More
important than precise details is the basic assurance that "every
Jew has a share in the World to Come."

The ideal woman, commanding as little of the traditional
learning as is compatible with reading of her prayers, still contributes to fulfilling the mitsva of learning and all its corollaries.
Without her the husband cannot fulfill his obligations and therefore cannot be a good Jew. As a bride she may bring him dowry
and parent-in-law support that enable him to pursue his studies.
As a wife she may earn the livelihood while he fulfills "his"
mitsva.

In her own right, the ideal woman is a good wife and mother,
and the "womanish mitsvos"—the three that are special to her—
concern her own area, the home. In order to be a good Jew, no
matter what else she does or does not do, she must "take hallah,"
light the Sabbath candles, and purify herself in the ritual bath
after menstruation. She must do a great deal more, for she is
freed only of the specifically masculine mitsvos.

The good wife and mother helps her husband to fulfill his
obligations. She is responsible for the observance of the dietary
laws and for maintaining or implementing all the domestic ritual.
Even when her husband performs the ceremony, it is her duty to
have in readiness the cup of wine, the loaf of bread, the knife,
the towel, the incense, or whatever is needed. She is not included
in religious ritual outside of the house, and in fact is not expected
to be familiar with it. Moreover, she does not have powers of
discretion even in household ceremonials. On any problem of
observance she must consult a man—her husband, the rabbi, a
respected scholar—and even if she knows the answer by experience she has not the right to decide for herself.

The formal demands upon women are revealed repeatedly
in comments on womanly virtue. "She was a perfect Jewish
woman, clean, patient, hard-working and silent, submissive to
God and to her husband, devoted to her children . . . her own
well-being was unimportant. . . . I don't remember my mother
sitting at the table when we ate, except for Friday night and
Saturdays. Those days she even sat on the whole chair. Other

times, when she was sitting, it was always on the edge of the
chair. I believe she never ate a whole meal, always some leftovers.
When I was older I asked her why she was like that and she said,
'Friday night, on Sabbath Eve, I am a queen, like every Jewish
woman. On weekdays I am just a woman. . . .!'"°

The woman's informal status is more demanding and more
rewarding than that formally assigned to her, for in actual living
the complementary character of her role is always to the fore.
She is the wife, who orders the functioning of the household and
provides the setting in which each member performs his part.
She is the mother, key figure in the family constellation. Moreover, the more completely her husband fulfills the ideal picture
of the man as scholar, the more essential is the wife as realist and
mediator between his ivory tower and the hurly-burly of everyday life.

It is the woman who manages the fiscal affairs of the family.
It is proverbial that a true scholar "doesn't know one coin from
another," but even in prosteh families the woman usually stores
and dispenses the household cash, and to a large extent decides
how it shall be used. She is the chief counselor, likely to have
power of suasion and of veto in any matter outside the World of
Torah. "What do you say?" is the husband's familiar query and
a common response is, "What can a silly woman say? I have only
a womanish brain, but if I were in your place. . . ." Often
enough the opinion so modestly prefaced is decisive.

The earning of a livelihood is sexless, and the large majority
of women, even among the sheyneh, participate in some gainful
occupation if they do not carry the chief burden of support. The
wife of a "perennial student" is very apt to be the sole support
of the family. The problem of managing both a business and a
home is so common that no one recognizes it as special. The
economic area is more nearly an extension of the woman's domain than of the man's. To bustle about in search of a livelihood
is merely another form of bustling about managing a home, both
are aspects of gezunt and parnosseh, health and livelihood.

Of course a woman sees that her house is clean, her children
fed, and all the regulations observed—even if she also runs a
shop, has a stall at the market, or merely helps her husband in

his store. She will comment constantly on the burden of it all, the ol. But her complaints are a kind of boasting. "See all I have to do, see how busy I am, see all that is demanded of me, how everything lies on my head!" The implication is not, please take it away from me, but rather, see all I can do—and secondarily, don't I deserve great credit for it? She is too busy to measure her shoulders against her ol and decide whether they are suited to each other. The cares and activities are all in the nature of things, as is the running obligato of complaint about them. When you run very fast, you pant; when you work very hard, you complain. It is all part of the process.

Clearly, although the woman's life is home-centered, it is by no means home-limited. She does the buying and often the selling. She is familiar with the market place and with the merchants who frequent it. Therefore, on the whole women have a better command of the local language than do the learned men. The women and the prosteh men converse freely in the language spoken by the peasants—Russian, Polish, Hungarian. The learned men handle the local language haltingly, if at all.

As full participant in the burden of economic support, the woman escapes the burden of a sheltered life. If anyone is sheltered, it is the scholarly man. Women and even girls move about freely. If business takes a woman to another town, she will stay with relatives, of course, for there are always relatives. But everyone assumes that she can take care of herself and even though an extremely high stake is set on womanly virtue there is no overweening fear that she will not be able to preserve her own.

There are many instances in which the man carries the chief or the sole support of the household. If he is not a scholar it is taken for granted that the primary economic responsibility is his. The important point is that, unlike the shul which is dominated by men and the home which is dominated by women, the market place belongs to both; and that the consequences of this threefold division permeate every aspect of shtetl life.

In effect, the arrangement expresses a functioning balance of power between the sexes. Verbally it may be differently presented, for the shtetl sees itself through the eyes of men and talks about itself through the words of men. It is set up as a man's culture, with woman officially subordinate and officially inferior. The man greets each day by offering thanks to God "that Thou hast not made me a woman." Each day the woman in her early morning prayer offers praise to God "who hast made me according to Thy will."

This view of woman is represented by the second creation story in the Torah, the story of Adam and Eve. Woman is inferior to man because she was created after him, and was made from his body. Talmudic legends explain that many physical and psychological differences between the two sexes must be attributed to the fact that man was formed from the earth and woman from bone. "Women need perfumes, while men do not; dust of the ground remains the same no matter how long it is kept; flesh, however, requires salt to keep it in good condition. The voice of women is shrill, not so the voice of men; when soft viands are cooked, no sound is heard, but let a bone be put in a pot and at once it crackles. A man is easily placated, not so a woman; a few drops of water suffice to soften a clod of earth; a bone stays hard even if it were to soak in water for days. The man must ask the woman to be his wife, and not the woman the man to be her husband, because it is man who has sustained the loss of his rib and he sallies forth to make good his loss again. . . ."

Moreover, according to the legends of the Talmud and the practices of the shtetl, woman is by nature sinful. The perfect wife is described weekly in the Sabbath prayer, but—"who can find her?" It was not for lack of precaution that woman became all too human. "When God was on the point of making Eve, He said: 'I will not make her from the head of man, lest she carry her head high in arrogant pride; not from the eye, lest she be wanton-eyed; not from the ear, lest she be an eavesdropper; not from the neck, lest she be insolent; not from the mouth, lest she be a tattler; not from the heart, lest she be inclined to envy; not from the hand, lest she be a meddler; not from the foot, lest she be a gadabout. I will form her from a chaste portion of the body.' And to every limb and organ as He formed it, God said, 'Be chaste! Be chaste!' Nevertheless, in spite of the great caution used, woman has all the faults God tried to obviate. The daughters of Zion were haughty and walked with stretched-forth necks and wanton eyes; Sarah was an eavesdropper in her own tent, when the Angel spoke with Abraham; Miriam was a tale-bearer, accusing Moses; Rachel was envious of her sister Leah; Eve put out her hand to take the forbidden fruit, and Dinah was a gadabout."

Woman is dangerous, not only because she herself lacks virtue but still more because she rouses in man a desire stronger than his will and his judgment. It is told that when Adam awakened from the profound sleep into which he had been plunged "and saw Eve before him in all her surprising beauty and grace, he exclaimed, 'This is she who caused my heart to throb many a night!' Yet he discerned at once what the nature of woman was. She would, he knew, seek to carry her point with man either by entreaties and tears, or by flattery and caresses. He said, therefore, 'This is my never-silent bell!'"

In the view of the shtetl, desire itself is not sinful, nor is it wrong to love so imperfect a being as a woman. The danger is rather that a creature so undisciplined and given to excess will not help a man to maintain moderation and righteousness, but on the contrary will incite him to break the rules he has accepted —just as Eve incited Adam to eat of the forbidden fruit. The danger that woman represents is less serious as a threat to man personally than as a threat to his fulfillment of the Law. If she causes him to transgress, she endangers herself also, since her personal future is dependent on her husband's Olam Habo, and since the final return to the Promised Land depends on the fulfillment of the mitsvos by all Jews. Eve herself suffered with Adam. Accordingly, the prohibitions affecting the relations between the sexes are for the protection of both against wrongdoing rather than of one against the other. They are equally, or even more, for the protection of the unborn child and of the Jewish community. It is to the interest of all to safeguard the Covenant.

The invariable involvement of the family and the community in the behavior of the individual is nowhere more evident than in the explanations offered and the attitudes expressed with regard to the rules for behavior between men and women. One of the "fences" erected to protect both the mitsva of learning and the sanctity of the home is that which separates the sexes during the daily round of activities. Extreme avoidance of women by men is the prescribed pattern of the shtetl. Usage with regard to this pattern varies from fanatic observance to nonchalant semi-conformity, and demonstrates the ease with which behavior spans the distance between the spirit and the letter of the Law.

The people of the shtetl give a number of reasons for the avoidance rule, all of them bearing on the need to insure fulfillment of the two leading mitsvos. A woman too freely contemplated would fill a man's thoughts with sex when he should be concentrating on study. It is striking that, despite the emphatic avoidance rule, sexual enjoyment is considered healthy and good —at the proper time and place, and in the proper context. To bring children into the world is the duty of every Jew and it is right for man and wife to enjoy intercourse as a means to procreation. Such enjoyment is not only permitted, it is prescribed. God does nothing without a purpose and since He made man with sex organs and appetite, the exercise of them must be good.

Excess in anything is bad, however, and not only bad but un-Jewish. The ideal Jew is moderate in all things. It is good for him to enjoy intercourse with his wife under correct circumstances. But it is wrong for him to entertain sexual thoughts or impulses toward her or any woman outside of actual intercourse. To contaminate study of the Law with extraneous thoughts is worse, especially if they are carnal thoughts. The Talmud says, "If one is studying the words of God and raises his eyes to say, 'Oh how beautiful that tree is!' he deserves the penalty of death."

The shtetl, with its veneration for the power of the mind, lays great emphasis on avoidance of untoward thoughts. There are even rules to help one keep the content of his mind in harmony with his duties as a Jew. Thoughts about business are recommended in order to avoid thinking of God in inappropriate settings. On Sabbath, when thoughts about business are forbidden they may be shut out by repeating harmless gossip to oneself. Again, if one finds himself in danger of becoming excessively gay or hilarious, the manuals of behavior counsel him to remember some sad event—possibly the destruction of the Temple.

Because it is sinful to be distracted by thoughts of sex while studying the Law, boys are married early so that their needs will be satisfied and they will have no difficulty concentrating on their books. The more talented the student, the more effort is made to have him marry young, even at fourteen or fifteen. Purity, in other words, is sought through immunizing rather than through quarantine. "There is no such thing as a Jewish monastery," says the proverb. The precautions taken are not against sex, but against the intrusion of sex at the wrong time and in the wrong context.

The precautions themselves are severe. The bride's hair is cut off and for the rest of her life she wears a wig or sheytl, in order to reduce her dangerous charms. A woman is not supposed to wear short sleeves, and in any case a man should not study in a room where a woman's arms are exposed. He should not listen to a woman singing, lest she arouse his desire.

The avoidance pattern also protects the home, for if impure thoughts are aroused they might be followed by the sin of fornication. The horror of this sin is increased by the menace that it holds for children conceived out of wedlock. It is evil enough for an adult to defile his own soul by violation of a commandment, but far worse to endanger the unborn child of God's Covenant. It holds a double danger to the child, since it makes him illegitimate and also may result in his being born deformed or subnormal. Protection is needed even against the man's desire for his own wife, since intercourse is forbidden during menstruation. Violation of this rule risks the same consequences to the child as if the two culprits were not married.

The woman is considered so potent a source of attraction that a man must avert his eyes in order to protect them both. Some men will not even speak directly to a woman. Most would avoid passing between two of them. And all pious parents would want their daughters to be raised in accordance with the strictest observance. An unusually loving couple had their only quarrel when the wife became addicted to advanced ideas and made for their two-year-old daughter some tiny shirts with short sleeves. "I'd die if she wears them!"° bellowed the outraged husband.

The burden of avoidance is more on the man than on the woman. She is expected to comply with sartorial regulations and

to refrain from obtruding herself, but the responsibility for not
looking at her, talking to her or touching her, is his.

A division of sexes at social functions follows naturally from
the division of interests and responsibilities, as well as from the
avoidance rule and the concept of feminine inferiority. At the
khumesh ceremony, when the boy moves from primary to inter-
mediate studies, the men sit at the table with the father and the
rabbi, while the proud mother and her women friends look on
from the corner. At weddings, the men and women stand in
separate groups during the ceremony and sit at different tables
tor the feast. Separation of sexes is obligatory and men precede
women. If friends come to visit on a Sabbath afternoon, as a
matter of course the men will sit together discoursing on manly
matters while the women gossip about their own affairs. In the
old days it was unthinkable for men and girls to dance together,
but in later years this prohibition broke down among the
"liberals" and the advanced.

Always, of course, the degree of observance has varied greatly.
Many of the prosteh have serenely ignored the rule, while among
the sheyneh this, like all the traditions, has been more rigorously
observed. The little shirts over which the parents quarreled were
finally given away, presumably to some poor family, and this disposal is in line with the prevailing assumption that the duty of
strict observance lies more heavily on the educated and prosperous than on the ignorant and poor.

Observance is more extreme also among the old than among
the young, and among the Hassidim than among the other Jews.
The avoidance pattern led to some embarrassment when an aged
Hassid who had moved to the city went to visit his niece one day,
sat down, and as usual said, "Give me a glass of tea." Carefully
keeping his eyes averted from the woman who served him, he
stirred the tea and began to drink in silence. Only when a strange
voice asked, "Is it strong enough?"° did he realize that he had
entered the wrong apartment and was being waited upon by a
stranger.

Such accidents are rare, since most men who practice rigid
avoidance learn also to avoid its pitfalls. They learn to glance
sideways with a look that sees and does not see. Some women

claim that the Hassidim see a great deal in those fleeting, skirmishing glances, and that they enjoy what they see. If a difficult social situation forces a very orthodox man to shake hands with a woman, he deftly slips his caftan over his hand to avoid contact. He avoids pronounced bodily contact even with men, shaking hands only with the tips of the fingers, or sliding his hand away quickly if the other is disposed toward a hearty handclasp—as if to minimize contact of two bodies where contact of minds is important.

The constant danger of confronting or touching a woman has developed in some extremely pious men an almost furtive manner. They enter a room sideways with averted glance, so that people say of a very shy person, "He comes in like a yeshiva boy."

The ideals of masculine and feminine appearance and deportment show the contrasts appropriate to the differences in role. The "surprising beauty" of Eve, as pictured by the shtetl, would be generous in scale. The ideal man is the scholar, pale and ascetic, but the wife of his hopes should be plump, with full breasts and hips. "A handsome woman," they will say, "such a fine double chin!" A matron not amply endowed by nature will hold her chin in when she sits in company, in order to give it a fulsome look. A woman's face should be sleek and smooth—wrinkles are a blight against which she will struggle with ointments and treatments that she strives in vain to keep secret from prying eyes. And she should be rosy. A woman should, in short, be a solid, healthy body, whereas a man should be a strong, transcendant spirit.

Because she is a physical being, the woman wears ornaments to enhance her beauty. A man who would not wear a ring himself is eager to see jewels on his wife's fingers. When she goes to shul on Sabbath, she wears the jewelry for the family. Presumably she is bedecked solely for the admiration of other women, since no man except her husband is supposed to look at her. However, a full description of every jewel worn by every woman will be current in the shtetl by nightfall. If a particularly elegant piece of passementerie has bloomed on Reb Kalman's Rokhl, many a woman will "make her husband the death" or "shorten his years" over it, dwelling on its charms and the fact that she has none like it.

In behavior the model man is restrained, poised, laconic. It is taken for granted that women are far more expressive, ready with tears, laughter and volubility. True, the ideal woman is silent and submissive, at least opposite her husband. But that ideal, unlike the man's, is commonly regarded as contrary to fact.

Whoever walks down the streets of the shtetl hears more women's than men's voices coming through the windows. The chatter in the women's section of the Synagogue has become a byword, so that a din is said to be "as noisy as the *ezras noshim*." When the chatter, quarreling or even the ritual wailing and weeping upstairs threatens to drown out the services, the men pound on the desks, cast angry glances up at the small grated windows, and shout, "Women, quiet!"

The sheyneh men would be ashamed to engage in loud quarreling, except over scholarly questions, for it would be said that they quarreled "like women in the market place." Women quarrel at home also, over children and household affairs or even over the holiday remembrance one owes to the other. Husbands may look on with neither embarrassment nor concern, for after all, "they're only women." No man wishes to have his wife go too far, however. The boisterous, strident, domineering woman is called a "Cossack woman," and although a grudging admiration for her vigor may creep in, one prefers to appreciate her as a member of somebody else's family.

Despite the balanced contrast of masculine and feminine roles, the mutual exclusion from the activities specific to men or to women is not categorical. The shtetl is not given to absolutes, and in this as in most respects there is flexibility and some degree of interchange.

Study is for men, yet some women do acquire a considerable amount of learning. If no man is available, a woman may say the Sabbath blessing over wine. If no woman is available, a man may light the Sabbath candles. Traditionally, women do not wear fringed garments, yet the Shulkhan Arukh tells what a woman must do if she should wear one. There was even a Hassidic woman who became a religious leader and acquired followers. It is typical of the culture both that this could happen and that when it did there was no way to deal with her. Yes, she was a "Rebbeh" and for a woman to be that runs contrary to sense and propriety. The ultimate solution was that she married, ceased to be a Rebbeh, and became a "real woman," that is a wife and mother.

The actual importance ascribed to the masculine and feminine functions varies according to the viewpoint of the individual and in any case is seldom a matter of comment. The shtetl is used to the arrangement and besides most people are too busy to give it much thought. "What could a man do without a woman?" is more than a popular saying, it is a constant theme. And how could women get on without men? Besides, this is the way it is and shtetl folk are used to accepting a status quo that they might not have recommended had they been consulted in the first place. Certainly few learned men would want to change places with a busy housewife, cooking, cleaning and perhaps supporting her family by running a small shop. On the other hand, probably few women would care to assume the duties and responsibilities of a talmid khokhem with his countless rituals, his endless study, his incessant discussions and arguments over remote and intricate subjects, his constant anxiety lest he neglect some regulation.

To a large extent, the formal status is dismissed as merely formal. Yes, the women will say, men think we don't count but they're stupid—what could they do without us? Could they get married? Could they bear children? Could they even be fed and clothed and housed decently?

As for the future life, let them say we can't get there without them. They couldn't manage this life alone, no doubt we'll have to do for them there too. Some of them say we have no souls of our own but that's silly. It would be silly to argue about it too, only—we know. Only a few would second the comment of one shtetl feminist who declared, "Women have real souls and men have recognized souls."°

When a woman does complain about the lot of her sex, she is apt to protest in terms of her formal status, exclusion from the World of Torah, consignment to the world of the week. When she explicitly prefers it to the man's, she is apt to reckon with her informal status. Similarly, when a man considers a woman's

role undesirable, he speaks of her formal status and when he en-
vies her it is in terms of her informal status. The man's-eye view
of the universe is the one that "stands in the books." The
woman's-eye view of the man's-eye view is her own affair.

Many women merely accept the man's-eye view and see themselves in a strictly supporting role. Such a role can be highly
gratifying if one is the wife of a scholar, proudly supporting him
and winning future bliss for both. It can also offer convenient
loopholes. "What do you expect? What am I after all, only a sinful woman. Naturally I make mistakes."

The pattern prescribed by the culture, however, allows full
scope for the "never-silent bell" to be a submissive partner or a
vibrant force in her home and in the community. A woman may
comply with all the formal demands upon her and still be an
effective manager of her domestic affairs, an effective business
woman and an active member of the community. There is room
for matriarchs as well as for patriarchs and it would be hard to
say which predominate numerically. "My grandmother was a
wonderful woman. . . . When we walked down the streets someone would always say, 'There goes Grandmother Leya's grandchild.' . . . My grandfather Yoysef, well, he didn't count for very
much."°

The wife of a nogid may keep her own private drawer full
of trinkets and small cash, from which to help the needy, and it
may be to her rather than to him that people turn for help and
advice. "She was always busy . . . her good deeds took up so
much time."° It is not unknown for a man to beg his wife on her
deathbed to transfer to him half her mitsvos, on the plea that
after all they were accomplished with his aid.

To a comfortable degree, in the day by day rush of life, each
sex is oriented to its own reality. If one's world revolves around
the activities of the shul, the domestic economy is seen as an
indispensable but secondary adjunct. If home is the hub of the
universe, the shul and its activities become a necessary luxury,
sometimes classed as a burden and sometimes as a privilege. In
either case, one can feel—mine is the real work of the world.

V

PEOPLE OF THE WEEK

Those who represent the humdrum daily round, as opposed to the spirit of Sabbath, are the "people of the week," *vokhendikeh mentshen*. They are principally the unschooled, the workers, the artisans, the peddlers—those who in general are called "prosteh."

The prosteh do not necessarily lack piety or elementary learning. Every ignoramus is prost, but not every proster is an ignoramus. On the contrary, some regularly spend their Sabbaths and evenings studying, in the groups and associations congenial to their humble station. Some are as strict as any rabbi in their observance of rituals and regulations, constantly seeking advice on points of interpretation or behavior too subtle for their skill.

These are not the majority, however. Nor is the other extreme in the majority, the prostak, who is blatantly ignorant and blatantly uncouth. Expectations and generalizations about the prosteh are built partly on the behavior of the majority, partly on the behavior of the prostak and partly on the prejudices engendered by that behavior. Who is prost and precisely what the term means will depend of course on the position of the individual who is speaking. All will agree, however, that a proster person cannot be learned, and that he will lack *savoir faire*. In short, he lacks the qualities that make one "beautiful." It is significant that it is far from unusual for prosteh people to be rich.

The majority of the prosteh, somewhere between the very pious and the prostak, exhibit the same subtle gradation that marks the various levels among the sheyneh. The upper levels of the prosteh merge into the balebatisheh, the respected burgher type, just as do the lower levels of the sheyneh. The balebatisheh, who devote a larger portion of their life to business, may often be richer than those learned men who give themselves to study, leaving the burden of parnosseh to their wives. The majority of the *balebatim* are merchants or storekeepers. These are the men who usually sit in the first rows—the "mirror"—facing the Eastern Wall. In their aspirations they identify with the sheyneh layt. Being less tradition-bound, however, they may be more free to give their chief attention to business, and also may grant their children more freedom in education. Accordingly, many doctors or lawyers come from balebatisheh families.

While the sheyneh layt are "of the Sabbath" and the prosteh layt are "of the week," the balebatisheh belong to both. They may be counted with the sheyneh on the Sabbath but during the week they belong to the market place. As a social group they have no distinctive pattern of their own, but combine in varying degrees the elements characteristic of the sheyneh and the prosteh.

Down below there are still the fine shades of difference, as between the shoemaker who makes the uppers and the one who makes the soles of the shoes. Those who are so inclined can usually find a reason for considering themselves not quite what could be called prost. Many will characterize their neighbors as "real prosteh" but will see themselves as a cut above, perhaps even as balebatish, because of some modest claim. Even if the visible badge is deportment, occupation or yikhus, the underlying trait reverts to education. A man who is truly learned cannot be a boor and no matter what his occupation, he will not be classed as prost. Uncouth manners or a lowly calling may be mentioned as evidence that a man is prost, but it is taken for granted that if he had learning his manners and his occupation would be different. At least by the sheyneh, these criteria are taken as signs but not as determinants of social status, the primary determinant being education. Some of the prosteh see eye to eye with the sheyneh, even across the class barrier, and some do not.

The schooling of the prosteh usually begins as the schooling of all the boys begins, but continues for only a few years. It leaves the average boy with an education slightly superior to what would be taken for granted for women—literacy in Yiddish, and ability to read Hebrew words without grasping their content. The pedagogical theory is consistent. One teaches women and little children by rote, confident that when the intellect develops sufficiently the precept will be embraced with enlightenment and affirmation. Meanwhile the pupil is safeguarded by having imposed upon him the conduct he will practice voluntarily and gladly when he reaches understanding. Book learning may be followed by apprenticeship at some trade, even for boys who are not so poor that they must attend the Talmud Toyreh.

Nevertheless, there is always the possibility for the son of prosteh parents to push through the Gates of Torah to a dazzling marriage and the status of sheyneh. The great Hillel himself was of a humble family and began life as a water carrier.

Even the least learned love to quote, and their speech is rich in allusions and references, often twisted, misquoted or manufactured. Sholem Aleichem's famous character Tevyeh is typical in his mangling of learned authorities. The main body from which the unschooled draw for verbal embellishment, however, is folk proverbs and sayings rather than the sacred writings. There are available not only the countless Yiddish sayings, but also the folk wisdom of the neighboring peasants. "A peasant proverb," they sometimes say, "is as true as Torah." Yet such a remark always recognizes a difference; *lehavdl*, they say, "let it be separated," meaning to differentiate between the sacred and the profane. The wisdom of the "others" is true, but their truth is of a different order from divine pronouncement. The phrase "lehavdl" is frequently used when "theirs" and "ours" are said in one breath.

The word prost may be used as simple definition, by way of placing an individual in a social group. Or it may be used as an evaluation, with implications ranging from the derogatory to the honorific, much as the word "common" ranges from an epithet meaning coarse to the honorable connotations of "the common man." The shade of meaning depends on the situation and on the values of the speaker.

The sheyneh tend to see the prosteh in terms of a stereotype. They expect the "typical prosteh" to be loud and coarse, quick-tempered as women, rough and violent as peasants. A "typical proster" is big, strong, broad-shouldered and fit for physical labor; or else he is wizened, underfed and miserable. His hands are stained and hardened by work.

He is hardly expected to be the best of fathers, since he cannot instruct his sons in the ways of the Law. He is not expected to be the best of husbands either, and if any Jew commits the outrage of wife-beating it would be taken for granted that he must be prost. The sheyneh, it is assumed, are too thoroughly imbued with respect for the sanctity of the home and with abhorrence for every form of physical violence except the pious punishment of children.

A glimpse at the market place has shown that in garb the prosteh stand midway between the sheyneh and the peasant. For greater agility in "chasing after parnosseh" the men may shorten or put aside their coats, and thrust their legs into high, heavy boots. Some even find it expedient to clip their beards and their ear locks.

The sheyneh may condemn the efficient attire, and the shearing of the beard—but what these humble folk do is of secondary importance, for they are "only prost" just as a girl is "only a girl," and like the girl, they are "something else again." All the more need for the enlightened and responsible members of the group to intensify their own traditionalism. They must stand as model and also as surrogate for all.

The qualities imputed to the prosteh are evident in the use of the term as an epithet. "Don't be prost!" is the equivalent of "Don't be vulgar!" "He has paws like a proster," may be said of a man who is unfortunate enough to have broad, stubby hands. Kheyder boys fighting a gang from another part of town throw at them the epithet, "prostak!"

The prosteh in exchange cherish their own stereotype of the sheyneh, and an important trait in that stereotype is hypocrisy. On the whole one can afford to feel less concern about what the community thinks and says if one has no obligation to be a model beyond reproach. "*I* am a proster mentsh," the rebel will say with as much pride as humility. "*I* speak right out what is on my mind. *I* don't have any high falutin' rigmaroles, and learned word somersaults!" Such a man sees the sheyneh scholars as pedants who exalt the formalities and the externals above the warm human traits. He resents the imputation that because he is "of the week" rather than of the Sabbath world, he is inferior. "Better a Jew without a beard," he insists, "than a beard without a Jew."

The "beard without a Jew" may be a pedant with a "Jewish head" but not a "Jewish heart." Or he may be merely an imitation, one who has come up in the world but is essentially prost despite his pretensions. For such a man, sheyneh and prosteh alike entertain only contempt, and when they refer to him as sheyn the term becomes ironic and derogatory. In contrast to the picture of the sheyneh as hypocrites, the prosteh sometimes refer to themselves as *amkho,* Thy People.

To some of the prosteh, even the truly learned look like parasites, sitting over their books day and night. "What do they do? Just squash down a chair, all day long." But the "vokhendikeh mentshen" do the work of the week, the humble, grimy, arduous work that makes possible the lofty glow of the Sabbath.

And what use do the chair-squashers make of their knowledge? Now and then a suspicion of hoarding crops out, as when a prosteh "commissionaire" took his business problem to the rabbi. His customers objected to his long black caftan, he lost business because of it, his parnosseh was at stake, what should he do? The rabbi studied the matter, tracing its implications through many volumes of commentary, and finally—straining to give the most humane interpretation—decreed that since parnosseh was at stake, the man might wear a shorter coat for business. Overjoyed the "commissionaire" ran out into the street, jumping up and down and shouting, "I can do it, I can do it! Oh the robbers—all the other things they must know and won't tell us!"

The vitality of the class stereotypes cannot obscure the fact that basically the sheyneh and the prosteh live by the same code. In both groups the dominance of the traditional pattern is accepted in a spirit ranging from affirmation through grumbling to resistance. Proportions differ, and the negative response is higher among the prosteh, yet any proster father longs to have a son become a learned man, even though he may swear that scholars are parasites living on the toil of honest fellows like himself. "Every Jew," says the proverb, "would like a seat on the East Wall of his shul."

Moreover, while each group harbors a stereotype of the other, each sees the other as an essential partner in the life of the community. One is the man of action, the other the man of thought. The man of learning or of wealth is constant adviser and constant helper. The prosteh not only do the heavy work but in time of violence they are strong-armed defenders. And violence is no stranger to the shtetl.

The prosteh sufficiently multiplied, become the crowd, the plebs—*hamoyn*. They are the ones made to be led, guided, governed by the elite. They seldom talk at meetings and gatherings. They are called to the Sabbath reading of the Torah only when they earn the right by celebrating some fulfillment of their duties as Jews—getting married or having a baby.

During the week it is the more humble workers who attend the very early services at the shul, while those who can afford to start the daily "chase after parnosseh" a little later, go to the "second minyan." The "first minyan" goes through the prayers more quickly and with less elaboration than the second, since the worshippers must finish as quickly as possible in order to get to their work. Since the "faces" of the community are not present to occupy their seats on the Eastern Wall, these places of honor are pre-empted by the more aggressive of the first minyan. The sober and devout, like the sheyneh, are quiet and not disposed to "push themselves" so that the honor seats are "grabbed" by the bullies, accustomed to elbow their way through life. Accordingly the first minyan during the week exhibits a disarrangement of the finely graded order of Sabbath seating, and those who are least learned, least restrained, least "Jewish" face the congregation from the exalted station of the mizrakh.

The Sabbath order is the one that counts. The whole shtetl, including the "vokhendikeh mentshen," lives from Sabbath to Sabbath, striving toward the climax of the week that makes all Jews equal and every man a king. For the prosteh, however, the world of the week occupies a larger part of the horizon and in that world they often learn to assert themselves more effectively than the ideal sheyneh. They are the realists, the hustlers.

For both sheyneh and prosteh the twin sayings hold true, "it is good to be a Jew" and "it is hard to be a Jew." On Sabbath the joy is most apparent and in the world of the week there is more to remind one of the hardship, the sorrow, the yoke—the ol. During the week one lives in *Golus,* the Diaspora. Sabbath is the time for remembering the privileges of the Chosen People and the promise of the future. In living from Sabbath to Sabbath, the people of the week lack the armor of learning that sheathes the sheyneh, and to this extent are more exposed. They are more exposed also by virtue of their greater contact with the peasants who for them chiefly represent the world outside the shtetl system. It follows also that the outside world knows the shtetl primarily through the prosteh. They are, as it were, the outpost of the culture. Just as for the Jew the Gentile is to a large extent equated with the peasant, so for the peasant "the Jew" is—with notable exceptions —prost.

The most conspicuous and most often mentioned earmark of the prosteh is their language. To "talk like a proster" means not only to talk inelegantly and ungrammatically but also that one is not above using "ugly words." The vocabulary includes expressions and tones of voice forbidden to the sheyneh. In the world of the week, "ugly words" are a commonplace, as are quarrels that may on rare occasions lead into fisticuffs. Quarreling is conceived as "un-Jewish" by the sheyneh. "They fight like prosteh" is as frequent a comment as "they quarrel like women" and carries the same implications about the behavior of the group.

When the sheyneh quarrel it is supposed to be only about some matter of scholarship. In a learned dispute one may become very angry indeed without violating decorum. He may even in an extremely heated argument grow so angry that he foams at the mouth. Two discussants will stand close together, gesticulating, shouting, perhaps seizing a button on the other's coat and twisting it to emphasize the words. In such cases the contact will always be between flesh and fabric, not between flesh and flesh.

In the ordinary affairs of daily life, however, the "beautiful Jew" is expected to be a model of restrained and dignified expression, and if he departs from this approved mien it is only when he "forgets" himself. If he gets so angry that he "jumps out of his vessels" he will be much ashamed, unless the topic is impersonal and erudite. On such a subject quarreling can be tolerated in the guise of argument or discussion. It is only women and prosteh who "really quarrel."

Among the prosteh any conversation may lead to verbal quarreling, although the shtetl is at one in regarding physical violence as "un-Jewish." Despite the contrast in deportment, however, the quarrels of all show a number of traits in common; in general one would quarrel only with his peers. Between people of disparate status, quarreling is avoided. One or the other will respond with physical withdrawal or with silence.

Vocabulary and intonation may vary at different social levels, but in any case the speech of altercation will be fluent and colorful. Words are a highly potent weapon, the medium for a high degree of virtuosity. They are, indeed, the only approved weapon except silence. An almost startling amount of imagination will be lavished on their use, whether the subject is blue vs. white fringes on the prayer shawl or the correct boundary line between the shoe stall and the dry-goods stall at the market.

Moreover, whatever the status of the quarrelers and whatever the subject of their dispute, it is beyond the bounds of decency to inflict real shame. You denounce a person for any or every sin you can think of, but refrain from mentioning the one thing that would bring to his cheeks the flush of serious shame. Shame is horrible to the shtetl. One of the regulations set forth in the Shulkhan Arukh is a prohibition against shaming any person. To shame him is worse than robbing him. It is called "drenching his face in blood" and any form of cruel bloodshed has no place in human behavior. If his daughter really had an illegitimate baby, if his son became converted, if his wife is suspected of infidelity, this is the one thing you will never throw up to him in an argument. Each week in her Sabbath prayer the housewife, asking for the well-being of her family during the week to come, pleads with God "may we not be ashamed!"

The curses of the uninhibited are countless and ingenious but they are carefully divorced from probability. "You should lose all your teeth except one and that should ache," "they should put a feather to your nose," "you should burn like a wick and they should put you out with benzine," "you should grow like an onion with your head in the ground." All may be uttered in genuine fury, but even at the peak of rage if you thought it could happen you would never voice it.

Physical defects are not in the category excluded from mention, for the strictly physical is never in the first rank of importance. To mention a deformity is not equated with shaming. On the contrary, the innumerable array of shtetl sobriquets draws as heavily on physical characteristics of all sorts as on occupation, status, temperament or kinship. "Berl Hunchback," "Shimen Flea," "Yenta with the Big Behind," are simple, straightforward designations, used as nonchalantly as Zelig the Tailor or Mottl the Shoemaker.

In a community where surnames have no functional existence, but represent a late imposition never fully absorbed, nicknames are almost a necessity of easy conversation. Men may be designated by their station or calling alone, without the name—The Rabbi or The Nogid (rich man); or they may be identified by the place from which they come: Mordekhay Pinsker or the Kotsker Rabbi. Individual temperament or history may also supply names: Avrom Shtiller or Yankel Soldat.

Although the prosteh are in general more inclined than the sheyneh to physical conflict, any member of the shtetl avoids overt anger or attack, especially against the Gentiles. Hostility often finds an outlet in humor, the humor of the oppressed with the special turn characteristic of Yiddish jokes. Sheyneh and prosteh tell countless jokes about each other and about themselves, the shtetl in general jokes and gibes at the expense of the goyim and no less at the expense of the Jews. Laughter is safe and in addition it serves as a safety valve.

It is to be expected that the superstitions of the neighboring folk should have gained the strongest foothold in that segment of the population least versed in the teachings of the Torah. A great deal of Eastern European folklore has been assimilated into talmudic legend, and many ritualistic Jewish practices have their parallel in the peasants' celebrations of their festivals. Nevertheless, there is a shtetl population of demons, spirits and witches who play a larger part in the life of the prosteh than of the sheyneh. The ignorant are more likely than the sheyneh to consult a fortuneteller, either Jew or Gentile. They are more afraid of the witches whose identity nobody is quite sure about, but who can transform themselves into anything they wish, and can work serious harm on anyone who displeases them. They are more likely to shudder for fear of *rusalkehs,* half woman and half fish, who live in the swamps and if they can lay hold of an unwary wayfarer after dark will "tickle him to death."

The difference is merely one of degree, however, and many superstitions are shared equally by all. A child of any social station will be protected elaborately from the evil eye, for example; and a learned man will be as fearful as the next one of going into the synagogue at night, for then the spirits of the dead go to shul to pray.

Avoidance of women is practiced less among the prosteh. They put it aside, with the long beard and the long caftan, as too cumbersome for their "chase after parnosseh." The bustle of the market place, to which women and prosteh men are native, brings time for encounters both friendly and belligerent, but not for elaborate detours and eye droopings. Again, of course, there will be a rigorous minority that practice avoidance with utmost zeal. For the most part, however, the moderate, almost subtle and almost instinctive separation of the sexes taken for granted among the sheyneh is not taken for granted among the prosteh. On the contrary, an easy intermingling is the rule, to which the occasional zealot furnishes an exception.

It is appropriate that barriers between prosteh men and women should be lowered, for the women of any class have much in common with the prosteh men. Both lack learning, and must read simple Yiddish books, rather than scholarly Hebrew *sforim.* Both are noted for lack of restraint, for volubility and excitability. They share familiarity with the local language, and an orientation different from that of the yeshiva, one more characteristic of the week than of Sabbath. In all these qualities they are, according to shtetl standards, less "Jewish" than the sheyneh yidn, and by that token, closer to the Gentile, the goy.

The contrast between the Jewish and the un-Jewish is corollary to, though not identical with, the contrast between the learned and the ignorant. At home and in the synagogue, prosteh and sheyneh alike are constantly confronted with the social superiority of the intellectual over the physical, and of learning over ignorance. This comparison is equated with the superiority of the Jewish over the non-Jewish way of life and consequently of the Jew over the non-Jew.

In the shtetl, reality supports such a comparison, for the neighboring peasants are illiterate, uninterested in the values the Jews hold highest, and more prone than the Jews to excesses of drinking and violence. It becomes easy, therefore, to identify the behavior of the prostak with the behavior of the non-Jew.

A series of contrasts is set up in the mind of the shtetl child, who grows up to regard certain behavior as characteristic of Jews, and its opposite as characteristic of Gentiles. Among Jews he expects to find emphasis on intellect, a sense of moderation, cherishing of spiritual values, cultivation of rational, goal-directed activities, a "beautiful" family life. Among Gentiles he looks for the opposite of each item: emphasis on the body, excess, blind instinct, sexual license, and ruthless force. The first list is ticketed in his mind as Jewish, the second as goyish.

Not only the character of the neighboring Gentiles has fostered and preserved this set of assumptions. The character of the contact between the two groups, from the Middle Ages to World War II, further supported them. That contact, almost exclusively on matters of business or of government, was peaceable for the most part, and in many instances friendly. Yet it was subject to explosions in which the Gentiles exhibited the violence, excess and unpredictability imputed to them. Most Jews knew, by experience or by eyewitness account, of pogroms. They had direct evidence of the strange fashion in which their neighbors might suddenly become pillagers and murderers. They knew equally well the reverse transition when, the pogrom over, these same killers once again became neighbors, customers, salesmen, and relations settled back into the old routine "as if nothing had happened." Nothing had happened—except that one's friend, one's uncle, one's sister, one's father, was now dead.

Occasionally the home of a rich man would have secret passages, leading to other key buildings, for use during pogroms. The passageways might fall into disuse, becoming choked with sand and dust, but they were part of the imagery of the children who played around them, just as the half-effaced memory was part of every Jew's mental equipment. Such houses would have an attic, too, designed to be a refuge as well as a storage space. In time of terror, the almost instinctive reaction was to take to the attic or the cellar, even though the pseudo safety offered by these retreats spelled isolation and the cutting off of escape.

There might be a shtetl that never saw a pogrom. "There wasn't much anti-Semitism in our shtetl. At least, it didn't affect us. We used to hear all sorts of stories, but we were good friends with all our Gentile neighbors. . . . I was never attacked or hurt by the Gentile boys."° There were many which for long periods were free. But there were also periods, for some, in which a child would become used to the shrieks from outside, the banging of doors being broken in, the wails for nonexistent help. "I sat in a chair reading while the grownups listened and trembled."°

Such a child the next day might peer out into the streets and see the Gentiles' pigs snuffing and eating the corpses of the people who until yesterday had lived next door. It was in character for the unclean animal to behave so, and inevitable that this scavenger activity would strengthen the symbolism of the pig as an object of disgust.

Such experiences and memories, quickly thrust into the background, nevertheless contributed to the total picture of the goyim held by the Jews. It could not be a simple, homogeneous picture, however. Like all the concepts of the shtetl it was composed of diverse parts and shadings. For there were goyim who protected Jews during a pogrom, even at their own risk. "We were hidden by the peasants, by Poles. The head of the village did not want to accept the pay that my father offered him for saving us."° There were also the many who could be bribed or bought to withhold or divert impending slaughter.

The attitudes of the shtetl toward itself and toward its neighbors can be understood only in terms of the minority group situation. Basic to the shtetl view of itself is the acceptance of itself as a minority, not by accident but by divine intention. The Chosen People are few among the hordes of unbelievers, and this is as God willed it to be. It is not their function to proselytize until all men accept the Truth, but merely to carry their own torch and their own burden, to fulfill God's commandments until in His time Messiah shall come.

There is no attempt, therefore, to convert others to Judaism. On the contrary, it is the duty of the rabbi to warn any potential convert against assuming so heavy a yoke and to discourage him if possible from joining the ranks of the persecuted. The duty is accepted the more wholeheartedly, since experience has shown that the conversion may become the occasion for open hostilities against the Jews.

The majority group is as much part of the design as the minority. They live without benefit of divine Truth and Law which, according to the legend, they themselves rejected. They remain, therefore, the victims of their own blind impulses and their own excesses. No more can be expected of them for they live in the dark. This is why a "good" Gentile deserves more credit than a good Jew, and a bad Jew is infinitely more reprehensible than a bad Gentile.

The view of the Gentile as an indispensable part of the universe and as a victim of his own limitations helps to explain the lack of intensity in shtetl attitudes toward the dominant group. The goyim represent, quite literally, an act of God. When they are persecutors they are also instruments of justice, punishing the Jews for transgressing the Law, and in any case they obviously do not know better.

The conception of the roles played by both groups is illustrated by the conception of the life to come. Heaven is not for Jews only, it is for "the righteous of the peoples." The good goyim will go to heaven also. They may not participate in the eternal pilpul, for which they would hardly be prepared or eager. But presumably they, like the prosteh and the women, will find entertainment to suit their capacities and their preferences.

Salvation, in other words, is not contingent upon acceptance of the approved creed. It depends rather on a righteous fulfillment of the role in which one has been cast. The requirements are far more rigorous for a Jew than for a non-Jew, and the penalties for failure are more harsh. This is as it should be, for the Chosen People carry the responsibilities summed up in *noblesse oblige.* Just as a Jew, especially if he is learned, carries responsibility for his group, so in the view of the shtetl the Jews as a group carry a responsibility for and to those peoples who are not "chosen."

Those who are not bound by the Covenant lie outside the close-knit system of the shtetl, and in this respect, they are lumped together. Being outside the system they are free of the demands made upon its members. They are not judged or ranked with regard to learning—the mitsvos have no claim on them. Within the broad category of unbelievers, however, the folk of the shtetl differentiate between different kinds of goyim and also between the character of a single individual in varying situations. The peasant of the market-place transaction is different from the same peasant when he starts a drunken brawl at the inn that evening. Any peasant is different from the powerful government official who decrees taxes, military service, or a pogrom. And all these are different from the helpful "shabbes goy" who comes to extinguish the Sabbath lights and is grateful for a piece of white holiday bread.

The peasant servant is a familiar character in the shtetl, often on affectionate terms with the family, and often fluent in Yiddish. Such a retainer may become more a stickler for religious observance than some of the household, and will see to it that the boys do not eat before praying, sharply remind any child who is careless about wearing his cap, the yarmelkeh, and take pride in keeping the milk pots and the meat pots rigidly separate. There is even a saying, "a peasant girl in a rabbi's house knows how to decide questions of dietary law."

On the other hand, Jewish children acquire from the shtetl servants a large part of their impressions about the non-Jewish world. These impressions are available not only to the children of the rich, for women of modest circumstances who work in a store or at the market often have the help of a peasant girl in the house. The girls tell the children wonderful folk stories and sing them lullabies in Russian or Polish, beginning their acquaintance with the local language of the peasants. Sometimes the servant will take them to the home of her parents, making sure that nobody gives them forbidden food. Sometimes she even takes them to a church, where childish curiosity may conflict with the shtetl-wide fear of entering the house dedicated to worship of "their" God. Ordinarily, any member of the shtetl would try to avoid even passing a church, and if it is unavoidable he will mutter a protective formula as he hurries by. Yet for all this, many Jews have been saved during pogroms by humane priests who gathered them into the churchyard for safety.

Peasant retainers often become a source of help when the pogrom strikes. On one occasion a rich man, a nogid, had been led out to be killed by a gang of rioters who were cheerfully executing the government order to "shoot up the Jews." But one of the troop was the sweetheart of the nogid's servant, and had enjoyed many a glass of tea, many a hearty snack in the nogid's comfortable kitchen. Seeing who was led out to be slaughtered, this youth called out, "Let him go, let him go, it's a good Jew." So the nogid was allowed to return to his home, to find his bruised wife lying on the floor where she had been thrown, weeping for his death, and to convince her that this torn and beaten man was indeed her dignified husband and no walking corpse.

Within a few days the peasant boy was again enjoying his glass of tea in their kitchen. "We were drunk," he shrugged. "Now it's over."

The burden of an ever-present anxiety becomes as imperceptible as a man's own beard. It is always there but seldom mentioned and for long periods of time hardly remembered with the conscious mind. Yet the one who wears it knows that it is part of him, a feature that is also a badge. Looking at the peasant the Jew often says, "He has no worries, what's he got to be afraid of? He gets drunk, he beats his wife, he sings a little song."°

The peasant, returning that look across the bodiless, invisible and undeniable barrier that separates the two groups, finds the Jew strange and unpredictable in much the same manner as the Jew finds him. "Jews are a contrary people," say the Poles. It is difficult to understand how a whole people can reject Christ, probably more difficult than for the Jews to understand how the non-Jews could reject the Covenant. It is odd for people to insist that Saturday is the Sabbath and to treat Sunday like any day in

the week. Their clothes are different and, to peasant eyes, un-
attractively drab. Their whiskers and long black coats seem both
dreary and inconvenient. Their food habits appear perverse, especially their refusal to eat that cherished staple of peasant diet,
pork. If every detail of their physical life is so outlandish, can
their bodies and organs be quite the same as those of a Christian?

The ritual of circumcision seems barbarous—why do they
want to torture babies? It plays its part in the potent stereotype
of the "bloody Jew" that has grown up about a people passionately opposed to the infliction of pain and to bloodshed. The
government forbids the Jew to farm or to own farmland, and
the peasant's whole life centers on his acres and his crops, so that
the Jew seems to live without a basic requirement.

The peasant has some respect for the studiousness of the Jew
and his mental alertness. Under special stress he may even appeal
to a very learned Jew for advice about his problems. Still more,
when he goes on a journey he may entrust his money to some
pious Jew for safekeeping. Yet, while he admires, he also distrusts
both the interest in learning and the shrewdness he imputes to
the Jew. The stories of mutual trust are undoubtedly outnum-
bered by stories of mutual deception.

Reciprocal attitudes are reflected in linguistic usage. Each
group will use animal terms in speaking of the other, implying
that it is subhuman. If a Jew dies, a peasant will use the word for
animal death in reporting the event, and a Jew will do the same
for a peasant. The peasant will say that a Pole *umiera* and a Jew
zdechl. The Jew will say that a Jew *shtarbt* and a peasant *peygert*.
A peasant "eats" and a Jew "gobbles" when a peasant is talking,
and when a Jew speaks the usage is reversed. The peasant will
say, "That's not a man, it's a Jew." And the Jew will say, "That's
not a man, it's a goy."

To each group the other represents the unbeliever. "A Jew
and a dog have the same creed," say the Ukrainians. And the
Jews say, "The peasants don't have a God, they just have a board
they call an icon, and they pray to that."°

Thus the two worlds hemmed into one geographical area,
interlocking yet discrete, see each other as having an advantage

in nonessentials and as inferior in all that matters most. Whether or not each defines the essentials to fit its own characteristics is irrelevant to the force and the effects of their mutual attitudes.

Through the years each group has had its impact on the other and the Jewish culture, representing a small fraction of the Eastern European population, has inevitably been the one more affected. Different forces, from different directions, have constantly chipped at the edges of the culture's hard, enduring core. Each class, each group has responded in its own way to the particular influence that touched it. But the very forces that wore away the periphery strengthened the center of the core by mobilizing and stiffening its resistance to change.

Despite the multiple impacts from without, until the late nineteenth century a very large proportion of the shtetl population grew up in ignorance of the world beyond. In the nineties, a boy of seventeen who stumbled upon a history of Europe translated into Hebrew was filled with amazement to learn that so many different ways of life could exist. One a few years younger refused to believe that there could be a place where nobody spoke Yiddish. Such attitudes were not confined to youth. The whole world was commonly assumed to be just one shtetl after another, until you reached Jerusalem, the grandest shtetl of them all. ". . . the whole world consisted of Slonim, Warsaw and a few towns in between and also America. And what was America? America was New York. . . . As far as we were concerned people lived only in Slonim and in a few places around there. We had heard of Moscow but it was just a name. People didn't live there."°

Space and time, for the ignorant as for the learned, were fluid, vague concepts, always less real than people and God. The geographical data of the Bible were fused and confused with the names of contemporary countries and cities that drifted in from time to time. A few days' drive with the village coachman might bring one to the mythical river Sambatyon, behind which dwell the ten lost tribes who were once visited by a medieval rabbi.

Isolation was most complete during the seventeenth and early eighteenth centuries. From then on the waves from without pounded increasingly against the Gates of Torah. By the end of the nineteenth century, emigration was in full swing and even the most remote shtetl would receive letters that had American and German stamps on them. Yet through the first third of the twentieth century the solid core remained, even though the peripheral area grew larger. It remained solid in the home shtetl, and in other parts of the world it has been memorialized in miniature—if not quite reproduced—by bearded men in long caftans who hurry by subway from the heart of Manhattan to their Williamsburg yeshiva.

The world of the week is nearest to the outside world and therefore offers the most obvious surface for erosion. Not only did the workers in the shtetl modify their traditional clothing in the interests of parnosseh, but often their work took them outside—to travel from one town to another or to take employment for a period in the city. Because of greater exposure to outside influence and less intense involvement with traditional customs, they were more likely than the sheyneh layt to adopt other clothes and other ways.

From the middle of the nineteenth century, the artisans and laborers, and also the intellectual youth, began to respond to the influences of the workers' movements in Russia and Poland. The activity of the nascent trade unions tied in with the rise of the Jewish Social Democratic movement, known as the Bund.* Striking against the social and economic traditions equated by the rebels with exploitation, the various workers' movements also hit at traditional orthodoxy. They even set up schools to combat the influence of the traditional kheyder—schools which rejected the Hebrew language and rejected the traditional curriculum. The language of these schools was Yiddish, the language of the people of the week, and the curriculum was that of the secular, non-Jewish schools. Many responded and at the same time many clung the more devoutly to the ways and the beliefs of the fathers.

Some of the wealthier balebatisheh merchants also found it expedient on occasion to lift their long, encumbering caftans. One whose business took him to the city often modified his clothing somewhat, at least while he was away from home. Inevitably his travels forced him to learn other ways and to make some con-

*Not to be confounded with the German Bund.

cessions in his orthodoxy. Many of these prosperous businessmen remained rigidly pious, nevertheless. Such a man might travel a great deal, but no promise of profit could induce him to travel on the Sabbath. And if morning found him in a railway carriage filled with Gentiles, he would put on his phylacteries and prayer shawl, turn to the East, and recite his early prayers, oblivious to his fellow passengers.

Economic forces were only one aspect of the attack from without against the tradition. From the early nineteenth century, the life of the shtetl was affected by government decrees aimed at "westernizing" the Jews. On various occasions in various localities, edicts ordered them to discard their characteristic costume—for the most part with indifferent success. More effective and more persistent were the decrees—again in certain localities—ordering children to attend government schools where they would learn secular subjects and the local language. At one time there was a rule in Russia that every rabbi must be able to speak the language of the country, a requirement that struck against rabbinical doctrine and practice, since it was the learned who were least apt to be familiar with the official language. One response was that of a rabbi who put aside the special hat that was his badge of office and wore a plain hat on the street, so that he would not be recognized and challenged to demonstrate his legal right to the position of rabbi. In Galicia, for a period, no Jewish couple could get married without passing a test to prove their mastery of the official language.

Some parents who were able to do so would buy off their children from attendance at the secular schools by bribing the local officials, just as boys were bought off from military service. Other boys would go half a day to kheyder and half a day to the government school. Or, if their parents could afford it, they might have a tutor at home for the sacred studies.

Many boys who attended secular schools led a double sartorial life. During the week they would wear clothes like those of their schoolmates, even putting aside the yarmelkeh. On Friday evening, however, they would again put on the traditional garb, and be identified with their families in celebrating the Sabbath.

Then they would return to the world of the week, with its forbidden clothing and forbidden books.

There were always some boys, however, who would desert
the kheyder to concentrate on studies traditionally condemned
as "treyf" and "possl," unfit and prohibited. Ironically, the
official oppressors provided such boys with the opportunity to act
out youth's revolt against home authority, and to capture some
of the freedom that hitherto only a few highly privileged girls
had possessed.

The economic and government-imposed restraints represented attack from without against the hallowed tradition. From
the mid-eighteenth century, however, there was ever-strengthening
attack from within. Its most effective manifestation was the Enlightenment, the *Haskala,* which emanated from Germany and
swept across Eastern Europe. It was the intellectualized form of
the rebellion against legalism and hidebound dogma which had
its folk manifestation in Hassidism. Characteristically, the revolt
of the intellectuals against mental tyranny was waged with
weapons of the intellect.

The Haskala was promulgated through the use of Hebrew,
"the sacred language." Only in this medium could the learned be
reached, since they would not read Yiddish or any other secular
language. For the first time, newspapers and magazines were
written in Hebrew, as were books of geography, history, even
novels and books of poetry--known as "the books with short
lines." The *belles lettres* were accepted, not as art for art's sake,
but because of their goal, the indispensable takhlis, which was
to widen the horizon of those who had lived in a strait and narrow world.

The youthful scholars, and some older ones, who could not
be swayed by the appeal of music, gay clothes, and carefree
pleasures, responded to the appeal of intellectual growth and
adventure. Frowned on and even persecuted by the staunch
traditionalists, they nevertheless flocked to the standard of the
Enlightenment. There developed a potent "underground" of
the mind and spirit, which added the romance of conspiracy to
the excitement of rebellion and new experience. Groups of boys

met in secret to read Schiller's poetry together in the woods. Popularizations of Darwin's theory, printed in small books in the Hebrew language, would be smuggled into the yeshiva itself and read under the sheltering mask of the Gemara. In attics and privies they would follow the novels of Mapu, a popular and prohibited writer who based his fiction on biblical themes, portraying the Jews as proud, fiery and independent—far from the resignation approved by the shtetl—and as glamorous exponents of the romantic love that ran counter to shtetl conceptions of the family and the proper subjects of study. In the dead of night, crouching over his dim candle, a pale yeshiva boy in yarmelkeh and traditional earlocks would pore over the pages of *Anna Karenina,* swaying back and forth as he chanted its words with the melody that was his only way of reading, and transported into identification with the dashing Count Vronsky.

Occasionally a teacher would be touched by the Enlightenment and would smuggle into the yeshiva a Hebrew textbook, perhaps on natural sciences or history. Anecdotes are told of how such a man, at the risk of losing his position, might go so far as to have the class read aloud the most interesting passages. Since any reading was done with the talmudic chant, the passerby would assume that they were studying some sacred work.

The effects of the Haskala were far deeper and wider in the city than in the shtetl. They were also more pronounced in certain regions than in others—more in Russia than in Poland, for example. Some localities were almost untouched. Yet even the smallest shtetl would probably harbor at least one of the *maskilim,* the enlightened ones—probably an isolated and somewhat suspect figure. The criterion for identifying a *maskil* would be, "He subscribes to a newspaper," and villagers would flock to hear the news even if they inveighed against the iconoclasm that made him acquainted with it.

The "enlightened ones" were known also as "fence breakers," those who tore down the protecting barricade against transgression, and as unbelievers, *apikorsim,* a word derived by a logical stretch of meaning from Epicurean. Respect for learning of any sort mingled with the anger and reproach heaped upon the fence breakers. A diploma is always an emblem of achievement, however misguided. There was even a curious saying, "A scholar cannot be a Hassid and an ignoramus cannot be an *apikoyres*."

More intense opprobrium was conveyed by the term "*Daytsh*," meaning one who dresses like a German. Since the German Jews were the ones most likely to adopt the ways and clothes of the majority, the name came to mean one who has been assimilated.

The yeshiva, the historic stronghold of Jewish tradition, was also the place where the Haskala took strongest hold. Since many of the yeshivos were in large centers, they were available to its influence, and the intellectual zeal of the yeshiva boys responded to the glimpse of broader horizons. Many of them became *externikes*, attending no courses but studying on the outside to pass the final examinations that would admit them to the university. Some dropped their yeshiva studies entirely, others continued at the yeshiva by day and carried on their secular studies through the night.

Most of them had to learn the local language in addition to the studies prescribed by the curriculum, since the young "genius" would be the last to know the language of the "unlearned." Some of today's eminent scholars, who hold advanced degrees from European universities and enjoy distinguished reputations, were yeshiva boys in their youth and knew not one word of the local language.

It became customary for young boys in the *gymnasia* to tutor the yeshiva boys. Students of fourteen or fifteen would teach a newly bearded yeshiva boy of nineteen or twenty. The maskilim turned to physics, Latin, algebra, with the same zeal they had been devoting to Talmud and pilpul. It was usual for them to cover in a couple of years the eight-year program of the gymnasia and to perform well enough in the examinations to overcome the handicaps of general reluctance to admit them, and of reaction against such outlandish effects as reading Latin with a talmudic chant, or reciting the events of history in broken Russian with a strong Yiddish accent.

Perhaps the intellectual effort required by these feats was no more drastic than the daily nine-hour study routine demanded of the three-year-old in the little children's kheyder. But there all circumstances and all people united to push him toward his goal. Here all but his fellow conspirators tried to block him from it, including the examiners with their raised eyebrows, offended ears, and official anti-Semitism.

The Enlightenment, in addition to its direct effects, opened the way to currents of political consciousness. Any student who broke away from the yeshiva was likely to become involved with one of the movements in which university students were active. Some were attracted by the labor movement, and joined the Bund. Some were inspired to activity in the Russian anti-Czarist movement. All these influences were carried from the university to the shtetl and developed its conflicting currents, attracting adherents and at the same time mobilizing the forces of the tradition.

The young people met in groups, often at great risk, to discuss their new ideas and plans. They read forbidden literature, written on onion skin paper that could easily be concealed in the heavy, scholarly tomes of the yeshiva or the university. This literature was in Yiddish, so that the workers could read it. Often in order to make it look harmless, the cover and first page would be those of a religious book.

Many of those who were not attracted by these movements became Zionists. As compared to the Haskala, Zionism represented a later and very different attack from within, holding out a nationalistic and materialistic goal that was at odds with the concepts of the shtetl. So great was the incompatibility that Zionism remained a comparatively slight influence until after World War I. The dazzling reaches of the mind opened up by the Haskala were a New Jerusalem to which the avid intellectual responded with ardor. It was after all a new development of the learning tradition, congenial to the outlook that tradition had fostered.

Zionism, on the contrary, directed its appeal to a different segment of the population and a different set of values. It offered, not light but an acre of ground—the very acre that was being earned through millennia of sorrow and hardship. In doing so it was felt to belittle the value of the sufferings endured, and the prerogative of God to work in His own way and His own time. It undertook to steal a march on Messiah. The initial reaction of the shtetl, therefore, was to reject Zionism as a crass and impious doctrine. As years went on, however, especially after World War I, Zionism took deeper roots among the younger generation.

It has been said that the forces from outside attacked the periphery of the shtetl culture while the hard core persisted. The periphery, however, is an integral part of the culture. The history of the Jews has been a history of acculturation. Since biblical times, in any setting, they have always been a minority. The peripheral area which serves as a bridge to the surrounding cultures fills several functions. It is an avenue to invasion, a buffer, and a source of renewed vigor. Each impact that chips at the outer edge may serve simultaneously to strengthen the core.

VI

THE REBBEH MAKES MIRACLES

Among those who fought fanatically against the impact of the outside world were the Hassidim, "the pious."

All over Eastern Europe, in hundreds of small towns, are scattered the residences of the Hassidic leaders, the Tsaddikim.* They are known as "courts," and a really prosperous one is "a kingdom in itself."° It contains living quarters for the "holy man" and his family, for his sons, daughters and their families, for the servants and for the guests. A besmedresh, a bathhouse with a mikva, storehouses, stalls for horses, and tremendous kitchens are necessary parts of the court. "The home and the *hoyf* (court) were extremely large. Imagine, it took over an hour to walk right through the garden. They had their own hothouse where they grew dates and figs and all sorts of foods that you couldn't get in town. Then they had their own mikva, their own carpenter, their own shoemaker, their own shokhet, they had all sorts of persons working for them. The people that worked for them were always called 'Reb.' The shokhet who worked on the hoyf was called 'Reb Shmil' but the shokhet who worked for the people was just called by his regular name. So the Rebbeh and his wife never really had to leave their estate. And each child of course had a suite for himself."°

The court is always crowded with people who live there or who have come to visit. The permanent members are the Tsad-

*As noted in the Preface, the present tense used throughout the book is essentially a historical present, describing the shtetl before World War II. This usage is to be borne in mind especially in connection with the description of physical manifestations, like the Tsaddik's court—as compared with general attitudes, many of which survive in more or less modified form under acculturation.

dik's family, his married sons and daughters with their families, servants, teachers of the Tsaddik's children, cantors and officials. Most Tsaddikim have at least two attendants, one—the gabai— who manages the "wonder man's" affairs and one who fulfills the functions of a personal servant. Among the permanent inhabitants also are people who make a living from the Tsaddik's visitors: dealers in ritual objects and books, vendors of food and liquor, innkeepers, and those inevitable participants in any shtetl crowd, the beggars. There are also the resident loafers who subsist by "turning around the court," joining in different celebrations, eating at the Tsaddik's table, and waiting for an opportunity to "catch" an extra drink.

The most important part of the crowd is the visitors, from the same locality or from out of town. They include people who have come to spend some time "near the Tsaddik," and those with personal problems who seek an audience for specific help or advice.

The size of a court varies with the popularity of the Tsaddik. During the High Holidays the residence of a very famous Polish Tsaddik contains several thousand Hassidim who come to spend the Days of Awe with their beloved leader. Some of the Tsaddikim count their followers not by the thousands but by the hundreds, and their courts are smaller in size, less sumptuous, but still always crowded with followers. "The Rebbeh was very well known. All over the whole world. Most of the people in town were able to live, to make a living because the Rebbeh lived there. They all made business from him. . . . The hotels, the shokhet, the shoemaker, etc. People came from all over the world to see him and they usually stayed for a long time."°

If a shtetl does not have a court, there will still be a small synagogue where the followers of a Rebbeh can come together for prayers, meetings and celebrations. If it holds followers of different leaders, it will have as many meeting places as there are Hassidic groups. Occasionally a Tsaddik comes down from his residential town to visit his followers in some small shtetl, and will confer on one of his Hassidim the rare honor of stopping in his home.

The central figure of the court is of course the Tsaddik or

Rebbeh, often referred to as "the Good Jew." For his followers he is the "holy man," the "master of miracles," "the interceder." For some he is the equivalent of a saint. "Do you know what a Tsaddik is? I'll tell you. In the Jewish religion there are 613 mitsvos. The average person cannot do all these mitsvos. But one who can do all these things, abide by all the 613—he is known as a Tsaddik."°
He is usually a member of a dynasty of Tsaddikim which traces its line back to the founder of Hassidism, the Baal Shem Tov, or to one of his original disciples. Each Tsaddik is a "grandson" of some famous originator of a dynasty.

The Tsaddik's chief activities are helping people who come to ask for relief and advice and comforting them by expounding "his toyreh," his teachings. He does not interfere with the strictly ritual life of the shtetl, which remains under the jurisdiction and supervision of the official rabbi, the Rov. The Tsaddik seldom has the diploma which entitles the Rov to exercise his rabbinical function, and which is conferred by a collegium of rabbis after the studies in the yeshiva are concluded. Therefore he does not make decisions in matters of Law. In contrast to the official religious leader of the shtetl, the Rebbeh does not achieve his high position through learning. The lack of erudition of some Tsaddikim has supplied a popular subject of jokes and mockery among those who do not share their beliefs. "The Hassidic Rebbeh could be an ignoramus. He was never examined and besides his position was a hereditary one so they usually were ignoramuses. It was like a dynasty."°

The concept of grade or "level" is the basis of the Tsaddik's position among his followers. He is the one who through his own mystical efforts, through his descent from and spiritual relationship to the great teacher Baal Shem or his disciples has attained the highest level a mortal can reach, the "level" of an intermediary between God and His sinful, unfortunate children—the people of Israel.

This position and the authority with which it is invested cannot be achieved through book knowledge, but only through mystical communion with God. Every human being has a divine spark, but only the Tsaddik has achieved the stage in which the spark becomes a divine flame that gives him the power to provide his followers with "children, life and livelihood." The Tsaddik draws close to God through his own efforts, which involve withdrawal from the problems of everyday life, constant prayer, meditation, and continuous cultivation of the awe of God and love for God and for Israel. He is helped in his efforts by zkhus ovoys, the merits of his ancestors who were descendants of the Baal Shem Tov or of his disciples. The mystical powers, once achieved, are transmitted by heredity from father to son and even to the son-in-law through the Tsaddik's daughter. They may be lower in one generation or more intense in another, but they are never lost completely.

Each dynasty and therefore each Tsaddik has a special *derekh,* a special way of dealing with God and with the Hassidim, and this derekh is expressed in prayers, melodies, teachings, everyday behavior. One will pray with his followers, another will have a separate room; one will improvise his "toyreh" at the table in the presence of the Hassidim, another will isolate himself for a few hours and then come back ready with a speech. Common to all Tsaddikim, however, is the basic obligation to participate in the life of their people, listen to their troubles, help them in their misery, use their powers to ameliorate the lot of the Jews and to intervene with God in behalf of His children. The Tsaddik must be the *melits yoysher,* the one who pleads in defense of Jews who are constantly punished by God for violation of the Law.

The human side of shtetl life—the worries, illness, misery, poverty—is his realm. He will listen to the sobs of a childless woman who can "cry out" her heart to the holy man. He will share with his Hassidim the burden of parnosseh, the struggle to support one's family. His duty is to listen to the complaints, to hear the pleas for help and comfort. With a word of hope, with a wish, with a magic formula, the Tsaddik will console the unfortunate Hassid. During the weekly teachings, in the vernacular and in simple terms not overloaded with pilpulistic reasoning, he preaches hope and joyful love of God. His God loses the severe features depicted by the Talmud and the Shulkhan Arukh. The attributes of justice, of punishment, constantly stressed by rabbinical scholars, are overshadowed by the attributes of compassion and love.

Yet for all his powers, a Tsaddik cannot function alone. He must have followers, and the more he has the stronger he is. To be nearer heaven he must feel the burden of earth, and the earthly element is in the daily life, the tsores or troubles of the Hassidim.

The Tsaddik who has achieved the highest level literally "talks with God." Through his exalted status, through his familiarity with the esoteric Kabala, through his knowledge of the mysterious undisclosed "Name" (of God), he is able to perform miracles in behalf of his followers. In the area of Eastern Europe where the Poles or Ukrainians have a special saint to help with each kind of calamity, the Hassid expects direct help in any crisis from his wonder man.

The miraculous activities of the Tsaddik are subject to countless stories, told by the Hassidim during the intermissions between prayers or at a festive table. The Tsaddik has the power of "jumping the road," which enables him to cover tremendous distances in order to help his Hassidim if they are in trouble. He has the *kuk*, the "look," which enables him to see what is going on miles away, and true believers are less concerned with the accuracy of this sight than with the miraculous power itself.

Visitors who come only to be near the Tsaddik may stay for a long time and become a temporary part of the "permanent crowd." They eat at the Tsaddik's table, pray in his besmedresh, participate in his celebrations and listen to his toyreh. A good Hassid must spend some time each year in the immediate circle of the Tsaddik. They come at all times but the greatest number come for holidays, and especially for the Days of Awe. At the season when the Hassidim of Ger start their annual pilgrimage to the court of their leader, the Polish railroad adds additional trains to accommodate thousands of the pious.

A fervent Hassid will often leave his family and stay away from home for months. "A poor Hassid who could hardly support his wife and children—when it came far yontev or far shabbes, this poor Hassid would leave his family and sometimes travel fifteen or twenty miles to 'come to the Rebbeh's table' to celebrate. And fifteen miles in the shtetl is like a hundred miles here by horse. He would take the little money he had and bring 'redemption.' When his sons got a little older he would take them as well

'to the table,' and he would leave his wife and daughter to celebrate their holidays by themselves and sometimes without a cent
to buy anything. . . . The wives of the Hassidim would go out
into the street and ask for money from people, they should help
them out for the holiday. And on the holidays they were rarely refused."°

Some may pawn their wives' jewels in order to obtain fare for
travel. Sometimes a group will take up a collection for the travel
expenses of their impoverished friends. Poor Hassidim will walk
for days and weeks to reach the Rebbeh's court, begging if necessary, stopping over on Sabbath in the houses of their fellow disciples. Before the High Holidays the roads in Poland and Ukraine
are crowded with Hassidim, walking in groups or traveling in
horse-drawn wagons. They stop at the inns to drink and sing and
dance, full of joy and enthusiasm.

"His wife accepted it as natural. In fact she used to encourage
it. She believed that if her husband went to the Rebbeh he would
come home and bring her a blessing from the Rebbeh which was
worth far more than food and money."° Not all of the women accept it, however. Some of them come to the Tsaddik's court looking for their husbands, or mothers looking for their sons. It is not
uncommon for a deserted wife to berate the husband she finds
celebrating with a group of other Hassidim. She may curse him
and drag him out of the court, reminding him of his hungry children and denouncing the influence of the wonder man.

As the court of the Tsaddik is a meeting place for the Hassidim from all over the country and even from abroad, people
often arrange business deals and marriages there. A bargain, a
partnership, a marriage concluded at the court have the advantage of being concluded between congenial people, bound together by devotion to the same leader, and also of being blessed
directly by the Tsaddik.

The temporary visitors, who come for specific help and advice, stay at the court only long enough to see the Tsaddik and receive his blessing and advice. "The Rebbeh was consulted by his
followers on any important matter. He would give advice on all
the questions bothering the people and he was a very learned man.
My own father became a tailor because of the advice of the Reb-

beh."° Most of the problems brought to him concern gezunt un parnosseh, health and livelihood. Someone is sick in the family, a man does not get along with his wife, business partners are quarreling, a merchant expects an important deal, a father wants to save his son from conscription. Each comes to the Tsaddik expecting a cure, an amulet, a blessing and advice. "Hassidim used to travel to their Rebbeh to ask him an advice; advice about a daughter who has to get married and the father has no dowry for her; advice about a match for his son, and so on."°

Women also bring their troubles to the wonder man, sometimes coming with their children. The sick are brought for miraculous cures. Insane girls or boys are led into the court so that the Rebbeh will "chase out the dybbuk." It is said that even Gentiles may come to a famous Tsaddik for help and advice, and the holy man's assistant may proudly show the name of a Polish nobleman on a note asking for help. "I want to tell you that even the Christians believed in the Rebbeh. On holidays, the Governor of the town and all the high officials used to come to the Rebbeh and greet him. The poorer people would often come for advice, like if a baby was sick and their people couldn't heal it. The Rebbeh was well known all over the world and everybody respected him."°

However high or humble the applicant, as soon as he arrives at the court he goes to the gabai, whose function is to write up the *kvitl*, a short note formulating the request. The kvitl has a standard form and must be written by the gabai, who receives payment for this service. The form identifies the petitioner by the mother's name and not, as is usual, by the father's: "Noach, son of Esther, from the town of Lodz, asks for . . . (a child, a cure, a blessing for business, etc.)" After interviewing the supplicant about his family, his background and his troubles, the gabai delivers the kvitl and an oral report to the Rebbeh.

On the reception day, the Rebbeh has all the notes before him on his desk and the gabai calls in the petitioners one by one. The holy man takes action for each case. One will receive an amulet, usually a blessed coin or a magic cabalistic formula on a piece of parchment. One will get a medicine, another the assurance, "God will help you." "The Rebbeh himself never promised miracles. He only wished that something would happen and said, 'God will help.' But he never promised that a miracle would happen to anyone. It was the people, his followers, who believed that he could work miracles. . . . My father used to tell me this story. . . . It happened before I was born, and my oldest brother, then a child, was sick with diphtheria. . . . The boy was gradually choking and was expected to die. They hired a special woman to sit with him and my mother was crying and wringing her hands. But my father insisted that he is going to the Rebbeh. But you can't just go to the Rebbeh when you feel like it, there are certain times when you can go, even if you were closely related to him. My father went anyhow. The Rebbeh was saying the Sabbath prayers when my father burst in yelling, 'Rebbeh, the child is dying!' And all the Rebbeh said was, 'Go home, God will help.' And this is the way my father tells the story. 'So I came home and seeing that it was shabbes I had to make holiday in the house. So I took a *seyfer* (religious book) and started to read and sing. All of a sudden the child raises his little head and says, 'Tateh, I'm hungry.' So I gave him a hard piece of bread and he swallowed it, taking down all the stuff that was choking him. And in a few days he was well. . . . Isn't that miracles?"°

In difficult problems concerning family relations or business deals the Rebbeh may give advice: to divorce the wife, to conclude a proposed marriage or to annul the betrothal, to dissolve a partnership, to buy or reject some merchandise offered for sale. In each case the advice is followed by a blessing. "Hundreds and hundreds of people used to come to him for advice. And he gave everybody personal attention. He listened to everyone's tsores and heard everyone's life story."° When the Hassid has a very important deal on his mind he may actually take the Rebbeh into partnership. In such an arrangement, the Hassid gives the money, the Rebbeh his blessing and they share the profits equally. Many Tsaddikim receive a substantial income from "participation" in the enterprises of their followers.

In return for the Rebbeh's advice or help, the Hassid must pay a *pidyan* or "redemption," which is given to the gabai and not directly to the Rebbeh. It is usually an amount of money corresponding to some variation of the number eighteen, which in Hebrew represents the numerical value of the word *khay,* living or life. One gives eighteen small coins, another eighteen hundred, a third eighteen times eighteen, depending on his finances or the importance of his request. Another system of calculating the "redemption" is by the numerical value of the name of the person for whom the cure or advice is asked. The numerical value of the Hebrew letters that make up the name Joseph is 156, so that a father who comes to ask a cure for his sick son Joseph might give a pidyan of 156 zlotys. The "redemption" is supposed to be offered voluntarily but quarrels and arguments and bargainings between the petitioner and the gabai are frequent, especially if the gabai knows that the Hassid is richer than he claims. "And when they go to the Rebbeh for advice they usually bring a pidyan to him. Sometimes it's the last penny they have. Some Rebbehs lived only on this and wouldn't give advice without a pidyan. Others, however, refused to take any money from the people who couldn't give it."°

Tsaddikim who are famous and have a great number of followers, especially those who are "grandsons" of the Baal Shem Tov or his immediate disciples, have often become extremely rich. Their courts have been referred to as "royal courts." Hassidim would proudly tell about the "golden chair" of a Tsaddik, about a seven-branch candlestick so high that the Rebbeh had to walk up on silver steps in order to kindle its lights. Such Tsaddikim dress in satin and fur, travel from town to town in their own luxurious coaches driven by four or six horses. Their wives, daughters and daughters-in-law wear precious jewels and are dressed in velvets and silks.

"The Rebbeh was very rich, and I mean *very*. The women of the Rebbeh were always dressed in the latest styles from Vienna, Paris, etc. Everything they had was imported. Even their sheytls were made of the rarest imported silks. They had three or four of them and every few months they were sent somewhere to Russia to the best hair stylists, to be styled in the latest fashion. And their dresses were exquisite, made of ermine, velvet and the most expensive silks. The Rebbetsin—the Rebbeh's wife—had fourteen rooms in her home. The house was decorated with the most exquisite landscapes, the size of a complete wall. I remember they had a white parlor, it was called 'Der Weisser Salon.' In each corner they had an oven made of white tile. That room was so huge that they had four parlor sets in it. One was green velvet which the Rebbetsin embroidered by herself. One was pure silver. There were four chairs and an end table. Over that set hung a sun clock which was an antique. It dated back to the days of Kasimir of Poland. A third set was made from mother-of-pearl. There was a tremendous crystal chandelier in the middle of the ceiling, and smaller ones coming out from the wall. And they had blue oriental rugs, very expensive ones."°

The life in the court is different from everyday life. It is somehow a constant Sabbath, a continuous "foretaste of the future world." "There was a 'holiday' atmosphere at the Rebbeh's hoyf, and they forgot all their troubles. Even when they gave their money away to the Rebbeh they had joy and pleasure because they were able to get a blessing from him."° There the faithful Hassid can "shake off" of his shoulders all the "yokes" that make up the round of life: family, children, the "chase after parnosseh." "You asked me why I leave my wife and children in poverty and come to sit at the Rebbeh's table. Now I'll tell you why. I am a man with eight children. I earn approximately eight rubles a week for my hard work. Could a kaptsn like I am possibly celebrate in the middle of the year just like that for no reason at all? Could I make shabbes in my own home in the middle of the week? No, never. So, whenever I have a chance I come to the Rebbeh to sing and dance and put a little bit of joy into my life."°

The focus of life at the "court" is the fanatical devotion to the Tsaddik. Everything that is done there is linked to him. The Hassidim pray in his besmedresh, eat at his table, listen to his toyreh, talk about his miracles. They wait for his appearance in public and after it has transpired they exchange their impressions.

Frequent celebrations mark the life at the court, always accompanied by drinking and often by dancing. When a Hassid arrives for a stay, he celebrates the occasion by paying for a round of drinks. When one is happy because of the Tsaddik's reception, it is again an occasion to celebrate with a *lekhayim,* a drink "to life." A betrothal, a wedding, the conclusion of a deal—everything is a reason to "make a cup." The more they drink the more joyful and happy they are, for great is their Rebbeh. They are drunk partly from alcohol and partly from their love and devotion. They begin to dance and sing, the "Rebbeh's nign," the special melody of the Rebbeh composed either by or for him.

Old and young, rich and poor together, with their heads thrown back they begin to move faster and faster around the table singing the Rebbeh's favorite "march" or a nign. Sometimes it will be a melody without words consisting only of "ay, ay, ayay-yay," sometimes a few words of praise for God and for the Tsaddik, repeated again and again. They drink but do not get drunk to a point where they would lose their yiddishkayt, their "human" aspect. When a Hassid drinks he does not fight or quarrel "like a brute," he merely grows happier and more joyful. Alcohol, they say, elevates the human soul to a higher level, makes the Hassid nearer to his Tsaddik who is only a few levels lower than God himself. The elevation is a group activity, a Hassid never drinks alone. "When ten Hassidim drink lekhayim they annul the sentence of death," because the emotions expressed in the libation are more powerful than fate.

Sometimes the behavior of the Hassidim in the "court" is strikingly different from their everyday behavior in the shtetl where they conform to all the rules of respectability. In the Hassid's court a man may behave like a Hassid even though elsewhere he is a "Shulkhan Arukh Jew." Bearded men, "fathers of children," respected burghers, may lose all sense of restraint during an important celebration in the court, such as the wedding of a member of the Tsaddik's family. On such carnival occasions the ecstasy and the excess run counter to the usual standards of behavior. Hassidim, their beards hidden in scarves and kerchiefs, their hats turned backwards, the corners of their long caftans thrust under their girdles, ride on horseback, shouting and brandishing wooden swords or whips. They gallop so for miles to meet the wedding party, provoking laughter among the peasants—and scorn among some of the other Jews—who jeer at the "Jewish Cossacks." On Purim, the maddest and gayest of all holidays, dignified patriarchs will dance burlesque travesties, their faces blackened with soot, and will play practical jokes on everyone they meet in the street.

Even the language of this exuberance is different from the

usual Yiddish. Words, idioms, whole sentences from the vernacular of the neighboring Ukrainian or Polish peasants have entered the language of the Hassidim, especially their songs. Sentimental stanzas from Ukrainian love songs are taken over unchanged and reinterpreted as praise of God, sometimes because of their similarity to certain Hebrew expressions, sometimes because of the mystical meaning read into them. On the anniversary of the death of the great Tsaddik of Kotsk, his followers sing a popular Polish song, "He has died, the old blacksmith who 'shoed' (the heels of) our boots."

They do not always celebrate and drink, however. For the most part there are days of quiet monotony, interrupted only by regular prayers. The Hassidim, their resources spent on celebrations and drinking parties, have to satisfy their hunger with a piece of dry bread and herring. But even on these gray, quiet days the Hassid has the joy of being with other Hassidim and the opportunity to listen to marvelous stories about the Tsaddik's performances and about the greatness of the "old Rebbeh," his ancestor.

As in the shtetl, the high point of the week is the Sabbath but this Sabbath has a difference. Here it is the Rebbeh who "makes Sabbath" for the entire court, and not each Hassid for himself. Each one present is considered an oyrekh, a guest of the Tsaddik.

With the minor exceptions due to each Tsaddik's "way," the regular Sabbath services are the same as in any synagogue. The major differences are in the behavior of the worshipers. The Hassidim are much more fervent in prayer, the swaying is more intense, sometimes even violent; the gesticulation is vivid to a point that sometimes seems to be not praying but arguing a case with God.

During each of the Sabbath meals, the Tsaddik "conducts the table." Dressed all in white, he sits at the head, with the male members of his family next, then the most important Hassidim in order of status through learning or riches. The crowd sits or stands around them. "The Rebbeh used to sit at the head of the table and there would sometimes be about two hundred Hassidim eating with him. No women, not even the Rebbeh's wife. Next to the Rebbeh sat the important visitors—usually the wealthy people who gave him a lot of pidyan. And these rich people used to come from all over the world—from America, from South Africa and all over. The poorer people or those with less yikhus sat at the end of the table according to rank."°

The menu of the meal is that of any Jewish family on the Sabbath. As each dish is served, the Tsaddik helps himself, then pushes it aside. This is a signal that the Hassidim may seize the leftovers, the *shrayim*. To "grab the shrayim" is the most important feature of the meal. Crowds of Hassidim jump, push, fight, in order to get the leftovers, for to taste of the Rebbeh's shrayim is a mitsva and a remedy for any trouble. "The Rebbeh used to make kiddush and cut off a little piece of hallah. Then he would distribute some pieces to those prominent Hassidim sitting around him. After that he would throw little pieces of hallah across the table for the other Hassidim. They would make a grab for them and hold on to it as if it were life itself. It wasn't the little piece of hallah. But the Rebbeh had touched it with his hands and therefore it was holy."°

The procedure is organized differently in different courts. In some the Hassidim seize anything that the Tsaddik has touched, in some the holy man himself divides each piece of fish or meat or hallah and distributes the parts with his own fingers to "the chosen ones," while other Hassidim "grab" the remnants. In still other courts, the Tsaddik hands out the shrayim for each Hassid, giving a piece to the nearest who will pass it to the next and so on to the end, so that each piece of shrayim is touched by the fingers of almost every Hassid at the table. "At the feast after the Sabbath goes away, the Hassidim used to have a big feast at the Rebbeh's house. A large table was set, on it were placed various dishes of different foods. The Rebbeh used to go around and taste a little bit of everything and then the Hassidim used to run to the table and grab whatever they could that was left. That was known as shrayim."°

A most important feature of a very different character is "saying toyreh," the Tsaddik's teachings. Usually the holy man "says toyreh" at the third meal of the Sabbath. The gabai strikes the table with his palm to stop the noise and announces, "Be quiet, the Rebbeh will say toyreh." The crowd falls silent, almost stops breathing. All heads are turned toward the Tsaddik, some bending forward to hear better, some cupping an ear with their hand. The Rebbeh begins to speak in Yiddish, quietly and slowly. His eyes are half closed. Sometimes he covers them with his hands, sometimes passes his hand over his beard. As he speaks, he sways the upper part of his body slightly.

Usually his speech is an improvisation based on some quotation from the weekly portion of the Pentateuch. It is an interpretation of the quoted text in a mystic-ethical manner. He cares little for grammar, for the exact translation of the words, for logical relations between the quotation and the whole text. His explanation is based on the "secret" meaning of the quotation, hidden from ordinary mortals but revealed to him because of his "level."

His simple words hold out hope to those brought up from earliest childhood in constant fear of violating one of the countless regulations. In the shul they have learned from rabbinical scholars that laughter and excessive joy are "un-Jewish," that they are in Exile because of countless sins and must constantly be on guard against committing more sins. In the court the Tsaddik teaches that the basis of man's relationship to God is joyful hope in His compassion, that excess is only human and if it is indulged in with devotion to the Holy Father it is not only permissible but even encouraged, that even in sin there is a "spark of God."

Dancing, singing, drinking can be the genuine expression of devotion to God. Any manifestation of deep religious fervor, no matter how unorthodox, may be heeded by God. A Hassidic legend tells about a Jewish shepherd boy who did not know how to read from the prayer book. On the awesome Day of Atonement he expressed his feeling by a loud whistle in synagogue. The congregation wanted to expel the boy for his "goyish" behavior, but the Tsaddik who was present announced that the "prayer" of the ignorant boy had opened the "Gates of Compassion" because of its deep religious feeling.

Many stories are told about Tsaddikim who put human need before ritualistic duty. It is told that the great Tsaddik Moysheh Leyb Sasower came late to the most important prayer of the year, the Kol Nidre chanted on the Day of Atonement. The reason was that on his way he heard a child crying. He entered the house and found it alone because its parents had gone to shul. He stayed with the child, played with him until he fell asleep, and only then proceeded to shul.

The words of the Tsaddik are beyond question, his activities are beyond criticism. His is an absolute authority no rabbinical scholar achieves. It is not based on learning like the authority of a talmid khokhem, and therefore is not subject to discussion. It is based on pure faith in his direct contact with God. If anything in Jewish culture has a similar authority it is the Torah which was dictated directly to Moses by God. Thus the relationship of the Hassid toward his leader is the uncritical attitude of a lover toward the object of his love, of a devoted son toward his mother. The element of rationality is swept aside.

This uncritical attitude to the leader does not modify the general attitude toward authority, but merely singles out one specific relationship as an exception. The Hassid shows the usual pattern as a citizen of the community, a student of yeshiva or besmedresh, a member of the congregation. He succeeds in reconciling his Hassidic devotion to the Tsaddik with his traditional duties and attitudes.

The characteristic attitude of the shtetl toward authority is reflected in the great number of Tsaddikim and the wide variation in their "ways." Each has his followers who believe blindly in his power and who fight against other Hassidim. In endless discussions where such epithets as "ignoramus, amorets, unbeliever, heretic" are hurled back and forth, different groups try to convince each other that their Tsaddik is the greatest and that his "way" is the true way. The history of Hassidism abounds in descriptions of fights between admirers of various Tsaddikim. "There were fights but not between Hassidim and their opponents. The fights were between Hassidim who were followers of different Rebbehs. One group backs one Rebbeh and another group backs a second Rebbeh and they begin to fight about them. I don't mean they actually hit each other. No, very seldom. But they talk with their hands and pull their jackets."° The "Umaner Hassidim" had to suffer real persecution when they made their annual pilgrimage to the grave of their beloved leader who was buried in the Ukrainian town of Uman. Children of the "Skverer Hassidim," who were the majority in this town, would throw stones through the windows of their synagogues and disturb them in their prayers by screams or jokes.

Another aspect of the shtetl attitude toward authority is evident in the limitations set even on the adherence of the Hassid to his Tsaddik. If the "Rebbeh's way" deviates too far, his followers may leave their leader and gather around another. The great Tsaddik Mendl of Kotsk, despite his tremendous influence on his devoted disciples, saw many of them depart from his court. It is told that once he dared to extinguish the Sabbath candles with his fur hat. Although many Hassidim accepted this act, seeing in it some "incomprehensible greatness" and esoteric meaning, a great number could not tolerate this desecration of the Sabbath and violation of the most severe religious prohibition.

The attitude to the Tsaddik's authority, like the tolerance of emotional excess and the exaltation of feeling over thought in religion, diverges from the characteristics idealized by the Jewish tradition. Yet Hassidism has been assimilated into the tradition, balancing and complementing—but never merging with—the stern rabbinical strain represented by its opponents, the *Misnagdim*.

The roles of the two socioreligious currents, and their curious interweaving, can be viewed only in relation to the origin and development of the Hassidic movement, which began in the early eighteenth century and came to embrace a vast majority of the shtetl inhabitants. Among the many elements that contributed to its rise, a few are clearly discernible. On the one hand, Hassidism was a response to the extreme misery of the Ukrainian and Polish Jews after the years of destruction, annihilation and pogroms at the end of the seventeenth century, when during the revolt of the Ukrainian Cossacks thousands of towns and villages were ruined and the economic basis of shtetl life was destroyed. "One-third of the Jewish population in Eastern Europe was killed off and the Jews were in a terrible state of despair."°

On the other hand, the moral basis of Jewish life had been

shaken by the tragic failure of the "false Messiah" Sabbattai
Zevi, who had promised the exhausted masses of Eastern European Jews the realization of their eternal dream—only to finish
up in conversion to Mohammedanism. After the brief, bright
blaze of hope shtetl life appeared more hopeless and the future
more bleak. The rabbinical reaction against the mysticism and
emotionalism on which the false Messiah had built his popularity raised the "fence" around Torah still higher by additional
rules. The talmudic scholars strengthened their domination by
making the mass of the prosteh literally prisoners of countless
regulations that were incomprehensible to the ignorant. The
shtetl folk had only the choice between complicated pilpul or
blind obedience. The traveling preachers, the *maggidim*, threatened terrible tortures in hell for each violation of a mitsva. God
was presented to the ignorant prosteh as a vengeful and jealous
guardian of the Covenant, with no hope for the transgressor.

The entire life of the shtetl was squeezed into the "four
square yards of the *Halakha*," the rational interpretation of rules
in the Talmud. There was no place for human emotions, for the
needs of "sinful flesh and blood." It was a period of unlimited
power and authority for the Shulkhan Arukh and its exponents,
the rabbis.

This extreme absolutism was contrary to the long tradition
of Judaism in which God's attributes of justice and retribution
are balanced by compassion and forgiveness, the severe traits of
the remote Father tempered by the warmth and indulgence of
the ideal Mother. The learned tradition includes not only a
rational exposition of man's obligations to God as expressed in
the Law, but also a parallel and complementary literary tradition
of emotional and poetical expression. From the Torah, where
dry enumeration of rules and regulations is interspersed with
stories of human suffering and passion, through the Talmud
where rational interpretation of laws—the Halakha—is inseparable from the poetic legends and tales—the *Agada*—through the
parallel development of the rabbinical commentaries and the
mysticism of the Kabala, these two lines developed into the coexistence of the "Shulkhan Arukh way" and Hassidism.

The Hassidic movement began as "the revolt of the un-

learned" against the rule of the rabbis. Its first leader was Israel
Baal Shem Tov, the Master of the Good Name, also called
"Besht" from the initials B-S-T. Besht began his activities as the
representative of the masses, the ignorant artisans and laborers
who were despised by the learned. According to the scholars,
only learning could insure Olam Habo, so that the untutored
innkeeper or peddler had little hope for salvation.

Besht and his disciples rejected learning as the sole road to
Heaven. Instead they emphasized the approach to God by individual prayer, by emotional love, by good deeds arising not from
study but from devotion to God and to the human being. "The
Baal Shem came and made them happy—he found some joy for
them in their miserable existence."° One of the Hassidic leaders
expressed the difference between a Hassid and a Misnagid by
saying, "The Misnagid is afraid of the Shulkhan Arukh, the Hassid is afraid of God." Instead of the gloomy and threatening
speeches of the maggidim, the Hassidic leaders preached joy and
hope; instead of vengeance and punishment, mercy and love.

At its outset, Hassidism elevated the prosteh to a position
in the shtetl hierarchy that they had never dreamed of attaining.
It is defined in a statement attributed to Besht: "Jews are like
unto a vine, of which the grapes represent the scholars and the
leaves the simple folk. The leaves of the vine have two important
functions: they are essential to the growth of the vine and they
have a task of protecting the grapes. Therefore they are of greater
importance, since the power of the protector is greater than that
of the protected."

Representing both a religious movement and a revolt against
the "Eastern Wall," Hassidism encountered violent resistance
among the rabbinical scholars and the "upper classes" of the
shtetl. The Misnagdim were ready to use any means to suppress
the "dangerous apostasy," including denunciation, jailing and
ostracism. At one time each group considered marriage with the
other almost as reprehensible as marriage with a non-Jew.

Despite their apparent irreconcilability, however, the two
socioreligious currents—the Hassidic and the rabbinical—were
merely two aspects of the same basic relationship of the Jew to
his God, based on the same Covenant. Hassidism stressed the

element of compassion in God, the hope of His mercy and under-standing. The learned scholar emphasized the element of divine justice and the obligation of the Jew to learn his duties. Both principles were basically complementary and both were inherent in the tradition. Each in itself represented an extremism contrary to the precepts and the spirit of the tradition.

Accordingly, neither could remain unmodified. After a period of antilearning extremism Hassidism began to incorporate within its ideology the ancient tradition of book learning and admiration for scholarly pursuits. The old respect for books and their contents reasserted itself and many Hassidim boasted not only about the magic powers of their leaders but also about their familiarity with the sacred literature. The Tsaddik's court con-tinued to fulfill its function of comfort and support for the humble, but it ceased to be a refuge only for them. Learned and unlearned, artisans and rabbis, prosteh and sheyneh began to "travel to the Rebbeh" for words of encouragement and help, while all continued to turn to the Rov for interpretation of the Law that governs every detail of shtetl life. In the end, the two elements were interwoven—though by no means merged—in the stream of the tradition. Tsaddic and Rov, Kabala and Shulkhan Arukh led a complementary coexistence.

The accommodation was facilitated by a countercurrent that threatened both, the Haskala or Enlightenment. The two con-flicting versions of traditionalism recognized a threat to both in the antitraditionalism of the Haskala and drew together to op-pose it. Thus a split involving all the members of the shtetl was narrowed by the appearance of one that involved only a minority.

The process of integrating Hassidism into the shtetl has pro-ceeded at different rates and has manifested different forms. To some extent differences have been related to the infinite number of Hassidic leaders and the variety of their "ways." To some ex-tent they have corresponded to social and economic differences. They have also reflected individual differences. According to a man's temperament, he might be a "hot Hassid," subordinating all else to his fervor for God and his Tsaddik. "Even if he knew that he will not have anything to eat for the next week, a thou-sand horses couldn't pull him (the Hassid) away from the Reb-

beh's table."° Or he might be a "little-Hassid." "My father was
sometimes called 'the little-Hassid'. . . . His Hassidism was
found in the religious ecstasy, not the fanaticism. But one thing
he never did was to leave us and take all his money to the Rebbeh. That he considered very wrong and that is why he was only
a little-Hassid and not a real one."°

Overriding other variations is the regional pattern of Hassidism, which shows a curiously clear-cut relationship to the prevailing character of the main geographical divisions of Eastern
Europe. Until its destruction by the Russian Revolution, Ukrainian Hassidism preserved its original characteristics as the refuge
of the prosteh and the unlettered. The Ukrainian Tsaddikim
were seldom noted for erudition, and their followers remained
the classical type of "ignoramus," the blind believer in the magical powers of the wonder man. Until its last days, the Ukrainian
shtetl witnessed the traditional conflict between the rationalistic,
scholarly misnagid and the emotional, untutored Hassid.

The complementary coexistence of the besmedresh and the
court has been most harmonious in the Polish shtetl, with
the Polish Tsaddik typically a great scholar and his followers
scrupulously observing the countless commandments and prohibitions of the Shulkhan Arukh. It is the Polish pattern for a
Hassid to spend his life over his books when he is not in the
Tsaddik's court, and for the child to absorb the traditional system in the kheyder and the Hassidic ideology at the Rebbeh's
court, where he is taken by his father.

The Lithuanian, the "Litvak," known as a cool, rationalistic skeptic, has been the most resistant to the Hassidic ideology.
Vilna remained an anti-Hassidic stronghold, surrounded by a
wall of heavy tomes. The ecstatic songs of the Hassidim had
little effect upon the Lithuanian talmid khokhem and the Rebbeh's miracles were good only as material for jokes about the
"Hassidic ignoramuses." Nevertheless, little by little, the ethical
aspect of the teachings of Besht, the ideals of love for God and
Israel, penetrated even into the Lithuanian shtetl and contributed to the formation of a strangely intellectualized Hassidism.
Rabbi Shneour Zalman of Lady, "The Old Rov," was the founder
of this form of rationalistic Hassidism, completely devoid of the

magical component and based on three principles: *"Khokhma, Bina, Daath,"* intelligence, understanding, knowledge. The first letters of the three words form the word *Khabad,* which is the official name of the movement, although it is also known as the Lubavitsher Hassidism, because the dynasty originated by "The Old Rov" officiated in the shtetl of Lubavitsh. In Khabad-Hassidism, the mystical relationship of man and his Creator is intellectualized to the maximum and the Hassidic principles of love and compassion toward human beings are based not on emotional sentimentality but on rational principles of ethics and philosophy.

Inevitably, as each group modified its extremism and allowed a place for the other in the shtetl world, the antagonism between Misnagdim and Hassidim lost much of its vigor. Intermarriage between the two has come to be resented less than before, even though some still oppose it. "There were objections to my marriage from both sides. At first his family didn't want it because Hassidim in general are not too happy when their sons and daughters marry into Misnagdisheh families. They prefer to have a Hassid marry a Hassid. And I suppose we can't blame them."° Nevertheless, such marriages are frequent, and often arouse no opposition. "My sister is married to a Hassid and a pretty good one too. . . . I don't remember anything being said against the marriage."°

That elements of antagonism remain is evident from the terms in which each group refers to the other and the characteristics with which each endows the other. "The Misnagid upholds the dry Torah, the facts of the teachings and he has no 'Sabbath Soul,' he has no inner flame. And of course he does not have that fanatic approach to religion which the Hassid has."° On the other hand, "The Hassidim have a completely different attitude to religion. They serve God with joy and delight and therefore they are so emotional when they pray. They are, however, in the main not too educated. . . . My own personal opinion is that the Hassidim are a happier element than the Misnagdim. They never worry about anything."° At its most extreme, the Hassidic picture of the Misnagid still resembles the "beard without the Jew." The Misnagid picture of the Hassid lends itself easily to humor and caricature. "You know before the New Year celebration when you go to the river and empty out your pockets. Well there was a big river near S— and the rabbi and the Rebbeh used to go with their followers. Our rabbi, that is the Misnagdisheh Rov, used to go with the officials from the town. They would wear their yontev clothes with high black hats and all walk down very stately to the river. But the Hassidim would make a seat with their hands for the Rebbeh and carry him to the river. He used to wear a brown fur hat, white long socks and a satin caftan trimmed with fur. But even they used to go to the river through the back of the town because they knew that if people saw them they would start to laugh. It was really a funny sight."°

Such a view makes it easy to say, "Hassidism seemed very outlandish to our family,"° "The Hassidim were more crazy . . . they took the Rebbeh's word for everything."° The unquestioning belief in the Rebbeh is hard for a Misnagid to accept. "It was very difficult for us to believe in a Tsaddik because we believed only in our rabbi. We didn't believe that he could perform miracles, but we did believe in his honesty and advice. He was a very honest man. He never took a cent from the community and therefore his advice to us was never biased."°

Forgetting that many a Rov went to the Tsaddik's court, the Misnagid is likely to cite the rabbi's indispensability as proof of his superiority. "The Hassidim themselves, whenever a problem about a deep religious question arises, will go to the Rov to solve it. Their Rebbeh simply doesn't know how to make decisions. You know the Hassidim themselves used to help support the Misnagdish rabbi. They simply had to come to him for help."°

A frequent conclusion, however, is that although "there is a great difference between the two groups . . . they both believe in God."° Moreover, for many people the line between them has become blurred. "In my shtetl there were no Misnagdim and no Hassidim. There were simple orthodox Jews who went to shul and prayed to God."°

The degree to which the two currents have been integrated within the shtetl society is evident in the frequent reversal of attributes. Although Hassidism began as the revolt of the unlearned, there are places where it is assumed that "prosteh people were Misnagdim. Misnagdim were usually not educated; they were poor and prosteh although they may have been nice people."° In such a shtetl the Hassidim would protest vehemently against the "slander" of claiming that Hassidim were opposed to book learning.

The blurring of boundary lines and the occasional interchange of traits does not negate the contrast between the basic characteristics of Hassidism and Misnagdim, but rather demonstrates the extent to which both have been absorbed by the shtetl. Each region, town and individual, in some way, adjusts the two contrasting and complementary aspects: justice and compassion, rationalism and emotionalism, learning and faith. The two words, "Hassid" and "Misnagid" which in the beginning symbolized two hostile camps, have come to represent popular personality symbols. Hassid means the zealot, warm and emotional; Misnagid is applied to those who are rationalistic, cold, skeptical and perhaps of dubious piety.

Part Three

... Into Good Deeds ...

I

CHARITY SAVES FROM DEATH

The varied meanings of the word mitsva show both the importance of the commandments in everyday shtetl life and the central role which "good deeds" play in the enactment of those commandments. Mitsva means commandment, but it may also mean the act that fulfills the command. It is a mitsva to dower an orphan, to get a man a job, to tend the sick. The helpful act may be large or small. "Do me a mitsva," a friend will say, "take this letter to the post office." Or he may say, "earn a mitsva" meaning, earn the credit you get for doing a mitsva. It is a mitsva to study, but it is also a mitsva to profit from nice weather and go for a walk on a sunny day. A tired woman will say after a hard day at home or in the market, "It's a mitsva that I should get to bed early tonight."

If a stroke of good luck comes, "It's a mitsva." Moreover, if one's sense of fairness is hurt by someone's evil acts and later restored by his downfall, one will say "It's a mitsva on him," meaning it serves him right. A mother will say to a child who fell from a tree, "It's mitsva on you, I've told you so many times not to climb trees."

A violation of the commandments, an *aveyreh,* is colloquially synonymous with any negative, undesirable act. It is an aveyreh to kindle fire on the Sabbath, but it is also an aveyreh to pay an exorbitant price for a purchase, or to wear a clean dress while doing dirty work. According to the same semantic logic, one expresses pity by the word aveyreh when something seems unjust. "What an aveyreh that he died so young!"

Thus mitsva and its opposite, aveyreh, have carried beyond the strict sense of commandment or violation of the command-

191

ment, and have come to stand respectively for what is socially and culturally good and what is not.

The mitsvos proper, the commands of God, are traditionally grouped according to their form and according to their function. Formally they are divided into the mandatory—"thou shalt"— and the prohibitory—"thou shalt not." Functionally, they are grouped in three categories, defining man's relations to God, to his fellow man, and to himself. The second group marks the area covered by maasim tovim, good deeds. In colloquial usage, mitsvos have come to be almost synonymous with maasim tovim.

The man-to-man commandments must be handled between human beings, although God supervises the relationships and punishes those who transgress. Sins against God may be pardoned by Him on the Day of Atonement, when the whole shtetl repents with fasting and with tears. Sins against men, although punished by God, must be forgiven by men. "God will forgive when a person sins against Him, but He will not forgive when two people sin against each other and do not forgive."° Accordingly, on the Eve of the great day, when each man's fate is decided for the year to come, the shtetl people go from one house to another, from one neighbor to another, and make the rounds of all their relatives, asking forgiveness for insults and misdeeds. People who "weren't on speaking terms" for the whole year meet and ask pardon, shake hands, embrace, and having forgiven each other, go to shul to ask forgiveness for sins committed against God.

Although only man can forgive the wrongs done to him by man, the good deeds, the maasim tovim, are credited by Him as well as by one's fellows. "In the hour of man's departure, neither silver nor gold nor precious stones nor pearls accompany him, but only Torah and good deeds." In the final accounting which will determine his fate in the world to come, he will be judged by "his mitsvos," and a large item in the final balance will be the maasim tovim he has piled up to his credit.

"Good deeds" include spiritual as well as material benefactions. One can give alms, words of comfort, a loan of money, wishes for good luck, advice, a pot of hot soup, and all are "good deeds"—maasim tovim, or mitsvos.

Charity is only one part of maasim tovim, but it is a very important part. The most popular word for it in the shtetl is *tsdokeh*. This is one of the Hebrew words which have been incorporated into the Yiddish vocabulary, and its real meaning is not charity but justice—"social justice" would be more accurate in this context. Tsdokeh covers all acts of giving, from *ndoveh*, the alms given to the beggar, to *gmilus khassodim*, a form of benefice in which mere material help is combined with "bestowing of loving kindness," and which is therefore of a higher quality.

Life in the shtetl begins and ends with tsdokeh. When a child is born, the father pledges a certain amount of money for distribution to the poor. At a funeral the mourners distribute coins to the beggars who swarm the cemetery, chanting "Tsdokeh will save from death."

At every turn during one's life, the reminder to give is present. At the circumcision ceremony, the boy consecrated to the Covenant is specifically dedicated to good deeds. Every celebration, every holiday is accompanied by gifts to the needy. Each house has its round tin box into which coins are dropped for the support of various good works. A home that is not very poor will have a series of such boxes, one for the synagogue, one for a yeshiva in some distant city, one for "clothing the naked," one for "tending the sick," and so on. If something good or something bad happens, one puts a coin into a box. Before lighting the Sabbath candles, the housewife drops a coin into one of the boxes.

It is considered "un-Jewish" to play cards, and the sheyneh layt seldom do so except on Hanukah when it is the custom and therefore correct. The prosteh layt, who often play, usually have a separate "bank" for the poor. If bets are made the stake is likely to go to one of the many community services. "I bet it will rain tomorrow and if I lose I will give so much to the Home for the Aged."

Children are trained to the habit of giving. A father will let his son give alms to the beggar instead of handing them over directly. A child is very often put in charge of the weekly dole at home, when the beggars make their customary rounds. The gesture of giving becomes almost a reflex. When anything out of the ordinary happens, one says a blessing and one drops a coin into the box.

The "social justice" of the shtetl is not wholly voluntary and not wholly individual. Much of it is, and there is wide latitude for individual performance. Nevertheless, it is firmly woven into the organization of the community—or rather, it provides the central mechanism by which the community functions. The interweaving of individual benefaction with collective community service, of the voluntary with the compulsory, of religious injunction with civic obligation is essential to the organization and the flavor of the shtetl.

The giving of tsdokeh, the performance of maasim tovim, are basic not only to the functioning of the shtetl but also to being a good Jew. A variety of proverbs, sayings, and comments, define the readiness to do good deeds as an earmark of the "real Jew." "One knows a Jew by his pity," it is said; one knows him by his "Yiddish heart," soft, warm, open to appeal; "a Jew is a pitying man"; "to sympathize with sorrow is a typical Jewish trait." This badge of group membership has been so worked into the structure of the society that it serves as a channel through which property, learning and services are diffused.

The patterns of giving and receiving represent a key mechanism in the shtetl, basic to individual relations and community functions, and paramount in the ethical system to which all relations and all functions are referred. Giving is both a duty and a joy; it is a source of heavenly approval and also a source of earthly prestige. The fortunate man is the one who is in a position to give. The unfortunate is the one who is under pressure to accept. Granted the correct situation, accepting is not necessarily painful—but under any circumstances, giving is counted among the great gratifications of life.

The good things of the world are seen as infinite and attainable. They are not acquired for themselves alone, nor for the individual alone; that they should be transmitted is part of their purpose and their nature. Wealth, learning and other tangible and intangible possessions are fluid and are channeled so that in the main they flow from the strong or rich or learned or mature or healthy to those who are weaker, poorer, more ignorant, younger, or sicker. For help of any kind to flow upward is "unnatural." Giving, however, is not an act of simple altruism, for the donor profits far more than the receiver.

The rewards for benefaction are manifold and are to be reaped both in this life and in the life to come. On earth, the prestige value of good deeds is second only to that of learning. It is chiefly through the benefactions it makes possible that money can "buy" status and esteem. The man who is known as a great benefactor receives honorific deference, *koved*. To "chase after koved," is a shtetl activity almost as important as to "chase after parnosseh." For the "love of koved," one will pour out his substance in charitable activities and in "buying" the preferred portions of the Torah during the Sabbath reading.

Moreover, to perform a mitsva through bestowing either goods, learning or services wins "the recording angel's credit mark." The sum total of the services one piles up determines his *zkhus,* his heavenly merits, of which koved is the earthly counterpart. One's lot in the afterlife depends on the number and qualities of his good deeds more than on anything else. Thus, he who performs a good deed is taking out "afterlife insurance in Olam Habo," the world to come.

A popular legend tells that when a man dies and his soul enters Heaven, it is received by his good deeds and bad deeds, and according to the amount of each the soul remains in Heaven or is sent to hell. A popular wish that may be used either as a blessing or as a curse is, "May this rise up to meet you," that is, when your soul enters heaven may it be judged by this that you have done to me.

The one who gives greatly is called *baal tsdokeh,* Master of charity, one of the most honored titles a man can win. When a person says with deep respect, "Oh Reb Duvidl is a groyser baal tsdokeh!," Reb David is a great Master of charity, it means that Reb Duvidl contributes largely to community services, gives alms to beggars, that he always has an oyrekh, a stranger-guest for the Sabbath or holiday meals, that he is ready to give a loan when his neighbor is short of money, that he will never refuse an invitation to a wedding or to a circumcision, that he participates in

funerals, visits the sick and the mourners in order to comfort
them. His wife, if he is wealthy enough, will supply a sick person
with raspberry syrup, which is the marvel drug of the shtetl; she
will distribute borshtsh or matsos before Passover. Reb Duvidl's
house is an "open house." A pauper, a poor relative is always
welcomed and never leaves "with empty hands." Moreover, the
real Master of charity gives much that is known only to him and
to God.

The Master of charity, who reaps koved on earth, becomes
in heaven the Master of zkhus. On earth as well as in heaven, the
accrued zkhus of oneself and one's ancestors becomes a great asset.
Each individual must constantly increase the sum total of his
merits through fulfillment of mitsvos and maasim tovim, and
usually he will make sure that others witness his activities. Everyone in the shul should see how much charity he gives, how he
fulfills his obligations to his wife and family—as witness her good
Sabbath dress, her pearls, her jewels, the education he gives to
his sons. Gladly or reluctantly the pious Jew goes to visit his poor
relatives on a holiday, and the shtetl will know that "the nogid
is going to visit the mishpokheh." He carries his little son to
kheyder and the shtetl will comment with satisfaction, "Reb
Nukhem is taking the boy to the melamed." For each mitsva,
large or small, he will receive koved, the acknowledgment of the
community that he is living up to his status and position. By a
display of fulfilled obligations he proves to the community that
his store of zkhus is mounting.

The ideal situation, however, is to have the community so
sure of your zkhus that there is no need to demonstrate it. The
man whose position is established beyond all question can afford
to neglect any display. The learned man can afford to dress himself and his wife modestly; the nogid who is known to give generously can afford the kind that is *tsdokeh beseyter,* secret charity.
In classifying the various degrees of social justice, Maimonides
put anonymous donation as number seven next to the very highest, which consists in preventing poverty. The great master of
tsdokeh can afford the luxury of secret benefactions. The stories
that are told of community benefactors make much of the good

deeds that spared the beneficiary the "shame" of public knowledge, or even of knowing himself who had helped him.

The importance of zkhus throws further light on the conception of yikhus. Zkhus, the totality of heavenly merits accumulated by the family, is reflected in its yikhus. Learning is the first criterion of yikhus, but next comes benefaction. The family of wealth can acquire yikhus because the nogid has the means to distribute tsdokeh, and to perform mitsvos and maasim tovim. Conspicuous charity thus becomes a familiar means of "social climbing."

It does not follow that the poor are free of the obligation to perform maasim tovim. Obviously the favored of fortune are in a position to perform more spectacular ones than the very poor and lowly, but in the afterworld they will be measured in terms of real merit. According to the code set down in the Shulkhan Arukh, "Even a poor person who obtains his support from the contribution of charity . . . is obliged to give charity from that which is given to him."

Regardless of economic status, general admiration or filial pride is often expressed through accounts of good deeds. "My parents were very generous. Even in bad times when we had several bankruptcies with our store, father still brought guests home to eat with us, and we did not have much ourselves. . . . Mother . . . literally took things off her back to give to the poor."°

Theoretically, the storing up of merits in heaven is the foremost reason for performing good deeds. More real and more immediate, however, are the social and psychological gratifications to be gained on earth. Moreover, aside from the earthly prestige and the heavenly rewards accruing to one for generosity, there is the increment of sheer pleasure. One aspect of shtetl life that has been least understood is the emphasis on joy in connection with religious and secular activities. Observance of the Sabbath is a joy as well as a duty; children are a joy; obeying a mitsva is a joy. It is not only that if one knows the rule one will obey it. It is not only that one has been trained from infancy to "earn a mitsva" whenever possible. In addition, there is a sense of pleasure that comes from the deed itself and from the feeling of identification with the people whose emblem is sympathy for those in need.

In the shtetl, many factors obscure or distort the joy of performing mitsvos. Nevertheless, it is always present in theory and often in fact. When a man is enjoying this pleasure he is apt to tell himself, "It's good to be a Jew."

The worldly rewards of maasim tovim are not restricted to prestige. Since "charity delays evil and increases life," there is practical advantage to be gained by doing good. Moreover, the Shulkhan Arukh points out a very realistic argument in the changing of human fortune: "One should also consider that the wheel of fortune is ever revolving, and that he himself or his son or his grandson will eventually have to beg for charity." The experience of the shtetl people, their political and economic instability and insecurity, confirm the argument of the scholar. There is perhaps also a feeling that if one is virtuous and gives freely, God will preserve him from becoming a recipient instead of a donor.

Good deeds lie in the realm of man-to-man, yet this relationship like all others is conditioned by the underlying relationship of man to God. As the Shulkhan Arukh reminds: "A man should consider the fact that he is constantly praying for sustenance from the Holy One, blessed be He, and just as he prays that the Holy One listen to his cry and supplication, so should he listen to the supplication of the poor." The names used for God bring home the comparison. God is invoked as "He Who feeds the hungry," "He Who comforts the widow," "He Who clothes the naked," "He Who heals the sick."

Moreover, the man of means feels that his money comes to him from God. It was God who enabled, perhaps assisted, him to acquire his possessions. Therefore he owes some to God, and the way to pay it back is through charity.

It is clear that the main rewards for benefaction lie in the perquisites of giving rather than in any direct return by the beneficiary. Nevertheless, there is a direct return. It is never made in kind, for the giving pattern is always complementary rather than symmetrical. The deed i :elf will not be returned, but the recipient may hope eventually to find himself in a position where he can extend similar help to others. This is a positive goal, since it is one of the greatest blessings in the world to put what you have at the service of others, be it wealth, learning or energy.

The chief direct return from the recipient is deference. The one who receives is in the position of a junior, and owes to the giver respect, esteem, and a certain subservience. Where you give deference you do not extend the helping hand, at least not overtly, and where you bestow publicly you do not defer. In specific cases additional returns are expected, but of a different order and degree.

The deference and respect rendered to the old by the young is part of the emphasis on being adult. Life is viewed as a constantly expanding area of gratification. It is a constantly expanding area of responsibility too, but the shouldering and discharge of responsibility is in itself a gratification. As one grows more and more adult—that is, older and older—he is able to do more and more, and to command more and more respect. In such a view, to receive instead of giving represents regression from adulthood and is accordingly felt as catastrophic.

It may be a simple and even a pleasurable experience to accept from one who is far above you in age, learning, or wealth—that is, who is unmistakably your "senior." But to accept publicly from one who is not obviously your senior may be felt as deeply painful. Accordingly, when a person gives material support to one who is his senior in age or learning, great pains are taken to save the recipient's face. For example, a wealthy younger man who may support a venerable scholar will give his contributions privately—perhaps sending money in an envelope by a little boy, or leaving the envelope unostentatiously on a corner of the table when he comes to call, or slipping it to the older man's wife. This donation would be regarded less as an individual benefaction than as a simple fulfilling of a community obligation. The wealthy man would reap far more criticism for withholding his generosity than praise for bestowing it.

The poor, the weak, the ignorant, feel that they have a right to ask for help, since the "have's" are under obligation to share with the "have-not's." It is correct procedure to ask for favors and services, if necessary with expostulations, cries and tears. Yet, though it is correct, there is an intense repugnance to asking material aid, and even the lowly will suffer much and go to great lengths in order to avoid it. There is comparatively little reluctance to turn to those who are wiser and more learned for advice and instruction, or for mediation in solving disputes. To ask for money or goods, however, is "something else." There is small fear of pauperizing a population accustomed to regard charity as social justice, because to receive can be so painful and to give can be so rewarding.

The horror of being the recipient rather than the donor is expressed in proverbs, sayings, even in prayers. The Talmud advises, "Make your Sabbath like an ordinary weekday (with respect to meals, adds the commentator) but do not have recourse to the assistance of your fellow creatures." The prayer after meals includes the plea, "We beseech Thee, O Lord Our God, let us not be in need either of the gifts of mortals, or of their loans, but only of Thy helping hand which is full, open, holy and ample, so that we may not be ashamed nor confounded for ever and ever." The family faced with economic problems repeat again and again, "May we not be ashamed, and may we not be in need of people." To be a recipient of material help is to be in the position of one who is weak, subordinate, dependent, and that means to be ashamed. "We had a grocery store which at some times went very well, and then at other times failed because people did not pay. Mother managed the store and taught all of us the business. At rush hours we all helped. . . . There were some poor Jews who used to come. We served them just like the others, but they did not have to pay. However, nobody was to see this, and they were helped just like the other customers. Mother used to say that to be generous you had to have three things: one, the means to give; two, a kind heart; and three (most important) good sense. With good sense you could make kindness go three times as far as otherwise. That's why these poor Jews were served like our other customers, so that they would not feel inferior and ashamed."°

It is a mitsva to protect a person from being ashamed, and an aveyreh to shame him. In performing a good deed, individually or collectively, an essential part of the arrangement is avoidance of the need for the beneficiary to request aid. The ideal arrangement is for the donor to offer assistance before the recipient has a chance to ask, even in the small details of life. In the case of a loan, ideally the lender should go to the one in need and say, "Will this be enough?" Always the benefaction should be proffered rather than solicited.

Illness is a special case, however. If someone is ill it is correct to ask what his wishes are. "You give to the healthy, you ask the sick." The hale have an obligation to succor the ailing, and in illness one can accept anything. The sick expect service from the healthy and do not feel obligated to make efforts in their own behalf. It is assumed that nursing, doctoring and feeding will be arranged for. Even the struggle for life should be supplied by the constant attendance of sympathetic relatives, their lamentations and their prayers. If one thoughtlessly inquires, "Do you want a glass of tea?" the answer may be, "Why do you ask; just put it on the table. Am I sick?"

If nobody offers assistance to one who needs it, it is better to have another person ask than to do it one's self. It is shameful to ask for one's self, but a mitsva to ask in behalf of others. A woman would wince at having to ask money for her own daughter's dowry, but would not hesitate to solicit it for a neighbor's daughter.

Ideally parents should be able to care for their children, but if they cannot, aid may be accepted for the child from outside sources. This help should be given in such a way as to save face for the parents. To be an orphan means to have no succoring parents, a condition which gives the orphan his special role as the most pitied individual in the community. If the parents cannot do things themselves, close kin should step into the breach, and if they in turn are unable to furnish aid, then help may be accepted from the community. Relatives will do all they can in order to avoid the humiliation of having a kinsman receive help from "outsiders," and if it comes to that, every effort must be made to spare the family as well as the individual. "Children do not accept food or gifts from strangers, but that is not because they distrust them, but rather because there is shame associated with taking. If one does accept, the situation has to be felt as taking a present but not needing it, for taking when in need is shameful."°

A boy who became sick had a mother who was "very poor, and she could not help him. Two girls got together, went from home to home and collected money for the boy. When they sent it to him they asked him not to tell his mother that the money was collected in this fashion . . . she would feel that her son received alms, and she would be ashamed."°

A "real Jew" is expected to "seek a mitsva." The man in shul, the woman at home, merchants in their stores, people in the market, even children on their way to kheyder are expected to be on the lookout for a chance to "earn" one. No one need look in vain, for each day brings many opportunities. It is a mitsva to lend a pot to a neighbor, to explain a difficult passage in the Talmud to a student, to watch the baby while the mother is out "chasing after parnosseh," to accept an invitation to a wedding or a circumcision celebration.

Each good deed performed is so much to one's credit. Conversely, each one missed is not only one credit the less, but is a violation of the command to help one's fellow, and therefore is punishable. The heavenly ledger may seldom be in the forefront of consciousness, but at least for some people the satisfactions of maasim tovim are associated with anxiety about failure to do enough. There is a sardonic saying about the anxious hypocrite who works for the sake of his own soul rather than for the welfare of others, "he will kill a man in order to earn a mitsva."

The various aspects of tsdokeh are not left to individual luck or caprice. The principle of social justice requires that every poor, sick, old or infirm member of the community must be taken care of, permanently or over a crisis. Accordingly, in each shtetl there are a number of institutions devoted to such community services. As a matter of course, they are centered round the synagogue which is the hub of all shtetl affairs. Each shtetl has its quota of organizations and often each congregation in a shtetl will have several. Since even small communities tend to have a number of congregations, there is no lack of associations, or *khevros,* devoted to charity. The number and alignment may vary somewhat from one shtetl to another, but the functions generally correspond to the classic division of activities included under tsdokeh.

The organization of *Malbish Arumim,* "Clothing the Naked," provides clothes for the needy, and the *Oyzer Dalim* distributes alms among the poor who are too proud to "go around the houses."

For a girl who has no dowry there is the association of *Hakhnosses Kaleh,* "Sheltering the Bride," which sends out collectors "around the houses," or uses its funds to provide her dowry, underwrites the marriage expenses, and sees to it that she has a "beautiful wedding" with prominent citizens of the community as invited guests. An orphan is taken care of by the association *Beys Yessoymim,* "the House of Orphans," which subsidizes an orphanage, and by a *Talmud Toyreh* organization which supports the free school for orphans and children of the poor. The *Bikkur Khoylim* provides medical expenses for the sick who cannot depend on their families to pay for the doctor or drugs. Members of this association visit the ailing person to help him with words of comfort, with money, perhaps with bed linens and other necessaries. This same association may be responsible for the *hekdesh,* the city hospice, a miserable construction on the edge of town, "somewhere out beyond the bathhouse."° In the shtetl vocabulary the word has become synonymous with the most wretched slum. The hekdesh may also be supported by members of the *Hakhnosses Orkhim,* whose task is to provide indigent strangers with board and shelter, usually by distributing them among the men of means if they do not find a host for themselves.

The Home for the Aged, *Moyshev Zkeynim,* is supported by yet another society, to take care of the very old people who either cannot or will not be helped by their families. Some of them feel it the lesser of two evils to be supported by impersonal funds to which all contribute rather than to be dependent on their own children—even though the children may plead for the privilege of supporting them. The dignity of age can better endure the impersonal than the personal benefaction.

When they die they will be buried by the "Holy Association," *Khevreh Kadisha,* which is in charge of "bringing Jews to Israel's grave." To this, as to all community benefactions, each contributes according to his means. Unlike most of the others, however, the Khevreh Kadisha serves all alike, the rich as well as the poor. When death occurs, the community takes over. The family, presumably too prostrated with grief to occupy themselves with practical affairs, are proscribed from busying themselves with funeral arrangements or with everyday affairs of living. They devote themselves to mourning the dead with the customary rituals and observances, while others arrange for the funeral, bring them food and perform any additional services that are required. A nogid who dies will have paid his burial expenses many times over in contributions to the Khevreh Kadisha. But when the moment comes he will be buried by the community, like any other member, as part of his automatic rights.

Aid for rehabilitation rather than relief plays an important part among individual and collective benefactions. The very highest form of tsdokeh, according to Maimonides, is that which prevents poverty. Cash is scarce in the shtetl, and sooner or later almost every family has an emergency for which money is needed, whether because of illness, preparations for holidays, or a business deal. Such money has to be raised by loans and a short-term loan, *gmilus kheysed,* is a great mitsva. "One who lends money to another in order to enable him to make a living gets a special credit." One would prefer, if possible, to borrow from an individual rather than from the community. Not everyone's credit is good enough for that, however. For those who cannot arrange a private loan, the *Gmilus Kheysed* association advances community funds, also without interest. "The people who had yikhus all belonged to the Gmilus Kheysed and if you wanted a loan, you had to go to them. They determined the amount you could borrow. From some people they took a pawn, but usually they didn't bother with that."°

If such a loan is returned, the payment by no means cancels out the mitsva. Often, however, what is phrased as a loan is made with no expectation of repayment. It is called a loan by courtesy in order to ease the distress of acceptance. Both the distress and the merit would be particularly great in the case of a person who was formerly rich and has become poor, since "he feels the sting of poverty and dependence more than one who is used to it."

An association that functions only once a year is the *Moës Khittin,* which provides the unleavened bread, matsos, for people who cannot afford to get it themselves, and also gives them whatever cash is necessary in order to observe fully the special dietary laws in force over the Passover holidays. Every Jew must have the means, not only to observe but also to enjoy the holiday, for enjoyment is mandatory. In some places there is no regular association for Passover, and the need is handled informally, as a recurrent annual emergency.

The officials of the associations, or khevros, are elected by the congregation, although the form of organization varies locally and regionally, as well as historically. There may be a central shtetl organization, or each synagogue may have its separate association which takes care only of its own. Some small places will not have a complete roster of associations, leaving certain functions to individual activity. Guild synagogues usually take care of their guild members, and Hassidic courts interest themselves in the followers of their own Rebbeh. Whatever the pattern of organization, however, every solvent inhabitant of the shtetl participates in one way or another in the good deeds of his community or his special group.

In all the community services it would be difficult to draw a sharp line between individual and group benefaction. In the shtetl there is no such line. The two types of benefice, organized and informal, duplicate and interweave in function and in participation. The same people are the leaders, either in private or in collective maasim tovim. Sometimes they act alone, sometimes they mobilize others to act. Sometimes the group activity is undertaken by group decision, sometimes through the prodding of one individual. At times one gives individually so that the recipient will not have to go to the organization; again, the organization gives so that he won't have to "go around the houses." An individual donor ekes out what an organization can muster; or an organization fills in when an individual can give something, but not all that is needed.

The problems of those who need help are accepted as a responsibility both of the community and of the individual. They will be met either by the community acting as a group, or by the community acting through an individual who identifies the collective responsibility as his own.

It is, of course, the learned and the wealthy who are active members, the men who sit on the Eastern Wall, the Faces of the community. It is partly by virtue of their community service that they are classified as sheyneh yidn. The very definition of "sheyn," as has been seen, includes services to the community and to the group. In this sense the status is also a vocation. A place on the Eastern Wall implies ability to serve the community on a grand scale. This holds for the learned as well as for the wealthy. It is assumed that a learned man is generous, not only with his wisdom but with any worldly goods as well. For a great scholar to be miserly is a contradiction, since study means knowledge of the mitsvos and there is a strong belief that to know is to do.

When a situation of emergency occurs—for example, if someone's house burns down or a family is evicted—the rabbi or some other leader will get up in front of the congregation, usually on the Sabbath after the reading of the Torah. If there are several synagogues in the shtetl and the emergency is acute, delegates will visit one after the other and mobilize the whole population of the shtetl.

The participation of the less active members is for the most part limited to financial assistance. The income of an association is provided by donations, by individual pledges, and by fund raising. An important part comes from the pledges made by those who are "called to the Torah," and a way of stimulating generosity is to have a man called up for one of the more important portions. The more important the portion, the greater a donation is expected, and on occasion being called may be a way of forcing a man's pocket rather than of honoring him. The one who is called whispers into the gabai's ear not only the sum but also the purpose, and later the gabai will announce: "Reb Abraham ben Isaac Halevi offers for the Talmud Toyreh twenty-five rubles, for Hakhnosses Kaleh twenty rubles," and so on through the list. Both the amounts and the allocation will be the subject of lively comment during the Sabbath afternoon.

Further regular sources of income for the associations are all the innumerable offerings made to celebrate joyful or sad occasions. The scholars explain that the sacrifices made in the temple are continued in the shtetl as money offerings for charity, because "The giving of charity is greater than all sacrifices." The poor sometimes comment bitterly that this arrangement permits a man to "buy off his sins with his charities." When a "beard without a Jew" makes a flamboyant contribution, they will say, "So, he bought an insurance policy," a place in the world to come. Even the cynics will admit, however, that maasim tovim do not necessarily require money—and also that the possession of money must be paid for with a constant stream of donations.

The tin boxes placed in the homes supply additional revenue for tsdokeh. Nevertheless, special fund raising is often necessary. For smaller emergencies, one or two women may undertake the collection. Perhaps a poor woman is having a baby, and a layette is needed. Perhaps someone is sick and doesn't want to go to the association.

In general the good deeds of women are personal rather than official. They may assist the associations on the side, almost as a "woman's auxiliary." More often, however, they give or solicit help in direct response to individual appeal. "My mother was always very busy. She was a very charitable woman and her good deeds always took up a great deal of time. . . . They used to call her 'the Angel.' "° Again and again one hears of the wife and mother who takes time from her work to help a sick woman. A prosperous housekeeper, balebosteh, would often bake much more than she needs in order to give the rest to the poor; or would make two barrels-full of borshtsh instead of just one, in order to distribute the rest. "My grandmother herself did a great deal. When I was ten years old, she started to make my trousseau. And for each piece of linen that I got, one was made for a poor Jewish bride. Or, she gave money to buy a small business."° Such a donation was not considered a gift. "Never should a Jew make a gift. The poor man borrows money for a specific purpose: to make a living. And he brings with him some object, some jewelry, as a security that he will give back the money. Every time that a Jew came to ask for a hundred rubles, to start a business, Grandmother would take such an object."° The object was taken less for surety than for face saving. "Grandmother explained to me that by bringing this, the poor man shows that he is not a beggar, that he is an equal, and that he only borrows the money."° The loan was not necessarily repaid. "Every time at Purim Grandmother sent some sweets to some poor families as a gift, and this object they left with her. That was meant as a gift from her to them . . . only I refused to go when I was older, I wanted a servant sent, but she said that the blessing of the poor people would fall on me, so she insisted that I go."°

For important and official fund raising, two respected officers of the association go from house to house, collecting money. It is perhaps in these house-to-house collections that the full burden of social justice is felt most keenly. It is beautiful to give, it is gratifying to give, to reap honor on earth and lay up rewards in heaven, to enhance the yikhus of one's family and the marriage prospects of one's children, to enjoy the warmth of feeling, "I am a 'real Jew,' I am obeying the Law." But the shtetl is a poor place. The proudest nogid of them all is not a rich man by western standards. And at every turn one must give. The coins that tinkle ceaselessly into tin boxes and outstretched palms are small coins, but their number is staggering.

One gives, and gives again, and then once more is asked to give. The fund raisers march into one's home. "We need from you so much," they say. They will not be bashful in their requests, since to ask for someone else is not a shame but a virtue. "He who urges others to give charity and causes them to practice it, earns a greater reward than the one who gives." There will be arguments, offers and counteroffers. It is too much, I cannot. But it is needed, you must. In the end they depart, probably neither empty-handed nor satisfied.

Everyone must give, down to the poorest. Everyone wants to give. But almost everyone is in financial straits himself and almost no one can give easily. If one has only two rolls for the Sabbath meal, how shall he satisfy the open mouths of all the little tin boxes? How shall he answer the call of the multiple associations, "not speaking about" the many special calls? At that point the poor man, looking at the nogid, thinks "with money one can buy a place in this world and the future world." But the nogid himself is turning out his empty pockets to satisfy the fund raisers that he has no more to give. When one is strained beyond his means, then "it is hard to be a Jew." In return for his donation, the nogid will receive koved, honor, from the community. But, as its Hebrew root implies, koved is heavy.

The sanctions that enforce support of social justice are phrased almost entirely as rewards rather than as penalties. The rewards are so far-reaching and on so many levels, that they are almost irresistible. The penalty is largely the absence of what one might win through maasim tovim. With regard to public opinion, however, the absence is so blatant that it becomes a negative sanction. Support of charitable activities is "voluntary" in the sense that one may give more or less generously and may complain loudly about the ol. It is also possible to refuse all contributions, but the social cost is so severe that few would brave it. Cold shoulders, wagging tongues, raised eyebrows are bad enough, but it may go further. There was, for example, a rich man who refused to give help to some of his relatives, and the community was so outraged that after he died the burial society refused to bury him. Finally they consented, but only for an exorbitant sum, so that in the end he paid posthumously some of what he had withheld from the kinfolk he should have succored.

Just as individual and group action merge, so it is impossible to draw a neat line between receiving generosity and receiving one's due. What one receives from the community, impersonally, is social justice and may be accepted as one's right by virtue of membership in the community. What one receives from an individual must be recompensed in the correct manner but, on the principle of social justice, it is one's right to receive—just as it is the donor's right to be recompensed. It is one's right for all the reasons that have been rehearsed, including especially the fact that to have is in itself an obligation. Moreover, an individual has significance only as part of a group. The compulsion to give and to share is not merely moral, not merely calculated in terms of earthly koved and heavenly zkhus. It comes partly from a sense of place and identification. To be isolated is hideous, pathetic and dangerous. Only when he has a functioning place in a group can a man be happy, "beautiful" and safe. "One should not live for himself only. You have to live for others."° The injunction, constantly repeated, may be interpreted to mean also, "You have to live *with* others." Otherwise you are not alive.

The attitudes toward receiving aid from an individual or from the community are complicated. One prefers, if one must be recipient, to receive from one's senior, and secretly; or better yet to receive secretly and also anonymously. In some ways impersonal help from an organization is easier to take than personal, because it is one's right as a member of community. There is far less shyness about asking from an organization—if one is willing to approach them at all—because one is asking only for his right. The organization is set up to give you what you need, that is its business. One is not asking a favor but only his just due. Nevertheless, it is better if a member of an organization sees the need and acts, sparing the person the unpleasantness of making his wants known.

If the need has been caused by some large calamity—fire, flood, pogrom—over which the individual had no control, there is no shame associated with asking. Then he is a refugee. Refugees from other communities or even other countries will also be helped. They may not necessarily be liked, but they are members of the larger community, the *Klal Isroel*—all of Jewry—and therefore it is their right.

While all the shtetl strains and pants to win the joy of giving and to escape the shame of public assistance, one group makes it a business to ask and to receive—the professional beggars, the *shnorer* and the *beytler*. The beggar is held in contempt, not because he accepts from his inferiors, for none is beneath him in status, but because he asks for donations. Nevertheless, he has function if not status. He is by definition an opportunity for good deeds, and as such helps the members of the community to amass credits in heaven.

Giving to a beggar rates only a minor credit. It is almost mandatory on certain holidays and celebrations and, if they receive less than their due, they do not hesitate to protest. "The beggars carried a large sack and put everything they were given into it. When they came to a house they would say '*Git a ndoveh*,' 'give alms!' And you couldn't refuse a beggar, you had to give him something. If you didn't have anything just then, you asked him to come a little later."° Such charity is given openly with no need for face saving, since the beggar has no "face." The professional beggar has his regular beat, and it is jokingly said that he may pass it on at death to his successor, or may give part of it as a dowry for his daughter.

The attitude toward the mendicant is mixed. As an individual who begs, he is despicable. Children who ask for things are told with grown-up disapproval, "Don't be a shnorer!" As an occasion for mitsvos, however, the beggar is an instrument of grace.

He is well aware of his utility, and it accounts in large measure for the arrogance of the shtetl beggars, which is a matter of amazement to strangers, and has been the subject of frequent comment and analysis by Yiddish authors.

The beggar is an important member of the shtetl. He is everywhere, in the market, in the shul, invited to weddings where special tables are set for him. When a nogid's daughter is married to a great scholar, word spreads throughout the region that a rich banquet will be held and beggars flock from far and wide to feast, receive alms, and dance with the bride. Their kingdom, however, is the cemetery. On the road to the grave, shnorers of all ages and both sexes are posted at small distances, stretching out their hands and repeating monotonously, "Charity will save from death!"

The respectable inhabitant of the shtetl may despise the shnorers, but he is cowed by their rages and their expletives. The shnorer is an artist in curses, producing the most elaborate and sophisticated examples on the slightest provocation, especially if one refuses or gives less than expected.

It is not only the verbal violence that intimidates the shnorer's benefactors, however. He presents the extreme example of an interdependence evident in any recipient-donor relationship of the shtetl. Despised and faceless, the beggar nevertheless feels himself at an advantage, because the more fortunate need him as an object of charity. It is he who opens for them the portals of heaven. Through their generosity to him they may win their way to happiness in the world to come. His impudence says tacitly, "Ha! you cannot get along without me." And their compliance tacitly admits, "It is so."

In other relations, the same interdependence exists. All maasim tovim represent a continuous stream of values, material and spiritual, from the one who has to the one who lacks. It is not a one-way stream, however, for the succor is reciprocated by a complex of social and psychological rewards. The one who gives and the one who receives are also bound together by a mutual need. One needs the help the other can bestow, while the other needs the opportunity to give help in order to win prestige on earth and merits in heaven. The one who receives may be less crude than the beggar in manifesting his consciousness that the donor needs him as an outlet for generosity. Nevertheless, the interdependence is clearly recognized. The privileged one needs the underprivileged, for only by performing maasim tovim can he enjoy the sense of being a good Jew in this world and the assurance of happiness in the world to come.

True, the ideal calls for the performance of good deeds "for their own sake," but even the most charitable and devout hold somewhere the thought of heavenly reward. "My mother was very hospitable and good to people. . . . She did it as a mitsva. . . . She helped a poor person, a needy person, in order to be a step nearer to Olam Habo."°

With regard to maasim tovim, as in most respects, the relations between man and man reveal the pattern of the relations between man and God. The covenant between man and his Creator is a bilateral pact. A member of the people who entered into it feels that he has the right to expect and to request the rewards promised in return for living up to the conditions of the bargain. The pact has a dual character, however. On the one hand there is a certain equality between the contracting parties with regard to mutual obligations and rights. On the other hand it is an agreement between the stronger and the weaker, and to this extent involves a relationship of subordination. The very inequality strengthens the right of the Chosen People to ask for help, since the strong has an obligation to the weak.

At the same time, despite His own limitless power, the

Almighty depends on helpless mortals for the propagation of His glory. The shtetl believes that His name is known on earth only because the Jews accepted His Torah. Had they refused, as other peoples did, God would have remained unknown on earth and would have had to watch humans worshiping other gods and goddesses. To describe someone who fails to find a customer for his wares, people say, "He lugs his goods around like the Holy One with His Torah (before the Jews accepted it)." It is not for nothing that He is bound to reward His people with health, livelihood and the "world to come." His own glory depends on it. Again and again they repeat in their prayers, "Do it for Your sake, for the sake of Your Name."

The prevailing pattern for interpersonal relations between nonequals reveals the characteristics of obligation, complementary function, formal subordination and functional interdependence. In all these respects, relations between donor and recipient, rich and poor, bear striking resemblance to relations between God and Israel.

II

"LIFE IS WITH PEOPLE"

The shtetl dispenses social justice by means of systematic benefactions in which the real motive power is informal, although an elaborate series of organizations exists and functions. In the whole machinery of community functioning the same combination is evident: the basic motive power is informal and operates largely without regard to—sometimes in spite of—the formal apparatus.

The formal apparatus is complex and variegated, exhibiting different forms at different times and places. For the outsider a detailed picture of it may be confusing. For a member of the shtetl this confusion does not exist—partly because each is habituated to his cwn forms but chiefly because the informal mechanisms are constant, and paramount. Moreover, regardless of local and temporal variations in specific form, the underlying relationship of shtetl autonomy to official government power is also constant.

As an "island" culture, a minority embedded in and subordinate to a majority group, the shtetl functions always within a conditioning element. In certain areas and in certain situations it is absolutely influenced by the "ocean" culture, as an island is coast-carved, storm-tossed and occasionally inundated by the surrounding waters. At any time its general climate is affected by them. Yet to a large extent it leads a life of its own.

The two groups, minority and majority, recognize different values, follow different customs, and to some extent have been subject to different laws. In Eastern Europe there have always been special decrees aimed specifically at the Jews, to enforce certain observances or more often to restrict movement or residence and to prohibit certain activities. In this they are not unique, for throughout Eastern Europe and especially in Russia there have been many instances of legislation particularly affecting special groups. Gypsies, for example, were prohibited from living in or even entering large cities in Russia. No other group in the region, however, has been the target of so much discriminatory legislation. The type of proscription under which they have lived is generally familiar, as is the fact that it has varied in different countries and at different times—for example, that they have been subject to more official prohibitions in Russia, and more informal interference in Poland. Where they might live, where they might go, what they might do for a living have been stringently limited, with major and much-discussed effects on their habits, behavior and attitudes, and on the stereotypes generally held about them. That legal edict has on occasion been compounded by officially condoned massacre has intensified the traits characteristic of the "island" culture.

Officially the functions of the shtetl community have been confined to religious, educational and welfare activities—those described in official parlance as "cultural." Even these have been subject to fluctuating outside influence and control, as when attendance at government schools and edicts requiring all to learn the official language have been enforced, or as in the appointment of a local government rabbi. Fluctuations have been due not only to the institution of new regulations but also to the varying enforcement of old ones. The constant need to adjust to sudden stipulations or to the revival of previously ignored ones has resulted in a high degree of adaptability and a corresponding adjustment to instability and insecurity.

In practice, a large measure of local autonomy has been granted to the shtetl. The government retains active jurisdiction in matters of criminal law. It levies taxes, exacts military service, punishes offenders against the law of the land, and issues special edicts. The whole area of local civil control, however, is left largely to the community.

The local representatives of the national government are always present, as are the police who enforce their rulings and are responsible for maintaining orderly behavior. Even though the Jews may constitute a majority of the local population, there is no question about the power and authority of the national majority. For the most part, however, in immediate day-by-day affairs, the shtetl is self-governing within limits that can be dismissed from the foreground of consciousness during certain periods.

The center of its self-governing authority, as of all shtetl authority and activity, is the synagogue, and in this capacity it serves as the House of Assembly. If there is a central community administration and council, it centers about the main synagogue of the shtetl. This was true of the community council, the *kahal*, which functioned for a period before the middle of the nineteenth century. It was true also to a great extent of the Polish *kehila*. In the larger cities, however, the kehila became an arena for conflicts between political parties as well as between the traditionalists and the "progressives."

The synagogue as House of Assembly is the town hall of the shtetl. Here community business is conducted, whether in the main central shul for the whole shtetl, or in a smaller shul in connection with welfare activities of that one congregation. All important announcements are made in the synagogue, from new decrees of the local or national government to announcements of a marriage, a birth, a death, involving some member of the congregation. No clear-cut distinction is made between religious and secular functions, since for the shtetl Judaism is not a religion but a way of life.

Adult males participate in the community activities, and among the most important meetings are those at which officers and delegates are elected. The actual mechanics of election vary widely, but a constant feature is the campaigning inseparable from all elections, the forming of factions, the influencing of the humble members by the *shtot balebatim,* the city bosses. These are of course men of the Eastern Wall, the ones who dominate all aspects of shtetl activity.

The meetings are not notable for parliamentary procedure. On the contrary, there is little order and more talking than listening. Any event calling for group action or consensus is the occasion for debate, dispute, disagreement and exhaustive weighings of the pro and the con. It is taken for granted that there will be differences of opinion and much taking of sides.

Majority rule is followed but not accepted. The minority may concede momentary victory but the issue is not considered settled. There is a tendency to believe, we were right, and it was mere accident that we were out-voted—the wrong people stayed at home. Dissent is most forcibly expressed by walking out of a meeting or by ostentatious absence from it.

Disagreement is characteristically associated with ideas rather than with individuals. There is no blind following of a leader on the theory that he is right and we will support him whatever he says. On the contrary, the leader's dictum is always subject to analysis and criticism. "Every Jew has his own Shulkhan Arukh," they say, meaning his own interpretation of the Law. They follow, not an individual, but their own version of the point of view he is currently expressing.

Neither do they obey orders blindly. Even the humblest man in the shtetl resents being told to do something that goes against his reason and judgment. He feels that it is not his duty to obey blindly, but to appraise the reasons for any act. Under compulsion he will obey within certain limits, but such compliance is strictly under duress and without acceptance.

The synagogue is the place where any individual is privileged to voice complaint or grievance against the community administration, or any of its officers and representatives. Just before the reading of the Torah a person who wishes to protest will stand up before the congregation, strike the stand on which the scrolls are to be placed, and cry out, "I forbid the reading!" It takes a strong spirit to stand forth in this way, for he may be shouted down or shoved aside. Members of the congregation will pound the reading racks before them, calling for silence. Others will register their support of the plaintiff, also by thumping on the wooden racks and shouting, "Keep quiet, let him talk!" The objectors will shout back, "Silence in the Holy Place!" with still more pounding on the racks. The little boys in the congregation join in with a will, yelling and thumping, with no clear notion what it is all about but with keen appreciation of the chance to make a fine noise and not be scolded for it. Startled by the sudden outbreak, the women upstairs will climb on their benches to peer down through the high, small windows, while here and there in the shouting group below an unperturbed few quietly go on with their prayers.

The women also have the right of interruption, and if one is too weak to pound hard enough for attention, she may demand that the sexton, the shammes, do it for her.

Within the area of shtetl autonomy the highest legal authority is the rabbi, who is also the highest religious and scholastic authority. He is the judge, and the law by which he judges is that set down in the sacred writings. Those who come before him are judged, not by the law of the land but by the law of the Promised Land, the sacred Law.

Shul and court are merged, within the area of autonomy, not only by virtue of the authority vested by the Chosen People in their Rov, their rabbi, but also with the express sanction of the official government. In his office or court, the *bes din,* the Rov judges strictly legal matters such as money disputes, strictly religious matters such as the ritual status of a meat pot on which three drops of milk were splashed, and matters like divorce which are considered to belong to both the religious and the legal spheres. The folk who appear before him may come as citizens to a court of law, as members of a congregation to their leader, or as both.

If the shtetl is large the Rov will have an assistant, called the judge or dayan, who will help him in both his religious and his legal duties. If it is very small, there may be only a dayan. Or again, a town may boast several rabbis with several assistants.

In a dispute, if other means have failed, the complainant will call the defendant to the rabbi, *rufn tsum Rov,* where the case will be decided. If the defendant refuses to go, there is no way to force him aside from the pressure of public opinion, but there are few instances of refusal to answer such a call. Some cases could be taken either to the rabbi or to the official court—for example, inheritance problems or failure to fulfill partnership contracts. In such cases the first choice is usually the Rov.

Certain kinds of wage dispute are examples of a strictly legal case that nevertheless could be handled only in the bes din, since it would not have legal status in the police court. The Law rules that a man must be paid enough to live, and therefore if he has six children he requires more than if he is newly married with no children. If the employer is too poor to pay him, that is another problem. These are legal tangles that the Rov puzzles over, between ruling on the breaking of a marriage contract and the case of a chicken with a lump on its gizzard.

The rabbi's decision will be enforced only by the pressure of public opinion. A salient feature of the civil machinery is the lack of enforcing power for the functions that are delegated to the shtetl. There are no police to implement the verdict of the rabbi or the decisions of other officials. Enforcement is solely by the combined authority of God and of man. As long as belief in the Almighty is effective, the Holy Books are the Law and the rabbi's interpretation of the Law carries weight. As long as concern about what people think is strong, the popularly accepted arbiter keeps his authority—and such concern is extremely strong in the shtetl.

It is taken for granted that the rabbi's judgments are not backed up by physical force. Words should rule, for they are the weapon of reason and all human behavior should be reasonable. The punishments decreed by the rabbi are most often imposed donations to charity, or penalties such as reading certain prayers and psalms, or fasting. Occasionally he will recommend a certain number of lashes. Since there is no mechanism of enforcement, it is left to the culprit to ask the shammes to administer them, or, if that official is unavailable, to persuade some friend to put the ruling into effect.

More severe is the penalty of boycott or ostracism and public shaming, for offense and penalty will be announced in the synagogue: "Do not buy of this man," or "Do not speak to him," during a specified period. Another familiar penalty is prohibition from being called to the reading of the Torah—one man who committed an act against the interest of the community was punished by "not being called to Torah for a whole year."°

The most extreme form of punishment is almost never inflicted and operates more as a threat, or even as a remote fear,

than as a fact. This is excommunication, *kheyrem,* the ultimate
form of ostracism and isolation, complete rejection by man and
by God. Few have witnessed the ceremony but it is referred to
with horror as extremely sinister, taking place in darkness while
black candles are being burned. The horror may be aroused
more by the significance than by the actual practices. Threat of
excommunication is the proverbial ultimate in menace—"even if
you ask me under threat of kheyrem," a person may say, "I
couldn't do what you want."

The Rov's authority is not absolute in the sense that his
verdict cannot be questioned nor appealed. No authority is absolute in that sense for the shtetl. If one questions the correctness
of the decision rendered at the bes din, he may go to another
rabbi; but the verdict of the first will be respected until another
authority upsets it. One can also take his case to the government
court, if it falls within that jurisdiction. That verdict will be final
and enforced, and there can be no going to the rabbi once it has
been delivered. Moreover, one comes under criticism for going
to "their" courts unless it is absolutely necessary. "They considered it a sacrilege to seek advice from the civic authorities, and
preferred by far to get their help from their own rabbi. To him
they would bring disputes of all kinds, usually with each point
of view represented by one speaker, and the rabbi would make a
decision."°

Not only can the decision be appealed, but one is free to
choose among the local rabbis the one to whom he will take his
case, that is to select his own judge. He is also free, before going
to any rabbi, to "call to men," *rufn tsu mentshen;* that is, to sub-
mit the case to one or more arbiters, whose decision shall be binding. They will of course be chosen from among the "beautiful
Jews."

Because the bes din belongs to the shtetl, cases will always
be taken there if possible, and it is chiefly the criminal cases that
get to the government courts. This suits the government well
enough. If localities will handle strictly local affairs, so much the
better.

Legal duties are, of course, only one part of the rabbi's functions. He is also a teacher, and an intimate personal adviser to

his congregation. Moreover, these religious leaders often command the respect and affection of the peasants. "The prosteh yidn and the peasants considered my grandfather a holy man, in fact they used to call him Holy Rabbi. They were superstitious; if my grandfather walked in the fields and it rained the next day, they said he had blessed the fields and had caused it to rain. And the Gentiles always came to him for advice, they never went to court. He was a very wonderful person and the peasants were extremely loyal to him. Once in a big storm, he harnessed his horse and went to shul because he had to say evening prayers. When he didn't come back for several hours my grandmother became very worried so she went to the peasant and asked him to look for my grandfather. It didn't take five minutes and in that big storm the whole town of Gentiles was out looking for Holy Rabbi. They found him in shul studying with some men. He had completely forgotten what time it was."°

The importance of the rabbi to the shtetl is tremendous, especially since he is appointed for life and serves as the center for community activities of all kinds. When a position falls vacant, usually through death, the new Rov is selected by the important men of the synagogue, after endless debate and investigation. On no subject is factionalism more lively, and even aside from appointments, the relative merits of different rabbis furnish matter for endless arguments that on occasion become open and sustained hostilities.

In some regions, in addition to the rabbi chosen by the people, there will be one appointed by the government. This "crown rabbi" is likely to be completely ignored by the pious, seldom referred to for advice or judgment, and usually disliked. Nevertheless, if the government appoints him, it is obligatory for the community to support him. Unlike their "own" rabbis, the "state rabbi" receives an outright salary, instead of living by some other occupation or having his stipend conveyed to him in some indirect manner that would maintain the convention of "not using Torah as an axe." He must be paid by the congregation, although it has no voice in appointing him. His functions are chiefly official: serving as a means of communication between the community and the government and issuing certificates of birth, marriage or death.

Welfare activities are supported chiefly, though not wholly, by more or less voluntary donations and contributions. The remainder of the community expenses are defrayed by taxes levied on religious objects and services—yeast, candles, the mikva, matsos, and meat. The meat tax is much the most important as source of revenue and also as economic burden. Jews can eat only animals or fowl killed by the licensed slaughterer according to the correct procedure. The kosher meat he sells is invariably and heavily taxed. It is not quite a temptation but it is a trial for the poor to see the peasants buying meat for less than half what they must pay.

The shtetl citizen carries a dual tax burden. The local taxes must be paid. In addition, the demands of the national government are high and there is no escaping the tax collector. "Everyone in the shtetl hated the tax collector. . . . If you didn't have any money to pay your taxes, he took away your candlesticks, your pillows or your samovar."°

Although the burden on the taxed is severe, the return to the community employees is proverbially less than they can live on. Most of them have a guaranteed minimum which is eked out by supplements or bonuses from the more prosperous men. The Rov receives no official salary, although usually some device is found to remunerate him. The *gaboyim*, the board or council, are paid only in status and prestige, and in many ways the honor costs them dear. Regular payments are usually given, however, to the cantor, the ritual slaughterer, the shammes, the teacher of the Talmud Toyreh, and the mikva attendants, male and female.

The ritual slaughterer, the *shokhet*, fares well since he provides the main community revenue through his occupation. He is apt to be a man of learning and status and may combine with his calling the duties of *mohel*, who performs the circumcision ritual. The other paid employees, however, sorely need the supplements slipped to them by the prosperous members of the congregation. This need, added to the fact that public servants are appointed by the board or council, further enhances the power of these "shul bosses" who are also "city bosses."

The appointed officers, whose duties involve the highest level of religious activities, are known as the Holy Tools, *kley kodesh*. These implements of God's Law include the rabbi, the cantor, and the shokhet.

Through its complicated network of organized group action and individual activity, the shtetl deals with crises and continuing needs, directed always by the leaders who take initiative in civil, charitable, educational, and religious affairs. In reviewing the organizations and their activities, it becomes evident that the system by which community problems are handled provides for certain kinds of situations, while for others there is a conspicuous lack of existing mechanisms.

There is systematic provision for meeting needs connected with problems and crises of the individual life cycle—the continuing needs of food, shelter, clothing, the critical needs of birth, marriage, illness, death, and education. Analogous mechanisms are lacking, however, to deal with situations that might be described as "acts of God," such as fires, floods, pogroms, which are frequent enough to be part of normal expectation. These arise from the external environment, over which the community is felt to lack control. The strictly human needs are systematically provided for, and when they occur steps are taken to meet them directly. The catastrophe that is visited from without, however, is met indirectly, by means designed to influence the source of the trouble rather than to control its overt manifestation.

Fires are frequent enough so that they are a constant and recognized source of danger. The closeness of the dwellings and their flimsy construction increase the possibility of the flame's spreading, once it has begun. However, responsibility for a volunteer fire brigade—if there is one—is left to the government. Effort is concentrated primarily on rescuing those in danger, salvaging household goods, and fleeing the flame, rather than on putting out or checking the fire. Later, when one is homeless, other members of the community will give relief and will help to rebuild the ruins. But the shtetl is unprepared to control the situation from the outset.

If an epidemic strikes the shtetl, prayers are of course offered up. Other steps consist chiefly in marrying off two orphans or cripples, so that God will be mollified by the good deeds of his worshipers. That is, one tries to placate or alleviate, rather than to control. "Whenever there was an epidemic in the shtetl they used to blame it on the people's sins. They tried to find the guilty ones and would expose them to the public. The Rov would pin up leaflets wherever people could see them saying that the reason why our children are dying is because the people are not pious enough: they don't go to shul; they don't keep kosher too well; and because the women don't go to the mikva. . . . Another method for getting rid of an epidemic, was to get two orphans if possible and to marry them off on the cemetery. This was done as a mitsva for God to show Him the good deeds the people are doing and by pleasing Him thus He would call back the plague."°

In this sense pogroms are treated also as acts of God. There is usually no defense organization. If organized resistance is attempted by the prosteh or by young people who have broken away from traditional attitudes, it is criticized by the very orthodox as "un-Jewish." One pleads with God for help and mercy. Perhaps one sends a delegation to the leader of the attacking group. But to fight back is the exception rather than the rule.

This passivity cannot be attributed simply to fear of death. There are too many instances of Jews who have accepted avoidable death rather than to violate the Sabbath. There are instances also like that of the shokhet, the ritual slaughterer, "a big husky man, strong as a horse," who allowed himself to be killed when he might have escaped by killing an unarmed assailant in a pogrom. "The funny part about it is that the shokhet is accustomed to killing and seeing blood shed. He even says a blessing over it, but yet he couldn't kill a man."°

Within the area where the community has autonomy and exercises control, the shtetl is run by the men who know and the men who give. Their leadership, like their earthly honor and their heavenly merits, must constantly be validated. If they want to preserve their status they must respond to any appeal of their fellows. The rabbi's house should always be open, the sheyneh layt have no right to refuse a call, whether it be to attend a wedding, mediate a dispute, or obtain permission for nearby soldiers to go to the synagogue on Passover. The burden of high status is

suggested by a familiar phrase used to describe someone who enjoys a lazy, luxurious life: "He lives like God in Odessa." In
Odessa, "the Paris of Russia" and "a city of heretics," people very
seldom mention God's name. "They don't bother Him, they
seldom stifle Him with requests and complaints."° Therefore,
"His life is easy there."°

Like everyone in the shtetl, the leaders live always under the
watchful eyes of "people," mentshen. Nobody is exempt from
criticism, and the sheyneh yidn the least of all. The familiar exclamation, "What can you expect of a prosteh?" gives to the common people a certain latitude. The nogid, however, is constantly
subject to approval or disapproval. The people give him deference
and honor, but they claim a right to know "how did he earn it?"
If they dare not criticize him to his face they do it behind his back.
If he is not living up to his position, "God will punish him," they
say wisely, or "there will come a day—" His behavior is constantly
tested and examined, and any fault may undermine his prestige.
No authority and no position is ever absolute and final; it must
be validated continually and visibly.

If one sins, however, it is worse to do it openly than secretly.
"Un-Jewish" behavior is despised and condemned, but public
violation of prescribed standards adds to the offense, because in
that case one influences others. Smoking on Sabbath in a privy is
bad enough but smoking at the open window is a crime against
the community. A sin that is unknown to the shtetl is regarded as
a sin against God, who will take care of it, but overt violation is
a crime against people, and people will retaliate. Atheists were
beaten by pious Jews, not because they ate on the Day of Atonement, but because they ate in public where they were seen by
worshipers going to or from the synagogue.

To sin publicly is a crime, but to insist on privacy if you are
not sinning is a serious misdemeanor. Again, the lives of the
sheyneh layt especially must be open to all. One of the worst things
you can say of a man is, "he keeps it for himself" or "he hides it
from others," whether "it" is money or wisdom, clothing or news.

Locked doors, isolation, avoidance of community control,
arouse suspicion. "You know, so-and-so locks his doors" is a comment which implies that "so-and-so" has something to hide. Locks

are against thieves and outsiders, but not against "home people," *heymisheh mentshen,* who are free to come in whenever they like at any time of the day. "To come in for a glass of tea" means to find out how your neighbor lives, what he is doing, what kind of household he has. Sipping the tea through a lump of sugar, you will tell him, "I don't want to interfere with your business, it's no concern of mine, but—" and this will serve as preface to a long series of helpful comments about your neighbor's way of bringing up children or of cooking a Sabbath fish. In the besmedresh everyone will hear that so-and-so spoke to his wife unbecomingly, or was reading a Russian newspaper, or gave a substantial loan to his poor relative to start a new business. The matchmaker does not wait until the father comes to him, but will remind him that "it is already time" for him to think about finding a son-in-law.

The authority of "mentshen," of people, is as compelling as the official power of the Rov and perhaps more so. "What will people say," is the constant reminder of parents to children, husband to wife, friend to friend, partner to business partner. Added to all the other pressures for conforming with usage and religious prescription is the powerful inducement, "because of people." "People will laugh," "people will talk," "we will be ashamed before people," "we will be unable to show our face to people." The wife of the impoverished nogid keeps several pots of water boiling —"people should think" she still has plenty of food to cook. An ignoramus sits with an open book before him on the Sabbath— people should think that he too is studying.

"What does one not do for people?" they ask. There are husbands who go into debt "over the head" in order to buy their wives a fur coat or jewels, or send them "to the country" for a summer outing. People "kill themselves" in order to give an expensive wedding and invite more guests than they can afford so that "people shall see." For the most part, however, such efforts are futile, for "people see everything, they know everything, one cannot hide from people."°

It is proverbial that "there are no secrets in the shtetl," and the shtetl itself jokes about the need of everyone to know all about everyone else's affairs. "If you want to know what goes on at my home," they say, "ask my neighbor." It is a joking point rather than a sore point, because basically the shtetl wants no secrets. One tries to hide his private lacks and weaknesses, but the great urge is to share and to communicate. There is no need to veil inquisitiveness behind a discreet pretense of "minding one's own business," for it is normal, natural and right to mind everyone's business. Withdrawal is felt as attack, whether physical or psychological, and isolation is intolerable. "Life is with people."

Whenever possible one "goes a little bit among people," the men to shul, the women to gossip with their neighbors. You dart into the house next door to relay the latest tidbit, and perhaps to borrow an onion. The door is never locked and nobody stops to knock. In the evening, you "sit a little bit" on the *prisbeh*, the low embankment that protects the base of the house, and "look at the people." Everywhere people cluster to talk, at home, in the market place, on the street. Everyone wants to pick up the latest news, the newest gossip. Everyone is interested in "what people say" about war, about the nogid's latest transactions, about the pregnancy of the rabbi's wife, about the illness of the melamed's youngest son.

News is never kept for oneself. It is immediately passed to the neighbors, spread from the Eastern Wall to the beggar at the door, and exaggerated in transit until it comes back unrecognizable. Whether the event is personal or general, it must be shared. When death strikes, the bereaved widow is more likely to rush out into the street crying, "He is dead," than to fling herself on the body of her husband. When a new regulation is announced, "circles of people," *reydlakh,* gather in the market place, talking, speculating, debating.

The freedom to observe and to pass judgment on one's fellows, the need to communicate and share events and emotions is inseparable from a strong feeling that individuals are responsible to and for each other. Collective responsibility is imposed by outside pressures on a minority group, but these pressures combine with and re-enforce the basic tenets of religious faith. The Covenant solemnized on Mount Sinai is with all Jews and with each Jew. Since it involves them individually and collectively, the punishment inflicted on any Jew may be for his personal misdeed or for an act of the group; and calamity to the group may be for collective behavior or for an individual sin. Again and again in the books studied from early childhood until old age, it is repeated, "All Jews are responsible each for the other."

If a member of the community fails in his obligations, if he "jumps the fence," and is "a sinner in Israel," the whole community may suffer from his misbehavior. God is just and does not punish without reason. An epidemic in the community, an unfavorable edict of the government, a pogrom, are the direct consequences of wrongdoing. Nobody is free from sin—"a man is only a man," "*a mentsh iz nur a mentsh*," therefore every member of the community has to be watched and controlled, lest the whole community suffer.

Just as the sins of the individual are borne also by his family and community, so the benefactions of the baal zkhus add to the welfare of "his own." Zkhus ovos, the merits of the ancestors, are invoked when one appeals to God for help, and may mean not only direct biological ancestors but also the patriarchs Abraham, Isaac and Jacob. In a family crisis one reminds God of the pious and outstanding scholars in his lineage, but the same scholars will be invoked by the community in a group crisis. The baal zkhus becomes a representative in heaven, entitled on the basis of his earthly deeds to ask of God favors for his family or community. Pious Jews will "go on the graves," that is, write specific requests and leave them on the grave of the baal zkhus, expecting him to use his influence in their behalf. The family invokes the zkhus of its ancestors, the Hassidim rely upon the zkhus of their Rebbeh, and the whole community counts upon the zkhus of its sheyneh layt.

Under the Covenant, people are interdependent, not only because the acts of one affect the fate of all, but also because each needs the others. The underprivileged depend on the privileged to help them with instruction, advice, services, material assistance. The privileged depend on the underprivileged in order to validate themselves as "real Jews," since the position of privilege is validated only through the sharing of values with those who lack them. This interdependence is evident not only in connection with charitable activities but in every aspect of human relations, personal as well as communal. The husband needs the wife for

her domestic and economic services and for aid in fulfilling the
mitsvos. The wife needs the husband for guidance, for performance of domestic ritual, and for final admission to Olam Habo,
the world to come. Parents and children are similarly dependent
on each other for fulfillment of earthly needs and of the holy Law.

Within this community where each person is linked and
identified with the group and all its members, the individual is
never lost. He is merged but not submerged. In the shtetl crowd,
each person has his own face, and his own voice. "Nearly everyone in the shtetl was a separate character—a 'type' all for himself."° Each one has a name, a nickname, a specialty or at least a
distinctive trait. One is a student, the other a specialist in military
strategy because years ago he was a soldier in the Russian army.
The cantor is an authority on music, but he may be challenged by
the tailor who considers himself a better expert, *meyvn*. The
shtetl accepts everyone's specialty and everyone feels free to challenge the connoisseurship of anyone else. It is a good day for the
congregation when three or four "experts" begin a "hot" discussion in the shul, during the interval between the afternoon and
evening prayers. Everyone can join in and offer a few "clever
words." No one admits defeat, everyone is right even if the others
do not agree. Faces are red, hands fly in excited gestures—if they
are not busy twisting somebody's button or lapel—all talk together, each wanting to "outshout" his opponent. Suddenly the
shammes hits the table with the palm of his hand and the argument is over—it is time to pray.

The community, a whole made up of many closely welded
parts, is felt as an extension of the family. "My shtetl" means all
the Jews who live in it and the bond persists even when members
meet in distant lands. Each shtetl has its known characteristics,
suggested in the many nicknames designating members of other
towns. Often the names are hostile or derogatory, for "my shtetl"
is always best and the one that differs is to that extent inferior.
People from Belz are called "Belzer jelly" because the fervent
Hassidim of that shtetl shake when they pray like "jellied fish
gravy." The women of Yanov are referred to scornfully as "Yanov
mares," in honor of the royal stables at Yanov, and the name survived longer than the royalty. The inhabitants of Glowno are

named for *teyglakh,* the small pellets of dough boiled in honey
because "Glowno folks speak as if they have teyglakh in their
mouths."

Despite local pride and prejudice, the region or country is
also felt as a wider community. The people who apply derisory
nicknames to inhabitants of a neighboring shtetl will feel a sense
of kinship with them as compared to outlanders, and will join
them in the cultivation of unflattering regional stereotypes. A
"Litvak," a "Galitsianer," a Hungarian, a Ukrainian, is "outlandish" everywhere but in his own province. The long caftan
and the fur hat of the Hungarian Jew are at odds with the custom
of Lithuania, and the man who wears them will be viewed askance.
In Poland the shorter coat will offend and its wearer will be given
the scornful appellation, "der Daytsh," the German. The Polish
Jew recoils from the "Litvak's cold rationalistic mind," and the
Lithuanian in turn scorns the Polish Hassid for his "fanatical" devotion to the Rebbeh. At the same time, all the East European
Jews feel closer to each other than to those from West Europe
who are known as Daytshen.

Beyond the regional or national boundaries, there is still a
strong sense of responsible identification with Klal Isroel, "the all
of Israel." The folk of the shtetl regard a sense of collective responsibility as another mark of the Jew. "Praying three times a
day does not make you a Jew. You have to be a Jew for the world.
That means you have to do something for other people as well."°
Especially, one has to take care of other Jews. "A Jew is always
concerned with the troubles of all other Jews . . . he is very conscious of the fact that his personal lot is dependent on the way
other Jews live and are treated."°

It is a standing joke, enjoyed as much by them as by others,
that when Eastern European Jews meet they will always try to
establish some bond of relationship or residence—and that it is
assumed they will usually succeed. First they find out whether
the stranger is Jewish, then comes the question of country, then
of province; next the shtetl. The ultimate tendency is to find common relatives. Once these data are established they feel secure.
"Among Jews one is never lost."

The transient who is a member of Klal Isroel is accepted by

the community as a guest who has claims to hospitality. If he wishes to move in and settle, however, he does well to establish ties with someone who belongs. If the stranger has relatives in the shtetl all is well for then "he is from our own." He can buy a seat in the synagogue and become part of the community organism. "Real strangers," however, are "something different," especially if they come from a region marked by different clothes and customs. Anyone who imports foreign ways is viewed with mistrust. The Talmud itself instructs the pious, "separate not yourself from the community," and again, "a man should never depart from established practice; behold, when Moses ascended above he did not eat, and when the ministering angels descended to earth they partook of food."

To leave the great community of Klal Isroel, that is to renounce the faith of the fathers, is the ultimate sin, just as excommunication is the ultimate punishment. It is one of the three sins that not even mortal peril can excuse. It is a social as well as a religious offense, since withdrawal is always felt as a hostile act.

When people die they remain part of the community, which includes the world to come. The dead are invoked for aid in times of distress, remembered in times of joy. A bride goes to the grave of her dead relatives to beg their presence at her wedding. When a person leaves the faith, however, he is pronounced dead forever. Funeral rites are held for him, his relatives solemnize a ritual mourning for his loss for an hour—a token ceremony. After that, mention of him or of his name is banned.

The most frequent reason for formally leaving the faith is marriage with someone who is not Jewish. To drift away from complete orthodoxy is of course very different from actually embracing another religion. To have one's child marry a goy means shame as well as pain and grief. One cannot "show one's face to people." Something must be wrong with parents to whom this happens, they have failed to make their children into "real Jews," God is punishing them. The person who sins is committing a crime against his parents, his community and his God.

Every possible pressure is brought to avert such a catastrophe. Rabbi, friends, relatives exhort the renegade to reconsider before it is too late. If all fails, the convert, the *meshumed,* is dead to the group. Yet nothing is final, no relationship is irrevocably broken. He can always repent and return. If he does not, then his children may—and sometimes do. Even if they do not, they will still be somehow vaguely regarded as Jewish. A "real Jew" is known by his "Jewish heart," his "Jewish head," his scrupulous fulfillment of all the mitsvos. But there is also a saying, "a Jew always remains a Jew." If you are born of Jewish parents, if you have any Jewish blood in you, then you have some bond with Klal Isroel.

The shtetl folk feel themselves united not only by bonds of blood, belief and usage, but also by their common burden and reward. In accepting the Covenant the Jews accepted the tremendous *ol fun Yiddishkayt,* "yoke of Jewishness." The burden is the complement to the rewards of belonging to the Chosen People, celebrated in one of the most popular Hassidic songs, sung at the Tsaddik's court to the accompaniment of dancing and often quoted as an expression of pride and joy:

> Whatever else we are, we are
> But Jews we are!
> Whatever else we study, we study
> But Torah we study.

Beyond the Jewish community—the immediate community of the shtetl and the world-wide community of Klal Isroel—lie the others, those who are not Jewish, the goyim. They too are part of the divine plan, but there is always lehavdl, the difference.

Recognition of the difference carries no denial of temporal and worldly jurisdiction. On the contrary, according to talmudic principle, the law of the land where one resides is the law one must obey, except where it would require change of faith. One must fulfill zealously all the duties of a citizen. One must also pray for the welfare of the rulers who govern one's country, even if they rule harshly, for authority is given by God according to His will.

Because of differences in laws and language, customs and values, it is generally assumed that the dominant group does not fully understand "Yiddishkayt." Experience has shown, however, that they do understand money, and bribery has come to be a routine part of dealings with their official representatives. In this respect the shtetl merely accepts the prevailing pattern of Eastern Europe where the "good official" is the one who can be bribed. Jews and non-Jews alike assume that "policemen expect to be bribed."° Efforts are made to meet their expectations by the individual involved or—if he is helpless—by the community, which draws together to present a solid front against the outsider. An incident involving a boy who had lost one parent and therefore was considered an orphan, illustrates not only the expectations of the official outsider but also the coexistence of unity and conflict within the group and the assumptions about social justice.

"There was a little boy my age who lived in the shtetl. He was an orphan. . . . Just his father was dead and his mother wasn't a strong woman and she couldn't take care of him very well. They were very poor and I remember how that boy used to walk around in those cold winter nights with torn boots. So **he comes** to the market on one of these busy days and he goes over to one of the stands where a man is selling these heavy boots that we used to wear in the shtetl. They were called *shtivl*. The man has a small shack which he calls a store and he has dozens of boots hanging from the wall and over the doorway. So the orphan stole a pair of boots. All of a sudden the storekeeper rushes out of the store into the market and starts yelling 'a *ganef*, a *ganef*,' 'a thief, a thief!' And people start rushing from all sides and the policeman comes and naturally they find the orphan boy who stole the pair of shoes, and the boy doesn't deny it. They return the pair of boots and the policeman is ready to take the boy to jail.

"All the Jews stand around and the women weep and cry, 'What are we going to do, how can we let the police take away a Jewish boy. . . . And he is an orphan, what will happen to his mother? We have to do something about it,' and so on. So one fat market woman, who is selling some sort of beygl, picks up one of her dozen skirts—you know, they wore two or three skirts, one on top of the other to keep warm, and the money was kept in a pocket sewn into the last skirt so nobody should steal it. She takes out some money and offers it to the storekeeper and so on until a collection is taken up and about $2.00 is collected. The policeman puts his hand in the back and the money is slipped into his hand and he lets the boy go. This the policeman always expected. Whenever he is called in to an affair like that he knows that he will be bribed to let the 'criminal' go.

"When the policeman goes away, then the real fireworks begin. The people start yelling that if the community took care of the boy, he wouldn't have to steal a pair of shoes. But the rich people are all too busy giving money to those who don't really need it instead of taking care of the orphans and the widows. So a committee goes up to speak to the big shots in the community. And the gabai begins to apologize that he didn't know that the widow was so poor and if somebody had only told him he would have seen to it that she and her family had enough to eat and to wear. And from that incident, the boy was always decked out in good clothes, and they always had food in the house. Now, I think, that could only happen in the shtetl."°

When communication with members of the official government is necessary, the shtetl needs people who can talk with them, who know their language, their ways, their preferences, and who if possible have special channels and contacts. The need is frequent enough that there is a special term for this sort of intermediary, who is called the *shtadlan*.

The pattern of the intermediary is well developed in the shtetl. The matchmaker is the middleman for marriage. The Tsaddik is the intermediary of the Hassidim in dealing with God —unlike the rabbi, the interpreter of God's law to laymen who for the most part address Him directly. In crises, however, they call on the baal zkhus, who is in effect a heavenly shtadlan. The cantor is also a sort of intermediary, in fact he is referred to as "delegate of the group" in whose name he addresses God. When one needs assistance, one tries to send an intermediary rather than to go and appeal in person.

For official business there are two kinds of intermediary, the professional who is paid for his services and the one who intercedes as a service to the community. The one who is paid in money commands little esteem, for it is well known that his methods are shady and his profits abundant. He is the *makher,* the "fixer." The intermediary who donates his services commands honor, koved. When he operates on an impressive scale he is a shtadlan, literally "one who exerts himself" in behalf of others. To be a shtadlan on a big scale requires outstanding ability and position, and such a man's efforts greatly enhance his prestige. The local intermediary may not be referred to as a shtadlan, but his services are similar, and similarly rewarded.

To be a successful shtadlan one must understand and to some extent conform with "their" ways, so that a certain amount of "un-Jewish" behavior may be forgiven the one who exercises this office.

Both understanding and flexibility were required of a nogid who, during a wave of pogroms, was delegated to persuade the Chief of Police to have his men protect the Jewish stores in the community. The nogid, who was on friendly terms with the officer, invited him to dinner in a private dining room of the local café. Although normally strict in his observance of the dietary laws, on this occasion he did not hesitate to eat nonkosher food, since the lives and livelihood of many were at stake.

After a full and merry meal the subject was broached, and as delicately as possible the nogid offered a bribe for protecting Jewish property from violence—that is, for performance of normal police duties. The officer regretfully explained that this time he could do nothing—he had "orders from the top." The nogid did not argue but, embracing his guest, flung him gently upon a couch that was next to the table and forced the money into his pocket.

No more was said on the subject. The meal over, farewells were casual and cordial. Next day a cordon of police surrounded the Jewish stores and homes, and throughout the duration of that particular pogrom they were safe.

In selecting a representative for matters of moment to the community it is important to choose a man who will command respect and recognition. When a delegate is sent out to raise funds, it is always an honored individual, one whom it would be hard to refuse. He is invited in, asked to sit down, given a glass of tea, and treated with deferential hospitality. "To such a man it is difficult to say no."°

If the community wants to plead for mercy against a formidable edict or to beg the leader of a bloody gang to stop a pogrom, the rabbi or one of the most illustrious of the sheyneh layt will be selected. The obligation of their status demands that they seize this dangerous opportunity to serve. In the days of pogroms in the Ukraine, when "Jewish blood was flowing in the streets,"° rabbis, negidim, learned men, had no right to stay at home hiding in cellars or attics when people called for their services. "They would walk right into the lion's den,"° saying their prayers on the way, accepting with resignation the jeers of drunken peasants. They would offer ransom for the shtetl, would bargain for the life of their community, and often would be killed on the spot. To do this was part of the ol and part of the honor of being a "real Jew."

When the weak appeal to the strong, the appeal is to mercy rather than to justice. Claims on justice are reserved for one's peers, or else for those who are assumed to be reasonable. One would say to the rabbi, "where is the justice?" but not to a government official from whom one has no right to expect it. In addressing such a man one begs for mercy, and to ask with tears and outcries is part of the pattern.

God is all powerful, but He is also a reasonable being, therefore one may ask Him both for mercy and for justice. Those two attributes, *rakhmones* and *yoysher*, are the two aspects of God which the Chosen People regularly invoke. One asks Him in justice to fulfill His promises under the Covenant, and one begs Him in mercy to forgive the transgressions of imperfect mortals.

The worshiper in the shtetl appeals to divine compassion because he is convinced that the trials visited upon him represent just punishment for some transgression, and only by invoking God's pity may he expect relief. Admitting that he deserves what is inflicted upon him, he asks for pardon. This appeal to the compassion of God is expressed, for example, in the daily prayers:

With abounding love hast Thou loved us, Oh Lord, our God, with great and exceeding pity hast Thou pitied us. Oh our Father, our King, for our fathers' sake, who trusted in Thee, and whom Thou didst teach the statutes of Life, be also gracious unto us and teach us. Oh our Father, merciful Father, ever compassionate, have mercy upon us. . . . Oh Thou who art merciful and gracious, I have sinned before Thee. Oh Lord, full of mercy, have mercy upon me and receive my supplications.

In order to be pardoned by God, however, one must repent. Hence the emphasis on *tshuva,* remorse or repentance. Every day in his prayers, and especially on Yom Kippur, the Day of Atonement, the Jew repents of conscious or unconscious failures to fulfill the pact. Not only may one have sinned without realizing it; in addition, since each is responsible for the errors of all, it is right to confess and repent the evil that other Jews have done. The "Confession of Sins" on the Day of Atonement contains about fifty specified sins for which each member of the community implores God's pardon. It is a routine confession recited with tears and moans by all members of the community, men, women, and children.

There are times, however, when the punishment seems to exceed the magnitude of the sin, and then the Jew will appeal to the justice of God. The Torah itself furnishes examples of such an appeal, occasionally even a kind of challenge to God's justice. The patriarch Abraham, pleading for the inhabitants of Sodom, cries out: "Shall not the Judge of all the earth do justly?"

According to a traditional Hassidic song, the great Rabbi Levi-Yitschok of Berditchev went so far as to start a "law suit" against the Almighty:

Good morning to You, Lord of the Universe!
I, Levi-Yitschok, son of Sarah, of Berditchev,
Have come to You in a law-suit
On behalf of Your people Israel.
What have You against Your people Israel?
And why do You oppress Your people Israel?

. . . . .

And I, Levi-Yitschok, son of Sarah, of Berditchev, say:
. . . I will not stir from here!
An end there must be to this—it must all stop!

Rabbi Levi-Yitschok based his appeal on his right to question God's justice—the right implied by a pact in which God and Israel are the contracting parties, each with duties and privileges. There is implied also a belief that God is a responsible, reasoning power with whom you can argue—provided you have lived up to your side of the bargain.

This faith in ultimate justice triumphs over temporal tests, holding that always in the long run there will be retribution for evil and reward for virtue. After centuries of suffering, permitted by the Almighty because of their sins, the Chosen People will reach the Promised Land. Whoever has abused them, it is pointed out, has enjoyed immediate gain and ultimate ruin. Cases are cited: Babylon, Greece, Rome, the Russian Czars, Poland. All enjoyed their moment of triumph and now all are gone.

III

"NO BREAD, NO TORAH"

In order to obey the commandments to the full, one must have the means to live. There can be no study, no donations, no "social justice," no zestful celebration of Sabbath and holidays, no proper rearing of children and setting them up to produce families of their own, unless one can meet the cost, no matter how modest the scale. In short, "if no bread, then no Torah."

The familiar saying does not imply that the good things of this world are valued only as tools for forging the future life. They are recognized as good in themselves, and to enjoy them is both a right and a duty. A common toast is "gezunt un parnosseh," health and livelihood. The joy of Sabbath, which all are commanded to relish, includes good clothes and good food as well as prayers and rest from labor. The Covenant promises not only happiness in the world after life, but also Olam Hazeh, this world. It grants to the Jews the right to ask God for gezunt un parnosseh, and to expect these blessings, provided they do their part.

Their part includes not only fulfillment of the mitsvos, but also a prodigious amount of effort. One does not expect the Almighty to snare his gezunt un parnosseh for him, but merely to aid by smiling on his efforts to help himself. "Work, and God will help." In this respect, God is regarded as every man's business partner. Economic failure is human failure, but no success is possible without divine collaboration. Therefore one owes his profits partly to God—and a hope of continued prosperity, as well as gratitude, suggests the wisdom of paying that debt by generous contributions to the charitable activities that are God's business.

Approved rabbinical practices demonstrate again and again that, from the strictly religious point of view, worldly gain is good and worldly loss is bad. It is correct for the rabbi to adjust the Law to the pocketbook of the person who asks if a chicken is kosher, it is proper for the fictitious Passover sale of the merchant's stock to be concluded in the presence of the rabbi, it is proper for the Hassid to consult his Rebbeh about his business deals and on occasion to court good fortune by taking the Rebbeh into partnership.

The pursuit of parnosseh is a never-ending marathon, engaged in by the majority of shtetl folk, regardless of age or sex. Only the very young, the very old and the very learned are excluded, and some of them also make a contribution. There is no leisure class in the shtetl, except for babies in arms.

Idleness is a sin and the loafer is scornfully dubbed "one who goes empty." A child who is not busy about something will be told sharply, "don't sit with empty hands!" If he is allowed to loaf he will grow up into a ne'er do well, a *batln,* and such a one is a disgrace to himself and his family. A good employer, mindful of the evils of idleness will keep his workers busy even in slack season. If there is nothing else to do, they can rearrange the goods in the store. The Shulkhan Arukh itself warns against lying in bed after one wakens in the morning, for rest should come only after hard work. It is against the background of constant effort that the peace of Sabbath takes on full flavor.

Even the wife of the nogid often helps her husband in his store. If not, she is busy with her household and her good deeds. Children help their parents at home or at work, except for the kheyder boys who toil long hours over their books. If the man is a scholar, the major burden of support falls on the woman. "As most of the men depended on the woman to make a living, my mother had to work."°

To be a scholar is, of course, no life of leisure. On the contrary, study is the noblest work of all, known as "work for the Creator." It requires the utmost in industry and zeal, from dawn to far past midnight. The scholar also may lend his hand at parnosseh on occasion, although a full-time student is traditionally inept at it. Sometimes he watches the store while his wife goes to market, looking up from his book to serve a customer—and probably selling the best quality pepper at the lowest price, for which she will "give him a black year" when she returns. "My breadwinner," she will call him sarcastically, a wifely term used only when it is contrary to fact. But, although she scolds, "she is proud of his learning."°

If the man is not a student, the load falls equally on both, since economic responsibility is a matter of family membership rather than of sex. "My mother worked all day in the store, and my father worked with her just as hard in the store. When we were children we used to help in the store, too."°

Children as well as grownups are likely to be pressed into service, especially before holidays. The very smallest does his part. "I used to pour out drinks and collect money (in our inn). I remember that I couldn't even reach the counter at that time."° Joint enterprise is considered more the rule than the exception. "Zalmen and Zalmekheh ran a bakery; they and their four children all worked together in the bakery. They were all so fat, all six of them!"°

The family enterprise is often carried on in the home, and frequently the "shop" is part of the main room in which the family live. Here food will be cooking, children crying, and an artisan carrying on his work in the corner. Sometimes a skilled workman will rent part of such a room for his business quarters, if his own house is too small. That a "store" can be conducted in one corner of a cramped living room suggests the scale of business enterprise in the shtetl. An outdoor stall is also a "store," and so is a portable bin with the total inventory of the month jumbled in a sort of magnified wheelbarrow.

Waking hours are working hours, except for Sabbath and holidays. There is no official work day. One toils early and late, squeezing in extra time whenever possible. If you work for someone else, "you stopped when your boss told you to quit" or "when the head worker stopped."° Disputes about wages or hours are taken to the rabbi or to selected mediators from the sheyneh yidn.

Neither time, space nor weather interferes with the pursuit of parnosseh. You go long distances through the storm to earn a penny. You freeze in winter and bake in summer in order to "have for the Sabbath" and to live as befits a "mentsh." And you will do anything that is not directly forbidden, no matter how difficult, how strenuous, how unfamiliar.

You try anything, but that anything must be within the area available. The limitations on means of earning a livelihood have been imposed from without, by the long series of government edicts dating back to the Middle Ages. Differing at different times and places, sometimes strenuously enforced, sometimes temporarily disregarded, their joint effect has been to prohibit the Jews of Eastern Europe from owning and operating the sources of raw materials, from free travel and from residence in large cities or on the land. The consequence of the prohibitions and restrictions has been that in basic production and in consumption their economic activity has been disproportionately low, while in distribution it has been disproportionately large. Above all, they have served as middlemen, although by no means as exclusively as is sometimes assumed.

The conditions and restrictions of the shtetl have made it possible for Jews to engage in the buying and selling of goods and services, and also in the conversion of raw materials into finished articles. Large manufacture is restricted to the urban centers, but many small towns are noted for one special item which may be produced in a small local factory, or may be made at home as piecework. There is room also for a vast number of artisans, skilled workmen, and unskilled laborers.

The great majority of the Eastern European Jews engage in commerce, trade, or skilled work. The familiar middleman mechanisms characterize the operations of the countless dealers in foodstuffs and other commodities, who earn their livelihood by moving rather than by making their merchandise. On a large scale such a dealer may be a nogid, buying and selling impressive quantities of important wares—dry goods, hardware, grain, logs. On a small scale, he may be a lowly "commissionaire," who discovers what some person has to sell, bestirs himself to find a customer, and collects a modest commission. In this occupation the sale itself may be the manufactured product, and into it go the enterprise, invention and energy that under different circumstances might produce more tangible results.

The sheyneh layt pride themselves on not working with their

hands. They are the merchants, the dealers, the large storekeepers. But the vast majority of the shtetl population either sell on a very small scale or else engage in skilled trades or in strenuous unskilled labor. In some areas the Jews have been almost the only ones to engage in certain trades, such as that of tailor or cobbler. The shtetl "shoemaker" is more likely to repair than to create. He is a master of rehabilitation, and can graft old leggings onto used shoes to produce a serviceable, if not a handsome, pair of boots. His is almost a seasonal occupation, like the tailor's, for in summer the peasants who account for a large part of his trade go barefoot.

In some places the blacksmith's art was considered Jewish at one time. It is interesting, too, that "the people of books" were regarded as especially adept at logging. Many of the pitch dealers who burned the pine stumps to extract liquid tar were also Jews, although some of them merely bought the finished product and peddled it to the peasants for their carts. In some large cities of Poland and the Ukraine, for a long time the teamsters and porters were almost exclusively Jewish. If you wanted someone to haul a heavy load, the badge of that office was not only a strap around the waist but also the earlocks and the fringed garment of the pious Jew. For, although many laborers modified their apparel in the interests of efficiency, many kept the key features of a "Jewish" appearance combined with the heavy boots of the workman; and some retained the traditional garb intact. Even blacksmiths, loggers, and the occasional farm worker might go to work wearing the solemn urban black caftan and hat.

In the shtetl there is less need of porters than in the city, but the coachman or driver, the *balegoleh,* is a well-known and indispensable figure. Using a carriage or a wagon in summer and a sleigh in winter, he takes people from one shtetl to the next. Another important unskilled laborer of the shtetl is the water carrier, who delivers drinking water from the town pump or well. If he boasts a horse, the water is drawn in a huge cask on four wheels. Otherwise he carries it in pails, either on a shoulder pole or by hand, to those who have pennies for payment. The others must fetch it themselves.

Before the turn of the century, Jewish inns and taverns were important as a social center for Gentiles and as a place where traveling Jews could get kosher food. During the twentieth century they became rare, partly because of edicts forbidding Jews to sell liquor, partly through the change in transportation methods from horse-driven vehicles to railroads and motor cars. The old figure of the Jewish innkeeper no longer existed as an actuality.

Comparatively few Jews have engaged in agriculture directly since, with a few exceptions, they have not been allowed to own farmland in Eastern Europe. There have been evasions, like buying land in the name of another, and legitimate cases of ownership as a special privilege after military service. Sometimes, too, a farm may be rented and worked, either by the lessee or by hired hands. Because there is so little money, competition is extremely keen, in agricultural as in all other products. In a region where most people go hungry at least part of the time, there is overproduction in terms of what they can buy and underproduction in terms of what they need.

The farmer grows attached to his fields and his calling, yet the shtetl holds that "even when he turns farmer, a Jew is not a peasant."° To the "real" peasant he appears a transplanted urbanite even after three generations on the farm. He is still oriented toward the town and the synagogue, going to the shtetl for the great holidays. In education, he appears benighted to his fellow worshipers, although far from the unlettered state of the peasants. Sometimes, individually or with a neighbor, he brings a melamed or a kheyder boy to the farm for a short time, so that the children can learn at least to read their prayers. He scrupulously adheres to the religious observances, "selling" his crop during the Passover period as the city merchant "sells" his stock. When work calls him out before sunrise, he says his morning prayers in the fields, carefully folding his prayer shawl and laying his phylacteries in their case before he begins to plough. On the Sabbath, his horse and cow enjoy complete rest, as befits good Jewish animals, unlike the peasant's horse who has to work for his master's Sabbath holiday—perhaps taking him for a Sunday canter to visit his friends. Peasants respect the religious observances of their Jewish neighbors, however, just as the Jew respects the devout pause for the Angelus.

Jews participate in agriculture more frequently as middle-men than as producers. It is common to "rent" an orchard in bloom, making a down payment or paying in full, and counting on God to grant a rich crop. The orchard has to be guarded night and day, at first from birds, and later from human night-raiders, equally intent on robbing the trees. The renter of the orchard arranges to have a member of his family there at all times, and it is not uncommon to see a learned scholar in fringed garment and skullcap studying among the trees, breaking off to chase the birds away and then returning to mingle with their chirping the melody of his reading-chant. If a man rents several orchards, he will employ guards to protect them—artisans like the tailor or shoemaker who have almost no work in summer, or kheyder boys who use their "between-terms" to earn a "little bit of cash."

Since money is scarce, few men have enough to engage in such enterprises by themselves, so that partnerships are frequent and often the operation is undertaken on borrowed funds. If neither drought nor blight nor thieves prevent, the crop will be sold to a dealer, who in turn sells to the retailer. There is always the danger, however, that a poor crop will wipe out both payment and profit. Characteristically, this type of speculation on the fruit market imports into the orchard—along with the prayer shawl and the skullcap—the methods of the city. It suggests, as do many local business activities, the extent to which restrictions on ownership and occupation have served to impose on the shtetl the features of large-scale urban enterprise, reduced to miniature and almost to caricature.

Since the restrictions have been on the ownership of agricultural land and not of cattle, they have not prevented Jews from producing as well as selling dairy products, and the Jewish milkman is very much a part of the shtetl scene. Dairymen who are prosperous enough have their own cows. Many others buy milk from a farm or estate and deliver it directly to their customers in the shtetl. Few milkmen own a horse and usually the pails are carried on a shoulder pole, sometimes a number of miles, for early morning delivery. If, in the haste and the summer heat, the pole rubs the skin off the milkman's arms and shoulders, he carries the pails in his hands, trusting that by the time the hands are worn raw the shoulders will have healed.

One group who live off the land are conspicuous by their absence, namely the hunters. The feeling against violent shedding of blood supplements the prohibition against eating meat that has not been killed in the prescribed way. Fishing is another matter, for fish do not belong to the "meat" category and therefore need not be killed by the ritual slaughterer. Moreover, fish is an important part of the diet, especially for Sabbath and festive occasions. A fisherman can lease the rights to a lake or stream from a non-Jewish landowner, and try to recover the costs by "lifting the price up to the sky." He may sell directly to the consumer or else to a fishmonger who will take the fish to market, often traveling all night because the merchandise is "the kind that won't wait." Desperate in his need to collect the cost as well as to make a profit, the fisherman sometimes flies into a rage at an unco-operative lake and curses it, "you should get killed!" or "you should burn!"

Whatever one's occupation and no matter how humble it is, it is endowed with importance. Even if a man's "store" is just a cartful of wares to peddle, he calls it a "business," a *gesheft*. Just as children are warned to be quiet because "the father looks in a book," so they are hushed with the exclamation, "the father talks about business, be still!"

One prays daily, and many times a day, for gezunt un parnosseh, and every day one prays to be spared from being forced into a "shameful" parnosseh. The shameful occupation is not necessarily wicked, but may be merely humiliating. On the other hand, the "beautiful" parnosseh is the one that brings a good income, even if it means long hours and hard work. The "light" one is the easy one, and is appreciated, but not prayed for. Each person longs for a parnosseh that stands high in the status scale, one that can be called "honorable," "fine," "noble," as well as beautiful. Each hopes that need will never plunge him into an occupation popularly rated "ugly" or "low." The great variety of terms commonly applied to parnosseh is in itself significant of the importance given to earning a living, both by the economic facts of life in the shtetl and by the values and attitudes that permeate every area of that life.

The elaborate rank order of occupations is, as has been seen, a secondary rather than a primary factor in determining social position. The position of the occupation itself is determined by the extent to which it fulfills the requirements of yikhus and respectability. The position of the individual who is engaged in that occupation is dependent on additional factors. Nevertheless, the ranking of occupations is carried to a fine point.

It is better to work for oneself than for someone else, and this is one reason why independent merchants and businessmen are considered fortunate. Everyone tries "to be his own boss" even if he pays for his independence with smaller profits and less security. It is a matter of profound preference as well as of status.

Storekeepers are graded according to the commodities they offer. "The grocery stores in our shtetl were in the hands of the Jews of mixed types. There were 'well-to-do,' 'not so well-to-do,' 'learned men,' 'common men.' The woolen stores belonged mainly to well-learned men. They were people who wore the traditional dress, had long earlocks and were very pious. They were usually those with yikhus."°

It is better, too, to be a salesman than to be an artisan. A salesman works with his brain, an artisan merely with his brawn. The shtetl folk feel that "head," *kop*—and especially *"yiddisher kop"*—is the chief capital in any enterprise, and sometimes the only one. Yiddisher kop is identified with *seykhel*, "brains" or "good sense." Every human being has seykhel but "yiddisher seykhel" is of a special kind and quality. It is characterized by rapidity of orientation and grasping of a problem, intuitive perception, and swift application to the situation.

Even a manual worker claims that his muscles are directed by head work. A good blacksmith handles the iron with kop, head, and scoffs at the Gentile blacksmith—who heartily returns his pitying shrug, feeling that Jewish hands could never match his own mastery of the forge. A good shoemaker beams on his product and declares, "a beautiful piece of work." Artisans are constantly pointing out the intellectual demands of their labor.

"You must put some head into it," they say. The apprentice will be instructed, "use your hands and work with your head," in figuring out the leather for the shoes, the wood for the house. Skilled workers look down upon the plain physical labor of teamster or porter, whose occupation requires "no kop." But no work is considered "headless" by the one who does it, as a little boy discovered when he questioned a grimy porter about how he could handle such enormous loads. The old man solemnly wagged his beard. "You see, you have to put some head into it."° A man who has no head, even for physical labor, is a *shlemil,* and for him there is only scorn.

The manual trades are prost but nevertheless respectable, even though a family of "big yikhus" would frown on alliance with a tradesman. A few callings, however, are definitely "low." "One of my cousins married a gravedigger; her family never visited her after that." Professional actors and musicians are considered "not kosher," not "real" Jews. An amateur who sings beautifully, however, or who plays very well on the right kind of instrument, is greatly admired. Stringed instruments are approved, percussion and loud wind instruments are not. The amateur of the shtetl will cultivate a fiddle, but not a drum or horn.

The cantor is not regarded as a musician, since he is a vocalist and his art is devoted to the service of the synagogue. As one of the "Holy Tools," he occupies a position of status. His duties require that he be at least moderately well versed in sacred lore. Nevertheless, there is a popular assumption that the cantor is likely to be a stupid man whose social standing is a result of his official role rather than of his individual gifts.

Those of the Holy Tools who are paid occupy a very special place, since they are both religious officers and community employees. The rabbi is, of course, in a unique position, since he is not supposed to receive direct remuneration for his rabbinical services and nevertheless must be supported. His support is a problem solved in devious ways. It is not incompatible with his dignity to be given a house, and this is often done. In addition it is common for him—or better, his wife—to be given a monopoly on the sale of candles, yeast and oil. Many rabbis are punctilious in avoidance of using the Torah as "an axe." There is a story about one who made his wife close her little shop each week as soon as a basic minimum had been taken in, so that people would not flock to buy there for his sake and take away parnosseh from other shopkeepers. Such attitudes are by no means universal, and at times the Rov himself takes steps to insure sustenance. In one case this was done with the co-operation of the ritual slaughterer. "We did have a Rov but he used to starve from hunger. . . . Finally he went to the chief Hassidic Rebbeh in another town and complained that he was starving from hunger and what should he do? So they decided that the rabbi should get half of the pay from what the shokhet earns. That, of course, means that the shokhet has to raise the price. If not, the rabbi would declare all the meat to be treyf. The shokhet was a nice man and was willing to co-operate. So, when the Rov declared his meat treyf he refused to sell it to any Jew. They couldn't buy meat in another place because it must be used soon after it is made kosher. Finally the people paid the higher price and the Rov no longer starved from hunger."°

Quite aside from such special arrangements, the shokhet—who stands high among the Holy Tools—works closely with the rabbi. His tools and his work are constantly supervised by the rabbi, who is empowered to revoke his license at any time they are below standard. In order to be ritually fit for use, or kosher, meat must be from an animal that has been killed with a perfectly smooth and sharp blade. Otherwise the animal suffers, and to inflict unnecessary suffering is a sin. For the same reason, the animal must be killed with a steady hand, and often the rabbi comes to inspect the operation and make sure that the shokhet's hand does not shake. The shokhet, then, highly skilled and usually learned, ranks as a meat surgeon rather than as a slaughterer.

The butcher, far lower in the social scale, buys the animal from a peasant and takes it to the shokhet who kills it in the approved manner. Then the butcher separates the parts that are kosher from those that are forbidden, which he sells to the peasants.

The scribe, or *soyfer,* although not quite a Holy Tool is close to them in yikhus and in function, for it is he who copies out the scrolls of the Torah. Every Jew is supposed to write a Torah in his lifetime, but very few could do so or would dare to try. Therefore, those who can afford it have the scribe do it for them and write the last word themselves, under his supervision. Since most people cannot afford a whole Torah, a congregation or association will sometimes take up a collection to present one jointly. Some individuals save penny by penny for years, in order to have the joy and honor of presenting a Torah to the synagogue. Now and then a scroll is presented in fulfillment of a vow, or in honor of some glad event.

The scribe's profession is exacting as well as sacred. He must always go to the mikva to purify himself before beginning to write. Returning, he puts on his praying shawl and pronounces a blessing before actually sitting down to work. He must also say a blessing each time he writes the name of God. The copy must be flawless, for it is against the Law to change a single word or mark in the Torah. Each letter of each word must be perfect. Even the traditional mistakes handed down through the centuries must be preserved intact. Moreover, the cantillation must also be perfectly reproduced. Other books are read with the traditional chant, but in the Torah each note is indicated so that there will be no danger of a mistake. There are about thirty-five different accent marks to indicate the tone, and each syllable carries such a notation.

If the scribe makes any error, the whole page of parchment must be cut out of the scroll, but it must not be thrown away for it is holy. There is a special place in the synagogue where such pages are kept, but an accomplished scribe prides himself on not increasing the collection. His pride of workmanship is an important part of his compensation for, although a great deal is paid to have the Torah copied, the work is slow and painstaking, and the parchment is expensive. Often a soyfer will teach his art to his son or to an apprentice, and this is one of the rare instances in which an apprentice would spend more time at learning his skill than in running errands or tending babies.

Domestic service is an occupation definitely disliked. There are in any case few real servants in the shtetl, since most people cannot afford such help. Nevertheless, a woman who spends most of her day "running after parnosseh" often needs at least part-time help, and may call in a peasant girl or a Jewish woman. An unmarried Jewish girl would not enter domestic service if she can avoid it. "A Jewish girl would rather work as a modiste. A maid would be an orphan whose father had remarried someone else. But even then, another relative would rather take her in."° She might go to "help out" in the home of a rich relative, but not as a paid servant. "For a Jewish girl to become a maid—there's a tragic story behind it."° If she were forced into domestic service she would probably go to the city rather than remain in the shtetl, where girls who work prefer some occupation like sewing at home or in a factory.

A married woman can more easily go out to work in a household by the day. If she is a widow or her husband is out of work, she can spend some days at the home of the nogid. Perhaps she will take one or two of her children with her, so that they may eat the leftovers from the nogid's table. Or else she will eat only part of what is given to her, taking the rest home to her family—in addition to the tidbits offered by the housewife as part of her daily good deeds.

The "moyd" in the Jewish household is likely to be scolded, nagged, and ordered about just like a member of the family. But she also is helped like one of the family, in such matters as finding a dowry and even a husband, and arranging a wedding in the style appropriate to her station.

The very small professional group is hardly represented in the shtetl, but belongs to the large town or city. A doctor or lawyer who comes back to visit his family and friends is treated with great deference. True, he has left the sacred studies to seek a university diploma, but any diploma is proof of scholarship and therefore to be respected. The professionals include fewer doctors than lawyers, since it is so difficult for a Jew to obtain a medical education. The professional category includes also anyone who can boast a diploma as certificate of special education and training. Nurses, veterinarians, even pharmacists are "professionals" in the shtetl, and are accordingly endowed with an impressive yikhus.

The shtetl itself never holds enough parnosseh for all, and

many have to travel in search of it. Going to and from fairs is hardly considered as traveling—one does that as a matter of course, the way urbanites go to the shopping center of town, to buy or to sell. Each town has its special market day, and to get to those within reach is part of business enterprise. The peddler, however, moves from one village to the next. Often a tailor, a blacksmith, a cobbler, go from place to place in search of trade. Such a traveling workman may settle down to finish an order, or to satisfy all the local demands, before he moves on to the next place.

The traveling store is a familiar institution. Its motley wares —dry goods, notions and foodstuffs—are jumbled in a push cart or in a wagon drawn by a scrawny horse. He is not a riding horse, but one who drags heavy loads through deep mud or dust, and over stony hills. He walks with the slow, disconsolate tread of one who never stops and never arrives. For all his jaded appearance, however, the Jewish horse is a companion and business partner, listening to the discourse of his master through long, plodding hours, and gently nodding his head as they move along. It is natural to return such devotion with affection and good care, although a Jew does not go to the lengths of the Polish peasant in showering more tenderness on his beast than on his family. This would be contrary to shtetl doctrine which counsels "beware a man who is good to his horse and beats his wife."

Some small dealers go out with empty wagons and buy hides, bristles, wool, grain, potatoes. "They sold cotton, needles, soap, candy, kerchiefs, dried fish, herring, etc. They would travel over the villages and sell them to the peasants. In exchange they bought hide, bristles, wool, corn and potatoes. There were two kinds of traveling stores, one who used to sell these articles and another who would go out with an empty wagon and only bought. Then they would sell the stuff they bought to the merchants in the shtetl. Hides and bristles were important industries in our shtetl."° Sometimes a kheyder boy takes a job as a helper to a traveling storekeeper during the summer "between terms," helping him with the horse and guarding the merchandise while the owner goes inside to conclude a bargain.

These travelers, like all others, try to plan their journey so that they can reach home by Sabbath. "We would go away for a week and return on Friday night. And if we did a good business, we came home earlier in the week."° If they fail to reach home in time, they will be well-treated guests in some shtetl, but for them and for their families it will be a "disturbed Sabbath."

The return home is especially welcome for those who travel among people who do not keep the dietary laws. "Usually the peasants would serve you a meal. The food wasn't too good and we could only eat dairy there. They used wooden dishes and cutlery and we would sit around their long table together with them."

It is customary to take one's own kosher milk pot and utensils if possible. But the need to depend on peasant hospitality and at the same time to subject it to the strain of constant testing for ritual purity sets up diplomatic prerequisites for the traveling trades.

The quarters one finds along the way conform to standards not of the shtetl and therefore appear below standard—as it may be suspected, the shtetl houses appear to the rustic population nearby. The shtetl may find that "the peasants were overcrowded. They had small houses and large families. They were kind of primitive. They all slept together and there was no shame about it. We used to sleep outside in the stable where they kept the hay and horses."° A corresponding description of the shtetl by a peasant might not sound much more glamorous. Economically and otherwise, each group sees the other as underprivileged and at the same time as enjoying unfair advantages due to their nature or position.

There are middlewomen as well as middlemen, and many women are peddlers or traveling venders. A woman as well as a man might go about, evaluating the orchards in blossom, buying the green fruit on the bough, and later selling it to dealers who in turn would sell it to a retailer. The woman would be likely to operate on a smaller scale and within a smaller radius than a man. Women are less apt to go away for extended periods, since the home requires their presence. They would seldom stay away more than a night or two. They are more likely also to stop with relatives than to seek hospitality from an unknown source—and "why wouldn't a woman find a relative in a nearby shtetl?"°

On the whole, there is singularly little fear of traveling alone beyond the limits of the shtetl. The men seldom evince anxiety about theft or assault, but assume that all will be well with them. The violence of the outsiders is unpredictable, but generally it is expected to be limited to periods of bloodshed and riot. During those periods one cowers at home. For the rest of the time, one moves about without evincing any special misgiving.

In addition to those whose work requires travel, there are those who work away from home in city factories, or who teach or attend school in another town. They may also be salesmen or clerks, but seldom in government jobs since Jews have generally been excluded from such employment.

Some of the city workers return regularly for Sabbath, or at least for the holidays in spring and in autumn. Others gradually drift away from the shtetl. Even those who return for the most part belong less to the shtetl proper than to the group that shuttles between two cultures. These are the ones who break away from the traditional artisan guilds, who join the labor organizations, who deal with their problems through unions and strikes rather than taking them to the rabbi. They bring in ideas strange to the shtetl, eat forbidden food, dress differently, and prefer secular pamphlets to the holy books. They have lost their veneration for Hebrew and accept Yiddish as the correct language even for books.

The urbanized workers have been among the chief carriers of change to the shtetl, especially at the turn of the century. At the same time they have imported into their city unions some of the shtetl patterns of group responsibility and aid.

In order to make a living one tries his hand at anything and often at a number of things. So few are able to support themselves by a single occupation that it is common for a person to have several, which he carries on simultaneously or successively. The carpenter may also be a coachman, and on the side he may assist the blacksmith during busy times. In summer the cobbler hires out as watchman to an orchard. "My father was a plasterer by trade, but that was no way to make an entire living, so he dealt in flax, too. The flax would be bought as is from the peasants and then my father and our whole family would prepare it for selling to the city merchants. And in the summer my father built small wooden houses for the peasants. . . . There were four other children of my mother's and seven by my father's first wife, though they were not all there when I was a child. I remember it was very crowded, though, and when we were all at work preparing the flax the whole house would be full of the dust from the flax and it would settle in everything."°

When all else fails a man may become a "little children's melamed," since "any Jew knows enough for that."° But the despised melamed himself often has to supplement his fees by turning to a number of trades, as did the jovial Borukh whose disposition was less typical than his economic state. "Borukh had several jobs. He was supposed to be a melamed but he never had enough children to teach. So he began fixing stoves. But he still didn't earn enough. So he made shirts for the Gentiles and finally he became a shoemaker. Yet, with all these jobs, Borukh was still a 'kaptsn in zibn poless' (poor man in seven edges). But he was always smiling and making fun of the fact that he was so poor and couldn't earn a living with all these jobs. He would say, 'God wants to be good to me and he always sends an Angel down to help me. But when he sends the Angel down to help Borukh, the melamed, Borukh is no longer a melamed, but he is fixing stoves. So the Angel can never find me. That is why I am a kaptsn.' "°

The "poor man in seven edges" blithely referred to by Borukh the melamed, means a man so poor that the hem of his caftan, instead of the customary four corners provided by the front edges and the slit in the back, is so tattered it has seven. It means further, to shtetl ears familiar with overtones that are explicit though inaudible, that each corner is weighed down with all the poverty and worries of the kaptsn. For all that, he is commonly pictured as a merry fellow, always working, never earning, and yet making a joke of his own difficulties.

There are many in the shtetl who "have no trade or profession," but few who have only one. And so the saying has grown up, "The best cobbler of all the tailors is Yankl, the baker." It is taken for granted that, no matter how many trades one follows, or how many people in the family work, the income is poor. "My grandfather worked in a factory. The whole family worked. My grandmother traded with the peasants. My mother sewed. They all worked very hard and they never made a decent living. . . ."°

Money is in coins, not in bills and profits are in pence. To say that a man has "a Yiddisheh parnosseh" means that his work is exhausting, exacting, uncertain and unprofitable. It is quite the opposite of a "beautiful parnosseh" which means work that is profitable, even though it may be hard. Even the nogid, who does have a beautiful parnosseh and is rich in comparison to his fellows, enjoys a modest standard of living. He may have a two-story frame house, but it is often dilapidated. If he owns a store it probably occupies part of the first floor. The symbols of his riches, aside from conspicuous benefactions, are chiefly food and clothing.

The nogid wears "silken" caftans, and has, besides the special one for Sabbath, another dedicated exclusively to holiday wear. His wife advertises his magnificence in the rustling folds of her black silk Sabbath dress, the gleam of her pearls, the flash of her brooches and earrings.

The plain man who works all week in order to "have for the Sabbath" is lucky if he can give his children new shoes for the "big holidays." He "starves every Monday and Thursday in order to have enough," but even so he never has enough. "We all worked but we were always missing ninety-nine cents to the dollar."°

Somehow most people manage to survive. "My parents didn't actually starve, but were always on the brim of starvation."° A melamed who took his family to a new town went to the market place and "tried to do business there. But he wasn't a business man and made hardly any money. The older kids used to do labor work . . . carry stones for new buildings and for that they would earn five kopeks. My mother used to stay with father at the market all day and they would come home with about twenty-five kopeks. The only food they had was when mother used to make a *kasha* (porridge) and everyone would eat."°

The most common diet is potatoes and herring and "sometimes they wouldn't even have herring and they'd have 'fish-herring' instead. They took potatoes and cooked them with pepper and salt and onions and that gave the flavor of a fish. Even that was too much. Some Jews were so poor that all week long they lived on bread and potatoes. Only on Friday night did they have a real meal."° And if, even on Friday night there is nothing "to make a Sabbath," then the family is really poor.

For the majority of breadwinners in the shtetl the prospects of self-sufficiency are low, and the need to "go to people" for help is an ever-present threat. Nevertheless, the pursuit of parnosseh is carried on with constant effort, constant anxiety, and constant hope. Economic stability is almost never achieved. If things go well today they may be bad tomorrow but by the same token, if the prospect is black today by tomorrow it may improve. In any case, one never stops trying. "I will worry out a parnosseh," he says, and feels that the worry—like the effort—is part of his prescribed activity.

It is often said, "The Jew is an optimist," and it is often said, "The Jew is a pessimist." Both sayings apply to the shtetl, and both characteristics relate to his conception of the Covenant. "The Jew lives on hope," is a common remark. The more rigidly he subscribes to orthodox beliefs, the stronger is his hope, *bitokhen*. "All's for the best," they say, and, "He that gave us teeth will give us bread." The optimism is conditional, however. All will work out well if one fulfills his duties to God and if he tries to help himself. There is supreme faith that God will provide, but only if man does his part. Especially, he will provide for the Sabbath. One works all week to no avail. Friday comes and there is nothing "to make a Sabbath." Again one goes out and with all the energy of despair somehow manages to earn a ruble. "God sent it to me for Sabbath!" and thanks are given to God for this manna from heaven.

If in spite of all efforts it does not come, then the question is, "How have I sinned?" But if hardship presses too far and if every effort has been made to do the right thing, then at last the question may be, "Where is the justice?"

In an economy so straitened, one lives on hope and also "one lives by miracles." As he pauses for breath in the daily round, any man of the shtetl can dream about the great stroke that will mend his fortunes. Perhaps a lottery ticket, perhaps a relative from America, perhaps a fat sale. He may sacrifice his last coin for a lottery ticket, dreaming of the big prize he is to win. Success will not come without constant effort, but neither will it come without luck, *mazl,* and one is always alert for the lucky chance. It is, of course, God who sends the luck.

The well-known *luftmentsh,* "the man of air," is the one who literally lives on hope and miracles. He has no fixed business, no regular means of support. He is a small-scale "commissionaire," darting about, seizing on almost anything, making a customer materialize almost out of thin air, selling to him almost by hypnotism, and collecting a fee that is almost invisible. Into each effort the luftmensh puts all the fervor and conviction of the artist shaping a masterpiece, although for the most part his efforts miscarry and his hopes of reward vanish into the air, his element.

Because earning a livelihood is so difficult, one of the best deeds a person can perform is to help another win parnosseh. The generous wife of a nogid will stay away from the inviting haggle of the market place and will even pay a few pence more, in order to buy from some poor woman who peddles her wares in a basket from house to house. "Let her earn a parnosseh," she will say. When she goes to buy at the market, "the women in the stalls will yell, 'Balebosteh, Balebosteh, buy something, I didn't have yet a beginning,' for the first sale is supposed to bring luck and others will follow."° If the rich woman will "buy for good luck" something she may not need, in order to "give a beginning," the women will bless her for the good deed as for any other form of charity.

Conversely, it is among the most evil of acts to prevent a person from winning parnosseh. To trespass on a place or a customer that belong to a competitor is despicable. One can be called to the rabbi and condemned formally if he violates the "established hold" of another. The hold may be a purchased monopoly, like the fisherman's, or it may be rights to the trade of a locality or an individual, accrued through long custom. "Sometimes there was a very interesting 'semilegal' arrangement—the *khazokeh.* It's a monopoly on a certain trade, although not written down, and if somebody else goes into your trade, you could go to the rabbi. You could have a khazokeh on a trade in a certain block, for instance, and no one else could practice this trade there. You would say, 'grandfather was a tailor, father was a tailor, I am a tailor.' . . ."°

Because pennies are so precious, it is unthinkable to let one slip through your fingers. You never refuse a job, even if it requires a technique you have not mastered. If you don't know how, then you learn by doing. Somehow you will "worry it out." You never say no to a customer, even if he asks for what is not in your shop. You persuade him to wait, or better still have someone hold him while you dart down the street to get a broad-brimmed hat or a larger pot or whatever it is he wishes. If he is not given what he asks for he might not come back, and that must never happen.

The storekeeper across the street, if he has what your customer wants, will lend it to you and later you will return the price. Perhaps this same storekeeper originally competed with you for the customer's trade. Perhaps he or one of his hired boys tried to buttonhole the buyer in the street and persuade him to come in. Now the customer is in your store, he belongs to you, and others will co-operate to help you keep him. It may be that the storekeeper you turn to for the hat or trousers the customer wants is your relative and therefore glad to help you. Even if he is not, he knows that tomorrow he may need a favor from you or one of your relatives. There is so much interrelationship in the shtetl, and so little stability, that cut-throat competition and mutual aid dwell side by side with no sense of incongruity.

A short-term loan without interest is extended as a matter of course if a man needs it and if his credit is good. There will be no fear of difficulty in collecting, for one who fails to keep his obligations in such a matter signs himself out of business. You never cheat those who trust and help you, and you never refuse a loan if you can give it. The guarantee of repayment is in the man's status and the informal sanctions associated with default.

In business ethics, to circumvent government regulation of selling is not regarded as lawbreaking or as wrongdoing. A man who sold tobacco without a license was regarded as a good man, even though the police were constantly raiding his shop. "In the shtetl he was considered a good man . . . because he was pious, went to shul, etc. He made a living selling raw tobacco. This was not legal unless you had a permit and he didn't have one. Whenever they were expecting a raid my aunt would have to carry all the tobacco in huge sacks to hide in our house."° Illegal selling of beygl is viewed as a respectable way for an "orphan" to help his widowed mother. When she has baked a fresh batch of the crusty, ring-shaped rolls, her six- and seven-year-old sons will take them out to hawk on the streets, packed in a basket covered with a piece of clean linen. They will sell as many as they can to anyone lucky enough to have a penny. Suddenly the alarm will be sounded in a whisper, "The 'sixer' (policeman)!" At once the children will disappear from the street; no one has seen or heard of them. Half-eaten beygl will suddenly be shoved into pockets or market bags. When the "sixer" is well out of the way the frightened boys will peek out to be reassured, and perhaps consoled by a sweet from some sympathetic passer-by. Everyone knows that if they were caught they would be beaten, and their baskets would be taken away with the beygl—of which the constabulary is very fond—and the precious linen cover. That they are guilty of selling without a license is a matter of concern to the government, but certainly not to their customers or to those who only wish they had a penny for a piping-hot roll. To flout customs regulations is considered no great sin. The government itself does not take small-scale smuggling too seriously. A lively traffic in cigarettes, matches, and liquor is carried on across the border.

Emigrants too are smuggled across, those who could not get passport and visa in order to leave openly. Far from officers and railroad stations, they are secretly shepherded "across the green border," that is the border that runs through woods and fields. During the great waves of emigration, the chief motive was economic. Some left the country to evade long-term conscriptions, some to escape pogroms, but the chief reason was the search for parnosseh. Even for those who went as a result of pogroms, the basic reason was often economic, for pogroms left stores looted and burned, and many sources of livelihood dried up. As living became more and more difficult, the dream of going to find a "beautiful" parnosseh in the United States became more prevalent and more compelling. It was a dream more inviting to the underprivileged than to the men of the Eastern Wall. The sheyneh layt would be the ones least eager to leave the shtetl where they held positions of eminence and lived a "beautiful" life. The vast majority of those who emigrated were "people of the week," especially young people for whom the economic future appeared to be a blocked road, and who saw their only solution on "the other side of the ocean."

Many contrived to bring their families after them, but many families who remained counted on assistance from the United States. During the thirties, even though there was also a depression across the sea, the shtetl could hardly have survived without help from the "new" country. Emigrants from one shtetl or from one region formed associations in the new land, and sometimes help would come from these. More often, however, it was from individuals. If you asked a man, "What's your parnosseh?" he might answer, "I'm a little bit a shammes, a little bit a matchmaker, before the holidays I sell palm branches for Sukhos, in the season I help out the tailor and besides I have a brother in the United States who sends me every month a little something."

All the circumstances and conditions that have influenced the occupational picture have played a part in shaping the attitudes of the shtetl toward money. For long centuries, its people have been forced into occupations directly connected with money transactions. During the same centuries, they have learned that cash money is the best form of riches to save during pogroms and to carry along during expulsions. They have learned too that money is the best argument in dealing with officials. With money one can buy relative freedom, exemption from secular education, from conscription. Sometimes one can buy life itself—one's own or that of one's fellows.

The leading attitude that has emerged from this background is that money is good, but only as a means to a definite end and not as an end in itself. It is accumulated in order to be spent and its worth is highest when it is in flux rather than when it is in the strong-box. The idea of saving in order to increase a savings account is foreign to the shtetl, where in any case there is no surplus for random saving. One saves in order to give a boy a better and longer education, to prepare a "nice dowry" for a daughter, to buy the children new clothes for the holidays, to spread a richer holiday feast.

Children are given money to spend, not to save. They are taught to spend rationally, however, not for "silly things," but for a purpose, for takhlis. They are taught to distribute "social justice," allowed to put the coins into the tin boxes, to hand the Friday dole to the beggars. They learn that constructive giving is a sure way to win approval.

Because it is the significance rather than the money itself that counts, one can be proud of spending a great deal or of spending very little. A man will boast, "I paid so much for my wife's coat," proving that he can afford to spend "with a broad hand," that he is devoted to his wife, and lives up to his family obligations. But he is equally pleased to announce, "I got this fine silk for so little," showing how clever he is to have bought it for less than its market price. To get a bargain is a sign of a "good head" or of good luck.

As means to an end, money is valued next to learning itself. Aside from its worth in attaining relative freedom and security, through charity one can buy social status and future happiness. Moreover, money gives power. The nogid has power through his money and though he may be the boss of the shtetl, he also can win friends in government circles, and serve his community as a shtadlan, or intermediary. The Jewish financial heroes have power through money—Rothschild, Brodsky, Baron de Hirsch. "Even the king listens to them."° They are heroes, not because of the amount they have but because of the way they spend it. "Brodsky was a millionaire . . . the richest Jew in Russia. . . . When the Russian Government closed the yeshiva, we appealed to Brodsky and he bribed the authorities to reopen it. This happened very often. Once, I recall, he was in the town and he came to say goodbye to the Head of the yeshiva. He wanted to give him money. But the Head of the yeshiva said that he had enough money to live on and besides, for teaching you don't take money. But there are poor students who need help. So Brodsky immediately gave the order that from that day on, every student should receive ten ruble a week. Can you imagine, ten ruble a week? It's a fortune— enough for a whole family to live on. Brodsky was a good person. Imagine, he gave ten ruble a week to those boys—ten ruble. A nice tsdokeh!"°

Those money heroes are popular personalities in shtetl day-dreaming. In the short hour between afternoon and evening prayer service at shul, the hungry and ragged will count and re-count the treasures of the Jewish millionaires, will discuss their financial operations, and will formulate their advice about the best way to handle all that wealth. Brodsky and Rothschild are not remote, semimythical personalities, they belong to the shtetl.

The undernourished luftmentsh, or the footsore peddler trudging along with his bony horse, knows that his chances of be-coming a Rothschild or a Brodsky are slight, and that "dumplings in a dream are not dumplings, but a dream." Nevertheless, with his traditional hopefulness, his bitokhen, he dreams about what he would do if by some miraculous luck, mazl, he would win a fortune with the eighth of a lottery ticket he bought instead of patches for his shoes. The contents of his dream in themselves point up the meaning of money for the shtetl: he would buy a seat on the Eastern Wall of the synagogue; he would build a new hospital, and get rid of Reb Khayim as President of the Talmud Toyreh association.

There is a tendency to associate possession of money with virtue, less on the theory that virtue is necessarily rewarded with riches than because the rich man is in a position to cultivate all the virtues. Since he can afford to fulfill the mitsvos in the grand manner, the expectation is that he will do so. The shtetl stereo-type of the virtuous man is not the self-denying saint, for asceticism is no virtue in the shtetl. The prototype of the good man is the nogid, richly dressed, well fed, surrounded by a family that lacks for nothing, busy with community services, and dis-pensing "social justice" with a "broad heart."

Nobody denies that a "poor man in seven edges" can be among the most virtuous of mortals, but nobody takes it for granted that he will be. The nogid is expected to be "good," at least socially, and any deviation from this expectation will arouse far more comment than will the mere fulfillment of his duty.

Money is good and money is important. Rewards and gifts take the form of money, and the most frequent punishment imposed by the rabbi is a fine—not paid to the imposing agent, but distributed as charity. Money is equated with gold, and golden is used as an adjective to describe what is best. It is the highest praise to say that a person has "a golden heart," "a golden head," or, if he is a good craftsman, "golden hands." If he has a fine character, his is "a golden soul." A guest at a party will refuse some delicacy by saying, "I couldn't eat a piece of gold now." There is no shtetl equivalent for the expression "filthy lucre," for the shtetl does not equate money with dirt.

If money is set up against the treasured culture themes, however—family, learning, identification with the religious tradition —it becomes secondary. "You can buy everything for money except father and mother and brains." Despite the great store set on money, the ideal man is the scholar who "can't tell one coin from another." Ancestor yikhus is better than money yikhus. The most desirable bridegroom is one who is learned, even though he is poor; and the woman, who is by definition ignorant and inferior, is the one who will handle money matters for the family. On Sabbath money must not be touched or even remembered, and "Torah"—which is "the best of wares"—must never be bought and sold. The ideal, of course, is to combine the two complementary elements, as in the marriage of the learned bridegroom and the well-dowered bride. In folk tales the hero is often both rich and learned, using his money to support the poor and the studious.

The importance of the money value is evident in the multitude of proverbs relating to it. Both their number and their character suggest a sense of conflict between the ideal formulation of values and the arduous reality. These proverbs and sayings are more apt to stress the power than the limitations of money. "Money is the world," is a theme more often sounded than the thought that you cannot buy brains, or that you cannot take riches to Olam Habo, "but only Torah and good deeds." Such proverbs are quoted more by the poor than by the rich, and are often tinged with bitterness at the extent to which the primary values are dependent on the secondary and are crippled by its absence. This spirit is evident in the saying that "a poor man is as if dead," or "a full purse is not so good as an empty one is bad."

The shtetl is habituated to a clash between what ought to be and what is, just as it is habituated to poverty, insecurity, and constant adaptation. Life is seen as a complex of contrasts which in the last analysis are accepted as complementary rather than as conflicting—Sabbath and the week, Jew and Gentile, the world of Torah and the power of money. Despite clash and contradiction, despite bitterness and revolt, the shtetl can agree that Torah is best but money is good—in its place. Its place is in flux and also in perspective.

The miser, who puts money before all else and wants it to hoard rather than to spend, is called by one of the shtetl's most scathing epithets. He is called a pig, with all the disgust and hatred lavished on that animal. Miserliness, in the view of the shtetl, is worse than un-Jewish, it is anti-Jewish. It blocks one of the key mechanisms for welding and conducting the community, and it denies some of the community's basic beliefs about human relations.

A Hassidic Rebbeh explained how it is that miserliness shuts a man off from his fellow men and from humanity itself: If you look through a glass window, you see all the world; but if you cover one side with silver, it becomes a mirror and you see only yourself.

Part Four

. . . Into Marriage . . .

I

MAZLTOV!

According to the Talmud, a Roman matron once asked a rabbi, "In how many days did the Holy One, blessed be He, create the Universe?"

"In six days," he answered.

"And what has He been doing since then, up to now?"

"He has been arranging marriages."

"Is that His occupation? I, too, could do it. I possess many male and female slaves, and in a very short while I can pair them together."

He said to her, "If it is a simple thing in your eyes, it is as difficult to the Holy One, blessed be He, as dividing the Red Sea."

He then took his departure.

What did she do? She summoned a thousand male slaves and a thousand female slaves, set them in rows, and announced who should marry whom. In a single night she arranged marriages for them all.

The next day they appeared before her, one with a cracked forehead, another with an eye knocked out, and another with a broken leg.

She asked them, "What is the matter with you?"

One female said, "I don't want him."

Another male said, "I don't want her."

She forthwith sent for the rabbi and said to him, "There is no god like your God, and your Torah is true. . . ."

. . . . .

The shtetl agrees that marriages are made in heaven. "Whenever a child is born, God calls out the one he is supposed to

269

marry." It is agreed also that a great deal of earthly activity is required in order to bring about the mating decreed by heaven, and that in many instances the correct combination is not achieved. As with parnosseh, the help of God must be supplemented by the efforts of man. If it becomes clear that the match is "not a *zivug*," a pair, divorce is not only possible, but comparatively easy. Nevertheless, the initial assumption is that a marriage is the happy enactment of divine will and that it is destined to endure forever, in this world and in the life to come.

A wedding is the most joyous and most elaborate festivity in shtetl life. It represents the fulfillment of the individual, who becomes fully adult only when he marries, and the basis for the perpetuation of the Jewish people, according to the commandment of God. It is the archetype of all festivity and rejoicing, the symbol of joy and completion. The Sabbath is a "bride"; an especially successful celebration is "as merry as a wedding"; one who is "called up" to read the last section of the last chapter on Simkhas Torah is a "bridegroom of the Torah," and one who reads the beginning of the first chapter, starting the new round for the year, is "bridegroom of 'in-the-beginning.'"

"Everyone" is invited to the wedding. Not to be asked when one should be is a deadly insult—and all relatives, friends, neighbors should be asked. Not to come, if one has been invited, is an equally serious offense. Old quarrels are put to sleep, if only for the occasion, so that all may celebrate together. The gayer the wedding, the more guests join in wishing well to the new couple, the better are the prospects for a happy wedded life. "*That* was a wedding. Who didn't come? Even the peasants from all around the shtetl. It lasted three weeks!"°

The actual wedding, the *khupa*, marks the climax of a long process, for traditionally the working out of divine matchmaking is not left to the whim or inspiration of the individual. On the contrary, arranged marriage is the classic pattern of the shtetl. Where external forces have weakened traditional usage, there has been revolt against that pattern. Nevertheless, the rule has survived in spite of exceptions, and some of its force remains even in new environments.

Like many traditional practices, the arranged marriage with

its attendant contract and dowry has been most prevalent among the sheyneh layt. "The religious people believed in a dowry."° Among them, the "marriage for love" was a romantic exception, to be discussed by current gossips and boasted about by one's grandchildren. "That was the man she really loved. She told me that when she first saw him, she felt like having the sun in her heart . . . that was a real romance."° Those who were considered prost, however, "were also different when it came to marriage. They married because of love."° This was a privilege of poverty. "My grandparents married for love. They could do it because they were just poor folks."°

The assumption is not that an arranged marriage is a loveless marriage, but quite the contrary. "First you marry, then you love." If two young people are appropriately mated, propinquity and joint responsibility will weld them into the perfect pair. Just as understanding and wholehearted acceptance are expected to follow the child's rote memorizing of the kheyder lessons that at first are gibberish to him, so connubial affection is expected to follow the mating arranged by dutiful parents for a boy and girl who perhaps have never seen each other. With the marriage, as with the boy's education, the facts on the whole have conformed to the expectations sufficiently to allow the persistence of both expectations and pattern.

The busy hub of the marriage negotiations is the match-maker, or *shadkhen,* a figure of considerable importance even though within the shtetl—as in the far places to which his fame has traveled—he is hero of innumerable jokes and almost no serious sagas. His little dog-eared book, in which are inscribed full particulars about all eligibles worth considering, is the social register of the shtetl.

To some extent he is a social arbiter, defining his client's status by the candidates he recommends. Surveying the prospects with his practiced eye, he will see the possibility of "a beautiful match," and ponder, "now, how to get the cat over the water." A really skillful shadkhen can "bring two walls together." Whether he modestly confines his activities to one shtetl, or is an ambitious traveler between city and town, he picks up an array of gossip and information that makes him both welcome and feared. Even families who know each other well often call upon his services for arranging a marriage, and his relationship to his preferred client "isn't just a business affair."°

Anyone in the shtetl may be an amateur shadkhen, and most are. A favorite subject for gossip, especially among women, is potential pairs. "Yossef's Senderl, now, such a bright boy, he would make a fine husband for Moyshe-the-Nogid's Gitteleh." But the shadkhen with his inevitable umbrella is the one who does what they merely talk about.

The arithmetic of matchmaking is complex and precise. Certain basic stipulations must be met before the more delicate parts of the calculations are even begun: for example, some relatives cannot marry, except in special cases to be ruled on by the rabbi; a member of the Kohanim must not marry a widow; the bride must not have the same name as the groom's mother.

These rules are met before a prospect is even discussed. Within the possibilities that remain, a balance must be worked out between the three essential variables: learning, yikhus, money. An excess of one can compensate for too little of another. The intellectual attainments of a penniless youth are expected to win him the daughter of a nogid, rich and respected, with a handsome dowry and some years of support in the home of her parents while he continues his studies—that is, of kest. If the youth has money or yikhus in addition, so much the better. "He had money and he was educated—where can you get a better combination?"°

Since the standing of the whole family is involved, the complicated rules of who-marries-whom are subject to infinite debate within the family circle and in the shtetl at large. "Naturally a family wants to buy honor for itself"° with the dowry of the bride, and will oppose any match that could diminish its yikhus. "In our family, we girls couldn't marry just anybody. I remember there was a fellow courting my sister. He came from Odessa and was a tailor. He was rich and he was good looking and he wanted to marry my eldest sister. So my mother (a widow) asked her brothers, and they said 'No.' How could she even think of marrying her first daughter to a tailor from a prosteh family? And if she married her oldest daughter to a tailor, to whom would she already marry her youngest daughter? To a musician? And my sister didn't marry the tailor. My sister finally married a third cousin of mine who was rich like Korakh. He was an educated man, too. I don't think she was very much in love with him, but they told her she should marry this man, so she did. I know she isn't sorry now, why should she be?"°

The yikhus determinant is clear in the very definition of the word by the common man—"yikhus is when a shoemaker's son doesn't marry a rabbi's daughter." Among some who come from "big yikhus" the feeling about choosing a mate on one's own social level is so strong that marriage between an aristocrat and a plebeian has been referred to as "intermarriage."° Such usage is extreme and rare, however.

The effort to work out an appropriate match has full talmudic endorsement. The holy writings point out repeatedly the evils of mesalliance. Like should be mated to like. A very tall man should not marry a very short girl; the old should not mate with the young nor the learned with the ignorant. Too much discrepancy in any respect opens the way to disharmony.

The bride's qualifications are defined chiefly by the extent to which her parents possess the three criteria of status, but in choosing a bride the money requirement may lead, depending on the combination offered by the bridegroom. If he happens to be the son of wealthy parents, he can afford to make greater demands for the learning and yikhus of his parents-in-law. The bridegroom is computed almost as if he were a disembodied intellect but the bride's personal qualifications are taken into consideration in balancing the marital account. If she is unattractive, or deformed, due allowance must be made in the dowry. There may be difficulty in marrying off such a girl, although it is generally assumed that some arrangement can be made. A large proportion of the jokes and anecdotes dealing with the professional problems of the shadkhen have to do with the half-serious implication that a handsome sum could cover almost any defect.

To the parents of several daughters, such jokes have a serious side. The girls must be married off in order, a heavy task at best, and if the eldest is difficult to dispose of, the younger ones may suffer—certainly not in silence. If the problem proves insoluble, a younger girl must secure the senior sister's permission before her betrothal can be solemnized.

From the moment a girl is born, her parents begin to ponder her *shiddukh,* her marriage arrangement. As she approaches adolescence, she is reminded to act with decorum, "You are a *kaleh-moyd* now," a bride-girl. Fond relatives, pinching her cheek, will say archly, "Soon the shadkhen will be coming." She herself may wonder anxiously if perhaps she will be a *farzesseneh,* "one who is left sitting."

The anxiety of the parents is proverbial, as is their relief when they have "given out their children in joy." A person who is in good spirits will be told, "You look as if you had married off all your children." A favorite toast is "a good match for your daughter," even if the prospective bride is only three or four years old. When finally their children are married, the parents say, "the ol, the yoke, has fallen off my shoulders!" Only then is the obligation discharged, leaving them free to enjoy the rewards of parenthood.

If the dowry is large enough, the "yoke" may be akin to pleasure. If it is small, enterprise, industry and patience are required; yet in the end it will be managed. But a girl who approaches the marriage canopy undowered is doubly unfortunate. Even if she is lucky enough to be taken "as her mother bore her," she might feel the lack for the rest of her life. "When I asked my mother why she always acted so self-effacing and humble she said, 'I came to your father without anything and I never forget it.' "° Relatives will forego immediate comforts, or even place themselves in debt for years to come, so that the bride, and they, "should not be ashamed before his family."

Even when a pair marries out of romantic and personal considerations and even among the very poor, it would not be seemly for the bride to come empty-handed: a pair of pillows, a white tablecloth, candlesticks, bedding, and tableware, are the irreducible minimum.

The contract will stipulate more than the amount of dowry and the years of kest, if any. It will also set forth, for example, the presents to be given the bridegroom—perhaps a gold watch, a silken caftan, a full set of the Talmud "printed in Vilna by Romm." For a really learned bridegroom "they would promise 'the little plate out of the sky!' "°

It is a reciprocal document, providing also for the treatment of the bride. She must be given new clothes, probably for Passover and the New Year, and other presents—a ring, earrings, a necklace or a fur coat.

In the course of negotiations, quarrels often arise, sometimes so bitter that the whole affair is broken off. Promises may be made and then withdrawn or broken. A trifle may "make the deal out." The saying goes, "Even a cat can spoil a shiddukh." Some unlucky young people are married only after several contracts have been begun and finally dropped. "She was engaged nine times and finally the tenth time she got married. It was a terrible experience to have a contract torn up so often."°

The stigma is far from fatal. Nevertheless, especially for a girl, a broken contract mists over the brightness of eligibility and is to be avoided. The family, too, is sensitive about the slight to its honor. People will ask why, is there something wrong with her physically, or with the brightness of the khossen, the bridegroom? Any irregularity in the procedure is ammunition for gossip.

The marriage negotiations are undertaken by the parents as part of their duty, and also as a way of building up the family prestige. The young people whose future is so elaborately negotiated may be hardly more than children. The late teens are the more usual marriage age, but the early teens are not uncommon. A father may tell his fourteen-year-old son, "Mazltov, you have become a khossen." A little later in the day the prospective bridegroom might be punished by his teacher, just like any other schoolboy who didn't know his lesson.

It is not taken for granted that young people would or should marry against their will. Many apparently accept—with or without inner pangs—the view that "parents always want the best for their children, and if I propose this match it is with good reason."° Those who object, however, often succeed in winning their point. Unusually strong-minded was a little girl of eleven who later, as a grandmother, told the story of her first betrothal. Her father said to her one day, "Well, my daughter, I congratulate you; you are a *kaleh,* a bride." That was all, but one summer day as she was sitting with her mother in the garden, she saw a boy coming toward them, and her mother said it was her thirteen-year-old fiance. "He was a thin boy in a very long caftan and long earlocks."° At that moment a chicken rushed out in front of the boy, who, confused and embarrassed, tripped and fell. When he got up he was covered with dirt, and "instead of cleaning himself he took a stick and went after the chicken. Oh, he was so ridiculous chasing after the chicken in his long caftan that I said to myself, 'No, he will not be my husband!' "° No persuasion availed, and in the end her parents had to break off the engagement.

Before the contract is actually drawn up, there is usually a review and inspection of the bride by the groom's female relatives and of the groom by the bride's male kin. The father and perhaps the uncles of the bride quiz the khossen to determine his knowledge of the Talmud and his adroitness in scholarly discussion. If the father is not equal to the task, he brings with him a learned teacher—"no children's melamed, but a real talmid khokhem."°

The girl, on the other hand, is scrutinized and questioned by the groom's mother and aunts. This "look," the *kuk,* usually takes place at some neutral place such as an inn, where the prospective in-laws gather by arrangement, but as if the meeting were accidental. By coincidence, the girl is usually able to produce a sample of her darning and embroidery, to be inspected by a battery of probing feminine eyes. It is commonly assumed that the groom's mother will be hard to please—"something is always wrong with the kaleh."

The mother, in fact, feels it a righteous duty to be critical. "She is after all his mother," she must make sure he will be well cared for, now he is leaving her. This girl can never give him all he needs, all he has become used to receiving. And yet, "when a boy marries he gives his bride a contract and his mother a divorce." A dutiful mother is bound to spy out all the flaws in her successor.

After enough questions have been answered to show the girl's familiarity with the running of a household and the scrupulous application of the dietary laws, she is often given a knot to untie, as a demonstration of her patience and diligence. To untie a complicated knot under the exacting eyes of one's future in-laws is a severe test of poise. That she is prepared in the sense of knowing what will come, is of doubtful help, for the tense anticipation and the preliminary barrage of questions are hardly calculated to make fingers strong, relaxed and nimble.

When agreement has finally been reached, the families and the approved witnesses—including the shadkhen and perhaps the rabbi—assemble for the "writing of the conditions." When the conditions are written, the two fathers, holding opposite corners of a handkerchief, exchange symbolic tokens. The joyful occasion is rounded off with the usual accessories to a celebration—food and drink. The final contract, to be signed at the marriage ceremony, is a standard and very elaborate form, written in Aramaic with spaces left to fill in the stipulations.

Once the contract has been drawn, the wedding date is set. There are certain times at which wedding ceremonies cannot be held and some that are especially favorable. One does not marry on the Sabbath, for example, although Friday afternoon is a most auspicious time, with the feast held on Saturday after sundown. One cannot possibly marry on Yom Kippur, The Day of Atonement, which is the most solemn and mournful of all holidays. It would be wrong to marry on a joyful holiday because mixing two joys would dilute them, and each should be savored to the full. Similarly, two brothers or sisters should not marry on the same day because, according to the Shulkhan Arukh, "one joy should not be made to interfere with another." One could not marry on a sad holiday because there can be no rejoicing when sorrow is prescribed. Neither joy nor sadness should be vitiated, although neither should be indulged in for too long a time.

A favorite nuptial day is Tuesday because when God was creating the world, at the end of the third day He said twice, "It is well." Monday, on the other hand, is unlucky, because He did not say it even once for that day.

Outside of the set limits, the marriage ceremony, the epitome of rejoicing, takes precedence over all else. Once the date has been set it is a bad omen to let anything interfere.

Correspondingly, it is a deed of good omen to help a marriage along or to play host at a wedding. The wealthier members of the community win honor and gratification by furnishing the feast for a poor relative or an orphan. "When there's going to be a wedding in the shtetl the biggest householder in town insists on being host. No matter how poor the family is, it's a great honor and a good deed."° Failing that, the nogid may insist on housing the groom, if he is from another town. "No matter how insignificant, a bridegroom gets this chance to sleep in a rich man's house."° It is because the facilitation of marriage is so blessed that one method of curing an epidemic is by arranging the marriage of two orphans with great fanfare.

The actual ceremony is the climax of long preparation and excitement. During the betrothal, which may be from several months to a year or more, the family of the girl is busy preparing her trousseau and making plans for the wedding. In many cases they also periodically entertain the groom who comes "on big holidays," sometimes bearing gifts. Theoretically this gives the young people an opportunity to become acquainted but "they are usually too bashful to become close."° The rest of the community is less inhibited and "the whole town goes on wheels each time the khossen comes."°

The week before the wedding builds up into intense activity and emotion. Quantities of food and drink must be prepared for a succession of feasts—not only enough for all present but enough so that they can take some home. It is part of the wedding hospitality to urge, "take this with you," and to wrap up choice tidbits to be sent to anyone who was unable to attend. The joy of the occasion must be spread far and wide in edible form.

For the bride, the week before her wedding may be a trying one. In some localities her hair, which will be cut after the ceremony, is dressed in tiny braids with a piece of sugar at the base of each "to assure a sweet life." By the time the cutting is done the sugar has stuck to the scalp and "she weeps for her hair and for the pain."° The custom of cutting the bride's hair is not universal but it is extremely widespread and often persists after emigration. Traditionally, from now on her hair will be cropped close and will be covered always by a wig, the sheytl, or else by a coif, cap or kerchief. The sheytl is usually made to look as much like her

own hair as possible and extremely elegant women in big cities
may import theirs from abroad, arranged in the latest style.

Whatever its fashion—and very little of that penetrates the
shtetl—the basic purpose is to keep women from being too attractive. And whoever the bride, she "weeps for her hair." She is expected to weep a great deal at this time even though it marks the
climax toward which all her life has been geared and all her training has been directed. In fact, her mother and friends advise her
to "cry herself out" in order to "make her heart lighter."

In preparation for her bridal night, she goes for the first time
to the ceremonial bath, the mikva. Here the nails of her fingers
and toes are cut very short by the attendant, who carefully gathers
the pieces and burns them, saying a prayer as she does so. If all
the pieces were not destroyed, after death one would have to
wander about trying to find them. She is then purified by being
immersed three times in the pool, above the top of her head. Each
time she emerges the attendant declares loudly that this is a
"kosher" daughter of Israel.

The order and form of observances and festivities differ from
region to region, from prosperous to poor, from orthodox to
liberal. In some form, however, the main features are always present. Like any important life event the marriage receives community recognition. The bridegroom is "called to the Torah" on
the Sabbath before the wedding and on the one following it. The
first time he is called he is honored by maftir, the reading of the
Haftorah. Both bride and groom must fast on the wedding day
"because on that day they are forgiven all their sins" and they
must not see each other until just before the ceremony. The bride
must not be left unattended for a moment, and she must be waited
on hand and foot, for on this day she is a queen and her khossen
is a king. She is surrounded from early morning by a flock of sisters, aunts, cousins and friends, as well as by the female relatives
of the groom, all of whom cluster around to help, advise, rejoice
and weep.

An indispensable figure in any large wedding is the "jester,"
the *badkhen,* who usually serves also as a master of ceremonies. He
is present with the musicians as the guests assemble, and as each

one enters there will be a fanfare, after which the name and yikhus
of the new arrival are announced in loud, impressive tones.

Throughout all the festivities the badkhen is at hand, to
move the company to laughter and also to tears. Both are conspicuous during the whole of the celebration. The bride weeps,
the parents weep, the friends and relatives weep. They are expected to do so. Tears are part of this as of many ceremonials, and
on this occasion as on others they mean many things. The badkhen
encourages the weeping by solemn words about the duties of marriage, by beautiful tributes to individuals and to sacred concepts,
by touching references to "the dear departed" who are not with us
today.

But it is also his role to dry up the shower with a sunburst of
gaiety. To be a master of his art he must command rapid transi-
tions between extremes as well as concentrated bursts of melancholy or of joy. At its highest, his performance combines the skills
of actor, poet, composer, singer, commentator. The badkhen may
merely be some local wit, drafted for the occasion. A really great
one, however, is known far and wide and is constantly in demand.
His solemn speeches sound vibrant notes of duty or of grief. His
ditties may enter into the realms of folk song. His jesting may be
simple and "folksy" or may draw on a wide range of learning—
satirizing and parodying the flights of pilpul and drily deflating
scholarship with free use of puns, homonyms and innuendo.

The bride wears white and it would be a serious breach of
etiquette for a wedding guest to do so, almost like trying to com-
pete with the queen of the day. When she is all dressed, preferably
in new clothes, she is enthroned on a chair piled high with
cushions for the ceremony of veiling. The groom in his black wedding finery is led in, supported by important relatives or others
worthy the honor of "leading-in." During the veiling and the
following discourse he avoids looking at his bride and keeps his
eyes closed or averted until he is led away with his party of men.

A large white veil or kerchief is thrown over the bride's head,
either by the khossen or by some honored relative. After she has
been veiled she is treated to a discourse on her duties and responsibilities as a bride, delivered by the khossen himself, by an
honored relative or by the versatile badkhen.

After grain has been sprinkled on the heads of the couple, to promote fertility, they are separated—each with his retinue—until they meet under the ceremonial canopy, the *khupa*, that gives its name to the ritual and symbolically to marriage itself. "He will lead her under the khupa," they say, meaning, "He will marry her." In the circumcision ceremony they bless and dedicate the infant "for the khupa," meaning he shall be educated and destined for marriage.

The khupa is sometimes a talis, sometimes a piece of cloth, plain or elaborately embroidered, held up by four poles. The ideal place for it is "under the stars," usually in the courtyard of the synagogue. The procession to the khupa is a gala affair. When the ceremony is literally "under the stars" the guests all carry lighted candles. In some places the houses along the way are brightly lit in honor of the occasion and the procession with its twinkling candles passes along a lighted pathway. Finally, when all are assembled word goes round, "They're leading the khossen!" and the groom appears, leaning on the arms of his escorts, followed by his parents and close relatives. Pale from fasting and from exhaustion, perhaps repeating over to himself the speech he must make later and hoping that he will not forget and "be ashamed," he may find the support more than symbolic. He looks neither to the right nor to the left, but straight at the khupa.

As he takes his place beneath it, again a stir goes through the crowd, "They're leading the kaleh!" Supported by two maids of honor and followed by her parents and relatives, "the kaleh's party," the bride enters and joins him under the khupa, standing at his right.

They stand before the rabbi with their parents and attendants and usually a cantor. The rabbi lifts the bride's veil, then slowly lowers it. Theoretically, if the khossen dislikes what he sees he can call off the wedding. In fact, the gesture is a vestige of a time when the lifting of the veil might give him his first glimpse of his bride. There is no vestige of a corresponding option on her part. She is not expected to have the decision nor to be concerned with the appearance of her husband. A man is not a body; he is a mind, a soul and a character.

Before the khupa are grouped the guests, men on one side, women on the other, listening, watching, weeping. But the bride under the khupa is expected to weep most of all. The rabbi pronounces the "betrothal benedictions" over a goblet of wine from which the khossen and the kaleh then sip. The goblet is thrown on the floor and broken for good luck. Supported by her "leaders" and followed by her "party," the bride circles seven times around the groom, reciting a prayer. This interlude represents symbolically the lapse of time between betrothal and marriage ceremonies, which are combined under the khupa. The rabbi reads the marriage contract which is then signed by the couple. The bridal veil is lifted once more, this time remaining up.

It is only after this formality that the real marriage ceremony is performed, and it requires less than one minute. The groom places the ring on the finger of his bride as he says, "Behold, thou art consecrated unto me, according to the Law of Moses and Israel." This solemn declaration is the actual oath of marriage and it is this that makes a marriage legal and binding. Essentially the act involves the man, the woman and their God. No document or dignitary is required to give it official status. Any man who puts a ring on the ring finger of any unmarried woman and recites the declaration in the presence of witnesses is married to her. There are cases on record, and countless tales, of situations arising from the force of this simple oath. In some, they say, it was used as an extortion device with wealthy girls. In one it was done for a joke and a divorce was procured immediately. Yet the girl came to grief later for she wanted to marry a member of the Kohanim and they are forbidden to wed a divorced woman.

The final act under the khupa is the breaking of the goblet from which bride and groom have sipped, following the rabbi's benediction. The shtetl has many interpretations of the symbolism in the shattered glass: that it illustrates the fragility of marriage, of human happiness, of life, or—most frequent of all—the destruction of the Temple, an event commemorated daily and many times a day. After the ceremony the unmarried girls will scramble to secure a fragment of glass "for good luck" in their own nuptials.

The shattering of the glass also breaks the prevailing stillness and solemnity. During the ceremonial there has been dead silence except for the sound of weeping. But when the glass is broken "the whole crowd explodes."° Everybody shouts "mazltov!" congratulations; there are kisses, embraces, peals of mirth, floods of tears; "everyone is loud and happy."°

After everyone has smiled and wept and talked to everyone else the party sets forth for the wedding feast, led by the badkhen and the musicians sounding fiddle, flute, horn, bass viol and drum. Behind them come the khossen with all the men, then the bride with all the women. If the feast is to be at an inn outside of the town they will go in wagons in the same order. The noise of the musicians is supported by the clatter of hooves and wheels on rough stones and the vocal effects of geese, pigs, and chickens scurrying out from underfoot.

As the procession passes, all the townfolk who are not in it look and comment from the street: what a beautiful khossen; how pale he is! You know he is a famous yeshiva student. Yes, they say her father bought him with a sackful of gold—ten thousand rubles, it is said. Still, his caftan is a queer cut, isn't it? And his earlocks, they look like corkscrews—those Galitsianer!

The bride also will be admired for her beauty and her beautiful dress, though with all his money her father might have gotten her a better one. She looks nice but they say she really has trouble with her liver. And all the in-laws, how blown up with pride.

They say it will be a fine feast; yes, they say a dozen chickens were killed for it and six geese, "not speaking about" all the beef and lamb. But with all his money he might have invited more guests.

At the home or inn the tables are prepared, one for the women and one for the men. Guests will be seated according to rank and if any mistakes his proper place there will be sharp reminders. "Look how he pushes to the top of the table!" In the final arrangement few errors will go uncorrected.

Before the feast is under way the khossen will give his speech, the *drosheh*. Usually it is "a little piece of Torah," a discussion and interpretation of some complicated text relating to marriage. The groom's speech is followed by the announcements of the *drosheh geshank,* the wedding presents. Some are money, and the

donor and the amount will be called out by the master of ceremonies between peals of music and appreciation. The other gifts
will also be announced with their donors' names—all the presents
of silver, china, and religious objects that are displayed on a table
at the side. Each announcement will be exclaimed at loudly, perhaps to be discussed in whispers later.

As the feasting, dancing and drinking begin, the badkhen is
at the height of his performance, shaking out laughs and squeezing out tears. The gaiety does not involve drinking to the point of
intoxication, however, for such excess is not "Jewish" except once
a year—on Purim. Any wedding guest who became really drunk
would be an object of outraged disgust. But to be even more expressive than usual, quicker to laugh or to cry, is well within the
bounds of festal etiquette.

A special feature is the "quarreling dance" by the new
mothers-in-law, who stamp, grimace, and lunge at one another,
dramatizing a mock quarrel. Finally they rush into each other's
arms and embrace. Another dance often performed is the *kosher
tants,* the only one in which it is traditionally correct for men and
women to dance together. They avoid bodily contact, however,
holding opposite ends of a large handkerchief as they turn, glide
and stamp to the music. Later the grandmother of the bride may
dance with a huge loaf of white bread.

Not only relatives, neighbors and friends are feasted. Any
big wedding includes a table for the poor and lavish distribution
of alms. To show that the entertainment is social justice rather
than charity, the bride in her snowy gown must dance with beggars in their dirt and rags.

The wedding supper is called "the golden soup" from a
chicken broth rich with globules of fat which is one of the dishes
commonly served. Fish, meat and sweets follow, with the hosts
urging all to eat more and more, and pressing on them tidbits to
wrap up and carry home.

The guests may revel until dawn and sometimes the wedding
festivities continue for a week or more, with the parents keeping
open house, the young people "beautifully dressed, receiving
everyone who comes to congratulate them, and cake and vodka

for all.''° In the midst of the festal atmosphere "the seven blessings" must be said, one for each day.

During the gaiety, the bridal pair are escorted to their chamber. Traditionally it is a much sought after mitsva to provide
the room for the wedding night if one is needed. The popular
stereotype of the groom is an innocent who is at a loss despite
his academic acquaintance with all the rules in the sacred writings. As a student he has read and reread the minute regulations
for connubial behavior but he may need days or weeks in order
to suit the act to the written word.

The bride is expected to lack even verbal knowledge about
this aspect of marriage. The many lectures on wifely duties to
which she has been exposed have dealt chiefly with housekeeping,
patience, piety and docility. Very brief formal instruction may be
part of the tearful week before her wedding but all that may be
left to luck and a husband as uninitiated as his wife.

If the bride—"it shouldn't happen!"—is menstruating on her
wedding night the ceremony is not postponed—"heaven forbid!"
—but she is "a bride who is not kosher." Great precautions are
taken to make sure that no rule is broken. Until the ceremony of
purification has been performed and the bride is "kosher" a little
girl sleeps in the bridal chamber, in the same bed with her, an
infantile chaperone to protect the newly married pair against the
impetuousness of youth.

From now on throughout her married life the bride must go
to the mikva seven days after menstruation ends. The ritual is for
purification, not for physical cleanliness. Before going there one
bathes either at home or at the bathhouse. If the shtetl is not very
large the same mikva is used by men and women on different
days, the men's day being Friday. The men go weekly, the women
usually once a month.

Regular visits to the mikva are one of the three womanly
mitsvos, without which "a woman cannot be a good Jew," no matter how many other acts of piety she performs. During the time
of menstruation she may not hand any object directly to any man,
including her husband. Nor may she touch any man, for this
would defile him. Otherwise she is permitted to go about her

duties as usual, except that she must not make or touch pickles, wine or borshtsh. If she did they would not keep.

The penalty of the man who touches her is severe. He would become impure so that he could not even pray before he had undergone elaborate purification. It is taken for granted that no man would wittingly commit so blatant a sin. The rules are set up to protect him from accidental pollution.

The mikva is a communal institution and commands the interest of the community. A substantial elderly nogid was startled when one of his cronies said to him heartily, "Mazltov, I understand you are going to have a grandchild!" On inquiring he discovered that "it must be so since your daughter has not been to the mikva for two months."° In a shtetl that had no mikva of its own, two or three women would have a peasant drive them to another eleven miles away. "Should it happen for some reason that one woman wouldn't go, the peasant would ask why not. Once I heard on Wednesday market day a peasant yelling aloud to a woman, 'Hey, Beautiful, why didn't you go to the mikva? Are you going to have a son?' And she waved to him and said, 'No, not yet. Next time.' "°

Although sex as a topic is taboo the affairs of the mikva are simple and open. "When she came back from the mikva everybody who met her on the street would wish her to conceive a nice son that night—of course not a girl! . . . You see, there was nothing to hide and nobody was ashamed of it."°

A wife is "ashamed" to mention it to her husband, however. When she is once more "kosher" she does not tell him so in words. According to the Talmud a woman must not invite sexual response verbally and in any case man and wife would never speak about "such things." She indicates that she is once more accessible by handing him some object, perhaps a pair of scissors.

When a wife is angry at her husband she may refuse to go to the mikva so that he "can't come near her."° The weapon is a potent one, and if it is used too long the mother-in-law may intervene, dragging the recalcitrant wife to the rabbi and insisting that she be "brought to reason."

Regular attendance at the mikva, despite the emphatic insistence on its importance, appears to be less universal than observance of other basic mitsvos. Some women who are otherwise rigidly orthodox do not actually go to be immersed although they scrupulously observe the avoidance rules and all the other regulations. Possibly they persuade themselves that the avoidance rather than the immersion represents the essence of the law. In any case, though the immersion in the mikva is commonly referred to as obligatory it appears at times to be neglected.

The monthly period with the additional seven-day interim means that for two weeks of each month a man may not sleep with his wife. "Half of the time she belongs to him, half of the time to God."° During the half month when she belongs to her husband they will scrupulously observe the regulations he learned so thoroughly as a student, and the reasons for which, if he was an advanced student, he debated as part of his yeshiva training. A blessing must be said before the two lie together and during the act no untoward thoughts must be entertained. There must be no disharmony or anger between them nor any thoughts of other women.

They must be in the dark and no living being must witness their pleasure, not even mice. It is said that an extreme zealot will chase the flies and insects out in advance. In crowded households there must be a long, quiet wait until the children who share the room are fast asleep. Only then will the husband go to his wife's bed. They always have separate beds, to make sure that there is no physical contact during the two weeks when she does not "belong to him."

There is a rule also that the body must be at least partly covered. The man wears his yarmelkeh even in bed and also the fringed talis koton that marks him as a Jew.

Any sexual indulgence except for procreation is sinful. The Sages have said that "the desire the man feels in his body was given to him by the Lord only for that purpose." Therefore it is wrong to have intercourse without feeling the desire for it and if he does not stimulate desire in her the act is considered compulsion, which is prohibited. The role of the woman is passive in this as in other aspects of her life. She is supposed to awaken the man's desire, but only at the proper time and place and never verbally.

The whole orientation is toward the children. Any violation

is a threat to them. Any deviation from the norm specified in the Talmud is associated with a specific defect and a child who is born mute, lame, blind, deformed or subnormal is regarded as evidence of parental guilt.

Divorce is an accepted mechanism as a last resort. One avoids it if possible for all the weighting is in favor of the match worked out on earth, presumably at the behest of heaven. Moreover, divorce carries a stigma for the individuals involved and for their families. Because it is available one may be able to prolong an unsatisfactory marriage without feeling trapped, and because it is socially undesirable one may put a perpetual brake on his dissatisfaction.

Like many shtetl prerogatives divorce is available chiefly to the man. The primary ground is infertility, which is attributed to the woman. Conception is credited to him but if it fails to occur the blame is hers. If after ten years she has not borne a child he may divorce her, and in fact is required to do so. There have been cases where a devoted couple were forced to part because they were childless. The social pressure was too much.

Another ground for divorce is desertion. This is sometimes difficult since it is apt to be the husband who leaves, and the wife can secure a divorce only by persuading the rabbi to persuade the husband to request one. If he, meanwhile, has gone to the United States or refuses to be wrested from the Rebbeh's court in a far-off city, the negotiations must be handled by mail. The absent father and husband is a commonplace in the shtetl and in many cases his absence does not seem to weaken the familial bond in the slightest. When it does, however, the wife may succeed in securing a divorce. The deserted wife is called *aguna,* abandoned, while the divorced one is *grusha,* the "chased out."

The procedure is extremely simple. The man presents the divorce contract to his wife, preferably in the presence of the rabbi and her acceptance of it dissolves the marriage. If the woman is unwilling complications arise, for in order to make it effective she must receive the document in her hand. Sometimes it is necessary to resort to tricks, such as mailing it to her in an envelope like an ordinary letter. The ceremony is referred to often in quarrels when an angry husband will shout, "I throw the divorce at your

feet." There can be many rage-relieving shouts, however, before it
is really thrown.

It is commonly assumed that divorce is more frequent among
prosteh than among sheyneh families. Certainly it is attended with
far less shame in the lower social brackets. The greater incidence
among the prosteh layt, who also tend more often to marry "for
love" encourages the belief of the sheyneh yidn that love marriages are less stable than arranged marriages. People who "play
at love" are unstable and in the end marriage crumbles, they say.

If a man or woman is widowed or divorced remarriage is expected and advocated. "It is not good for man to be alone." A
widow can get along somewhat better than a widower although
for her also remarriage is favored. It may be more difficult to arrange since there is always the problem of dowry and after one
marriage she may not have as active support from parents and
relatives as in her girlhood. Nevertheless, efforts will be made. A
second marriage, especially of a woman, will be comparatively
quiet and simple.

A man is considered far less able than a woman to "do for
himself," especially if he has children. How can a man run a
household, keep the little ones clean and in order? No male can
handle a baby, or wash a child—and the fact that under the
scourge of necessity men sometimes manage to do it is merely an
exception to prove the rule. Actually, the ideal man is almost completely inexperienced in coping with his physical environment.
The world of things is an unknown jungle to him. While his wife
handles household, children and budget, he exists in a realm of
thought—where, to be sure, he may contemplate the physical
measurements of the Temple or the proper means of connecting
two houses in order to consider them as one "private domain" on
the Sabbath—concrete concepts, conveniently abstracted. If only
the milk pots and meat pots could also be etherealized into intellectual abstractions, no doubt he could cope with them too. As it
is, he had better find a wife promptly.

If a man dies childless his unmarried brother is obligated to
marry the widow in order to perpetuate the line. Neither the
widow nor the brother may marry anyone else without a formal
release from the other.

The rule of remarriage extends to the very end of one's life. No matter how old a person is when his wife or husband dies, he is not too old to marry. It is not merely that man should not be alone. Age is not necessarily equated with decline nor is it considered in itself a reason for retirement. In all areas a person expects and strives to be an active participant as long as he lives. Life is seen as a path of expanding gratification. The older one is, the more mature he is, the more ripe, the better as a human being. Aged couples expect to enjoy as well as to help each other. Age is good. Old people are "beautiful." If a man of eighty marries a woman of seventy-five, they expect it to be a good marriage in every sense of the word.

One always expects it to be a good marriage. If it is not then somehow one's inclinations or the labors of the shadkhen have miscarried. In that case one has missed the zivug, the match planned in heaven. The responsibility is man's and not God's, for man is always free to choose between good and evil, the right path and the wrong one. If he fails to make the correct choice, then he must try again. The fault is his own.

It need not always be assumed that the zivug decreed in heaven is the easiest and happiest for the individual. There was, for example, a rabbi who married a shrew and she nagged him constantly. Someone said to him, "Why do you take this? She's the scandal of the entire town, always pecking at you. You ought to divorce her!" The rabbi answered, "I don't believe God means to punish me. He gave me this woman because if she had married somebody else that man would have divorced her and taken another wife. Thank God, He gave this poor woman to somebody who could tolerate her."°

Marriage is both a climax and a threshold. From birth on every step is directed with an eye to the khupa and if that goal were missed life itself would seem to be by-passed. Once attained, however, marriage is merely the background for the great goal, the great achievement, the great gratification—children.

II

PEACE OF THE HOME

A person is part of a family. There is no fulfillment of one's duties or one's pleasures as an isolated individual. If a man is not a husband and father, then "he is a nothing."° A woman who is not wife and mother is not a "real" woman. To be an old maid or a bachelor is not only a shame, but also a sin against the will of God, who has commanded every Jew to marry and beget offspring.

In the family unit, the father and the mother play complementary roles. The two are not spoken of as "parents" but as *tateh-mammeh*, as if in recognition of the duality that composes the union. "The tateh-mammeh will be angry," says the boy who does badly at kheyder, or, "The tateh-mammeh will be pleased" if he does well. When little children play house they say, "We are playing tateh-mammeh."

The woman of the house is mother of the whole family including the father. She is the one who tends, cares for and above all feeds the family. When she offers food, she is offering her love, and she offers it constantly. When her food is refused it is as if her love were rejected. She is characteristically remembered as "never sitting down" except for the Sabbath meal. She eats the leftovers, hastily, as she works.

All the temporal, domestic responsibilities are her domain. She is the one who directs and supervises the daily life of the household, comforting the punished culprit—not by spoken sympathy but with bread and jam—scolding and slapping for minor offenses.

There is, of course, never an absolute cleavage between temporal and spiritual affairs. In ordering the material welfare of her household, the mother is responsible also for the physical aspect of its Yiddishkayt, by which is meant the total way of life of the "real Jews." It is her duty to insure fulfillment of all the dietary laws, to guard against any contamination of kosher food by treyf, of milk food by meat food, of Pesakh food by everyday food. All the intricate apparatus of domestic religious observance is in her keeping. Every member of the household depends on her vigilance to keep him "a good Jew" in the daily mechanics of living. If she is an efficient and skillful housekeeper, if she conducts a *"Yiddish hoyz,"* if in addition she keeps harmony in her family, then she will be known as the mistress of a "beautiful household," a real balebosteh.

The realm of the father is the spiritual and the intellectual. He has the official authority, the final word on matters of moment, however he may be advised or coached—or opposed—in private by the mother. "When he talked everybody was quiet, and when he slept no one made any noise."°

The father is a more remote figure, psychologically and often literally. He may be away from home a great deal and this is more or less as it should be. "Children, household, is not a man's business."° The father may spend much of his time at shul studying in the company of his peers. He may be a traveling merchant or an itinerant artisan. "A woman prefers a man who smells of the wind and not of the hearth."° She may be less pleased to have him withdraw for long periods to the Rebbeh's Court, or even emigrate to the United States.

His absences become part of the family picture. "My father used to come back every six months or so,"° it will be said casually. Even when he is there, he is not an active participant in the family circle but is busy with his own affairs. "He is a guest in the house."° When he enters, the hubbub drops, at least temporarily. Voices are subdued in deference to his august role.

Between parent and child exist a host of rights and obligations to which each refers explicitly and freely. Basic to all, however, is the one that is seldom demonstrated verbally or physically, although it is constantly invoked in absence and in retrospect—namely, parental love. A parent never says to a child, "I love you," never praises him to his face, seldom kisses him, after he is four or five. But your parents, especially your mother, "will love you always no matter what happens."° The stereotype of the "Yiddisheh mammeh," familiar in many lands, has firm roots in the shtetl. No matter what you do, no matter what happens, she will love you always. She may have odd and sometimes irritating ways of showing it, but in a hazardous and unstable world the belief about the mother's love is strong and unshakable. Countless mothers of the shtetl have supplied supporting evidence—the mothers that have pawned their pearls and gone hungry to give their sons education; the mothers that have pled with hostile authorities to win their sons' freedom; the mothers that have trudged miles through the snow; the ones that have waited and believed.

The quality of the affection is so taken for granted that any question about it comes as a surprise. "She loved us, so how could she be angry even if we did hurt her?"° This love of shtetl parents for their children is sometimes labeled by outsiders "unconditional" but perhaps "unbreakable" would be more accurate.

Aside from the crises that evoke heroic action, the mother's love is manifested chiefly in two ways: by constant and solicitous overfeeding and by unremitting solicitude about every aspect of her child's welfare, expressed for the most part in unceasing verbalization. "What have you done, what are you going to do, are you warm enough, put on another muffler, have you had enough to eat, look, take just a little of this good soup."

In addition to the affection which is perceived, not as an obligation but as a fact, the parent has certain formal obligations to his child. Children can expect from their parents support, religious instruction, and preparation for adult life. For the girl that preparation involves practical rather than spiritual education, and includes her marriage arrangements. To a son the parent owes a series of ceremonies beginning with circumcision, as much "Torah" as is feasible, and assistance in finding a good wife. These formal obligations are apt to be felt as parental wishes, for the development of the child is a direct gratification for the parent and what happens to the child in an almost literal sense happens to the parent. His marriage and his achievements reflect honor on the parents, his failure or disgrace is a direct reflection on them. Until the boy is Bar Mitzvah his father is specifically responsible for his sins, and a dutiful son may look forward to the day for this reason. "As a child I was always anxious to become Bar Mitzvah so that my father wouldn't have to pay for all my sins."°

Inherent in the picture of parental, and especially of maternal, love is the idea of boundless suffering and sacrifice. Parents "kill themselves" for the sake of their children. The *ol fun kinder,* the yoke of children, is eagerly sought but it is also constantly bemoaned. The great goal of parenthood is "to make the children into people," and to make them into good Jews. To this end, parents toil ceaselessly and if necessary deprive themselves. "When my father was out of work or he didn't have enough pupils, my mother had to go to work. She would earn a few pennies and she would give us to eat while she herself starved."° Parental sacrifice is not shrouded in silence—silence is not a shtetl habit. Children are reminded constantly of all their parents have done and suffered in their behalf.

The ideal shtetl mother, toiling constantly for her family, is an eternal fountain of sacrifice, lamentation, and renewed effort. When misfortune strikes she cries out with tears and with protests, but her efforts never flag.

Parental love is also expressed in worrying, which the father does in manly silence and the mother with womanly outcry. Worry is not viewed as an indulgence but as an expression of affection and almost a duty. If you worry actively enough, something may come of it. You "worry out" a dowry for your daughter, a parnosseh for your son. Or else you "worry yourself out," as you "cry yourself out" or "pray yourself out"—that is, so thoroughly as to achieve catharsis and then proceed to some more constructive exercise.

The intensity of one's worry shows the extent of identification, another proof of love. "Oh, it should have happened on me!" cries the mother whose child has hurt himself. "It should be to me and not to you!" And she wrings her hands—"breaks her fingers"—over his scratched face. Even before anything happens, a good mother worries about it and there is magic in her worry. It not only proves her love but it may keep the misfortune away.

The obligations of the child to the parent begin with obedience and respect. No commandment claims more vivid adherence—to the letter and to the spirit—than the injunction to "honor thy Father and thy Mother." That a child owes his parent obedience goes without saying, but what he speaks about more often is respect, *derekh erets*. This term, literally "the way of the land," has come to mean the respect that must be shown to any older person, but above all to parents. "It is something that is never given to someone who asks for it."° On the contrary, like social justice, it should be offered automatically. "No sooner did we see the adults than we would stop fighting, because no matter how angry you are, you still retain derekh erets for an adult. You never stand up against an adult."°

Both parents are entitled to derekh erets. In speaking about the feeling toward the tateh-mammeh, however, a difference is usually made. It is the mother who is celebrated in countless folk songs—my love for her, but far more often her love for me, her constancy, her boundless sacrifice. "There were no other mothers like those!"° On the other hand, "We used to shiver at the mention of my father . . . not because we were afraid of him, but because we respected him so."°

The father enjoys "enormous" respect, from "the very smallest up to the married sons."° "You should see him, how he comes home from shul, all his children are around him; they help him to take off his coat and his boots. The mere fact that he is in is a holiday for the family. He does not speak to them; he sits down at the table. Often he closes his eyes and meditates."° Like a deity, he can thunder with his eyes. "Sometimes a child is noisy, so the father opens his eyes, looks at the child out from under his eyebrows, and that is enough. He does not have to speak to the child, he only looks."°

Respect for the father is a constant, but its components are variously defined. There is repeated insistence that it is not rooted in fear. "A Jewish child is never terrorized at home. That 'look' is not a threat, it is only a reminder to behave."° Reasons are given to support this view. "If it were fear, then the respect would be asked of the child and my parents never asked for anything."° On the other hand, the possibility of fear may be conceded. "I don't know whether or not that was fear or respect, but when father came into the house we all became angelic."° And occasionally there is explicit recognition: "According to my mother, her mother was smart and sweet and good. She supported the family. The father was tolerated and feared, but not loved."° Yet the word used for fear carries the meaning of awe rather than of fright.

The respect that envelops the father extends to his possessions when he is not present. Father's chair, father's shoes, are a part of him and therefore live in the aura of derekh erets.

The father is the one who wields the lash, for major offenses are referred to him and he administers punishment to scale. He punishes chiefly for some infraction of the moral or social code— especially if the culprit has "shamed" the family in the eyes of the community, or has been guilty of un-Jewish behavior. His punishment must be accepted as one accepts the visitations of God, since he acts for one's good. "When I was spanked by my father and I considered it unjust, I sulked. My grandmother urged me, 'You should kiss the hand of the father after he spanks you. He knows what he does, and he does it for your good.' "°

Any criticism of him would constitute disrespect. "He knows what he does!" One may not always understand, but one must accept. He is The Jew, The Man, the one who most literally is made in God's image.

Mother's slaps and scoldings are of a different order. For one thing, they are more frequent, since she is at home more, even though she may rush off to the store or her market stall every day. Then, too, they often reflect the domestic climate rather than one's own offense. They come easily and are easily forgotten, while paternal discipline is less frequent and is long remembered.

In different households, on different social levels, shades of feeling and usage vary widely. The contrast between the parents is a general characteristic, however, as is the obligation to show to each the appropriate derekh erets.

To a large extent the obligations of the child to the parent proceed from his role as an extension of the parent. Children are under deep obligation not to shame their tateh-mammeh. "What have I done that God should punish me with such a child!" is the outcry of one who feels disgraced by the behavior of his offspring. Whatever the child does that is wrong is sensed and verbalized as an affliction to the parent. "If I did such a thing my mother would wear a rag around her head!"° That is, she would have a headache from grief.

Vulnerability becomes a weapon, especially for the mother. Her suffering serves not only as a rebuke for the past but also as a control on the future—"if you do that, you'll bring me to the grave." Almost any illness may be traced to *tsores fun kinder,* troubles from children. "She had gallstones because her daughter ran around with a musician."°

All the sacrifice, all the suffering, all the solicitude pile up into a monument to parental love, the dimensions of which define the vastness of filial indebtedness. The debt cannot be paid in kind, but must be tendered in the reciprocal currency appropriate to the relationship. A large part of this return is through emotions, attitudes, and the behavior that makes them manifest, chiefly the varieties of derekh erets. An equally important part is the joy that parents reap from their children.

The shining reward a parent expects for all his care and sacrifice is that he should "gather joy," *klaybn nakhes,* from his child, or "draw joy," *shepn nakhes.* The translation is hardly adequate, for nakhes can range from transitory pleasure to deep gratification, tinged with exultation. The shtetl is a place of many tears and moans, but nakhes is frequently invoked. One klaybt nakhes from a good meal, a new dress, a beautiful song; or from a business success, an honor bestowed on husband or child, the marriage of a daughter. The whole shtetl may klaybn nakhes from a "beautiful speech" by the rabbi or the building of a new besmedresh.

It is hard to be a Jew but it is good to be a Jew, and the rewards are often remembered. It is hard to be a parent but it is good to be a parent. Just because it is so hard there is constant insistence on the compensatory nakhes. Because parenthood is so important, nakhes fun kinder is the epitome of joy. If one says the word nakhes alone, the immediate association is—fun kinder.

At every feast there will be a long succession of toasts, including health, long life, nakhes fun kinder and nakhes fun kinder's kinder. A bitter and frequent reproach of parent to child is, "I have no nakhes from you." If a child does wrong or fails to make good, he robs his devoted parents of nakhes.

The nakhes of a child's achievement is more important than any tangible gains it might bring. Through the child's success the parent is validated, just as through his defects the parent is disgraced and condemned. "Whom God would punish, he sends bad children." And why would He want to punish? Only because one has sinned. Therefore the fate of parent and child are one and inseparable, through bonds of affection and also through the decrees of justice.

The formal obligation of child to parent, as set down in the Shulkhan Arukh, and as phrased on the prisbehs where women sit and gossip, includes old age support. Children should want to support their aged parents; they should offer them support. The material part of filial obligations, however, is the part least emphasized by the parents. On the contrary, it is often rejected, especially by the father. "When the father gives to the son, both rejoice, when the son gives to the father, both weep."° It is a wound to a man's self-esteem to be forced to accept help from his junior, and many aged fathers would rather support themselves miserably by menial labor than be dependent on the bounty of their children—even though the children are eager to assist. "Better to beg one's bread from door to door than to be dependent on one's son."° Old age and dependency should not be equated, at least not for men. A mother can far more easily accept help from her children. Not that she prefers it. As long as possible she refuses their presents, insisting that she needs nothing, feeling that her role is to give and not to receive. But if necessity forces her to let them support her, she may even klaybn nakhes from their ability to offer her luxuries and may boast proudly, "They do everything for me; they watch me like an eye in the head!"°

It is only when the child supports the parent that a difference is made between mine and thine. As long as the parents are heads of the house, money belongs to the whole family, and is administered by the mother. All of the funds are pooled and drawn upon for household expenses, but the mother also has her private hoard of coins, known as her "knot," *knippl,* because it is frequently knotted into a handkerchief. This private treasure she draws upon in emergencies—when a child is sick, when the melamed's fee must be paid, when someone needs a pair of shoes. It is added to slowly, expended quickly with whatever pangs, and is one of those secrets known to all.

Sons and daughters who work give their wages to the mother, as does the father also. Even when the children are carrying most or all of the economic burden, the parents still feel that they are "supporting" the family. Isn't it their home?

One's own children are "my own—my own flesh and blood," and therefore no substitute is conceivable. The stepparent, especially the stepmother, is stereotyped as cruel and unmotherly, even though she may be devoted and helpful. The person who has lost one parent is "an orphan," and no verbal distinction is made between this misfortune and the loss of both parents. The complete orphan is the most unfortunate of creatures, without parents and without a home. Occasionally an orphan is able to exploit his sad situation and to gain privileges and favors because of it.

A household may include three generations, but the nucleus is the senior parental pair. They with their children and often their married children and their grandchildren form a closely integrated constellation. The senior male is the head of the house, and it is he who sits at the head of the table, except on the rare occasions when he may give his place to some honored guest. There is no set rule of residence, but it is far more frequent for a married couple to live with the bride's parents than with the groom's. The arrangement will probably be covered by the marriage contract, and its classic form is the kest. A three-generation household is regarded as a right family group, one that belongs together. True, there may be wrangling between mother and daughter, for "no kitchen is big enough to hold two women." On the other hand, the arrangement often offers great advantages to the father-in-law and son-in-law. It is proverbial that the bride will have trouble with her mother-in-law and, in fact, with all her female in-laws—a problem dramatized in the quarreling dance between the mothers-in-law at the wedding. It is equally proverbial that a father may find in his daughter's husband the son of his dreams. "The father-in-law," it is said, "mirrors himself in the son-in-law."

A man's own sons are born to him and he cannot control, although he may try to influence, the traits they develop as they grow up. Sometimes he is disappointed in them. There is a saying that "bright men have dull sons," and the sons of rabbis are stereotyped as stupid—although often they are quite the contrary, and many a nogid is proud to claim one for a son-in-law. The father is less close to them than their mother is, and the relationship tends to remain formal and distant. "Respect for our father was in our blood, but I couldn't quite say we loved him."° When a father chooses a husband for his daughter, however, ideally he can go out and "buy" just the kind of man he yearns to have as a son. Many obstacles may prevent the realization of his ideal. He may not have enough to offer, or he may not be able to find the perfect candidate. Nevertheless, the possibility is there, and most shtetl folk would probably agree that a man has a better chance to klaybn nakhes from his son-in-law than from his own son; or at least that the relationship is apt to be closer and warmer.

A man's relations with his mother-in-law are also apt to be smoother than those of his wife with his own mother. In fact, "the best thing to be is a son-in-law—everybody likes you."°

The populous household is likely to include more people than there is room for. Adults, children and babies, all are busy growing up or taking care of the young, "chasing parnosseh" for the joint establishment, performing the countless rites and prayers, carrying on the community services, or studying the Law in some island of serenity within those vibrating walls. In such a home a favorite phrase is, *sholem bayis,* the peace of the household.

Sholem, peace, is an important word in the shtetl, and an important concept. The Hebrew root of the word includes the meaning of peace, health and unbroken wholeness—three major ideals of the culture. Violence is anathema, quarreling is "un-Jewish" or at least low-class. For evidence of dissension to get abroad is a disgrace and there is a horror of being shamed. Moreover, there is always the possibility that the world outside the shtetl may crash down and peace in a larger sense may be destroyed.

The most common daily greeting in the shtetl is *"sholem aleykhem,"* "peace to you." The daily prayer is for peace. And in the household the constant call for sholem bayis invokes peace and unity.

The domestic sholem is a highly volatile if not a negative concept, invoked more often as a lack than as a presence. "Where is the sholem bayis?" they will ask. "He has destroyed the sholem bayis," one may charge. It would be more difficult to quote a characteristic way for saying, "We bask in sholem bayis, it is here."

"Household peace" might be described more as a state of dynamic equilibrium than as unruffled serenity. A happy household is a swirl of people, all busy, all talking. There may be arguments and nagging, mutual recriminations. All this is part of being expressive, part of showing one's affection and interest, part of sharing in the experiences of one's family. None of it fractures the sholem bayis. Only when a serious quarrel erupts is sholem bayis destroyed, and that is more apt than not to be marked by withdrawal, physically, or from verbal communication. The most serious way to destroy sholem bayis is not through rich participation in the constant expression of feeling and opinion, but through disrupting the household by pulling out an essential piece of its structure.

This concept of peace is sometimes difficult to grasp for those not reared in the shtetl. Every problem in the family, as in the community, is subject to lengthy discussion, with full probing of every possible side of every question. The domestic version of pilpul closely follows the pattern of the yeshiva. Life would be dull without constant discussion, and that is impossible without constant disagreement. Disagreement leads to excitement, and to heated argument. Nevertheless, until the boiling point is reached, sholem bayis is not jeopardized.

The equilibrium is possible because affection and anger are not in the least incompatible. A parent considers it his duty to exhibit—and probably feel—anger in correcting his child. Such anger does not interfere with love, but rather is one of its manifestations.

Any evidence of ill will and hostility, especially within the family, is cause for anxiety. Nagging and bickering are not evidence of either, being simply an emanation of personal interaction. It is necessary, however, to guard against any suspicion that sholem bayis is in danger. Whatever the family tensions, its members will try to keep a harmonious front so that "the whole shtetl doesn't need to know the mammeh and the Goldeh are quarreling again." In the name of sholem bayis there is always someone to shout, "Don't yell, what will the neighbors think?" although "at that very moment the neighbors may be having a quarrel of their own."°

The definition of a quarrel shows the characteristic gamut of variations from the family that is sheyn to the one that is prost. The sheyneh will retreat more quickly into silence and withdrawal and will flinch from the shame of real quarreling. It will be commented on with distaste if members of such a family "fight like a shoemaker or a tailor and destroy sholem bayis." Probably the prosteh layt are responsible for the saying, "When parents don't quarrel they have weak characters," as well as for its opposite—"When a man and his wife fight there is no food to cook."°

Verbal communication of varying intensity is the norm. When tension rises to crucial heights, or there is a special need to exercise coercion, withdrawal of some sort is the effective weapon. Silence is more impressive and more painful than speech. A pattern of quarreling is that as one person grows more vociferous the other becomes more silent. Frequently it is the man who becomes ever more mute and finally retires in dignity, perhaps to the besmedresh, theoretically the victor. Men, at least sheyneh men, are supposed to be more silent than women in any case.

Sometimes, however, the wife or mother retires into silence, and when she does so it is more conspicuous in contrast to her usual loquacity. Withdrawal from verbal communication is painful to herself and to others. At times the self-imposed silence may continue for surprisingly long periods, although this is extremely rare within a family circle.

A helpful device used when one member of the family is not speaking to another is an invisible third person. To this imaginary witness the "silent" one will say, "I ask you, have you ever seen such foolishness in your life?" or "Look at him, carrying on like that." Other members of the family are also used as means of communication: "Tell your father (in his presence) that it's time for him to eat." Or, "I wish that wife of mine would stop spending so much money!"

Silence is also employed opposite more distant relatives, or friends. Sometimes two individuals or two families will refuse to speak to each other for very long periods of time. The feud may be interrupted to celebrate some great occasion like a wedding or a funeral, and then be resumed again. The formal apologies and reconciliations of Yom Kippur often last only twenty-four hours. In the end, a third party may intervene to heal the breach.

Another form of passive retaliation is refusal to eat. This, again, employs an extremely important means of attitude communication, for food is the symbol of the mother's devotion. A child soon learns that he can coerce his seniors into yielding on almost any point by refusing to eat. Similarly, a man can coerce his wife, or a mother her children by refusing to eat. The rejection of food means rejection of loved ones and of life itself. It is intolerable and excites acute anxiety.

Tears are less a part of quarreling than a part of the vocabulary for expressing grief or joy. Emotion is supposed to be expressed. When a child of five failed to weep before the body of his dead grandfather, "Somebody pinched me to make me cry."° A young man who returned for his father's funeral was stony with grief until "my brother said, 'Look at Berl, he isn't weeping, he doesn't care.' Then I cried and cried and couldn't stop."° At weddings, at funerals, at the Yom Kippur services, tears are almost obligatory. When the kheyder boy celebrates the beginning of khumesh, his mother weeps for joy. In the daily give and take, however, tears are not a part of altercation, unless the woman is of the silent type who resorts to weeping instead of scolding. "My mother never yelled, she cried."°

The activity of the household is heightened by the frequent running in of neighbors, to borrow a pot or tell a bit of gossip. Sociability is further increased by the habit of renting out rooms to people not in the family. Many of the callers are relatives, for family ties continue close even when one is no longer part of the household. Several times each year, aunts, uncles, cousins—the entire family, *mishpokheh*—will gather to celebrate some event, or one of the holidays. They may, for example, celebrate the Passover feast at the grandparents' home, with grandfather at the head of the table, all the men on one side and all the women on the other. To the patriarch, such a gathering represents the ideal nakhes of family. All the children that have been "given out in joy" assemble with their children and their children's children. Perhaps Rivkeh and Pessie are not speaking, but today they will treat each other courteously for the honor of the day, for the nakhes of the *bobeh-zaydeh,* the grandmother-grandfather, and for sholem bayis. For days in advance "di bobeh" will be telling her neighbors, "My gantzeh mishpokheh are coming. Such an ol! Such a nakhes!"

Human relations are expected to endure. There is seldom a final end to anything. Certainly a brother is always a brother, a sister always a sister. There may be quarrels and misunderstandings, but in time of crisis a family hangs together and cares for its own. If parents cannot give their children the support and help that is their due, other members of the family are expected to step in. Perhaps an uncle, an aunt, a grandparent, or even a more remote relative will take responsibility. It is always assumed that those who can will do, and those who have will give. When there is no family, the community acts, but this is so painful to pride and so damaging to yikhus that every effort is made to forestall it.

Nothing so strongly demonstrates the sense of family cohesion as the assumptions about the help one can count on as a matter of course from relatives. It is taken for granted that if a brother's child is sick and the brother cannot pay for the best of attention, if he has a daughter to be dowered, a son to be educated, a more prosperous brother or sister should shoulder the expense. It is "only natural" that the brother or sister who emigrates to the United States "can't rest" until he brings more of the family over. It may be less that he cannot bear to live without them than that one just "naturally" behaves so. At times, however, extreme personal devotion enters in. "Mother moved earth and heaven to get my aunt Soreh over (into the United

States). It was quite a financial strain on us, and all the money we could possibly save went for the *mummeh* Soreh. When they came to America, they lived with us and it was quite an ordeal. . . . Mother felt it was her duty, and we all loved mother very much, so we put up with them. But they were not a very attractive bunch of people."°

For children to live with an aunt or uncle in another town while they go to school is hardly considered as assistance. Especially if the couple is prosperous and there are no children in the house, it is taken for granted that the opportunity to perform this mitsva is really a boon to them—and in addition they reap the joy of having a child in the house. "When I was maybe seven years old, I left home and went to the yeshiva in Pinsk. . . . I lived there with my aunt, my father's sister."°

If a relative waits to be asked for help, he is a niggard and a boor. Nor should he inquire, "Do you want help?" He will say simply "How much?" Or, without comment, hand over a sum that is certain to cover the need. If he has to be asked repeatedly, it is as if he had refused.

Assistance does not necessarily imply affection. The giver may disapprove of the recipient, the recipient may suffer pangs of wounded pride at having to be helped—or, on the other hand, may feel "He certainly could give more." The mechanism is one of social justice within the family circle; and like the broader social justice, it derives its impelling force from the fact that all are part of one integrated whole. This is the way mutual obligation works out. There is no choice for a conformist. For a miser or a misanthrope there might be, but he would be aberrant, and —who would envy him?

"Uncle Froyim's brothers and sisters were jealous; either they complained that his wife was a Litvak and overly thrifty— that at their home they ate nothing but 'head-meat,' or that Froyim smuggled to make all this money; this latter they said only in undertones. Later, they claimed his wife had a bad influence on him—that he had been changed completely by her and that she had extorted money from him for her own family. His wife, it is true, had brought her sisters from Novgrodek and had given them dowries. Uncle Froyim, members of his own family would say, on the other hand refused to help his own relatives. Khayeh Goldeh, for instance, got money from Froyim for years—she felt, as the oldest sister, she had full right to this help; Froyim helped to support her husband and her daughter and gave the girl several dowries before she finally got married. He was really reluctant to give all this help, but it did not seem to me that he ever refused to give it—just that they had to ask and ask."°

The patterns of assistance which exist within the immediate family are duplicated, although in attenuated form, in the extended family—all those who are related either by blood or by marriage; that is, all the mishpokheh. Even the in-laws, the *mekhutonim,* claim and render the obligations of kinship.

Kinship ties, even distant ones, entitle an individual to food, lodging and support when he comes to visit. In a strange town or city you seek out a relative to stay with, and there is usually one to be found. He may be your uncle, your seventh cousin, or the nephew of your brother's mother-in-law. If a man needs a job, a wealthy relative must give him one if it is at all possible. If not, he must help him to find one.

Again, it cannot be assumed that the assistance is always joyously extended. On the contrary, so constant are the calls that many a nogid bemoans his own fortune. A favorite curse is, "May you be rich as Korakh and have as many relatives as there are stars in the sky!" But again, there is no choice. The obligation is real and unalterable.

These mutual obligations act almost as a form of insurance in an economic system as unstable as that of the shtetl. Today's nogid may be tomorrow's obgekummener. It is a mitsva to help those in need, and it is a useful thing to have others indebted to one for past favors.

Despite all the sardonic quips and sayings, and despite the very substantial "ol fun mishpokheh" there is no serious attempt to deny kinship. On the contrary, people are constantly trying to acquire new relatives by tracing a relationship with new acquaintances.

For the shtetl, the community is an extended family. Within it are similar interrelationships, a similar network of obligations and duties. Within it, as within his family, a person is highly individualized and at the same time pre-eminently a part of the whole. Beyond the shtetl there extends the Klal Isroel, the whole of the Jewish people, of whom he is also a part.

III

THE PARENTS' CROWN

"Ye shall be fruitful and multiply," is the first commandment in the Torah. God has commanded His people to help fulfill His promise that the children of Israel shall become as many as the sands of the sea and the stars of the sky. Children are always wanted in the shtetl, not only because it is so written, but also because no adult is whole without children.

Aside from scriptural and social reasons, children are welcomed for the joy they bring, beyond the gratification due to the parents—the pleasure of having a child in the house. A baby is the toy, the treasure and the pride of the home. It is taken for granted that any household would welcome a child. "I decided to leave B— and live with my aunt in Lyov for a while. They were always glad to have somebody there because they had no children."°

A house without children is a gloomy place. When all the sons and daughters have been "given out" in marriage, the parents are "alone" even if they are together. "No children in the house" means no brightness in the home.

It is good to have many children. "The more children the more blessing." A woman who had only two "considered herself childless" because "if you had two children it was like not having any children at all."° Children show that the marriage is blessed, that it is a "match," a zivug, approved by God. The idea of increase has come to be associated with blessing in almost any context. If leftovers from the Sabbath chicken last a surprisingly long time, someone will say, "There is a blessing in the chicken," and if money increases rather than dwindling it will be said, "There's a blessing in the money."

Increase in people is good, a large crowd is better than a small one. Many relatives are better than few—the bigger the mishpokheh, the stronger and more secure you feel. To lose any member, close or distant, beloved or not, is grievous.

It is common to say that people are "blessed with children," *gebentsht mit kinder.* A particularly great blessing is the "child of old age," who is apt to be much petted and pampered. "My father was so proud and happy he gave my mother wonderful gifts," said such a son, "but Mother was a little embarrassed."° The child of old age is often called "the scooped-up," the word used for the tiny loaf of Sabbath bread which is baked from the scrapings of dough left after the large loaf has been made, and usually given to the youngest child.

Children are wanted, but boys are wanted more than girls. A boy can become an illustrious scholar and can marry into yikhus. Moreover, it is the boy who says *kaddish,* the prayer of mourning for the parents after they are dead. Three times a day, during the year after a parent dies, a dutiful son goes to shul and says kaddish, thus helping to insure the heavenly well-being of the deceased. To be without someone to say kaddish after you die is a tragedy. The reason usually given is that the prayer said on earth will diminish the sufferings of the deceased in hell and increase his joy in heaven. Behind this post-talmudic explanation, however, is the fact that through the kaddish the deceased remains in the community, will continue as part of it, while the one who says the prayer feels a continuing bond with him and a comforting knowledge that someone else will say kaddish for him when he goes. It serves as a link between the community on earth and the community in heaven, keeping the individual a living part of each. To say the prayer is of tremendous importance and to neglect it is a deep sin. If there is no male member of the family to say it, then someone must be paid to do it. So important is the mourning prayer, that a proud parent will lovingly call a son "my kaddish."

True to the spirit of the shtetl, the actual words of the famous prayer for the dead are quite impersonal. It does not beseech for the well-being of the dear departed, but for the welfare of Israel.

A girl is also a blessing, and receives the affection and care showered on all children. She too may make a marriage that will enhance the family yikhus, but in order to do so she must have a dowry and marrying off daughters is likely to be a serious problem. Therefore they say, "many daughters, many troubles, many sons, many honors," and "if you have daughters you have no use for laughter."

When a young couple are married it is assumed that "each year they will have a child." A wife who is disappointed in her hope of becoming a mother prays earnestly for children. If her prayers are not answered, she or her husband, or both together, go to the Rebbeh, asking him to "bless the womb." Often he gives amulets and charms to help. To be childless is a source of guilt and bitter shame, a condition that draws pity from all but also arouses suspicion that there is some reason for this punishment. The woman especially is to be pitied, since after ten barren years her husband is enjoined to divorce her.

The child who comes to bless a household is regarded as an individual from the moment of conception. In a sense his life cycle begins with Creation, for all human souls were created by God when He made the universe, and are His contribution to the human being. The rest comes from the parents—and no mother ever forgets that her child is her "own flesh and blood." Father, mother and God are partners in producing the child. Here, as always, God will do His share and grant His blessing on the result, provided humans do their part in full accordance with all the commandments.

The life of the individual soul continues from Creation into the hereafter, and life on this earth is "just a passageway" between two disembodied states. In the life before life, the individual studies and is happy; and in the life to come he will do the same thing. Moreover, in that life he will be concerned with good deeds, for he will be importuned constantly by his relatives and community on earth, and sometimes he will return to perform good deeds. He may appear in a dream to remind the sleeper of a neglected promise, or to give good advice about family or business. The folklore abounds in anecdotes of fathers, mothers, grandparents, rabbis, who appeared in dreams to save someone

from disaster or to point the way to success. Heaven is concerned
also with marriages, which are planned there. Thus the triple
dedication to Torah, marriage and good deeds is paralleled on
high, strengthening the bonds between the earthly and the
heavenly communities.

Although the life before birth and after death is free of
earthly pains and troubles, the life on earth is good. All the precepts point to making the most of it, none of them to belittling
or despising the things of this world. "A worm in a horseradish
thinks the horseradish is sweet," and will struggle against leaving
it.

A legend tells how the soul clings to whatever life it knows,
rebelling successively against conception, birth and death. When
a woman has conceived, the Angel of the Night carries the seed
before God, who decrees "whether it shall be male or female,
strong or weak, rich or poor, beautiful or ugly, long or short, fat
or thin, and what all its other qualities shall be. Piety and wicked-
ness alone are left to the determination of man himself." God
then designates a soul who is brought from Paradise and commanded to enter the seed. The soul protests against leaving a
happy life and pure state, but "God consoles her: 'The world
which I shall cause thee to enter is better than the world in which
thou hast lived hitherto, and when I created thee it was only for
this purpose.'" She is then forced to enter the seed and "Two
angels are detailed to watch that she shall not leave it, nor drop
out of it, and a light is set above her, whereby the soul can see
from one end of the world to the other."

Before she is finally shut into the mother's womb, the soul
is taken to Paradise, where the righteous enjoy eternal bliss, and
to hell, where sinners suffer eternal punishment, and is carried
through the whole world to see all of it. When the time comes
for her to emerge from the womb into the open world, the soul
again protests and "the Angel replies: 'Know that as thou wert
formed against thy will, so now thou wilt be born against thy
will, and against thy will shalt die, and against thy will thou
shalt give account of thyself before the King of Kings, the Holy
One, blessed be He.' But the soul is reluctant to leave her place."
Then the angel touches the baby just under the nose, making

the cleft on the upper lip, "extinguishes the light at his head, and brings him forth into the world against his will. Immediately the child forgets all his soul has seen and learned, and he comes into the world crying, for he loses a place of shelter and security and rest."

In his life on this earth, the individual grows increasingly stronger—in theory the older one is, the less vulnerable. It is the very young who are weak and need protection. Danger is greatest immediately after conception and the pregnant woman must be guarded in every possible way from anything that could threaten the child. Actually, precautions begin before conception, when she leaves the ritual bath, the mikva, in which she has been purified. She must not look on anything deformed, lest the child she may conceive that night should suffer. A careful woman looks first at the sky and only lowers her eyes if she has some assurance that they will fall on a pleasant sight.

All sex regulations are designed to promote and safeguard conception, and Friday evening is a most auspicious time for it to occur. In the Sabbath peace and joy, when all are festive, relaxed and free, it is considered appropriate to obey the first commandment. It is imperative to observe all the conjugal rules, for otherwise the baby will not be "kosher" and may therefore suffer some physical or mental abnormality, or if not that, some disadvantage in later life. To circumvent conception is equivalent to "shedding blood," always a heavy sin.

Abnormality could be the result of accident rather than of sin, however. It is extremely important for a pregnant woman to avoid looking at anything that might harm the unborn child. On leaving the mikva a woman has to be careful only until she has seen her first object, but a pregnant woman must be on the alert every minute of every day, for fear she might "mislook herself." For example, a midget was born in a shtetl "because a circus arrived when her mother was pregnant and the mother looked too long at a midget who was performing there."° If a pregnant woman is walking with someone, her companion "will always warn, 'Look away, a clubfoot is coming,' or 'Look away, a hunchback is walking toward us.' "° If a mother "mislooks herself on an animal," she may give birth to a monster and it will be said that she bore a calf or a dog. An ugly or misshapen person is commonly referred to as "a mislooked one."

The pregnant woman must be pampered and humored as well as guarded. "She must not listen to not-nice things, or look at them. She must take special care not to be frightened by anything . . . a cat once jumped on a pregnant woman and frightened her. When the child was born, it was deformed."° During pregnancy, "when the woman imagines that she wants a lot of things, her husband gets her anything she wants, for example sweet things. Whenever the family comes to visit her, they also bring her presents."° And of course, "she must avoid all heavy work."°

Specific practices vary in time, in space, and in the degree to which the family has been touched by outside influences. On almost any detail a wide range of usage can be cited, not only among the Jews but also among the neighboring peasants. The basic outlines of the pattern, however, and above all the basic attitudes toward children and child rearing, are stable, and are familiar to any member of the shtetl.

Almost at the beginning of pregnancy a midwife is engaged. She comes to visit the prospective mother and "can foretell the date of the birth merely by placing her hand on the woman's belly."° The visits continue, at first once a week and later every day. "The midwife was respected and loved but there was no status or yikhus involved. She was paid. If it was a boy she usually got more pay because at the circumcision all the guests left something for her. She was paid according to the means of the family."°

The child will stand in a special relationship to the woman who attends his mother at his birth. He pays her visits and she participates in all the festivals and celebrations of his life. He gives her gifts, especially when he is married, and he mourns at her funeral. She calls the children she delivers her "babies" and she in turn is known to all the community as "granny," di Bobeh.

There are mothers, especially where outside influences are strong, who begin preparing a small wardrobe as soon as they know they are pregnant. A widespread usage, however, is to make no visible preparation, for if swaddling clothes and tiny shirts are assembled in advance the evil spirits would have notice, and every effort is made to keep the birth from their attention. After the baby is born female relatives will rush about preparing necessary clothing and food.

The impulse to keep malign spirits safely uninformed is so deeply ingrained that it has become a verbal reflex for the shtetl. One avoids mentioning the date of a birthday, or the exact age of a person. The answer to a question about when one's little brother was born might be, well, let me see, it was two days after Passover and a month after Gittel got married and a week before Uncle Shmul went to America—even though the exact date is known. If a person must tell his own age, he would be likely to say, "Forty to one hundred and twenty," meaning, I am forty years old and may I live to be a hundred and twenty. Moses lived that many years and this is accepted as the best life span and is mentioned when age must be revealed—a habit disconcerting to officials trying to record the ages of people in court.

When "the time comes," the midwife is sent for and the men are hustled out of the house. Even the husband is not allowed in the room, but usually the wife's nearest relatives are at hand. She is encouraged to shriek and moan in labor, to "cry out" the pain so that it will hurt less, and is urged to work to bring the baby forth. "Scream, child, and try hard," the midwife will say, a formula favored in many situations. "There was no secret about labor, but some women were afraid to let anyone know because of evil eye. But if you saw a woman going to the shokhet with a chicken in the middle of the week you knew that someone was giving birth or had given birth in the family, and you usually asked, 'A boy or a girl?' "°

If the birth is easy, that fact might be kept a secret because if it were told, "the baby might get an evil eye." Extreme labor pains are a punishment from God, and if the delivery is very difficult every effort is made to persuade Him to relent. "The women from that family would go to the cemetery—they would beg the dead to pray to God and help the woman. . . . The men would go to shul and say psalms."° They would "run to the Rebbeh," they would "call to people," and organize minyans for prayer. They would open the Ark and cry out aloud in prayer before the Holy Scrolls, or as a last resort tie one end of a very long string to the Ark and the other end to the woman's bed. If nothing avails and the woman dies, the child is removed and, if dead, it is buried separately.

As soon as a baby is born there is great rejoicing, especially if it is a boy. Somewhat less ado is made about the birth of a girl, but a boy baby is the occasion of boundless excitement and festivity. "When my parents learned that the baby was a boy, they were so happy they danced a *kasatski* at my bedside."° There is a constant stream of visitors who come to congratulate the new mother and see the new baby. Neighbors and relatives bring food, and her female relatives come in to do the work. If the baby is male, the young kheyder boys come every evening for a week to say the *krishmeh* at the bedside, the prayer that the child himself will say each evening when he is old enough. The explanation for bringing in the kheyder boys is that the baby should get used to the environment of the kheyder as soon as possible. Like so many of the prayers for individual life events, the krishmeh is not personal but is the well-known affirmation, "Hear oh Israel, the Lord our God, the Lord is One. . . ."

The mother entertains from her bed, for she must remain there a week and in some regions must live entirely on liquids. Elsewhere she is indulged with delicacies and sweets. So tenderly is she pampered, that the word for a new mother, *kimpetorn,* has become a byword for indulgence. If a person demands excessive attention, he will be told, "you are not a kimpetorn." A hale adult will reject oversolicitude by protesting, "Why? Am I a kimpetorn?" After the prescribed period of rest the mother gets up from bed, purifies herself at the mikva, and is ready to return to her normal life.

The baby, the center and cause of the flutter, is enfolded in precautions as palpable as its swaddling bands. Immediately after birth it is cleansed with oil, the cord severed, and the body bound in strips of soft linen from the shoulders down. Then the small human bundle is laid on a soft down pillow, its head covered by a little cap, and placed next to its mother. Perhaps a boy's forehead will be soaped and the hair removed so that he will grow up to have a high, broad brow, the symbol of wisdom.

The windows are kept closed to shut out any vestige of cold or draft. The shutters are tightly fastened to keep out the strong light of the sun, harmful to newly opened eyes. No moonlight must enter, for that brings the danger of spirits. External nature is barred from the dim, warm, draftless room almost as effectively as from the abode of the past nine months. The human contacts, however, are all-pervasive.

No less care is taken to guard against evil spirits and forces. The umbilical cord and placenta are buried in the earth where no malign influence can reach them. Throughout the first week a curtain is hung around the mother's bed where the child lies also, and curtains are hung at the windows and door. Psalms printed on pieces of paper are pinned on the curtains, in order to keep the infant from harm.

During the period before the baby is named, it is in especial danger from Lilith, Adam's first wife, who wants to snatch all babies in order to make up for her own demon children who are killed daily. If it laughs during the night, the mother must slap it quickly, for Lilith may be playing with it. The pattern of laughter swiftly followed by tears is one that will soon become familiar to any shtetl child. The baby who laughs at night, however, may be responding not to Lilith but to the angels with whom it is still on speaking terms. They come in the dark and praise a good baby, who gurgles with joy at their words. But if they say it is a bad baby, then it cries and must be comforted.

There is also especial danger from the evil eye during the first week. "Nobody is supposed to look at the child except the mother, father and the 'granny.' But if they do, they must 'spit' (say ptu!) three times and also say, 'to keep the evil eye away' and 'no evil eye!' "°

Precautions against the evil eye continue throughout infancy, in fact through life, although the danger decreases with the years. Praise of the baby or boasting about him is an invitation to the evil eye, and arouses great anxiety. "The evil eye could be gotten through too much staring at the baby because of its beauty or health, from jealousy, or from excessive verbal admiration. So, if a neighbor praised the baby too much he would be warned by the parent or friend: Do not praise him so much, he may get an

'evil eye!' "° Efforts are made to keep outsiders from looking at
it too much. "The mother, grandmother or any person who took
care of the baby at that particular time would distract his attention by turning it in another direction. The expressions most
heard were, 'Look at the lamp, there is something wrong with
it today,' or 'Look at the lamp, how clearly it burns today.' "°

Any complimentary comment must immediately be followed
by the exclamation, "No evil eye!" and this is true at any age.
Moreover, any common trouble might be caused by evil eye,
since nothing happens without reason. When baby yawns too
much or cries too much, someone must apply the usual emergency
procedure, "spitting" three times and exclaiming, "No evil eye!"
Excess of any kind may be dangerous as well as unbecoming, in
baby, child or grownup, and must be stopped at once.

Additional steps are taken to protect the infant. Sometimes
a red ribbon is tied around one arm, or an amulet is fastened
on. Girl babies may wear tiny gold earrings, perhaps set with
turquoise for additional protection.

If, in spite of precautions, the baby seems to have incurred
the evil eye, more drastic measures are taken. A professional
"talker-away," *opshprekher,* may be called in to "talk away" the
badness. On occasion a peasant woman will be summoned, just
as on occasion the peasants consult the Rebbeh. There is mutual
respect for magic practices and practitioners. Moreover, there is
a large area shared in common. Many beliefs and usages are the
same among the local peasants and the Jews, although different
explanations may be given.

The difference between boy and girl—a difference that begins
with their reception into the world and continues throughout
their lives—is evident in attitudes, in activities and in periodic
rituals. In a sense the culture ignores its females, although they
are present, active and often forceful. When informants tell about
babies, it is typically the boy and the boy's development that are
described. "The baby" of the shtetl is a male, cared for chiefly
by women and girls.

The girl has no formal *rite de passage* until her marriage,
which marks her as a full adult and formally incorporates her into
the community—through her husband. The boy is the center of

periodic ceremonials, beginning on the first Friday night after his birth with the *ben-zokher*, "male child." The next day on the Sabbath, is the *sholem-zokher*, "peace (and welcome) to the male child." The delighted family keeps open house, men, women and children come and go, and all are regaled with brandy, cake and cold boiled chick-peas, which are a nutlike delicacy specific to this occasion.

The circumcision ceremony that inducts the male child into the Covenant with God is know as the *bris,* or covenant. Like similar ceremonies, familiar in the Orient and Africa, it marks the formal acceptance of the male by his special group or community, and the acceptance by him of the duties and privileges attached to such membership. For the shtetl, it is a community that includes both God and man, and into which he is accepted by community representatives. The father's role is minimal in the ceremony and the mother is not even present—the excitement, it is explained, might spoil her milk.

The bris takes place on the eighth day after birth and the preceding night is known as "the watch night," during which mother and child must not be left alone for an instant. A number of men, preferably a minyan, stand around them and pray to protect the infant from the harm that is especially potent just before the ceremonial. "Everyone" is invited to attend the celebration on the next day, and refreshments are prepared by the relatives.

To officiate at a bris is both a mitsva and an honor, and the participants are selected with utmost care—the two who present the baby, the one who holds him, the one who initiates the healing process. The more illustrious the participants, the better the auspices for the child's future. The godparents furnish the clothes in which the baby is dressed for the ceremony. Their participation sets up no mutual obligations between them and the child, but it does mark the beginning of a lasting, personal relationship.

The ceremony begins when the *kvaterin,* or godmother, brings the baby from the mother's bed to the *kvater,* the godfather, who hands him to the *sandek* or "syndicus," the one who holds him while the ceremony is performed. The sandek, wrapped in his prayer shawl, is usually seated on a special chair known as "the chair of Elijah," which is kept in the synagogue and taken to any house where a bris is to be performed.

A piece of cotton is dipped in spirits and put between the child's lips so that he will fall asleep easily. Then the operation is performed by the mohel, a pious Jew who has studied the procedure. To serve as mohel is "a big mitsva" and, although it is often done for pay, the ideal is to do it purely as a service, and to refuse any money. The operation itself is so trifling that in a society where any physical symptom provokes exaggerated anxiety, it arouses no concern. Attention is centered on the solemn prayer of dedication that accompanies the physical act. "Our God and God of our fathers, preserve this child, his father and mother, and let his name be called in Israel Mordekhay, the son of Tsvi-Hersh Halevi. Let the father rejoice in him that came forth from his loins, and the mother be glad with the fruit of her womb. . . . And it is said, He hath remembered His Covenant forever. The word which He commanded to a thousand generations; (the Covenant) which he made with Abraham, and His oath unto Isaac, and confirmed the same unto Jacob for a statute, to Israel for an everlasting Covenant. . . . This little child, Mordekhay may he become great. And as he has entered into the Covenant, so may he enter into the Law (Torah), the nuptial canopy (khupa), and into good deeds (maasim tovim). . . ."

In the old tradition, the greatest honor of all is that of the *metsutsa,* performed by a venerable and pious man who sucks the first drop of blood. Then the wound is tied around with cotton, to be changed daily by the mohel until within a few days it has healed. Nobody worries about that part and even the baby makes little of it.

The ceremony over and the principal returned to his mother's arms, all celebrate the reception of a new member, with brandy and honey cakes, hearty "mazltovs" and innumerable toasts, "may you have pleasure in your children and your children's children, and in their children." A long line of members yet-to-be is present in spirit and hailed with enthusiasm. God is increasing the number of his Chosen, His people are fulfilling their part of the pact, the promise of the future is one step nearer to fulfillment, and in the present a living source of joy and honor to the family has been added for all to admire—"no evil eye!" As always, the festivities are accompanied by the jingle of coins, presents to the midwife and often to the mohel, contributions to community services.

For the first-born male there will be a ceremony four weeks after birth, called "the redemption of the first-born," again with feasting, toasting, and the exchange of glad congratulations. This ceremony, the *pidyan ha-ben,* is another strong link binding to-day with centuries long past. In ancient times the eldest male was dedicated to service in the Temple, but his father could buy him off by making a contribution to the priests, the Kohanim. Today the first-born son is also "redeemed" by a small payment to any member of the Kohanim, those who are descended from the priestly tribe. The amount is calculated to equal the five shekels originally paid to the priests of the Temple, and varies with the currency of the country. A token arrangement with the priest-hood and with God, it maintains the old tradition which is viewed as merely suspended until the day when once more there will be a real Temple with its officiating attendants. The vestigial nature of the symbolism is suggested by the fact that the Kohan who receives the token payment is free to use it as he will, re-garding it as a simple part of his private income.

Whatever the baby's sex, its name will be announced in the synagogue on the Sabbath after its birth, special prayers will be added to the service, and the father will be called to the reading of the Torah. In honor of the event he will donate as large a sum as he can to the community activities, although probably he will strain his resources less for a girl than for a boy. After all, he may remind himself, there is the girl's dowry to think of—a thought that will be present from the moment of her birth. Following the services he will "make a kiddush" in the synagogue, treating all the congregation to brandy and cakes.

The public announcement of the name, the special prayers of the congregation, and the series of festivities celebrating the boy, dramatize the extent to which a birth is a community affair. The child is born into a family but also into the community. If the parents are poor, clothing and food will be sent in at once, for the shtetl takes care of its children from birth to burial. The evening prayer of the kheyder boys, the "watch night," the group participation in the bris, the observances at the synagogue, the offerings to community welfare that mark the festivities, all confirm the closeness with which the strand of the individual life is woven into the texture of the group. That individual strand will always remain distinct, it will never lose its own identity and its own continuity; but as long as the newborn child remains in the shtetl, its identity will be defined as much by the fabric as by the thread.

It is customary to name the baby in honor of someone who is dead, very often a grandparent, sometimes another relative or a distinguished person, perhaps a great rabbi. It need not be a person of the same sex, for names can be masculinized or feminized. Because it is believed that the child will exhibit some of the attributes of his namesake, the name of a weak person or a failure is avoided. "I was especially interested in the Grandmother Sarah, because I was named after her. She was supposed to be a very clever and nice woman. . . . The Grandfather was . . . a sort of *shlemil*, and I remember that Mother used to wonder whether it was such a good idea to name children after him."° A boy is often named for a learned member of the family, and as he grows up he will constantly be reminded to become a scholar like that one. He is named for his father only if the father is dead. It is a misfortune not to have someone named for you after you are gone, for a namesake is another link with the continuing community.

If a woman has lost several children, names are designed, not to honor the deceased and edify the child, but to trick the Angel of Death. In such cases the baby may be called something like "old one." "When you have a child that is weak and sickly, you give it a nickname like Alteh or Alter which means old, so that it should live out its years and scare away the Angel of Death. And the nickname usually remains."° Or the child may be named Khayim, which means life.

Another way to trick the Angel of Death is to change the name of a sick child, so that if death comes to claim little Moysheleh he will not be found. A child named Vigdor will be in his crib and since the word is all-important, this child is obviously not the one designated. Death will continue the fruitless search for Moysheleh, and Vigdor will recover.

There are other devices to prevent the premature death of children whose mother has lost a number of babies, one being to "sell" the child when it is quite young, to a mother whose children "stay with her"—that is, to one whose children are healthy and who never lost a baby. In order to fool death effectively, a token payment of real money must be made, and there should be a show of the customary bargaining over the price. "In a case like my mother, who lost four children before she had me, you sell your child at an early age to a family where there are a lot of healthy children. I was sold to a woman by the name of Goldeh. I remember I was scared because I thought I would have to leave my mother and father to live with them. But all they do is buy the child for about ten kopikes and when the transaction was over, I went home with my parents."°

A pregnant woman who had lost three babies was sure she had sinned and that God was "punishing her by stealing her children."° Therefore she sent her husband to the rabbi to find out what to do in order not to lose this one. "First, my father wasn't allowed to name me after a dead person. When I would be born and they would have to name me, he should go to shul that Saturday and the first name he hears from the Torah, that's the name I should be given."°

Such a child is a "blessed-by-God," and is guarded and pampered as if he were breakable or soluble, and might crumble or melt away. He is dressed in special clothes of pure linen made at home by hand, as special precaution against the danger that wool and linen might be mixed. It is "a crime for a Jew to wear such a mixture."° All children are carefully guarded, but a "blessed-by-God" is absolutely forbidden to "scream, cry, climb trees, pick berries, tell a lie. In short, I wasn't allowed to do anything."° On the other hand, "nobody was permitted to scream at me, to hurt me, or to say anything bad to me . . . because I was 'blessed-by-God.' . . . They had to love me and be good to me. . . . If somebody would say something bad to me they would always yell, 'Woe is me, you are looking for troubles, he is blessed-by-God!' "°

Belief in such devices is strong. A woman of fifty who had been "sold" by her mother remarked, "My mother never lost any children after she had me."° And the "blessed-by-God" stated, "It never happened that if somebody should hurt me, they would not be punished afterwards. They 'catch a black end.' "°

If all precautions fail and the baby dies, there will be great reluctance to mention it later. Often children are almost grown before they discover that brothers or sisters who came before them had died in infancy. There is a fear that mentioning the Angel of Death will attract his attention. The desire to use every possible means of discouraging him is natural enough in a community where children are wanted and the infant death rate is high. "Most of the families had three, four and five children, and sometimes there were families with ten and eleven children. But one thing that happened often was children dying young."°

The first months of the baby's life are a constant bath of warmth, attention and affection. At first it sleeps with the mother, then it is placed in its own cradle or swinging crib, near her bed. She may hold a string attached to the baby's cradle, which she rocks incessantly, even in her sleep. If the accustomed motion stops, the baby wakens and cries. Then it must be picked up, carried about and crooned to until it falls asleep again. All its wants are attended to by the mother, or by female relatives. The father may play with the infant, sing to it, talk to it, but there is a strong feeling that the serious care of a baby is woman's work, and men are incapable of handling a baby without damaging it.

The swaddling to which it is subjected is also warm, for it is laid on a pillow and wrapped with firm, soft cloths. The reason given is its welfare, and the very gestures with which it is confined convey tenderness and solicitude, although when it is done "the baby is like a mummy."° Its fragile body must be protected from the rigors of a harsh world, its back and legs must be kept straight. "Mother was very careful about this swaddling. She used to put her hand on the knees and arms so as to keep him really straight. She used to show us other children who had, for instance, bad legs, or a little boy in our neighborhood had his head a little bit inclined on the shoulder . . . and Mother used to say, 'Yes, they didn't swaddle it right. Their Mothers didn't take care of them, that's why they look this way.' "°

During the first few weeks the wrappings are snug and the baby is literally "like a mummy." As protection against light, cold air and evil eye, most of the face is covered so that hardly more than the nose peeks out between the cap pulled far down over the forehead and the coverings drawn up over neck, chin and mouth. Later the whole face is exposed, the arms are freed, and the wrappings are relaxed, so that the restraint is almost cozy against the soft pillow.

Several times a day the swaddling is removed and the baby is massaged and allowed to move freely, always with an obligato of loving coos and murmurs. Once a day it is bathed with warm water, the hair brushed, and as soon as there is enough, a boy's hair will be shaped into earlocks. These locks, *peyos,* are never to be cut as long as he lives.

Wrapped and pillowed, the baby is carried around a great deal by grownups and by older brothers and sisters, for if it lies down too much its lungs will be weak. As if to make up for the insulation and comparative immobility enforced by swaddling, it is almost never allowed to remain still or unattended. Conditioned to expect constant notice, the baby promptly signals any lapse in attentiveness, and a large part of its time is spent in motion. If it is not being carried, then it is rocked endlessly, hour after hour. The combination of swaying and singsong will be familiar from the cradle on. In the kheyder, the yeshiva, the shul, one rocks and chants as he studies. The man of the shtetl habitually sways and croons when he studies or thinks, even if he is pondering a business problem. If he does not sit rocking back and forth he walks about, hands behind his back, humming a nign under his breath. To sit motionless and silent for a long time is contrary to shtetl usage.

Another familiar pattern will be the swift alternation of mood which modulates but does not interrupt a basic relationship. The mother tenderly rocking the cradle suddenly flares up at the neighbor who comes in to return a noodle-board a week later than promised. In her anger she rocks the cradle roughly, jerking it back and forth, back and forth. The startled baby cries and the mother yells, "Be quiet." Perhaps she shoves her breast into the open mouth to still the wails, holding the baby in arms tense with rage. The storm passes, the arms relax, the voice croons softly once again.

The mother talks to the baby constantly, telling it about its future as it lies in the crib, "talking out her heart" to it. It is sung to, petted, addressed with endearments that usually end in the diminutive "leh": little cat, little bird, wee one.

The father sings to it, visitors coo over it, speaking in baby talk and in a special singsong voice. "Father, mother and close relatives like brothers and sisters use baby language to the child. They say all kinds of funny things to try and make the baby laugh."° Even when talk is not directed at the baby, the room is always full of words. The father murmurs to his books, prays at the wall, the mother talks to the father, everyone talks to everyone else. From the outset of life the shtetl child associates verbal expression with warmth and security, and silence comes to be equated with rejection and coldness.

The warmth and affection of this outer womb in which the baby lives comes to be associated also with food, for he is offered the breast whenever he seems to want it. The mother is proud of his appetite. "He eats so much, I don't have enough milk for him," she will boast proudly. "I'm all dried up, he sucks me dry." And visitors wanting to compliment her will exclaim, "the baby is so heavy I can't lift it."

If baby cries, the first assumption is that it must be hungry. That there must be some reason is taken for granted, just as there must be a reason for all human behavior. Crying is not "natural" nor is it naughty, but merely baby's signal—and a thoroughly effective one. If the child is not hungry, then it must be wet, cold, in pain, frightened. If no other cause appears, it must be bewitched, in which case immediate steps are taken to counteract the magic. In any case, if it cries it will at once be fussed over, cuddled, comforted, and attended to. This is not viewed as "spoiling" a baby, but merely as normal and correct procedure. That a complaint should evoke a response is always expected.

Even when the baby does not cry, there is no slackening of the anxious care for its physical well being. It is guarded against drafts almost hysterically, for a blast of cold is the bane of the shtetl. It is guarded even against fresh air, taken outdoors only briefly, well bundled up, and merely to be whisked into the house of some friend or neighbor. Overheating can never hurt, but a chill might be fatal. It is watched for signs of stomach disorder. The big sister, who may be still a small child herself, is treated to a constant barrage of warnings when she carries the baby about—not to drop it, not to squeeze it, not to run with it, not to jar it.

To suckle one's own child, her "own flesh and blood," is regarded as a rewarding and desirable experience, pleasurable for the mother as well as for the child. "They loved to breastfeed their children. I think it's the greatest thing in the world. I'll never forget when I fed my son how he sucked and pulled that milk. . . . Modern mothers are crazy, they don't know what they are missing when they give their children bottles, not the breast. It is such a thrill, you have no idea."° Moreover, the attributes of the nurse are believed to be transmitted to the child. Therefore mother's milk is better for the baby, and the milk of a Jewish woman is more desirable than that of a Gentile. It is even believed that a child knows the difference between his mother's milk and another woman's, and will choose his mother's. Human milk is obviously far better than that of an animal, which might affect the baby's character adversely. Aside from such misgivings, there is widespread belief that bottle feeding is harmful and the child would be unlikely to survive.

The wet nurse, like the midwife, has a special and lasting relationship to the child. Her own child is the "milk sibling" of the one she has nursed. Although it is better to have a Jewish nurse, in many places even the orthodox employ a peasant woman if they need, and can afford, the luxury of a wet nurse. Undoubtedly this practice has contributed to the mingling of Jewish and non-Jewish superstitions and magic practices, so that it is often difficult to tell which group has borrowed from the other. The wet nurse is a highly important personage in the house. She must be fed sturdy, milk-giving foods and plenty of them—beer, eggs, cheese, meat. Her diet may be better than the mother's, and often there is a rivalry between the two in caring for the child and winning its devotion. Everyone waits on her and she is able to become the tyrant of the house, since if she is upset her milk may be affected and if she is displeased she threatens to leave. Yet often she becomes a firm friend of the family, and the attachment between her and the child is stable and permanent.

For about six months the baby is fed only on breast milk. Then gruel and paps are added, or a brew made of water mixed with hard bread, toast or zwieback. It must be warm but not too warm, and in order to be sure the mother tastes each spoonful before putting it into the baby's mouth—just as she automatically protects her child from any threat. If any tongue is to be burned, "It should be on me!" Sometimes the baby is given a pacifier of chewed bread wrapped in a cloth. If a child learns to speak before he is weaned, he should be taught to say the "before-meals blessing" before he takes the breast, and there are legends that the great rabbis did so when they were babies.

Nursing is believed to avert pregnancy and, despite the great urge to have children, the mother who has several toddlers may prolong it for this reason. Although in theory it is impossible to have too many children, a hard-worked and impoverished mother of eight or ten may secretly feel that to be overblessed is to be overburdened. If she does become pregnant while the child is still nursing, he must be weaned at once, for otherwise he would be draining strength from the new baby. Whenever it occurs, weaning is sudden. Some hold that the best day for it is the Sabbath, and that the child should be given his mother's breast for the last time on the threshold of the door, because then he forgets it more easily. If he cries for it after that, it may be given to him, but covered with mustard or pepper in order to repel him. Then he himself will reject what he has cried for. The child is weaned directly to a cup or spoon. Solid foods are gradually introduced into the diet, and by the end of the second year the baby eats what adults eat and sits at the same table.

In keeping with the usual differentiation between strength and weakness, a boy is apt to be weaned earlier than a girl, and a strong child sooner than a sickly one. It would be dangerous to return to nursing, once the child has been weaned, and if he still needs human milk it may be fed to him from a cup or spoon. Under no circumstances may a child nurse beyond the age of four, for it is written that no "adult" may suckle at the mother's breast. It is not considered desirable to suckle a boy longer than a year, for otherwise he might become stupid.

Long before this, orderly toilet habits have probably been taught, for that begins some time after the first six months. The training is firm and even insistent, but anxiety centers on the child's well-being rather than on repugnance for the function. If elimination is not effective, he cannot be well. It is necessary to discharge bodily excreta just as it is necessary, through verbal expressiveness, to discharge emotional tension. The great remedy is "out," *oys*—talk out, laugh out, cry out one's feelings. One should even eliminate before praying, and a blessing must be said after doing so: "Blessed be Thou, Oh Lord our God, King of the Universe, who hast created us with orifices and openings." Failure to achieve catharsis is bad, for it is dangerous to retain what should be expressed.

A child is encouraged to good performance by verbal stimulus, and praised if he does well. If he misbehaves, sounds of disapproval are made—"pheh, pheh!"—and he is shamed, though mildly, "a big boy like you, a year old, you're not a baby." If he persists in misbehavior, he may even be slapped. Basically, however, all body processes are regarded as natural and not disgusting, provided they are confined to the proper time and place. There is no need for euphemisms in referring to the toilet and "accidents" are accepted until quite late even though the child may be rebuked by the exclamation, "A kheyder boy already and look at you!"

The baby who is welcomed so eagerly and sheltered so anxiously, is nevertheless hurried out of babyhood. For all the kissing and cooing, all the baby talk and coddling, there is no effort to keep him infantile. On the contrary, he is treasured as a potential adult, and the admiration of his audience is most evident when he shows signs of precocity. Early sitting, teething, creeping, crawling, standing, walking, and above all early talking, give tremendous satisfaction to parents and family. A smile, an unexpected gesture, an imitation of an adult's expression, will be taken as a sign of exceptional intelligence. "Everything the child says is a bright saying and everyone likes to hear the baby say and do things."° The whole family, parents, aunts, sisters and brothers, will proudly tell neighbors and relatives, "The child has smiled." They rub his gums to make the teeth come quickly and when a baby of three months cries, someone will suggest hopefully, "perhaps he is teething."

Slow development is a cause of serious anxiety. If a baby is late in walking or talking the family tries to cover up his deficiencies but they grieve and worry in private. Moreover, if development is out of order it causes concern. For example, the lower teeth should come in first and the upper ones later. If the order is reversed, it is bound to mean something regrettable.

Even after the baby can crawl or walk, he must never be away from a watchful elder eye, to make sure no harm comes to him. As soon as the little boy can get about by himself, he draws more attention from his father, and sometimes will be taken into father's lap to "study" with him. The bearded head in a yarmelkeh and the tiny head also in a miniature yarmelkeh bend over the "little black points" in the book. The mother is too busy to look long on this foretaste of her son's entrance into a man's world, yet she may realize that he no longer belongs exclusively to her. His body is still hers, her "own flesh and blood." But the mind and spirit belong to the father and soon they will lead the body out beyond the four safe walls of home.

IV

MAKING CHILDREN INTO PEOPLE

Babyhood is brief in the shtetl. Often it is ended by the arrival of the next baby, but in any case the process of babying is at the same time a prodding toward adulthood.

Growing up is not a transition of the total child through graded phases. There is no nursery life in the shtetl, no kindergarten phase, no recognized period of adolescence. Children mature in segments or streaks, so that one segment may become comparatively adult while another remains immature. Limited indulgence is shown them and in certain situations they will be excused on the ground of being "only a child." But increasingly, the area of indulgence contracts and the demands enlarge.

For the boy, especially, the process of growing up is segmented. From the moment he enters kheyder he is a serious student, expected to concentrate on his books for eight or nine hours a day, with no easy stages from picture book to primer to solid text. The method of study is graduated from rote memorizing, through commentaries to original pilpul, but there is no gradation in the amount of effort and attention demanded from him nor in the basic subject matter.

When the same boy leaves the kheyder and races home, he is still a little child who wants to play in the street. And, despite his new dignity, he is still swaddled in the ministrations of his mother, still bombarded with her constant admonitions: "Be careful, don't run too fast, you'll fall down!" "Don't climb a tree, you might break a leg!" "Keep out of the draft, you might catch cold!" "Be careful, you'll knock out an eye!"

To some extent neither the boy nor the girl will ever stop

being a baby to the mother. She will never stop feeding, hovering, worrying about health, warmth, safety. In certain areas each sex remains always "a child" to the other sex, and this contrapuntal maturity plays its part in the interdependence of men and women. The man is always "a child" with regard to physical needs and domestic arrangements, dependent on mother, sister, wife for the arranging if not for the supplying of proper food, warmth, clothing, health care, and for alleviation of, or sympathy with, any physical or mental suffering. From the time he starts to study, however, he is adult with regard to matters of the intellect, religious rituals and community affairs. In these matters the woman is always junior to the man. From the time she can first carry a new baby about, however, she is a "mother" to little brothers and sisters, to her husband, even to her father. On occasion either sex may cultivate maturity in the other's specific area, but such exceptions merely prove the rule. That the woman's specific area of maturity is considered inferior to that of the man, does not alter the complementary balance.

Despite the persisting, but steadily contracting, areas of indulgence, from the moment a child is able to help with the younger ones or with the family parnosseh, or to go to kheyder, it becomes a responsible and functioning member of a group. "When you were five years old you were supposed to be responsible for yourself."° There is no effort to shield children from personal quarrels or family problems. Everything is discussed before them except sex, and that is not discussed before anyone. Children do not, of course, enter into adult deliberations, for that would be *khutspeh,* "nerve," the opposite of derekh erets, respect. A child who tried to speak up in an adult discussion would be told to listen and learn, so that understanding might come later. But he is expected to participate silently. "When I was ten years old, I was a whole person, a gantser mentsh."° And parents will say reprovingly, "be a person," *"Zay a mentsh";* or "you don't behave like a mentsh."

To be a mentsh means to be a complete human being. One must be both "a mentsh and a Jew," for it is possible to be one and not the other. A "whole person" means a real adult, and in praising children it is customary to say, "He sits like a mentsh" or he eats or talks like a "mentsh." The "beard without a Jew" is not a mentsh, but a hypocritical façade. On the other hand, a Gentile can be a "real mentsh."

Unlike the baby, who is smothered in kisses and caresses, the "small person" is seldom kissed except on a few special holidays. "Maybe she did it when we were very small. But as far as I remember when I was five she never kissed me. That, too, is Jewish. A child at this age takes part in the life of the house. It is some- how considered as an adult person. And it is not shown any affection. But that of course does not preclude the unique love of Jewish parents for their children. . . ."°

The withdrawal of kisses and caresses is gradual, with no sharp break to indicate rejection. The child who appeals for demonstrative affection will be told, "Don't ask for petting like a baby," but he may be kissed or patted while the mild reprimand is delivered. He learns and sees that the ways of adults are dif- ferent from baby ways. "Jews never kissed in public, even wives."° To a diminutive mentsh the mother shows special approval by an occasional pat on the head, a soft stroking, or a pinch on the cheek, but for the most part her affection is expressed in solicitous scolding and unremitting interest. The pinch can be painful, and children often shrink from the affectionate nips of grownup visi- tors. That same pinch, embellished with a sharp twist, is used for punishment as well as for endearment.

The mother is apt to be more demonstrative to a son and the father to a daughter. When a tiny boy climbs on father's knees as he studies, he will guide the small fingers over the letters and reward the child with a smile of approval or a pat on the head. A kheyder boy no longer sits on father's lap, and their contact grows increasingly distant and dignified. The father remains in closer physical contact with the daughter, although the rabbinical tradition forbids her to sit on his lap after she is nine. As she approaches adolescence his caresses dwindle, but the emotional distance between father and daughter is likely to be less marked than between father and son.

The mother demonstrates her affection more freely to the son. Perhaps because he is away from home so much more than the girl she feels that he needs more mothering when he is there.

Moreover, he is the only male toward whom she may display affection.

Parents make a great point of having no favorites, insisting that "all my children are the same to me." Their protestations are seldom taken seriously. There is too much difference between individuals, either because of their position or because of their nature. The first-born male, the youngest child, the brightest boy, the sweetest or prettiest girl—each has a special role and a special position and everyone, including the parents, knows that each has a different share in the parents' affection. Nevertheless, it would be shocking for the parents not to insist, they are all the same to me. The youngest is apt to be everyone's pet. "He gets the most love of all because all the brothers and sisters make a big fuss over him."°

The baby is praised to his face, told how good, how clever, how sweet he is. Once he has become a mentsh, however, there will be very little direct adulation. Children may know, or even overhear how their parents boast to relatives and neighbors about their prowess and achievements, but a dutiful parent avoids saying to a child anything that might "spoil" him.

Nevertheless, the mother is always there and the home in which she reigns is the never-failing haven of refuge. The child who has been hurt always can run to her, sure of a response that proves she cares and shares, even though her sympathy may be mixed with rebuke. She will wipe away his tears. She will cry out, "It should hurt me for you!" When his sobs are quiet, she will give him a *potch*, a slap, because he has been told "how many times" not to climb trees; and she will stanch the new flood of tears with bread and jam. The shtetl is used to tear-stained little faces streaked with jam, and shtetl children know well the flavor of mingled sweetness and salt, enjoyed to the accompaniment of their own subsiding sobs and mother's worried scolding.

Apparently the flavor of sweetness outlasts the salt. Like the child who is hurt, the grownup who is sick or wounded will automatically call out to mother. She can always be counted on to administer scolding mixed with jam, and to point out that pain and punishment are retribution for wrongdoing. The principle of the Covenant reaches into the earliest years, and "God will punish," *Gott vet shtrofn,* is a refrain familiar even to the toddler.

Distances are short in the shtetl. It is only a step from baby-hood to being a person, from laughter to tears and back again, from riches to poverty. In the mother's moods, opposites are al-most simultaneous. If the child pesters her while she is panting to finish her Sabbath preparations, her sharp "devil take you!" or "go in the ground!" will merge swiftly into a blessing, "you shall grow strong and healthy for me!" Her phrases often include "for me" or "to me" as if whatever the child does or experiences is for or against her. And often her impatient exclamations, like her sudden slaps or pinches, seem to express impersonal resent-ment of general circumstances and difficulties, rather than a personal rebuke.

The mother's myriad terms of endearment change color with her mood. "My crown," "my jewel," "my heart," may take on tones of irony when she is displeased. If she calls her little son "my breadwin-ner," the appellation is always ironic, but playfully so. The same term addressed to her husband becomes less playful and more biting, for it is used only facetiously. A number of names are used interchangeably between parent and child, for example "little father," and "little mother."

Whatever the fluctuations in mood, home and mother repre-sent security and solace. The necessity to leave home for educa-tion or for apprenticeship is frequent, and is usually remem-bered with pain. "I hated to go home for vacation because I knew how hard it would be to leave again,"° said a yeshiva boy.

Usually the child manages to overcome his homesickness, but not always. An unusually gifted boy of nine was unable to endure a seven-mile separation when he was sent to live with an aunt where there were "better and more modern teachers. They were afraid that the teachers in B—would spoil my head. . . . But I was terribly lonesome for my mother. I was so lonesome I thought I'd die. And my mother was very lonesome for me too. I kept running away to see my mother. And it wasn't because my aunt was bad to me. She was very good to me. But I was lone-some and I used to cry. Finally it reached the stage where I ab-solutely refused to leave my mother. So mother packed up her be-longings, sold the house and the whole family moved to my

aunt's town. . . . In Europe, of course, Torah came before anything else."°

That a child should cry when he is hurt or unhappy, is a
matter of course. No one will say, "Be brave and don't cry." The
shtetl places no value on the suppression of tears, nor are they
considered essentially the mark and the prerogative of childhood.
On the contrary, weeping is accepted as a normal means of expression and, on occasion, a legitimate weapon. It may signify
grief or pain, joy or anger, or the futile expression of a child who
rebels against his parents and dares not "talk back." One does
not run away to hide his tears, for they are nothing to be ashamed
of and at times they are correct procedure. True, they may be
an expression of weakness, but at the right time and place they
are accepted as an appropriate expression—even a required one.
Grown men are not expected to weep as often or as freely as
women and children, but for them too tears are in order during
certain rituals, or as an accompaniment to pleas for help, either
for themselves or for their community.

When it is time to weep, one weeps, and the ability to produce tears is taken for granted. "Now you weep," says the zogerkeh
who leads the women in the shul. During the services for the
Day of Atonement, everyone weeps. The tight-throated singing
of the cantor often sounds like weeping, and at certain points he
weeps for the whole community, of which he is titular "delegate."

Weeping serves also as a means of catharsis. You "weep out,"
"moan out," "cry out," "sigh out," your trouble. Afterwards you
say, "Oy, it's lighter on my heart!" Relief brings renewal of energy
and of effort and once again you set about the task of "worrying
out" a solution to your problem.

Whatever the function, in the shtetl tears have takhlis, purpose. They do not necessarily indicate a loss of control, for there
is no pressure to control them.

It is the business of every person to become a parent, and
it is the business of every parent to make people out of children,
makhn fun kinder mentshen. Parents are assumed to know their
business. The children are expected to accept instruction and
discipline, and whether they understand just why is unimportant.
"You were told that you mustn't do certain things, but you were

never told the reason why. But we understood that it just wasn't right. And we obeyed."° Let them learn first, and understanding will follow. They will understand in time to instruct and discipline their own uncomprehending offspring. And the children who are reared to obey without question and without understanding, grow into adults for whom no authority is absolute and final, who feel it both a right and a duty to exercise their own judgment and intelligence. Only in intellectual matters are questions in order, and here they are encouraged and approved. For the kheyder boy or the yeshiva student to ask searching questions about the sacred writings, is proof of ability.

Any explanation of parental edict that is offered is apt to be in terms of sanction rather than of reason. The authority of the parents is backed by the ways of the group and the commandments of God. Someone may say, it's a mitsva to do that. More often, "we were told, 'It is done' or 'It is not done.' That's the only reason we were ever given."° The other chief formula is, "it is not appropriate," *es past nisht*—a theme that runs from childhood through adulthood and from the lowest to the highest social level. Grownups as well as children are constantly reminded of what is becoming or unbecoming to their particular role or status. An irrefutable argument is, *"es past nisht far,"* it is not appropriate for a child, a boy, a girl, a kheyder boy, a boy from a sheyneh family, a married man, a bride. Any category carries an explicit array of prohibitions and the most enveloping of all is, "es past nisht" for a Jew.

A mentsh must never fail in derekh erets. All older people merit respect, but to give parents respect and obedience is an absolute imperative. In some families linguistic deference may be shown by using the second person plural *ir* or the third person nominal to parents. Usage within the family varies in different regions and different social groups. To strangers and to seniors in age or status, the courtesy form of address is regularly employed.

To "talk back" is a punishable offense. *Azzes ponim,* "dare the face" is one term for impertinence to those who are superior in age or status and therefore should be shown respect. It is always used in condemnation. Khutzpeh is another, used when a person speaks or acts in a brash, shameless manner, especially when he demands more than is his due. Khutzpeh, however, may command a certain admiration, if a person shows unusual boldness or daring.

The punishable offenses are legion and punishment is often corporal, from the quick slap of the harried mother to the father's premeditated strap. When parents punish there is no claim that it is done more in sorrow than in anger. That they are angry is understood and admitted. The shtetl parent freely vents his rage at a wayward or undutiful child. The child may fume inwardly at what he feels is the injustice of the parent. Neither assumes, however, that the child is loved only when he is good and that love need be withdrawn in order to make way for displeasure. "The love of Jewish parents for their children is absolute. The child is everything."° Corporal punishment is inflicted in anger, but also in line of duty. This is the way a good parent makes his child into a mentsh and a good Jew.

Punishment "doesn't do any harm" and if it occasionally falls where it is not deserved, no matter—let it serve for a time when it would be merited. The punishing authority is always right, and if you did not commit the precise sin for which you are now chastised, no doubt you have done or will do something that merits a beating. In the long run, justice will have been done—just as in the long run the punishments dealt by God to His people are justified. Resorting to physical methods, forbidden between proper adults, is correct toward children, for this is the method that children, the unlettered, the unenlightened can understand.

Children apparently become more accustomed to verbal and physical discipline than to the "look" occasionally administered by an outraged father. There are frequent comments that scolding and beating are easier to bear. "My brother put it very aptly once when he said he would rather have the daylights whipped out of him by my mother than get one look from my father."° The significance of the look is strong in a culture where the evil eye is a constant threat, and it extends beyond punishment and magic. The Rebbeh who can see across space and time is said to have "the look." The examination of the prospective bride by the family of the khossen is also referred to as "the look."

The language of the eyes is given great weight in daily life, and people are often characterized by their eyes. "He has a pair of thieves' eyes," means that he looks shrewd and clever, "he has a pair of compassionate eyes," means that he must be generous and kind. One can "devour with the eyes" or "murder" with them, and if someone gives a withering look it is said that "he opened on him a pair of eyes."

Money is employed both as punishment and as reward. A child who has misbehaved will be denied the expected penny, and one who has done especially well at the kheyder will be rewarded with money. Food may be used as a reward, but never as a punishment. Even if a mother is angry, or is "not speaking" with any member of the family, she is still concerned about feeding them. She will silently bring out the food and never ceases to worry if they do not eat properly. The children, on the other hand, can hurt her by refusing to eat. "No food is ever hidden from the child, only sweets. That is given to the child only at certain times, for instance, after a meal or as a reward for being good. But food is never taken away as a punishment . . . if a child doesn't want to eat, the mother usually caters to the child, giving it whatever it asks for and likes, and this way tries to arouse the appetite. If there is a shortage of food, the children eat first, adults later."°

Children must obey and children do obey in the shtetl. They obey their parents and the Law. At the same time they are taught that man is always free to choose between right and wrong. God has defined, and parents have interpreted, what is good and what is evil. God has ordained many events for the group and for the individual. He decides at birth whom one shall marry. But the choice between good and evil depends on the individual. If he chooses evil the fault is his, although others will suffer for it. "Man always has that choice."°

If he chooses the right, it will attract less notice, since it is assumed that one does the right thing if he knows what it is. Children are punished for wrongdoing much more often than they are rewarded for doing well, just as the grown man is more criticized for deficiencies in community service than he is praised for performing good deeds.

Behind all parental prohibitions and injunctions stands God, the final arbiter of what is good and what is bad, the source of the mitsvos that underlie so many acts. He will be displeased, He will punish, or else He will reward. The shtetl child has a vivid awareness of God, though usually not a vivid image of Him. There is an occasional tendency to identify Him with the male head of the family. The father's punishments must be accepted like the punishments of God. "I can't remember what I imagined God looked like, but I do remember that I always wanted to know what was the difference between God and my grandfather."°

Most often, however, He is conceived as a disembodied and all-pervasive presence. The degree of abstraction represented in childish conceptions of God, as remembered in later years, is in keeping with the tendency to equate spirit and mind with the male principle, and with the emphasis on meaning rather than on matter. It is also in line with the prohibition against "graven images" and the statement repeated daily among the Thirteen Articles of Faith, "He does not have a body." When imagined in human form, He was most apt to be "just an enormous head."° He was seldom imagined in human form, however. "He didn't look anything like a human being. He didn't have a head or a body or legs or arms or anything."° Perhaps "he was just a flame, a huge yellow flame."° But more typically, "I thought that God was in the sky, but that you couldn't see Him. He was invisible. I was afraid even to mention the word God. If I did by accident, then I immediately put my finger in my mouth and bit it. . . . Then the sin would disappear. If you mentioned God, you had to wash your hands first. Most of the time God was talked about as 'Der Oybershter in Himl,' the All Highest in Heaven, rather than saying the word 'Gott.' "°

A point of contrast with other Gods became also a point of superiority. Other Gods were localized, specialized, corporeal. The God of the peasants stayed in one place as contrasted to "our God . . . who flew around in all the skies and took care of everybody. . . . The goyisher God hung on a wall with little lamps all around. What could a God do hanging on a wall?"°

To "believe in pieces of wood or pictures" came to be associated with believing in the physical rather than the spiritual and intellectual values. "I grew up with all the stereotypes that Jews had about the goyim. . . . And I, as well as all the other Jewish children, developed superiority complexes with regard to goyim. And this is not surprising."°

It is the less surprising since the chief non-Jewish contacts were with impoverished, illiterate peasants or with formidable officers of the law. The peasants were often as poor as, or poorer than, their Jewish neighbors. "Always, by the time late winter had set in, the peasants would be without bread or any other food. When spring came they were not so bad off already, because they could eat grass and other things, but in late winter they were often desperate. I can remember them coming in the store wearing nothing but an old coat of ragged wool, and under it a thin hand-made linen shirt, coarsely woven. They would beg my mother for bread and offer to give her their shirt in exchange for a loaf of bread. My mother, poor thing, would give them bread and tell them to pay her when they could—she didn't have so much herself—and they would weep and kiss her hands. I remember all this very well, and I remember what the Czar would try to turn these peasants into—relief service of any kind was forbidden by the Czarist authorities because they feared such things would unify the people. Jews and Gentiles had always gotten along well, given the opportunity. The peasant people would always run to the Jews when they were in trouble—a sickness, a letter, a hungry family. The Jews themselves would starve 'every Monday and Thursday' in order to have enough, but they and the peasants were friends."° Against this background it is not surprising to find the "poor peasants" frequently described as objects of charity. "My grandmother who was so poor would give her whole worldly goods away to the needy. And it made no difference whether she gave it to a goy or to a Jew. When a goy took sick my grandmother would go to see them and take care of them. And she never went empty-handed. She always took a white roll, milk, butter, sugar, etc. You know, to them the best medicine when they were sick was a glass of strong tea with sugar. She never discriminated between Jews and goyim when it came to help. Something worked in her head that all people must be the same and therefore should be treated as such."°

Instruction in the discharge of social responsibility puts need before group identification. "If a child gets coins for distribution among the poor he would be told again and again, don't make a distinction between the Gentile beggar and the Jewish beggar . . . any helping of the needy is a mitsva."°

Such a child sees the peasants as deprived of the highest joys and values, yet he sees them in a position of comparative power. The kheyder boy runs home through the dark, trying to elude the attacks of the peasant boys. He sees, too, that the Jewish father, clothed in the authority of God, is helpless before the worshipers of the other God. His complex picture of the differences between the two groups is affected also by the character of parental "do's" and "don't's." The chief reasons for injunctions are "because it is fitting," "because it is a mitsva," "because you are told." The chief reason for prohibitions is "because that is 'un-Jewish' " or, as the shtetl puts it—goyish. A "real" Jew does not fight. A "real" Jew does not steal. Although it is known that a Jewish underworld exists and that individuals do sink to perfidy, it is still held that such conduct would be impossible for a "real" Jew. A common response to charges that one has done so is, "A Jew a ganef?" "A Jew a thief?" The phrase, "a Jewish robber" means one who is no robber at all. Ideals of honesty in business are strictly Eastern European, with bargaining and sharp dealing as an accepted sport, art and profession. But stealing is "something else" and within the Eastern European definition, a real Jew is incapable of it. A "real" Jew will not hurt man or beast. "Pity for all that lives" is a basic requirement and if anyone neglects it the question will at once be raised, "Where is your pity for all that lives?" One must never overwork or beat an animal, take a calf from a cow, overstuff geese, keep animals confined except when strictly necessary in order to produce food for human beings.

Above all the children are constantly reminded that a "real" Jew is moderate, restrained and intellectual, and they are chided for betraying these ideals. "A Jewish boy doesn't climb trees." "A Jewish boy doesn't ride a bicycle." "A Jewish boy doesn't laugh like a fool."

Visitors to the shtetl have remarked that the children's eyes are solemn and that they "grin but do not smile." In comparison to children whose primary business is play, this is a common impression. Nevertheless, they do play. It is not "Jewish" to skate, whistle, shout—but many shtetl boys do so. "I was a very wild boy, used to climb on every tree and roof. I always carried a needle and thread to mend my suit before I got home from my wild climbings."° "We used to like to catch birds. . . . You would cover the bird with your cap not to let it escape. We did this even though we were not allowed to take our hats off. . . . Of course we were not supposed to catch birds. It was a 'pity on living things.' Mammeh wouldn't let me do it so I could never bring a bird into the house."°

Only sons of very sheyneh and very orthodox parents are apt to be restrained entirely from dirtying their hands and rumpling their clothes. For them life is a sedate round of study. There may be very few such boys in each shtetl and they may feel lonely, watching the other boys from afar. The minute grading of the social order is paralleled by a grading of restrictions on children. The more sheyn a child is, the fewer other children may he play with, and the more rigidly he must observe the code of the model man. The more prost, the more companions are permitted, and the more license in what one plays. Moreover, in the lower social levels there is less punishment for using "ugly words."

"I had one friend who was the son of a rich man and I could play with him. But we used to study together most of the time and on Saturdays we were taken to the melamed together so that he could listen to what we had learned that week. And we had to know the whole works—all the commentaries. The only games my friend and I could play were indoor games. And indoors we had to be quiet, and we had to be directly under the eyes of an adult in the house."°

Perhaps the other boys sometimes pity the overprivileged few, and certainly in later life they sometimes pity their own boyhood selves. "I was definitely envious but at the same time I was aware of their lower status. I wore better clothes. I traveled in a carriage. I had better food, and although I was annoyed by the extreme care I received, I also realized my exclusive position.

Whether I enjoyed my position very much is another question. . . . I used to stand in the window in my room and look down over the other side of the street where the boys used to play. . . . They used to walk barefoot in the mud and make mudpies, build castles, and so on. I would have loved to go out and do the same thing. But at the same time, I remember this as clear as if it was today, I wiped my hands of that imaginary dust and mud with which the other children were playing. I already knew what I was supposed to do and what I was not supposed to do. And certain things became disgusting to me. So I used to stay in my room most of the time and study my lessons, and think."°

Except for the very sheyneh, most boys find some time to play —even those who spend long hours at kheyder and those who help their parents in the store and those who at eight or nine are apprenticed to a trade. They also find time to fight, although fighting is "un-Jewish" in the extreme. "Do not hit anyone because your hands will fall off," is the adult injunction, which some children take literally and more do not. "When adults see children fighting, they bring the children together, they have to kiss each other or shake hands, they sit down and they are watched by the parents for a long time to see that they don't get into a fight again."° They are instructed to play only "clean and kosher games" and "by unclean they mean games like fighting."°

Nevertheless, they fight. A gang from one street fights a gang from another street, boys of one kheyder may fight the boys of another. In these clashes the bitterness of class difference often bursts forth, for the boys of one street are apt to be prost and the other gang "balebatish." They fight with tongues as well as hands and the word prostak is a favorite epithet. Nevertheless, noses become bloody and clothes are torn. When the boys come home after such a battle they are apt to get another beating from their fathers, for disgraceful behavior. "They used to play soldiers but very often this was more than a sport. A real war used to break out between the boys living on two streets. The boys from our street, the balebatisheh boys, would fight against the sons of the coachmen, shoemakers, horse dealers, butchers. But this was anger, not for fun, and when the mothers used to see such a war they would pull their hair from their own heads. . . ."°

"Sometimes when there was a quarrel between the two groups they would settle it by choosing one boy from each group to fight it out and the boy who won made his team the winners, and there would be no big fight. From the fine group I was always chosen. I was the strongest; and I never lost. No butcher boy ever beat *me* up!"°

There are also fights with boys who are not Jewish. They enter these fights only with reluctance and would avoid them if they could. To lose is painful, to win may prove dangerous. ". . . We had to go through the Gentile streets. This always meant a war with the goyisheh boys and their dogs. So we never went alone, but in groups. But every time there was a war—a fight. It would all start with insulting songs and would be returned with insulting songs. Then the fighting began until their parents stopped it. I used to wonder. The parents of these children were very friendly with our parents, so why did the children hate us?"ᵒ

These fights are not fun. Going to and from the kheyder, one avoids certain streets, hoping to elude the gangs; and one tries never to go alone. "Before Shevuos and Sukkos and other holidays we also had to pass by the goyisheh streets to get trees, branches, twigs, etc. to use for the holidays. And of course there was always a war. But we never went alone, but in large groups, and we always got what we needed."°

More painful than a bloody fight is the shearing of an earlock, a trick occasionally practiced on a boy unwary enough to pass one of the danger streets alone. It is a trick learned from parents who sometimes during a pogrom will shave off half the beard or one earlock of an adult Jew. To lose these symbols of Yiddishkayt is a deep pain and humiliation. The most common device for concealing the loss is to tie a rag around one's head and pretend that one has an earache or a toothache.

Dogs are associated with fights, but not with boyish games. To the people of the shtetl the dog is not a pet, but a symbol of brute strength and unpredictability. Whatever his breed, he is a bloodhound. The watchman on the estate of the absentee noble is accompanied by fierce dogs, hoping to surprise adventurous boys looking for nuts, fruits, berries or firewood. The outlying peasant houses are always guarded by dogs whose inclinations and masters prompt them to snap at the long caftans of the shtetl boys. The boys always run and the dogs always chase them. His role in the shtetl has stereotyped the dog as the dangerous beast. When melted wax is thrown into water to discover what has frightened a baby, the figure most often seen is that of a dog.

If an older child is frightened, two remedies may be suggested —to say the prayer called Krishmeh, or to urinate. One invokes divine aid, or else one eliminates the poison bred by fear. In either case the typical shtetl attitude is—get rid of it.

One outlet for boyish noise and violence is winked at by adults. Now and then a pig wanders from the street into a court-yard. When this happens, the boys in the neighborhood congregate to torment him. They attack him with sticks, they drive him from one corner to the other, they terrify him until he screeches in mingled fear and rage—and the screech of a pig is a sound more reminiscent of the torture chamber than of the barnyard. "When a pig gets angry he is dangerous like a lion."°

The grownups do not interfere. Cruelty is forbidden, one must have "pity on all living things." Noisiness is forbidden, rowdiness is forbidden. But this is a pig. The pig becomes a scape-goat before he escapes.

A large number of the "don't's" issued to children are based on superstitions shared with the peasants. In addition to dangers from divine wrath, earthly elements and irresponsible mortals, there is constant menace from the devils, ghosts and spirits that swarm the earth. Countless phrases used almost automatically in daily conversation pay tribute to the fear inspired by the super-natural population on earth and in heaven. "No evil eye" is the most common. Another, attached to any report of misfortune, is "not for us be it said" or even "not for us be it thought." One may announce, for example, "Ayzik's Gitteleh broke her leg, not for us be it said." Any statement remotely resembling a future plan is hastily followed by the phrase, "God willing," or "not making any vow." One does not say "I am going to Lodz tomorrow," but rather, "I might go to Lodz tomorrow, not making any vow."

If a dead person is mentioned in connection with someone who is alive, a protective phrase must also be added, "You look just like your (dead) father—wishing you long years!" In any case it is propitious to follow a person's name with some well-omened exclamation, such as "may he live to be a hundred and twenty." To count people is very risky, as the Angel of Death may regard this as incitement to diminish the number. Therefore if it is necessary to count the members of a gathering it is well to fool the bad spirit by saying, "Not-one, not-two, not-three," etc.

An unwary child may endanger his parents if he is careless in his play. If he walks backwards, for instance, his parents will burn in hell for as many years as the steps he takes. If he kicks up in back with his feet, he curses his mother with the left foot and his father with the right—the right hand position, like the head, being always the symbol of the superior as compared with the left or the foot. Throwing food behind him similarly threatens his parents.

Other practices would endanger the child. He must not play with his shadow, for that would make him stupid. He must not play with fire or he would become a bed-wetter. He must not stick out his tongue at a mirror, or it would fall off. He must not eat the first crust of the bread or he would become stupid.

The cleavage in activity between boy and girl begins early, for he may be only three when he is carried off to kheyder and the girl is left at home to help her mother. From then on their work and their play will be different. Even if the girl does go to school, it is for a shorter period, and shorter hours each day, and her main job is to be helpful at home.

The earliest work is baby tending. "The children grew up one after the other, and each one took care of the next."° But the care is apt to be given by the girl. When she goes out to play she carries the baby with her, "wrapped like a cabbage" in layer after layer. When it is her turn at hopscotch, she hands the baby to a friend and then reclaims it after her jumpy tour of the plotted squares. "When my sister was born—I was about ten then—I took care of her. So much so that when she woke in the middle of the night she would call for me, not for my mother or my father."°

A girl is always a mother to someone. If there are no small children at home, she will be told to help out her aunt or a neighbor. A big sister often figures almost as a parent to brothers or sisters who are considerably younger than she. If the mother should die, a sister usually slips into her role—not necessarily the oldest sister, but the one temperamentally most suited to the part.

To be a "mother" to a younger sibling—or for that matter to one's own child—does not necessarily mean to share his inmost thoughts and feelings. Inmost thoughts and feelings, unlike money, learning, and gossip are not freely shared in the shtetl. Despite a lack of privacy about overt affairs, it is possible for each individual to maintain his private inviolability. "If you want to know what goes on at my house ask a neighbor" is a saying balanced by, "You never know what goes on in another person's 'innards.' " You seldom want to know and he seldom wants to tell you. Each person has his "own four yards of earth." Perhaps the intimate swirl of shtetl life would be difficult to bear without the capacity for inner retreat.

In household matters, the girl's instruction will be by example rather than by precept. While the melamed is drilling his lessons into her brother, the mother at home is following the principle of "learn by doing," which is the one generally accepted. She gives few or no instructions and a daughter is supposed to learn how to bake halla, to sew, to keep house, by watching and picking things up for herself. The prevailing pattern is followed, of noticing what is done wrong rather than what is done right, and taking the satisfactory parts of the performance for granted. Later, when the girl marries and has a home of her own, the mother may be proud of her accomplishments, but they are apt to be more appreciated in her own home than in that of her parents.

In contrast to the series of rituals celebrating her brother's progress from one phase to the next, the girl has no ceremony from the time she is named until her marriage contract is signed. When she first begins to menstruate, if she tells her mother it will probably be with tears of fright, since any forewarning is unlikely. "I thought I was going to die. I didn't know what was wrong with me. . . . The only thing I could think of was that I was very sick or something like that."° In response she will be roundly slapped on both cheeks. After the tears induced by this treatment are dried, it will be explained that this is in order to make her rosy and beautiful. "I was very startled; the first thing she did, she slapped me on both cheeks. I looked at her and said, 'What does that mean?' 'Oh,' she said, 'that is, that you will have a wonderful color, all your life. My mother did that the same way with me. When a girl gets her menstruation she should be slapped in her face; the blood will go always to her face and stay there—and you see, that's true.' "°

This is the closest she comes to a *rite de passage*. Nevertheless, from this time she is increasingly reminded that girlhood is an apprenticeship for womanhood. "You are a bride girl now, a kaleh moyd," she will be reminded constantly. Until she is married, the menstrual rules do not apply to her at all. Menstruation is a physiological fact for the girl but a social fact for the matron.

Perhaps the girl feels left out when her brother is wrapped in his father's prayer shawl and carried to the kheyder. Perhaps, on the other hand, she glows with motherly pride, especially if she is the older sister who has been as a mother to him. To what extent her greater freedom may compensate for her lower status is a matter of individual temperament and experience. If her little brothers tease her as some do, crying "We are the ones who will say kaddish, but what will you do?"° then she may feel, "boys are luckier than girls,"° or "a girl's life is much harder than a boy's."° When those same brothers are penned into school twelve hours a day, beaten by the melamed for not knowing their lessons, scolded at home for being negligent about their yarmelkehs and their talis kotons, her burden may seem more light. And she, like her mother, may be "too busy to notice much."°

If the girl is left out, the boy is thrust out, when he is carried from his mother to the melamed—thrust out from babyhood and from the safe, enfolding warmth of the feminine world. The event is not without forewarning. For weeks grownups have been pinching his cheek, telling him he is a big boy now and soon will go to kheyder. Perhaps he has even been taken to play about "there where Torah is" in order to become imbued with the atmosphere of learning, just as his mother has taken him to the woman's section of the synagogue to give him a preview of the ritual world that will one day be his element.

From the time he enters kheyder, he will go to shul with his father and sit in the men's section. He will look more manly too, for his baby curls are cut off and his head cropped close, except for the precious earlocks. Barbers are expensive and the mother is likely to shear him herself, to the accompaniment of her tears and his. When all is done and his head is inexpertly shorn in ragged "steps" he looks like a "real" kheyder boy. If his mother could not nerve herself to sacrifice his hair she would do him double injury, for the other boys would jeer that he "looks like a girl—braids like a girl!" Except for the one lock his mother treasures as a memento, the hair that is cut off will be burned so that he will not have to go hunting for it in order to enter the future life.

The entry into the kheyder, then, marks a change in the boy's appearance as well as in his activities and his status. All are changes freighted with a mixture of deprivation and gratification, the loss of infantile privileges, pleasures and protection, the gain of rewards pointing toward manhood. The new world will be male, with the melamed teaching derekh erets, respect, as well as Torah, sternly instructing with no leaven of indulgence and permissiveness. Any direct and quasi-maternal care received by the smallest children in the kheyder will come from the melamed's assistant, the belfer, who sees that the little ones wash their hands, pronounce the correct blessings, keep their heads covered—incidentally demonstrating the possibilities and the limitations of interchanging masculine and feminine functions.

The world the boy enters is far more exacting than the one in which his sister remains, and if there is room for her to envy his male prerogatives, there is also opportunity for him to envy her feminine freedom. "Girls could do what they wanted,"° say many men. "Boys could do almost anything they liked,"° say many women. Such comments, however, are likely to be voiced in retrospect from outside the shtetl, or else as a result of outside influences.

Grownups in the shtetl are constantly telling the children that childhood is the carefree time of their life, warning them that all too soon they will grow up, and at the same time pushing them toward maturity. They say of an irresponsible person, "He's carefree like a child, no troubles, no worries." Yet to the child, existence may seem anything but carefree. The boy of three or four already knows something about the "yoke of Jewishness," ol fun Yiddishkayt. When he is four or five he has to know khumesh and is beaten by the melamed if he fails. To a five-year old, the routine of daily prayers, the stringent demands of the kheyder may not spell freedom and irresponsibility.

Although each year adds new responsibilities, most of the children want to grow up. They imitate their elders as much as possible, copying their gestures and intonations. "I used to walk with my grandfather. He too would tell me a lot of stories. He would walk with his hands folded behind his back and I would copy him."° They tell each other what they are going to do when they are big. Children below thirteen are not supposed to fast, but many of them insist on doing so. "I hid in the woods all day so that they couldn't make me eat."° Babies are petted, the youngest child is pampered, and still they want to grow up. Indulgence is with the infantile, but all the social rewards are with maturity. By the time one is old enough to recognize himself as a junior, the advantages of seniority are visible as a goal worth pursuing.

For the boy, the threshold of official maturity is his Bar Mitzvah—literally "Son of the Commandment"—a ceremony celebrated on his thirteenth birthday. Ritually, he is now an adult, and can be a member of a minyan. During the ceremony the father, who so rejoiced to assume the burden of his son's conduct, gives thanks to God "who hast freed me from the responsibility of this child."

When the boy is Bar Mitzvah he is called to the Torah for the first time as an individual. Heretofore he has been called only as a child with a group of other children, on the holiday of Simkhas Torah. For several weeks in advance he has been studying the rules for handling and putting on phylacteries, and it will now be his duty to wear them daily for his morning prayers. He may even achieve the dignity of a prayer shawl, although in many places this is reserved for his wedding day.

He also learns the appropriate chapter of the Shulkhan Arukh, with accompanying commentaries. Moreover, he works out with his teacher an elaborate oration, a drosheh. Like the ones he makes when he leaves the little children's kheyder and when he is married, it is an interpretation of the Law, presented as a discussion of some talmudic problem. On each successive occasion the discussion reaches a higher level of erudition and discourse. Whereas in the first juvenile display of learning the questions were asked by the melamed, they are now propounded by the youth himself, for his own answering. Sometimes a boy is sent to a special teacher to prepare for the Bar Mitzvah, perhaps a learned friend of the family who performs this service as an act of friendship and a "good deed."

The more orthodox the family, the more simple is the social celebration—"it's more religious that way."° Father and son go quietly to the synagogue and the boy, with no fanfare, puts on the phylacteries for his prayers, as he has learned to do during the preceding weeks of training. On Sabbath he is called to the Torah like a real man. Elaborate gifts and parties are associated with a less "religious" observance. The social part of the truly orthodox Bar Mitzvah is a simple reception, a kiddush in the synagogue and at home, with brandy and cakes for all. The high point is the declamation of his speech during this celebration, with parents beaming, friends admiring, and everyone preparing to discuss later the merits of the "little piece of Torah" to which he treats them.

For boys not destined to make study a career, the Bar Mitzvah often is an economic as well as a religious landmark. Many leave the kheyder on their thirteenth birthday, and some are at once apprenticed to a trade. Some of course are apprenticed earlier, or are taken out of school to help in their father's work.

Like most life cycle celebrations in the shtetl, the Bar Mitzvah ceremony emphasizes the group as much as the individual, for its significance lies in his new relationship to the community. At once he is guided on toward the next step. Hardly has the boy been Bar Mitzvah than he is reminded that he is now a potential bridegroom, a khossen bokher. Anything not in line with male adult duties is frowned on as "foolishness" with "no purpose." He must begin preparing for marriage, just as he had prepared for Bar Mitzvah and for each phase of kheyder. At each phase there is a straining and a training toward the next. Each comes as a definite change, but usually a change for which the groundwork has been laid. And at each stage a portion of babyhood is renounced, while a new share of the "yoke" is accepted.

"If a boy is Bar Mitzvah and still likes to play, people make fun of him and tell him that he is supposed to be a mentsh. And girls the same thing. If a girl is over twelve and is still playing her mother will say, 'Give her stones to play with. You are a child, not a bride-to-be.' "°

From the time of his Bar Mitzvah the boy, now officially adult, will have less and less to do with women. He has long since ceased playing with girls, only very small boys do that. If he so forgot himself, his companions might chant a verse at him, "Donkey-ass, donkey-ass, jump out, jump out!" or they might jeer, "Shame on him, playing with a girl!" Even the older boys would point out that it is not becoming, "es past nisht."

From the outset the chief burden of avoidance is on the male. Girls are less often warned against playing with boys, although they too understand that "boys of eight or nine no longer play with girls."° The reasons are left vague, as always. "Only once my mother told me that one doesn't play with boys. But why I shouldn't play with them she never told me. It was always like that."° As they grow up they will become more and more aware of the rules against intermingling of sexes.

Little girls have their own games, one of the favorite being "papa-mamma." "We played ball and jackstones. We also played hide and seek. But the most popular game was papa-mamma . . . just the girls played that game. Sometimes the little boys would play with us but not the boys our age."° Like little girls anywhere, in their game of "house" they reproduce the situations with which they are familiar. "The father was always in shul or away at work with the brothers, because we were just girls. . . . The mother remained at home to cook, sew, take care of the children. . . . Sometimes a child would get sick and we had to call a doctor. . . . Or a stranger came to be fed. . . . At other times somebody got married—something was always happening. And it was fun to play."°

The reluctance of the girls to play the parts of men seems general, and the shtetl pattern of home life makes it easy to avoid the necessity. "We played papa-mamma most of the time and we had so much fun. . . . We had no boys and the girls didn't want to play boys' parts so we would imagine that they were on a trip.

. . . Let's say I was the Rebbetsn (wife of a Rebbeh). So I would take a large rhubarb leaf with some small grass and put it over my head and that would be a hat with a feather sticking out. Then from a long piece of grass and a stick I would make a lorgnette. And I would walk around like the Rebbetsn, give orders to the servants, sit in the garden and smell the flowers. I went to shul and prayed like the Rebbetsn, in fact I even hiccuped like her. They had a special kind of hiccup, I think it was put on. . . ."°

The girls have comparatively little time for play, but they make the most of what is available. Usually there is a baby or a toddler to be included, and occasionally the big sister rebels. "I had to take care of my younger brothers and sisters. When I was going somewhere they were always following me and I was chasing them away so they were complaining to my mother who was insisting on my taking them with me."° For the most part, however, baby tending is taken for granted. If the baby must be rocked, the girl says sadly, "I can't come out to play today." Or else baby is taken along. It would be highly unusual to see a group of girls playing with no nurselings on their hands.

The boys have even less time for play than their sisters, and at different hours, for they are in kheyder or at work from early morning until nightfall, except for Sabbath and holidays, and an annual excursion with the melamed to the fields.

They also have a number of games that they play in the kheyder itself, bookish games, appropriate to the setting. Each locality has its own variants, handed down by one generation of students to the next. One of the simplest, for very young children, is to make a book into a "windmill" by folding the pages into each other in such a way that when it is stood up the pages turn by themselves, like the wings of a windmill. Or two boys choose different pages and count the number of times a given word appears on each. The one whose page has that word most often is the winner and has the right to give the loser a number of slaps on the back. Cheating is punished by ostracism.

Many of the games draw on stories they have been studying. Characters from folklore, from sacred writings, from the shtetl streets, jostle each other and are linked with themes reflecting life as the kheyder boy has observed it. Kheyder studies make their way also into some of the outdoor games. The study of the Prophets is reflected in tugs of war between teams that represent the Jews and the Philistines.

Outdoor games are not encouraged by parents, especially not by the mother whose solicitude is most actively focused on the physical welfare of the child. Both parents are concerned constantly with "making the child into a Jew and a mentsh," but her endless stream of admonitions and reminders has to do with physical well-being. Children must not hurt themselves, they must not get into a draft, or get chilled. Above all, they must eat enough. Fears of overeating are negligible. Few households in the shtetl provide opportunities for it, but in any case food represents the mother's love and how could there be too much of that?

Warmth also is associated with parental affection and protection. The fear of chill or drafts is extreme. Even in summer, little children are bundled into layer upon layer of wrappings "like an onion," and the mother whose child is not too warmly dressed would feel guilty of neglect. There is always room for one more muffler, and no one ever outgrows the need for incessant health hovering.

If, despite all precautions, a child actually does become ill, both natural and supernatural remedies will be sought. All members of the family unite in the interests of health. No expense must be spared, and if the parents cannot pay for medical care, near or even distant relatives must step in, for the obligation of the well to succor the sick is absolute.

Nothing is worse than illness. Even the loss of parnosseh is feared less than the loss of gezunt, health. Illness of one member upsets the whole household, arouses the anxiety of everyone from parents to distant relatives and neighbors. With sighs, advice and money, all participate in efforts to cure the ailment.

In times of illness the women take command, the men are helpless. Their only contribution is the recital of prayers and psalms. Silent and haggard they watch from the corner the busy activities of mothers, aunts, grandmothers and female neighbors.

Since the cause of illness must be something that has gotten into the child, it must be eliminated, and the universal method is the enema administered either by a member of the household or a "professional." A familiar, and to the children a dread figure in the shtetl is the enema woman who devotes herself exclusively to this art. Her apparatus in its most primitive form is a calf's bladder and a goose quill, and her treatment is threatened as a cure for any ailment, including naughtiness.

Whatever is wrong, the mother will first try her own remedies, perhaps compresses or tea with raspberry syrup. The neighbors will join in with advice taken from their experience and household history, bringing in nostrums handed down through generations.

If all the "women's remedies" fail, the *feltsher* or *feltsherkeh* is called—a man or woman who has a rudimentary knowledge, not of medicine but of medicines. His battery of cures includes chiefly castor oil, gargle, and cupping, with leeches for very severe illness.

In extreme cases, with both reluctance and fear, the doctor is called. He arrives by carriage or sleigh, a figure of awe, waited on hand and foot and deferred to by everyone. He sits in state while the family stand about him, the women craning and staring. His instruments, his learning, his foreign appearance and manner— he is usually a Gentile or a highly assimilated Jew—inspire wonder and uneasiness. Everyone competes to bring him whatever he asks for—a spoon, some water, a towel—and to fetch his coat when he is ready to leave. As he goes, the father timidly shakes hands with him, shyly pressing the fee into his palm.

If the doctor gives up hope, the last resort is the Tsaddik with his amulets and prayers. During any illness, of course, prayers are offered, charity distributed, appeals taken "to the graves." At the same time the resources of local *znakhors,* medicine men or women, are not neglected, and their innumerable charms, herbs, magic formulas are brought into service. Placing the child in a hospital is avoided at any cost. No care can equal a mother's care and no place can be as good for him as home.

Sicknesses that are transitory and to be expected in the course of normal life, are freely discussed in the family and neighborhood. Chronic diseases, or those that leave a physical or mental defect, belong to the area of concealment. The family tries to hide them and neighbors pretend not to know about them for they are a reason to be "ashamed before people." The other illnesses are a passing misfortune. These are a major visitation and there must be a reason behind them.

Mental illness belongs to the category of the hidden in those families that can afford to contrive concealment. Parents will seldom give up hope of curing the shameful condition, going from doctor to Tsaddik and from the Tsaddik back to "the Professor." The ultimate shame is to consign the afflicted one to an asylum and if this happens it will never be mentioned. Not only is it a disgrace to the family but it can be a handicap in marrying off the other children. Marriage itself is regarded as one cure for minor mental instability.

Among the very poor, concealment is impossible and every shtetl has its *meshuggeneh* or "crazy people." The meshuggener may be an object of childish fears. "I was told to go to sleep but I was afraid to sleep alone. I saw a meshuggeneh in the shtetl . . . she was a woman of about forty, dressed in rags and always was singing and speaking. And she made us be afraid. She used to sing at night, I heard her and I was afraid."° At the same time, the "crazy ones" are the butt of children's mockery and pranks, and often the intervention of adults is necessary to protect them from childish cruelty. "There was a crazy man at whom the little boys always threw rocks."°

Within the limits set by physical humanitarianism, the adults themselves consider such village characters a legitimate target. "They would laugh at them and make fun of them in public."° Against the setting of a normal family who could be shamed and injured by it, insanity is the stuff of tragedy. Detached from the related group, the "meshuggener" is a comic.

Despite the agonies of grief, shame and secrecy, and the handicap to matchmaking, a man does not necessarily lose status because of insanity in his family. "The people didn't stop buying meat from the shokhet because he wasn't responsible for his crazy daughter."° "The whole shtetl knew that the Rov's son was crazy but they accepted it as a '*shtrof fun Gott*' (punishment from God). And it did not harm the respect the people had for the Rov."°

Bodily defects and deformities are a source of shame and anxiety to women but not necessarily to men. The body is a primary part of the woman, a secondary part of the man. The only hope for a malformed girl is to conceal her defect or else to have it "covered with a dowry."° The boy can compensate by his achievement in learning, business or trade. It is not unusual to see a hunchback or cripple with a beautiful wife and a brood of healthy children. There is no squeamishness about mentioning a person's physical deformities, as there is about mentioning a source of real shame. The attitude is reflected in such simple descriptive nicknames as "Shimen Hunchback" or "Kalmen the Lame."

For the healthy body, hygiene is primarily ritual. The mikva is for purification rather than for cleansing, and one is supposed to bathe before the ritual immersion. The many hand-washings, first thing in the morning and before each meal, are religious rather than sanitary. The weekly scrubbing of the whole family from head to foot is as much a Sabbath observance as a matter of personal hygiene, although the same purpose is served.

The body itself is respected, for it has been given by God. Because it is His gift, it must not be altered. Whatever traits it displays are heaven-sent and it should be preserved intact for the return to heavenly life when Messiah comes. Hair and fingernails that have been cut off must be gathered and burned. If death is bloody, the blood that has been shed must be buried with the body, if necessary with the earth on which it was spilled. After a pogrom, tragic burial parties try to dig up as much as possible of the ground which holds the victims' blood, in order to bury them whole. Whatever belongs to the body is clean as long as it is still part of the living organism, but becomes repulsive and even dangerous once it has been separated, whether it be hair, nails, blood or excreta.

The body is respected primarily as the container and squire of the mind and spirit. Excellence of mind and spirit are conceived as Jewish—the "Jewish head" and the "Jewish heart" are "the sign of the 'real' Jew." Physical superiority is not Jewish in the same way, but is rather ascribed to the goyim.

Ideals of beauty reflect the exalting of the spiritual over the physical. The beautiful baby and the beautiful woman are round and rosy. As the boy becomes adult, he is expected to grow increasingly thin and pale, that is, to undergo a progressive etherealization, until he becomes the "beautiful" old man—pale, emaciated, aflame with inner light, the epitome of the complete and "real" Jew. His ideal pallor and emaciation are associated, not with physical weakness, but with spiritual vigor. A mother will press food on a young scholar and cry out "How thin he is!" but she will be proud of his studious appearance. The ideal son is one on whom you can endlessly urge food with no danger that he will ever seem not to need it. A yeshiva boy who worked in an orchard over the summer came home strong and ruddy and was berated by his family—"Look at you, coarse and red, like a prostak, like a coachman!"° The wealthy father wants his daughters sleek and blooming, to show how well he has fed them. His sons should be pale and thin, to show how well he has educated them.

The child learns, then, to respect the body as God's gift and as the container of mind, heart, and soul. "I was so angry I almost jumped out of my vessels!" is a familiar expression that implies the attitude. The role of the body as container is suggested by the frequent reference to a brilliant scholar as *keyleh*, vessel. "What a vessel that is!" a proud father-in-law will boast of the khossen.

Respect is appropriately concentrated at the head, evaporating as the feet are approached. A division between the upper and lower parts of the body is symbolized by the girdle men wear when praying, when writing Torah, and often when studying. More than respect is concentrated at the head. It is the focus of attention and concern. In a sense, the head is the man. Its qualities determine his qualities, and his fate. Jewish portraits and paintings characteristically depict a head that is real; if the body appears, it is apt to look like a dummy covered with clothes. Children sometimes picture God as "just a big head."

The words for describing the quality of a person's head are countless, and invoke almost every variety of image: animal, human, inanimate, abstract, emotional. One may have a big head, a heavy head, a pointed head, a horse head, an iron head, a stuffed head, a flying head, a head on wheels, a head on screws, almost as many kinds of head as there are kinds of adjectives. A cat's head means no memory, and children are often forbidden to play with cats for fear of losing their ability to remember.

Because the head is the container of the brains, it is treated with tender care. Baby's heads are covered from the moment they come into the world, and the head of the male is always covered. In handling babies one must be breathlessly careful not to touch the head unless absolutely necessary, and then with extreme gentleness. When children are beaten the head must not be hurt, and the characteristic cry of the mother to the flailing father is, "Only not on the head! Be careful, careful, not on the head!"°

The symbolism is pervasive. The head of the table, the head of the bed, the head of the fish which the approving husband presents to his wife, each carries its honorific connotations.

The importance of the face is evident in a multitude of expressions suggesting that what happens to a person's status happens to his face, and what he is, is revealed in his face. Disrespect is "daring the face," to humiliate is "bringing shame on the face." A noble person has a "luminous face," the leaders are the "faces" of the community.

The heart, contained in the body, has fewer descriptive terms than the head, though it too is used as symbol of the man and of the Jew. The hidden entities, the mind and the heart, must be revealed. The mind shows itself through the eyes and through the discourse of the mouth. The heart shows itself through the eyes, the words, and the deeds. But the container, the body, must be concealed. Nakedness is shameful, even between man and wife. Even to members of the same sex, the body is exposed only in the bathhouse or when men and boys swim in the river. A son, however, must never see his father's nakedness. As soon as children can dress themselves they are taught to be "modest" and "decent." The body itself is not in the least disgusting, but to expose it would be so.

One part of the body that comes close to disgust is the feet, especially the toes. They are furthest from the head, lowest, and nearest to the ground. An orthodox Jew's feet are never uncovered, he may even sleep in socks.

Possibly the association with death contributes to the repugnance for feet. Dead people are picked up by the toes, and when one talks to a corpse, especially in making a request, one grasps the toes. The association with dirt seems stronger, however. Feet are always treading the mire, always in a position symbolic of inferiority. If by accident a book or a piece of bread falls to the floor which is the realm of feet, it is hastily picked up, dusted off and kissed.

V

THE KOSHER HOUSE

Just as the body is the container of the mind and spirit, so the home is the container of the family life. The house means the household, and its quality comes from the people who live in it. A "beautiful house" is a harmonious household. A "broad house" is an open house, where nothing is lacking, where all who enter will find hospitality and help.

Every house must have a housewife, a balebosteh. It cannot be a real house without one. Nor can it be a beautiful house without "Yiddishkayt," which means more than having a mezuzah on every door. That the mezuzah will be there is taken for granted. Yiddishkayt, however, means full and "beautiful" observance of the traditional ways, the responsibility for which rests chiefly on the balebosteh.

Nevertheless, there is a physical house. Its outer aspect may vary, according to local architecture and the economic position of the people who live in it. Certain features and certain characteristics of its interior, however, will be constant.

Unless the family is unusually prosperous, there will probably be not more than two rooms, and may be only one. The usual interior is plastered and whitewashed. The floor may be of boards but more often the earth serves as a floor, swept and sanded.

The door will be locked only at night, when all doors and shutters are carefully fastened. During the hours when people may drop in to "catch a chat," a locked door would be an outrage. Nobody knocks before entering, but after coming in the guest or neighbor will ask politely, "May I come in? Do I disturb you?" The invariable answer is, "Come in, come in, sit down, have a glass of tea." Everyone is always busy but no one is ever too busy to welcome a guest. In summer the neighbor may merely put her head in at the open window, and stand for hours gossiping, with her feet outside and her head in the house.

The ideal in housing arrangements provides a separate room for sleeping. The wealthy few may have separate bedrooms, one for parents and one for children, but a family is considered fortunate if it has a special sleeping room for parents and children together. Father and mother always have separate beds, preferably on opposite sides of the room, with the baby's cradle or crib close to the mother's bed. Perhaps a child will sleep with the parents, or perhaps a number of boys or girls will sleep in one bed, laid in rows with their heads alternately at the head or the foot, in order to give more room, and all covered with one large, warm comforter. A really good bed is soft and high, with feather beds, eiderdowns and soft pillows. If a family has to move, every effort is made to take the precious bedding along. It is an important part of the wife's dowry, and as soon as a girl is born her mother will start "plucking feathers" for her bridal outfit. These same feathers are a delight to marauders during pogroms. They love to rip open the featherbeds and send the contents snowing through the air. In the streets, after a pogrom, a swirl of feathers is as common as a stain of blood.

When the family overflows the bedroom, a child or two may sleep on a wooden couch in the kitchen, or on one of the long kitchen tables, commonly called "benches." Or a few chairs may be put together, close to the wall.

If a daughter marries and her husband comes to live in her parents' home, a new room may be made by hanging a curtain to form a partition. A curtain may also be used if the house has only one room, to separate a portion of it for a bedroom.

The ideal arrangement also calls for a special place to eat on Sabbath and holidays, different from the one used for ordinary meals; a place too where the father may study. It could be in the bedroom, in a two-room house. This would be quite satisfactory.

If separate sleeping quarters and Sabbath eating place cannot be arranged, it is no major misfortune to accommodate the family to one room, where everything happens—cooking, cleaning, sewing, baby tending, studying, perhaps tailoring or making shoes in one corner. Each person carries on his own activities, undisturbed by the others. In the evening, they may gather about the table to use the same light. On one side the father studies, swaying and chanting over his books; on the other the son also studies audibly; meanwhile the mother sews or picks feathers, while in a corner the daughter rocks the baby, softly singing a lullaby. If a neighbor should come in and not hear the variegated hum of activity the immediate question would be, "What's wrong? So still in the house!"

Even if a large family lives in a one-room house, the balebosteh will try to give it a special appearance for the Sabbath, to make it look "Sabbath-like," *shabbesdik*. Everything will be cleaned, the oven covered with a board, the table will have the white Sabbath cloth and the candlesticks. Only by putting your head inside the door, they say, just by sniffing the atmosphere of the house, you can tell whether it is Sabbath or weekday.

During the week the Sabbath clothes will be put away, all together. Storage space is divided according to weekday and holiday clothes, not according to individual ownership. The candlesticks and Sabbath cloth will be kept in mammeh's cupboard which holds an amazing variety of things, including raspberry preserves—"may we not need to use them!"—and chicken fat, *shmalts,* if the family is lucky enough to have some.

The mother always knows where things are, although nobody else does. To be a good housekeeper means that one keeps the house clean, observes the dietary laws scrupulously, never mixes the various sets of dishes, towels and cutlery, always has a fresh cloth for the Sabbath meals, is a good cook, and knows where everything is in the house.

Beneath the orderly surface, however, confusion may exist for all except the presiding housewife. Closets, cupboards and drawers are usually locked and the woman of a prosperous house carries an impressive bundle of keys about with her. The keys are the symbol of her status, and she jealously guards the closed drawers to show that she and she only is the balebosteh in the house. Every storage place is crammed to capacity because almost nothing is thrown away. Discarded clothing and rags will be kept for years—"It's a pity to throw them out, one never knows when they will be needed."

The most important wall of the house is, of course, the eastern one. Sometimes it is marked by a special picture or embroidery, showing the direction one must face for prayers. Such a decoration is called "the mizrakh." If the eastern wall is not clearly marked, a guest in the house will ask when it is time for prayers, "Beg pardon, where is the East?"

However modest the house, the balebosteh will try to give it some touch to make it pretty, though often the touch is slight and almost pathetic. She will make curtains for the windows, or hang up a picture of a famous rabbi, or set flowers on the window sill. The climate of the room is not conducive to healthy plant life, however, and before long they may look "like tubercular flowers."

In decorating her home she will draw chiefly from peasant art. Any household embroideries are apt to be copied from peasant themes. Jewish folk art is chiefly verbal. There is a rich lore of stories, songs, sayings, proverbs, but very little Jewish handicraft, aside from ritual objects. The covers of the Torah, the cases for the phylacteries and prayer shawls, are lavishly embroidered with traditional designs handed down through centuries—the dove, the lion, Hebrew letters, stylized scrollwork. Wood carving and elaborate silverwork decorate those ritual objects that offer scope for it, but there is no specifically Jewish art. There is no equivalent of the peasant embroideries, or the elaborate paper cutouts made by the Poles. The reason obviously does not lie in lack of manual facility, for the shtetl has produced many highly skilled craftsmen—goldsmiths, diamond cutters, watch makers. The free election of the folk, however, appears to be verbal or at least audial rather than visual or tactile. "In the beginning was the Word," and the word still leads all forms.

Aside from the spoken word, the outstanding folk expression is through song. In addition to the ritual music, the melodic chanting of prayers, the individual melodies of the Tsaddikim, countless secular songs are sung in the shtetl. There are the lullabies constantly crooned to babies, work songs describing the labors of the artisan or complaining about the difficulties of his toil. There are the love songs in which young girls celebrate romantic themes, frowned on by the tradition but enjoyed by those who are not too sheyn to indulge such fantasies. The Hassidim especially are known for their love of song, extolling the exaltation of wine, the joys of faith, the exploits and miracles of the Tsaddik.

No matter how few rooms a house has, and no matter how many functions the kitchen may serve, it is still dedicated primarily to cooking. The great stove of tile, porcelain or brick does duty as a furnace in winter—and unfortunately, in summer too. Except in very hot weather, something is always cooking on the stove, if not for today then for tomorrow. In winter, when the fire is never allowed to die down, there is always hot water boiling, ready for tea. But unless the family is very poor there is likely to be also one of the long-simmering soups or stews or boiled dishes that are central to cookery.

The cooking equipment is dictated by the nature of the dietary laws, strict observance of which is absolutely essential to the Yiddishkayt of a house. A good balebosteh has in her keeping the dietary rectitude of her whole family. The importance of observing the dietary laws is evident in the deprivations to which people will subject themselves in order to avoid violations. Travelers who do not carry kosher provisions with them will go hungry or subsist on dry bread rather than risk eating forbidden food. When water is scarce they will use it for the ritual hand washing rather than for drinking. If the shokhet dies, a whole shtetl may go without meat or import it at great expense until a new ritual slaughterer arrives. Army conscripts have lived on bread and potatoes for years because nothing else seemed safe, except when they were garrisoned near a Jewish town. Whenever that happens, the community feels a responsibility for feeding the Jewish soldiers on kosher food as long as they are near. Sometimes, too, kosher food is sent to prisons for the Jewish convicts.

Inability to observe the rules is felt more as pain than as danger. The Law makes it clear that life and welfare come before the dietary regulations. Nevertheless a very pious Jew prefers to keep to the letter of the rule, even though he knows it would be permissible not to do so. This is what he must do, but even more, this is what he wishes to do.

Dietary considerations are the more important since food plays so large a part in religious, social and family life. Feasting and fasting are major elements in the holidays. Food is conspicuous in all social celebrations and even a casual call is a signal for some sort of refreshment. Feeding her family is the duty and the gratification of the housewife, who thinks of herself not as one who eats but as one who gives nourishment, and who equates rejection of her food with rejection of her love.

The kitchen is the real schoolroom of the girl, where she learns by watching and by doing rather than by direct instruction. The infinite details of "keeping kosher" come up one after the other in the form of household crises, and part of her cooking course consists in hurried trips to the rabbi for advice, or to the neighbor to borrow a pot, a cupful of sugar, a bit of tea. The intricacy and the multitude of dietary problems could make of housekeeping an exacting life work, but for most women they will be combined with the "chase after parnosseh." Nobody assumes that the variety of demands is too much for one individual, although the busy housewife seldom neglects to point out the enormous burden that "is all on my head."

The daughter of the house learns by observation what she must do in order to observe the all-important dietary laws, the laws of *kashrus*. If she should ask for reasons, her mother will tell her, it is done this way, this is how it must be. Meanwhile her brother at the kheyder is taught the rules, but not their application. He will learn that the basis for kashrus was given to Moses on Mount Sinai. He will study the laws catalogued in Leviticus, and the interpretations of them developed in countless commentaries. The girl's knowledge is practical, his is academic. He learns, for example, what parts of the hind quarter of beef must not be eaten, and the reasoning behind the prohibition, but he might not recognize a hind quarter if he saw it hanging in a shop. She will learn to avoid certain cuts, although she will not know the explanations he can recite so glibly. She learns how, he learns why. If any question comes up about the fitness of the food in the kitchen, a man must be consulted, either a rabbi or a learned scholar.

Everyone in the shtetl knows, of course, that one must eat only food that is kosher, or ritually fit; and that food which is treyf, or ritually unfit, must be rejected. Men, women and children know that in order to be kosher food must be of the right kind, be prepared in the right way, and be uncontaminated by any substance or circumstance that could make it unfit. They are most commonly concerned with the laws of kashrus in connection with animal foods, although some vegetable foods are forbidden—for example, untithed grain, crossbred grain, and the fruit of a tree that has been bearing for less than three full years.

Everyone is familiar too with the foods that are permitted: quadrupeds that both ruminate and have cloven hoofs, birds that do not eat carrion, and fish with scales. All other animals are ruled inedible, as are their milk and eggs. This excludes carnivores, rodents, shellfish, birds of prey, eaters of carrion, and reptiles. Probably the peasants know as well as the Jews that pork and its derivatives are forbidden, for this prohibition is the most conspicuous one in Eastern Europe, where the pig furnishes the major source of meat to the majority of those who are not Jewish.

Although girls are not burdened with esoteric explanations, they are fully acquainted with the basic consideration to which a large part of the dietary regulations is ascribed—namely, the humanitarian one, which is paramount in these as in all other laws. They realize that the principle of "pity for all living things," is applied not only to people and to the animals they keep about them, but also to those animals designed by God to be the food of man. Any child knows that in order to be kosher the "permitted" animals must be killed in a way that causes a minimum of pain, and this is the blanket explanation for the rules about slaughtering for food. Hunting is forbidden, since it may inflict death in a cruel way. The shokhet's blade must be so keen that there is no brutal tearing of flesh or skin, but only one swift, almost painless stroke, which must sever both trachea and jugular vein. The constant inspection of the rabbi enforces this ruling and serves as a reminder that although human welfare requires the killing of animals, it must be done with as little suffering as possible. It must be done by one who is trained in the art, and never by a feeble-minded person, a deaf-mute, a drunkard or a blind man. In contrast to this picture of the slaughterer as surgeon, the shtetl views with horror the methods of the peasants. "How they slaughter pigs. I saw it once and wouldn't ever want to see it again. It's horrible. The man sits on the pig's back and plunges the knife in again and again. And the pig yells. It was just horrible."°

A little girl knows as well as her brother that an animal which has died a natural death or has not been slaughtered ritually is just as treyf as one of the wrong kind. The defects that can make an animal treyf even after it has been killed in the approved manner are academic knowledge to the boy, but vivid experience for the girl who hears her mother bargain for the chicken, goes with her to have it killed by the shokhet, and witnesses the final "koshering" at home, with alternate soaking, salting and rinsing until all free blood has been drained off—for blood that has left the living stream is abhorrent as well as forbidden.

A humanitarian explanation is also given for the ironclad rule against mixing dairy, or *milkhik* foods with meat and poultry, or *fleyshik* foods. The basis is said to be the command that "thou shalt not seethe the kid in the milk of its mother." For the girl, however, the problem is so compelling that the rationale may sink into the background. It becomes a matter of constant vigilance to keep the separation of milk foods and meat foods absolute, in time as well as in space. They must not touch each other, they must not even be stored in the same place, they must not be cooked at the same time and they must not be eaten at the same meal. They must not be eaten from the same dishes nor with the same tableware, nor must the two categories of dishes or pots be allowed to touch each other. In a house where the main room is used for many purposes besides cooking, the separation in space demands ingenuity, energy, and unremitting concentration. The boy too must remember to keep "dairy" and "meat" separate in time. Six hours must elapse after eating meat before milk may be taken, but less time is necessary before following milk with meat.

Fortunately for the housewife, the bulk of the shtetl diet is drawn from the third class of foods, *parveh*—neither milk nor meat, but "neutral." These, which may be eaten with anything, include flour and its products, eggs, vegetables, fruits, salt, sugar, condiments, beverages, and most fortunate of all, fish. Next in importance come the dairy foods, of which great quantities are used. Meat is so scarce that the meat dishes and utensils are the ones least used. The traveling artisan or peddler takes a milk pot with him, knowing that he will have little use for a meat pot. When the meat pot is used it means Sabbath, holiday, a special event, sickness in the family—or else a very rich house.

The ideal minimum is two kitchen tables, one for preparing dairy foods and one for meat foods. A house too poor for these will have an extra "meat" board to put on top of the "dairy" table on the rare occasions when meat must be prepared. Even the poorest, however, must manage two separate sets of dishes, cutlery and cooking utensils, one for meat and the other for milk.

There must be two additional sets for use during the eight days of Passover. The minimum need of the humblest house-keeper, then, is four complete and separate sets of cooking and eating utensils. In usage the minimum may be reduced, but not by much, even though the shtetl is well versed in reducing a minimum. The wife of the rich man will have six sets of every-thing, one pair for special Sabbath and holiday use.

If a neighbor runs in to help during an illness, her first question will be, "which are for meat and which are for milk?" There is always a difference in appearance as well as in place, but each household has its own system so that no one can know without asking.

The problem of keeping kosher is many-faceted. The eco-nomic stress in itself is considerable. Not only is kosher meat more costly than the other, but after one has paid for a chicken with painfully earned coins, it may turn out to have a spotted liver or to be otherwise unfit. One runs to the rabbi asking advice and if possible he will find it kosher. But it is not always possible and then there is no Sabbath—joy is gone. A housewife buys very few eggs during the year and if she does invest in one there is a special reason. But when she opens it, she may find a fleck of blood and then there is no help. Nothing can make that egg ritually fit to eat.

After provisions have been brought home they still must be protected. If the baby is just beginning to run about and get into things, he may ruin the food for a whole day by splashing milk into the meat pot. And again, one drops everything and runs to the rabbi wailing, what shall I do, must I throw it all away?

Whenever possible, the answer is no. Waste is wicked and to be avoided. There are innumerable methods of "re-koshering" food that has been contaminated by contact, rules for the amount of fleyshik necessary to dilute the ill effects of a few drops of milk. But the methods are complicated, the running to the rabbi is time consuming and difficult, and the strain is unending.

Dishes and cutlery can be purified more easily than food, although it is far better to keep them pure than to make them so. A knife is simply thrust into earth, and in most houses the kitchen floor or a flowerpot is used for purification. Dishes are scalded with hot water. Yet, although it can be done, one runs a house as if it were impossible. The different dishes are of different colors and patterns, kept as far apart as possible and never mixed.

The concept of kosher has broad application. Cloth can be kosher or not, depending on whether it mixes linen or silk with wool. A woman on emerging from the mikva is kosher and if she has not been purified, she is treyf. The menstruating bride is not kosher.

The terms are also used figuratively. A "kosher person" is one who is honest, and dishonesty is described as treyf or non-kosher. "A thick-souled, treyf bone" is one way of referring to a mean, untrustworthy person. A vacillating individual is "neither meat nor milk." A treyfeh parnosseh is a dishonest calling, and a frequent wish is for "a beautiful and koshereh parnosseh." Illegal, forbidden literature is "treyf."

Whatever the application, kosher means correct and acceptable. "It means all right, the way it ought to be."°

The complex observance of kashrus is only one aspect of the girl's kitchen apprenticeship. There is much to be learned about the cooking itself. Economic limitations and gastronomic preferences conspire to make most dishes elaborate and time consuming. Shtetl tastes do not run to food that is in a state of nature. There is much chopping, kneading, rolling, simmering, seasoning. Food usually means cooked food and for the most part it is served warm—even if it is only milk with bread, or only bread with water, well seasoned. When it is warm it must be very warm. Tea and soup should be scalding hot, so that it must be blown on and sipped slowly, with "ah's" of appreciation between sips.

Well-cooked food should be soft and tender, if it is not chopped like chicken liver and gefillteh fish. Fat is a sign of opulence and savor. Fat meat is better than lean. When the housewife buys a chicken she blows on its rear feathers to make sure that the part underneath is yellow with fat. Soup should have globules, "eyes" of fat swimming around in it.

There is little taste for raw vegetables, aside from radishes, cucumbers and onions. Vegetables as such are in any case not a favored part of the diet, except for carrots. Beets are used only in borshtsh. The favorite vegetables are dried legumes—peas, beans, lentils.

Good food is spicy, but it should be accented with highly flavored relishes and pickles, including cucumbers, peppers, green tomatoes, apples. Horseradish is a household staple. As background to all this flavor there must be an abundance of starchy foods—noodles, potatoes and above all bread. Many of the holidays have their own characteristic breads, including the festive hallah for Sabbath.

The daughter of the house learns to be far more concerned with the taste, temperature and texture than with the appearance of the food, for eating is a gustatory rather than a visual pleasure. Most of the food is nondescript in color and there is little effort to appeal to the eye with garnishes, color contrast or arrangement.

Except for Sabbath, holidays and special occasions, the prevailing rule is a minimum of fixed meals. The women and children eat when they are hungry, the men when they return home. Just as the infant is fed when he wishes to be, so the child and even the grownup for the most part follows a self-demand feeding schedule. Thoroughly cooked food is better adapted to such a schedule than the kind that spoils if it is not eaten at once.

Despite the irregularity of eating hours, meals do have names, and the basic pattern is for breakfast, lunch and dinner or supper. There are numerous names also for eating between meals, a regular and respected practice. Children are always entitled to a snack. The husband will say, "Have you something to take in the mouth?" unless his wife anticipates him and urges, "Don't you want to bite into something?" or "Take something to support your heart." Food is never locked away. "No matter what you were doing or how busy you were, you stopped several times a day to drink tea with jam. The meals were divided in such a way that it seemed to me we were eating all day."°

Special delicacies or sweets are known as *nasheray,* and the pleasant exercise of eating them is *nashn,* to nibble. Sweet things in general are feminine or childish. Women traditionally like to nibble on sweets and small children get sweet buns with jam or fruit. At a celebration there may be cakes for the women and snacks of meat or fish for the men. On Purim when one plays the fool, men eat sweets, and it is the only holiday on which sweet foods are required.

It is "natural" to give men the best food. A man needs good food to keep up his strength. One keeps out the best for him, and insists on his eating it. A woman eats constantly, nibbling and tasting in the course of cooking, seldom sitting down to a real meal except on special occasions. For her eating is incidental, feeding others is important.

If there is a scarcity, however, it is "natural" to feed the children first. Parents, especially mothers, will go hungry in order to make sure that the children have enough to eat. And what children eat is always diminutive. "Little Hershl, do you want a little piece of bread with a little bit of jam?" one will ask. Father eats a beygl but the same roll when given to a small child is a "little beygl," a *beygeleh.* The little boy puts a "little nash" into his little mouth, for everything that a small child has or is given is made diminutive by the suffix "leh."

Food is always good, always good for people, always a token

of good feeling. There is no malicious food sorcery in the shtetl. To give food symbolizes not only maternal love but also the friendliness of the household to its visitors. Not to offer a guest "honor" in the form of food, or at least a glass of tea, would be equivalent to rebuff, and not to eat in another person's home would be equally bad manners. A rich man especially would not dare to refuse. One way in which he pays for his good fortune is by consuming the refreshments served him by the poor relatives he visits on a holiday. Each kind of cake, each kind of preserve must be tasted and if he skips one, the hostess will point it out— "But look, you didn't try my honey cookies!" She knows he has just called on Sister Pessie and will probably go from her home to Uncle Vigdor. Will he pass over her food because he has enjoyed Pessie's too much, or because he expects the fare at Uncle Vigdor's to be better? The nogid in turn knows that in order "not to be ashamed" before him she has probably sacrificed or borrowed for the elaborate plateful of snacks. To eat is his social duty and besides—good food never hurts anyone.

It is a reflection on the housekeeper if food is not ready to be served at once when somebody drops in. This would be unlikely, however, because with the lack of set mealtimes, food that can be served at once is a standard feature of the home. It would be a very slipshod or very poor family that did not have on hand herring, bread, tea, and possibly boiled potatoes, as well as the usual jams. These foods are all "parveh" and can be eaten at any time, without concern about conflicting with milk or meat foods.

The only excuse for not eating a host's food is if the house is "not kosher." In the home of a Gentile one may eat only parveh food, and only from uncontaminated vessels. The risk of mistake is so great that it is best to eat only in a Jewish home, or else to bring one's own food and pot along. There is little occasion for a Jew in the shtetl to eat in the home of a Gentile, although Gentiles are often given much relished refreshments in Jewish homes.

Aside from kitchen duties, the mother needs and uses the girl's help constantly in the strenuous labor of housekeeping. There may be too many daughters to supply with dowries but there are hardly too many to cope with the demands of the household. The flurry of Sabbath cleaning comes only once a week but each day brings its accumulation of chores. Yet, no matter how many helpers she may have, a good housekeeper feels she must be everywhere and have a hand in everything or at least an energetic eye on it.

Washing the clothes once a week or once every two weeks is among the most arduous of the household tasks. The shtetl plumbing consists of a barrel of water, brought by the water carrier and stored in one corner of the kitchen. Above it hangs a jug with which the water is dipped up, and a basin into which it may be poured. Dishes are put into the basin and water poured over them. For the frequent hand washing demanded by the ritual, water is dipped up and poured over the fingers.

There are no bathing facilities in most shtetl houses. One uses the public bathhouse or the river, where separate sections are reserved for men and for women. The bathing costumes are informal but discreet. "There were no such things as bathing suits in our shtetl, so the men and women couldn't go bathing together. There were separate parts of the river where the men and women bathed. The part where the men were supposed to bathe was pretty deep and we youngsters couldn't go swimming there—it was too deep for us. So we used to bathe where the women went swimming. The women didn't bathe in the nude anyhow. They wore long undergarments."°

Wash day is the time when muscles must substitute for non-existent water pipes. The recurrent crises of house cleaning or laundry work are "a terrible time."° A man takes care to stay away as much as possible while they are in process. The clothes must be rinsed in boiling water, beaten, wrung out, rinsed again. Only after the preliminary work has been done are they taken to the river. The laundering techniques vary widely, but the strength and energy requirement is constant. "Washing clothes was a big event in the shtetl. First we would put all the clothes in a big tub with soap. Then the clothes were put in a container which was like a barrel made out of a tree trunk that was hollowed out. . . . Water was boiled and poured over the clothes and left there until the water cooled off. Then we took the clothes to the river. That was my job and it was very heavy. There we would rinse it and soap it again and beat it with a board made out of very heavy wood about one foot long, six inches wide and two to three inches thick. It was flat all around but had a handle on the top. We would beat the clothes with that and then rinse them again. After that we brought the clothes home to dry. Only special clothes were ironed—linens, shirts, etc., but most of the clothes were rolled on a piece of wood that looked like a rolling pin, and another piece of wood about the same length, with jagged ends, was used to pass over it. It was a difficult job but the clothes came out fairly neat."° When wash day is over the men folk will return to the house and the balebosteh will groan proudly, "I can't straighten out my bones!" On such a night she will sigh, "It's a mitsva, now I can sleep a little."

For odd moments and in the evenings there is the never-ending work of patching and mending torn clothes, making over the garments the big ones have outgrown for the younger ones who are outgrowing their current hand-me-downs. "Mother was always very thrifty. She saved everything that could be used. And she made our clothes by hand."°

When a dress can no longer serve as a dress it may be converted into an apron. When the apron is beyond repair it can still furnish a few patches. A man's caftan can be transformed into a boy's jacket. The fine coat father got for Rosh Hashanah ten years ago may end its days as a little boy's trousers. There is good reason why nothing is ever thrown away, for as long as there is enough cloth to thrust a needle through, something can be done with it.

Each season is marked by special household tasks. As summer wears on there is a bustle of preserving and pickling. The balebosteh goes about red-faced from her hot stove, which "cooks" her temper as it boils the plums—"may we eat them in health!" In winter, if one is lucky, there are geese to set and during the winter nights there will be feathers to pluck until "from plucking feathers it's dark in the eyes" and by daylight the flying fluff must be recovered from all the corners of the house. "There was a lot of work to do in the summer time. We had to can pickles and cabbage for the winter and that was a lot of work. In the winter we would set geese. We would feed geese until they were good and fat. Then we would kill them, remove the feathers which were used for bedding and then separate the meat and the fat. This was a long process. First you had to remove the fat together with small pieces of meat. The fat was called 'shmalts.' The fat from the geese wouldn't harden completely when cooled, but would form a sort of soft jelly which we used to spread on bread. The whole family would help on the winter nights, and when we were finished, we would help my aunts."°

The house that is also the "face" of the family, changes expression with every changing phase of family life. When there is joy or sorrow, when there is weekday disorder or holiday festivity, the interior of the house reflects the family mood.

The greatest change of all is shown when the soul of a person leaves its earthly container. Then the house, container of the family life, is shrouded in the trappings of death. "All the mirrors in the house were covered up. There were several superstitions about this. One was that you might see the Angel of Death in the mirror; another was that the image of the dead person would not leave the house and would remain in the mirror."° The windows that have been kept so tightly closed during illness are flung wide open, the rooms are left disordered and neglected.

Death is the greatest of all evils. God's highest gift to men is life and to cling to this gift is a primary obligation. "Man has been given life by God, and he has to keep it. Negligence in keeping life is a sin. Life should be sacrificed only for very worthy aims, and not be thrown away by neglecting the health. Jews are known to have sacrificed life for their faith."°

Aside from obligation, "the worst life is better than the best death." Even the words for death or dying are avoided in everyday language by means of countless euphemisms, for "one who mentions death is not sure of his life." One does not die, but "goes away," "closes his eyes," "falls asleep," "stretches his feet," "ends his days." When a great scholar dies, people say that "he has been taken away," "he took leave," "he was invited"—meaning, invited to the "upper yeshiva." The expressions used for the death of such a man will be in Hebrew and not in Yiddish.

The cemetery is located far from the center of the shtetl and is also referred to only by indirection. It is "the House of

Eternity," "the House of Graves," "the House of Life," "the Good Place," "the Holy Place." Only in reference to a Christian burial ground is the word for cemetery used.

As long as a person is alive, hope will not be abandoned, and the community as well as the family is mobilized to fight death. Prayers, charity, changing of names are used in addition to treatment and drugs. When the end seems almost inevitable, extreme measures are taken: running to the graves of the ancestors, weeping and screaming in front of the Ark in shul "to cry out" the dying from death.

While these activities are under way, the dying person must not be left alone even for a second. On the contrary, the more people in the house, the better it is. He must not be touched, however, for that might hasten his death and every second of life is precious.

Meanwhile, members of the most important society in the shtetl, the Khevreh Kadisha, or burial society, are taking care of the last ritual. The dying person must repeat the final confession of sin as it is read to him. Like the Yom Kippur confession it is a standard form. If he is unable to speak for himself a member of the burial society will recite it for him. This service will be performed for women by elderly matrons who belong to the Khevreh Kadisha, and whose duty also is to sew the shroud in which the corpse will be wrapped.

When death actually arrives, the first exclamation of those who are present or those who hear about it will be, "Blessed be the True Judge!" Even the ones most deeply bereaved will utter this acceptance of the decree they have striven so passionately to avert. "The Jew knows that the Lord decided to take the sick man's soul. He mourns very deeply, but he submits himself to the will of God."°

Every effort is exerted to prevent the Angel of Death from accomplishing his purpose. Once he has succeeded, however, and the person has died, family and community as soon as possible must be rid of the body from which the soul has departed. Just as fingernails or blood become unclean or dangerous, once they have left the living body, so the body itself becomes evil, once life has left it. Within twenty-four hours the corpse must be cleaned, purified and buried. Speed is so important that if death occurs on a holiday, the body may be buried by a non-Jew if it is on the first festive day and by Jews if it is on the second festive day, although any other work must be avoided.

While the corpse is still in the house, it lies on the floor with a candle at the head and the feet toward the door. Relatives, neighbors, friends and acquaintances come to "ask pardon" of the deceased for all possible insults or offenses they may have inflicted on him during his life.

The corpse is prepared for the funeral by being washed, purified, and wrapped in the shroud prepared by the members of the Khevreh Kadisha. A man is dressed in his festive white kittl and covered with his prayer shawl. Men may be purified by either men or women, women only by members of their own sex.

As in any life crisis—circumcision, Bar Mitzvah, wedding—the community takes an active part. "The entire shtetl is invited" and it is one of the most important mitsvos "to accompany the dead." "As many people accompany the dead body—so many Angels will greet the soul. Therefore it is a duty to go to a funeral."° Absence from the funeral is a sin and also a direct insult to the departed, an insult for which there will never be an opportunity to ask forgiveness.

Weeping and wailing, the funeral cortege brings the dead to the House of Eternity. If the deceased was a nogid or a scholar the body is carried by the most important citizens of the community; otherwise, it will be borne by members of the burial society. The procession always takes the longest road to the cemetery to show the departed how reluctant the community is to separate from one of its members.

At the cemetery an official of the burial society will cut a gash in the clothing of each member of the immediate family, a ceremonial representation of rending the garments in grief. Friends and relatives gather about the open grave to pay final honor and respect to the dead. Because no priest may have contact with a dead body, members of the tribe of the Kohanim are forbidden to enter the cemetery and they must wait at the gates until the ceremony is over.

The body is buried uncoffined, but the walls of the grave are boxed with boards. For the burial of a learned man it is preferable to use the boards of the bench on which he sat while studying Torah. A bit of earth from Palestine, the Land of Israel, is placed under the head of the deceased. After the grave has been covered with earth and a member of the burial society has said appropriate prayers, the nearest male relative—son, brother or husband—says Kaddish, the prayer for the dead.

On returning home, the mourners begin the seven days of intensive mourning, "sitting *shiveh*," or sitting seven. During this time they sit either on the floor or on boxes, without changing their rent clothes. They should not talk too much, nor leave the house; they should not even study Torah, because studying Torah is a joy. The only books they may read are moral treatises or volumes of sad import, such as Job, Lamentations or Ecclesiastes. "For seven days the family refuses all life and all comfort. They sit on the floor and they don't cook; they eat whatever visitors and neighbors bring."°

To visit the mourner is an important mitsva, and the house is always full of guests who come in without greeting, bringing food or caring for the small children. The mourners will eat hard-boiled eggs, beygl, or other round or circular food—for example, peas and lentils—as roundness symbolizes mourning.

During the entire shiveh period, prayers are said in the house of mourning. Only for the Sabbath services does the mourner leave the house to go to shul. He interrupts the shiveh as the rejoicing of all Israel overshadows the sorrow of the individual. On Sabbath he must fulfill all public ritual, but must not change his clothes or bathe because this belongs to his private life and within his private life he continues to be a mourner.

After shiveh comes *shloshim,* the thirty days of less intensive mourning during which the mourner is allowed to take care of his business, to go to shul, to eat regularly, but must not take part in any festivities or celebrations. After this period the mourning is officially ended and the mourner has the right even to remarry. Who is a mourner and the detailed etiquette of mourning are explicitly prescribed, and cannot be changed. And just as grief must

be expressed in the most intensive way during shiveh, so it is forbidden to be excessive in the expressions of sorrow after the prescribed mourning period is over.

For a year after the person dies, a near relative will say
Kaddish in shul three times every day. On certain holidays
the family will participate in the prayers for the dead during the
service "Remembering the Souls." On the anniversary of the
death they will light a candle at home and in the shul, study
actually or by proxy a chapter in the Mishna, and distribute
charity in memory of the soul of the deceased.

After death, the soul is supposed to go to Paradise, *Gan
Eyden,* or—if it is the soul of a sinner—to *Gehinom,* Hell. These
places are part of the "real world" as differentiated from the in-
substantial world in which we dwell. The picture of them is extremely vague, however.

To some extent it seems that, although the body is buried
and theoretically the soul has departed, the deceased continues to
live within the community. In his grave he listens to the complaints of the living, by night he attends service at the local shul,
he may even be met in the street after midnight. He participates
in the life of the family and the community by appearing in
dreams—giving advice, threatening those who may intend some
wrong to the community, or merely expressing his opinions on
current events.

Except when their services are needed in the role of heavenly
shtadlan, the living are not wholly at ease with this participation
of the deceased in their activities. Therefore precautions are taken
to discourage their return. Upon leaving the cemetery after visiting the dear departed, it is expedient to put an extra pebble on
the grave. And people sometimes say that the long road which the
funeral party takes to the cemetery is not so much to show love
for the deceased as to make him lose his way if he tries to come
back.

VI

GUT YONTEV

The seasons are measured less by their workaday activities than by their characteristic holidays. Just as the week is lived from Sabbath to Sabbath, so the year is lived from one holiday to the next. The holidays themselves have their own grouping and their own rhythm. There are the strictly religious holidays on which work is forbidden and the post-Biblical ones on which it is permitted. Each of these groups has some days that are "glad" and some that are "sad," some that are "easy" and some that are "hard" to prepare for, some marked by feast and some marked by fast. The feast is often preceded by fasting, and the fast preceded and followed by feasting.

The feasting as well as the fasting is a mitsva, one is commanded to rejoice as well as to grieve. "It stands in the book" how one should feel, which thoughts are permitted and which are prohibited, and compliance with the command is expected to be so wholehearted that the prescribed feelings become spontaneous.

A religious holiday, like the Sabbath, means translation into a different life. A new dimension is added and the daily burden is laid aside. The clothes one wears, the food one eats, the very aspect of the house in which one lives are different from those of the weekday world. The atmosphere is steeped in history and symbolism. Time and space are welded into a close unity. One lives in communion with ages past and with all the far-flung members of the Chosen People who in all parts of the earth are celebrating at the same time, in the same way.

A holiday, like a personal event such as birth or marriage, is never restricted to the home or to the synagogue, but is partly in each. Some are centered more in the family, some more in the

381

community, but any major event is shared with the group. The observances are always a mixture of ritual prescribed in the sacred writings and folk custom that has become interwoven with the written law. Prescribed ritual is uniform among the orthodox, but the folk customs vary widely from one place to the next, although only the learned would recognize a difference between the two.

Each holiday, like each Sabbath, brings its combination of anxiety and joy. As it approaches, the work of preparing for it looms mountain high. So much to be done, so little time. For most families the cost in itself is a problem. Will there be enough money to "make holiday" as it should be done? Will there be enough to buy new clothes for Passover, to provide all the special foods that are essential? The daily prayers are intensified, "may we not be ashamed before man and God," may we not have to "go to people" for assistance, may we not need to borrow. As the day comes closer, worry, fatigue, tension, increase. But when the holiday arrives all that part is forgotten, all workday cares are thrust aside. Then one relaxes, expands, enjoys, and wishes to all, "Gut Yontev!," a good holiday.

It is always either *far yontev* or *nokh yontev*, "before the holiday" or "after the holiday." In the case of the Passover, *Pesakh*, the most exciting of all for the children, preparations begin months in advance. During the winter special fat is prepared, and kept separate from any possible contamination by common food. The real "far yontev" begins after Purim, four weeks before Passover. Raisins are bought and special wine is brewed, untouched by any substance or utensil that is not *peysakhdik* "Pesakh-ly." One place in the house must be purified for storing these supplies, the borshtsh that will be brewed a month in advance, and the unleavened bread when it is ready. As the Passover stores increase the space in the house shrinks, until at last there is hardly room for the family to carry on its daily life. Yet that life too must go on until the last moment. The baby must be tended, the weekday food cooked, the work clothes kept in order, the needs of the father taken care of, the breathless search for parnosseh maintained. "The hands and the feet fall off of me" cries the housewife and her head "bursts" with all it must remember and foresee. But when the time comes all will be ready, and she too will be ready to soar from the maelstrom of far yontev into the peace of the holiday world.

Although New Year's Day comes in the autumn, the shtetl feels that the annual cycle begins in the spring, with the celebration of Pesakh, the Passover. Urbanized though its people are in occupations and in habits, they share with their agricultural neighbors the feeling that the year begins with the springtime rebirth of nature. Moreover, their holidays—however modified in rationale and interpretation—stem from their own agricultural antiquity. "To us in the shtetl, Pesakh was considered the beginning of the year. People were hired from Pesakh to Pesakh, new clothes were bought, and so forth."°

The new clothes are an important feature of the holiday. In the poorest as well as the richest family, the child is given new spring clothing on Pesakh. If they cannot afford to buy him a complete new outfit, he will at least get something—new shoes, a new hat, or a new scarf. At the shul there will be much comparing of new things and the children will display what they have received, no matter how modest it is. There is no greater disappointment to a shtetl child than to have nothing new for this holiday. If the family is moderately well off, his parents also may expect, or at least hope, for new clothing to celebrate Pesakh. Sometimes it is stipulated in the marriage contract that the bride shall have a new outfit for the holidays. "Twice a year, for the special holidays, we would get new clothes. The new clothes would be for shabbes and the holidays, and the other clothes we would begin to wear for everyday use."°

The outstanding feature of Pesakh is, of course, the unleavened bread, the matsos, to symbolize the flight and deliverance of the Jews from bondage, carrying their unleavened bread with them into the desert. To celebrate the Exodus, the orthodox must abstain from all leaven during the eight days of Passover. The very dishes from which they eat, the house in which they live, must be peysakhdik, untainted by any contact with leaven which for the time being represents impurity. Each family and the community as a whole wage an active campaign to banish during the Passover all *khomets*—all food tainted directly or indirectly by leaven. It is because of this that the merchant must "sell" his stock, so that nothing which is khomets remains in his possession over the holidays.

In the home, Pesakh is honored by the major house cleaning of the year, far more drastic and dramatic than the relatively restrained cleaning that takes place before the New Year, or the weekly upheaval of Sabbath. For those days the house is scoured and polished, for Pesakh it is also purged. All the furniture is taken outside, every corner is swept, dusted, scrubbed. If possible, the walls are freshly whitewashed. "Preparing for Pesakh was a hard job, especially for the women. The whole house had to be taken to pieces and made kosher for Pesakh. Some stuff, like foods, were prepared during the winter and stored, but the actual cleaning was left for the last week or so."°

In the course of this domestic catharsis, innumerable treasures are bound to turn up—things that were mislaid and longed for, things that have been forgotten and come with the surprise of discovery. To a small boy or girl the process has all the tang of a treasure hunt. The shtetl mode of housekeeping, where many objects are jumbled together in closets and cupboards, enhances the suspense and pleasure of this annual review. "Everything was taken out of the house; the walls were whitewashed, the furniture was scrubbed with boiling water. Then we used a kind of sharp grass to take off the dirt from the furniture. Then it was scrubbed with a knife and rubbed with a piece of white iron while boiling water is poured over again. . . . Any new things bought have to be taken to the river and rinsed three times. . . . The floor is covered with straw, the stove has to be burned out completely. You put a lot of wood in the stove and let it burn. The house is a real 'upside-down.' "°

When the whole house is clean, the peysakhdikeh dishes are brought out and made ready for use. They always seem prettier, shinier, brighter than the everyday ones, and probably they are, since they are used for only eight days each year. If there are not separate pots and cutlery for Pesakh, the regular ones must be koshered. "Silver cutlery . . . was cleaned with sand and 'sour salt,' a sort of silver polish. Then it was tied with a string, taken to the bathhouse in a clean kosher cloth; there the bathman takes it with a stick, dips it into boiling water three times, says a few prayers, and your silver is kosher for Pesakh."°

The frenzy of cleaning is fun and it is also exalting. Even children who have grown up far from the shtetl have known indirectly the sense of purification, of joy, and of "newness" special to Pesakh. It is like the weekly joy of Sabbath raised and magnified.

Meanwhile the larger family, the community, is actively preparing. The synagogue must be cleaned like a home. Arrangements must be made for hospitality to any soldiers in the neighborhood. Each Jewish soldier will be a guest, an oyrekh, for the eight days of Passover, sleeping in barracks but eating all his meals where no khomets can intrude.

Delegates from the society Moes Khittin go from house to house collecting for matsos, potatoes and wine. The poor must be given unleavened bread and peysakhdik wine for the ritual. But they must also receive potatoes since the compact matsos are too expensive and too unsubstantial to fill hungry stomachs.

Usually the matsos for the whole shtetl are baked at one place. "Before Pesakh a special bakery for matsos was put up. All the people in the shtetl would make their matsos there. . . . The person who owned the bakery usually hired girls for rolling the dough . . . then they hired a kneader to mix the dough. This too was usually a woman. Then there were boys who were 'water pourers.' They had to have separate people for this job, because the kneaders mustn't touch the jug of water. Then there was the hole-maker who put holes in the dough, the one who measured the flour, and the one who watched the dough, because the dough must not be left alone. There was a huge oven which was in the same room as the hole-maker."°

The climax of the preparation comes when "everything is cleaned up and is nice and neat. . . . Then you have to get rid of the khomets, that is, of the food that is not used during Passover."° If there are any stores of common food in the house, they must be locked away and "sold" to a non-Jew for the eight days of Passover. The negotiation is performed through the rabbi, as is the temporary "sale" of the merchant's stock.

On the evening before Passover the father with the excited children swarming about him, puts a few crumbs in the corners of the newly cleaned house. Later, "he takes a wooden spoon and a feather and collects all the crumbs he put into the corners. He shovels them into the wooden spoon with a feather because you mustn't touch them. He ties this around with a cloth,"° wrapping it carefully so that none of the pollution will leak through. Then he puts the bundle of impurity away in some high place where it will not be touched.

The next morning the crumbs and the spoon are burned—not in the cookstove, which has been koshered by being burned out and cleaned, but in a neutral fire. Often "the neighbors get together, build a fire, and all throw their spoons in. They say a prayer until the crumbs and the spoons are burned. This is called 'burning the khomets.' Then you sweep out the straw that was on the floor, the table is set, everything is nice and clean, and you were ready for Passover."°

By now "the holiday is at the door," and so much is still to be done. There must be cooking for the Eve and the first day. "All the relatives will come," all must be fed, and "we should not be ashamed." Perhaps the whole family will go to the grandparents for the first day's celebration, but each household wants to be at home on one of the two days, and to receive "the whole mishpokheh."

Every effort is made to have the whole family together for the most important feast of all the holidays, the famous Seder, on the first two nights of the Passover. Those who are away try to come home, parents try to assemble all their children and their children's children. Going to grandfather's for Seder is a very frequent shtetl memory. The memories include the menu, with its unleavened bread and all the dishes made from matso-meal instead of flour. They dwell chiefly, however, on the long and dramatic service that begins before the meal and continues after it.

Not only the house is different on Pesakh. One's father is different also. The mother is dressed in her best, with all her jewels, and whatever new clothes the holiday has brought her. Everyone wears something new, and everyone is as clean as the house. Even the holiday guest, the oyrekh, has a special look of brightness, though it is sad for him to be away from his home on Pesakh. But the master of the house is so changed that to awed round eyes he looks almost like a different person. At other times he wears black, but for the Seder he is robed in white, a flowing garment girdled at the waist. If he is a nogid, it may be of gleaming satin, girdled with silver or with a knotted silk cord. In any case, it will be white, the symbol of purity and cleanliness, for this most exultant holiday of all the year. The only other time he wears white will be for the most solemn of all the holidays.

He looks different and he sits differently, for he reclines among pillows, as "a free man." He looks and he sits like a king, and on Pesakh even more than on Sabbath, he is a king. On Pesakh, unlike Sabbath, it is his wife and not the blessed day that is the queen.

The table is also changed, with the best cloth, the candles, the peysakhdikeh dishes. The goblets before each place will be filled with the special Pesakh wine, unless perhaps the women and children are given mead. Each person is expected to drain two cups before the meal and two cups after. There is an extra goblet for the prophet Elijah, who is expected to join the company when the moment comes. Strange dishes are set before the father's place, symbolic dishes that he will serve at the proper moment. Also before him, under an embroidered cover, are three matsos, symbolizing the tribe of the Kohanim, the tribe of the Levites, and the remainder of the Klal Isroel.

When all is ready, the father signals the youngest child, perhaps with his eyes, perhaps with a spoken "nu?" The child, quivering with excitement, stands up to ask the four questions he has been rehearsing for weeks. They are important questions, and difficult for a very small child, perhaps not more than four years old. The younger he is, the more will his listening elders melt with delight if he performs well. As for the child, this is his hour. The holiday hangs on him, for with his questions he will set off the whole ritual. The Seder itself will be performed to answer his questions. For the rest of his life this will remain one of his most vivid memories—how the great festival unfolded to answer him, and in doing so enhanced the understanding of why it is good to be a Jew and why it is hard to be a Jew.

The questions will not be asked by a girl unless there are no boys in the family. But if there are no children at all, if they have married too far away to return for the holidays, or if—"not of us be it said!"—the couple is childless, then the family is poor indeed. In that case the wife must ask the questions, and the king and queen are as paupers in their own palace.

The child begins in Yiddish, "Papa, I want to ask you four questions," then at once chants the first one in Hebrew, loudly and clearly, after which he intones it in Yiddish: "Why is this night different from all other nights?" As soon as he has finished the fourth, with its Yiddish translation, all who are at the table begin to read aloud in Hebrew, "We were slaves in the land of Egypt, . . ." and continue through the *Haggadah*, the history of how the Most High liberated his Chosen People from bondage in Egypt.

The reading is constantly varied and interrupted. Some of it is chanted in singsong by the father, some parts are sung by all at the table to well-loved melodies, some are chanted by the father while the others murmur with him. He conducts the service as the director of an orchestra conducts a score, signaling when it is time to take a sip of wine, when it is time to spill out the ten winedrops, symbolizing the ten plagues of Egypt.

The father and the older brother pour off their symbolic plagues with a steady and practiced hand, but the child's hand wobbles with excitement and the ten drops become a pool in his saucer. The father's hands are also deft and steady when he prepares the *afikomen,* breaking off a piece from each of the three matsos and wrapping them in a napkin, which he hides among the pillows on which he leans.

The reading is further interrupted by distribution of the ritual foods ranged in small dishes before the father, symbolizing phases of the Exodus, hardships that led up to it, or the ceremonial in the Temple. A saucer-full of horseradish represents the bitterness of their lot. The father has a generous helping, between two pieces of matsos. The child has "a little bit," spread thin between the matsos, but even so the sharp bite sends tears threatening to overflow. He blinks them back fiercely, for he knows that it is childish to choke over the bitterness of the lot of the Chosen People, and that a boy big enough to ask four questions and start a whole holiday on its course should be able to swallow down horseradish "like a mentsh." The clay from which the children of Israel fashioned bricks to build the pyramids of Egypt is represented by a mixture of chopped apples, nuts and wine. There will also be a burned bone commemorating the sacrifice in the Temple.

The father slices a hard-boiled egg, dips it in salt water and passes a morsel to each, a reminder of mourning and tears to guard against excessive joy. The mourning, the child will be told, is for the destruction of the Temple.

When the child is a father, he will do it all in exactly the same way, with exactly the same gestures. He will know every move, his muscles will even remember how one expands and reclines on pillows to show he is a free man. Nevertheless, before every Seder he will read over again in the Shulkhan Arukh how everything should be done. He will check the table to make sure that all the required objects are laid out. He will review the directions sprinkled in Yiddish throughout the Hebrew text of the Haggadah, so that everyone will know exactly the point at which each act and gesture should be performed. They are dry and impersonal, crisp as stage directions, up to the last one in the first portion of the service—the one that announces, "Shulkhan Arukh, The Set Table," and adds, "Now you eat and drink, and may it do you good!"

The instructions are fully followed. The meal is brought in and compliments fly, praising the matso balls, the matso-meal pancakes, the chicken, all the rest. At the end of the meal, the father reaches for the pieces of matsos that he buried among the pillows, knowing they will not be there. He gropes busily until the child can no longer restrain the beaming confession that he has "stolen the afikomen." Without the eating of the afikomen the second phase of the Seder cannot begin. After earnest discussion, during which the father promises the child "anything he wants," the afikomen is triumphantly returned and the services can continue.

When everyone is well fed and tired of eating, the second part of the reading is begun. It is far less standardized than the first section, subject to variations in length and in procedure. Whatever is added or taken away, however, the high point of this section is the throwing open of the door. Child mythology holds that at this moment the prophet Elijah enters the room, and many a child has evidence that it is so. Perhaps the wind blows in from the opened door, stirring the wind in Elijah's goblet, and then the child knows that he has "seen" the prophet sipping from the glass. He did not see the lips but he saw the movement of the wine as it was being drunk. The prophet has arrived today, Messiah will come in the future.

At some point there will be the story of the kid that "my father bought for ten zuzim." It is a children's story but by now the children are tired with excitement, food and wine. Sleep begins to muffle the chanted words, the wine in the half-empty goblets is ringed by a ruby mist.

The second Seder is a replica of the first. For the children, the high peak of excitement is over. They have been told that something about the calendar requires an extra day's observance for most major holidays, that time is different in different parts of the world, and the real holiday is timed by Palestine. They understand that only by observing two days can it be made certain that all the Jews in all the world will be doing it together. They feel the significance of everyone joining, all of Klal Isroel offering the same prayers on the same day. But the first thrill comes only once a year.

The first two days and the last two of Passover are full holidays. The four in between are "the profane within the holy day." The dietary restrictions remain in force. No leaven, no "khomets" may be eaten. Otherwise life goes on as usual, with its accustomed work. When the eighth day has ended it is "after the holiday," nokh yontev. The peysakhdikeh objects are once more stored away, to be used next year—"God willing."

As spring gives way to summer, it begins once more to be far yontev. This time it is "before Shevuos," another of the "glad" holidays and one that also is centered in the home rather than in the shul. The fifty days between the two glad holidays

of Pesakh and Shevuos are a period of semimourning, commonly
explained as a tribute to the memory of the students of Rabbi
Akiba's yeshiva, who died during an epidemic. During these
days there must be no weddings and no haircutting, and the
very pious fast every Monday and Thursday.

The muted period is broken, however, by a joyous day devoted to the pleasure of the children, *Lag ba Omer,* the Thirty-
Third Day in Omer. This is the one day of the year when the
boys, with their melamed, go out into the fields and woods to
enjoy the outdoor world that otherwise is nonexistent to the
kheyder. Each brings his lunch in a package, and all the mothers
vie to give the best "nasheray" and the most savory tidbits, so
that they will not "be ashamed" when all the food is opened and
pooled in a common meal. The boys play outdoor games, long
caftans flapping about their legs, earlocks bobbing as they run
and jump, or shoot at a target with bows and arrows. The
melamed, who all the year round bars the kheyder door against
any spirit of play, accepts the antics of this day as part of the
approved regime. How happily he accepts it is "something else
again" for occasionally it furnishes opportunity to work off accumulated resentments against the presiding authority of the
schoolroom. Excess in this direction is usually checked, however,
by the realization that tomorrow the melamed will again reign
in his own realm, wielding the scepter with nine tails.

Originally related to the beginning of harvest, in the shtetl
Shevuos is said to celebrate God's gift of the Torah on Mount
Sinai. Nevertheless, its activities and its spirit hark back to rejoicing in the gifts of the earth. It is one of the rare holidays on
which children go to the woods to collect "the greens for yontev,"
branches for decorating home and shul. The expedition is
counted as a frolic, even though it may require braving hostile
gangs of boys in the streets they must pass.

The great feature of Shevuos is the dairy dishes served in
all possible combinations—blintses, kreplakh with cheese, pot
cheese and sour cream, cheese strudel with raisins and cinnamon.
Although meat is eaten for the evening meal, the holiday stands
for all that is most delectable among the "milky" foods.

Despite the fifty days of semimourning, the spring holidays

are happy rather than sad. When summer has passed and autumn comes there begins the cycle of the Days of Awe. The first day of the month of Elul ushers in a period of repentance leading to the holiday of the new year, Rosh Hashanah. As always, one tries to be at home for this period, and to plan so that duties will not take him away from his own family and his own shtetl.

This is the time to take stock of one's soul, in preparation for the high holidays when each person's good deeds are weighed against his bad ones, and his fate is sealed for the year to come. On Rosh Hashanah the fate for the year is inscribed on the tablets of heaven. On Yom Kippur, the Day of Atonement, it is signed. On Oshanah Rabah it is sealed and after that it will not be changed. For the shtetl, each year begins three times. January 1, the official date, belongs to the government. It is important for taxes and official transactions, but otherwise it matters little. Pesakh is the beginning of nature's year. God's year begins with the Day of Judgment on Rosh Hashanah.

From the beginning of the month until Rosh Hashanah the shammes makes nightly rounds, pounding on the shutters of each house and calling, "Jews, get up, it's time to go to 'pardons'!" The girls and women lie quietly under their warm covers, while the men and boys leave their beds, dress, and go to the synagogue for prayers of repentance and entreaty, intoned with voices that quaver and wail. During the day there is less laughter than usual, for this "far yontev" is building up to a climax of solemnity.

The Days of Awe belong more to the synagogue than to the home. On the morning of Rosh Hashanah the family go to shul together, exchanging sober greetings before they separate to go to their places. Mother and father shake hands, wishing each other, "May you pray out a good year!" The same wish is exchanged with others who are entering for the long service of prayer.

The high point of the New Year service is the blowing of the *shofar,* the long ram's horn sounded only during the Days of Awe. It must be perfect, free of any crack or flaw, and the sound it utters will be a symbol of the year to come. All wait in hushed suspense as one of the shul officials dictates to the "Master of the Sounding" the notes that he and all know very well. Then he blows, his face red, his body tense, for he represents the whole community and all the responsibility is on him. The sound of the shofar must be full and steady, for the welfare of all.

After the service all the congregation shake hands, wishing each other "a happy New Year and a good inscription," voicing hopes that the book of judgment will bring health and parnosseh "for you and your wife," "for your children and your children's children." After Yom Kippur the wish will be for "a good inscription and a good signature."

As further augury of a good year, the evening meal always ends with a sweet, perhaps an apple dipped in honey. Sweetness is spread in all the corners of the house, for the father goes about with a dish of honey, smearing a bit of it in each corner with a feather, murmuring a blessing and a wish, "May we have a sweet year." To the children who follow and watch him, this folk custom is as impressive as the religious ceremonials dictated by the holy writings.

Rosh Hashanah is the portal of the Ten Days of Repentance that lead to the "Sabbath of Sabbaths," the greatest of all the holidays, the Day of Atonement which is also the Day of Pardon. Not only do the men continue their nightly prayers in shul. Everyone uses the ten days to go about asking of all the people he knows forgiveness for any offenses, conscious or unconscious, that he may have committed against them. On Yom Kippur, God will be asked for forgiveness, but since only man can pardon the sins against man, it is essential to approach with a clean conscience the day on which one's fate for the year will be "signed."

True to the rhythm of the shtetl, the most solemn of all the fast days is set between two feasts, and "it is as much of a mitsva to feast before and after as it is to fast on Yom Kippur." Part of the feast will be furnished by part of the ritual of absolution, for early on the morning of Erev Yom Kippur, the Eve of Yom Kippur, the shtetl is busy with the "beating of the scapegoat." Actually the beating of the goat might more accurately be called the whirling of the fowl. In the ancient days, which at this period seem so close to the present, the scapegoat was sent out into the desert, carrying the sins of the community. The shtetl rationale has transformed the quadruped into a fowl, and instead of being sent away to the desert, it is consumed by the family at the Yom

Kippur feasts. Since "the Law is for man and not man for the Law," the family economy is further respected in the choice of the "scapegoat." If there are too many members for the budget or the appetites involved, or if no fowl is available, a fish may be used by some or by all. The fowl, or the surrogate fowl, is whirled about the head of the penitent, with an appropriate prayer. A man whirls a rooster, a woman a hen, children a cockerel or pullet depending on their sex. If a woman is pregnant she may use a hen and an egg, or else a hen and a cockerel and pullet, for the unborn child. It is even possible to substitute a donation to charity for any living animal, and to say over the money that is given the same prayer that would be uttered for the fowl or the fish.

That day is a busy one for the ritual slaughterer. All the women come crowding with their hens and cocks, all in a great hurry to have them killed so that they can rush home and prepare the three feasts—two before and one after the Day of Repentance.

The second feast of Yom Kippur Eve is prolonged until sundown, and all are urged to eat as much as possible to prevent suffering from hunger and thirst. It is well to finish off the meal with a small piece of bread and a glass of water, symbolic sustenance for the fast. The meal itself is preceded by the ritual of lighting candles as on Friday night, except that on Erev Yom Kippur the mother prays longer and cries more, "to cry out and pray out a good year" for herself and all her family.

The emphasis on feasting before and after the fast brings into prominence the importance attributed to abstaining from all food and drink on Yom Kippur, and also the fact that the purpose is not to mortify the flesh. Man's welfare is God's concern, the fast is not designed to harm the body but merely to help the soul. The soul is not helped by physical suffering per se, but only by the symbolism and by the turning of the mind away from earthly things. There is no virtue in fasting to the detriment of the body. On the contrary, such an exercise is forbidden. Pregnant women, children, sick people, are enjoined to eat even on fast days. The practice is ecstatic but not ascetic. There is even some feeling that for the healthy, fasting is beneficial. "It is good to give the stomach a rest."°

The values of fasting are manifold, and different ones are in evidence on different occasions. Some pious Jews fast every Monday and Thursday, for half or all of the day, feeling that the lightness of the body brings them closer to God. One may fast to show that he is too unhappy to eat, and this kind of fast may become almost a weapon with which to coerce God. Just as the child can bully his mother by refusing to eat until he has his way, so mortals may attempt, by refusing food, to force God to grant their requests. The most famous instance of fasting for coercion concerns three Tsaddikim who decided that the Chosen People had suffered enough and it was time for Messiah to come. They announced that they would not eat until he arrived. People flocked from far and near, begging them to eat and not to attempt the impiety of bringing such drastic pressure to bear on the All High. Man should accept the will of God, they maintained, and allow Him to bring Messiah in His own time.

The fasting on Yom Kippur has a special quality and intensity. There are other fast days on which abstaining from food and water is taken almost as a matter of course. On *Tisheh b'Av* one fasts and goes about his business as usual. Yet the Yom Kippur fast is viewed as an ordeal. By noon, children are being sent from synagogue to synagogue, to see how relatives are surviving their deprivation. "Run and see how Aunt Sara is feeling," a father will whisper to his little boy at about eleven in the morning. And the child will return solemnly with word that Aunt Sara is bearing up, though she has had no nourishment for over twelve hours. Grownups have little bottles of aromatics to sniff when they begin to feel faint.

The faintness is not necessarily imaginary, for the shul is always crowded, the prayers are intense and unremitting, emotions are in a state of prolonged climax during the whole of the day, windows are closed tight, the air is filled with chanting, weeping, and the fumes of as many candles as there are closely packed, swaying, hard-breathing human beings in the tense, crowded room.

After the second feast of Yom Kippur Eve the whole family goes to the synagogue. Before setting out, the father blesses all his children, laying his hands on their heads, and kisses each one as if they were going on a long journey. From then until sundown the next day they will not leave the shul except to sleep, and will not eat, drink or wash, except for the morning "fingernail water."

The overture to the entire Yom Kippur service is the powerful and gloomy *Kol Nidre,* sung by the cantor while the congregation weeps and moans. This ancient prayer sets the mood that will be maintained until the next sundown. For this holiday the mother lays aside all jewelry and adornment, and the father once more wears his flowing white kittl. The men remove their shoes and a zealous few put beans in their socks, so that for part of the day they stand with discomfort. All day the prayers, the songs, the confessions of sin continue. Sometimes the father takes his small son under his prayer shawl with him, and the boy sees his father's tears fall on the prayer book from which he is reading. Upstairs the mother is weeping as she prays, and before the Eastern Wall the cantor weeps for all the congregation and for all of Israel. Each weeps for his own sins and for the sins of all, each confesses to the sins of all, for each is implicated in the acts of all.

During the morning service, as on other important holidays, the descendants of the priests, the Kohanim, bless the congregation. For these moments the unimportant division by tribes becomes meaningful, and on this occasion the Levites must act as servants to the Kohanim. When the Kohanim file out to wash their hands for the blessing, the descendants of the tribe of Levi follow to pour the water over their fingers. Even though the Kohanim may be prost and the Levites sheyn, the child sees that the priest of God must be served. When the Kohanim return, he sees the "Faces" of the community vacate their proud places at the Eastern Wall so that the Kohanim may stand on the seats, raising their hands in benediction.

What happens next, no one must see. All the men cover their heads with their prayer shawls gathering the children under the ample folds. Those who have no prayer shawls shield their eyes with their hands. All know that the Kohanim, standing at the mizrakh, cover their heads with their prayer shawls, join the thumbs and forefingers of their upraised hands, and turn from side to side as they chant the blessing. But anyone who looked would be struck blind, for between the third and fourth fingers of the upraised hands there flickers the flame of God, a brightness no mortal eye could survive. When the blessing is ended, all return from the places assigned by their order in the Temple to the places assigned by their order in the shtetl. But the child knows that if the Levites grew proud and refused to serve the Kohanim, the Kohanim might withhold their blessing and then disaster would surely strike the whole community. No such situation arises, but the possibility marks the merging of the past and the present.

The end of the day is announced by the blowing of the shofar, and everyone in the shtetl assembles to hear. Even the girls who had to stay home tending babies, the old women who were away caring for the sick, the children who are too small to stay in shul all day long, try to be in the yard of the shul when the shofar sounds.

Everyone pours out, and again the wishes are exchanged, "May you have prayed out a good inscription and a good signature," followed by a whole litany of hopes for wives and husbands, children and children's children. "Relatives kiss each other—even husbands and wives."° Finally all return home happy, purified, purged of all evil. They will "take something into the mouth to support the heart" until the meal is ready. As they eat they will ask each other, "How did you fast?" They will compare experiences, contrast this year with last, inform each other who fainted, who grew weak, discuss the performance of the cantor. After the anxiety of struggling to discharge all sin, they will bask in a conviction that surely the inscription and the signature ought to be favorable.

Far yontev treads on the heels of nokh yontev, for Yom Kippur is hardly ended when it is time to build the booths for *Sukkos,* the Feast of Tabernacles. They must have four walls and be covered with branches, and during the eight days of Sukkos males must take their meals in the booths. Those who are fortunate enough have a private *sukkah* for their own family. Among the less prosperous, a few neighbors may join together to construct one, and there is also a community sukkah for those who cannot build their own. Each man has his own food brought there by wife or daughter, and eats in company as if he were at home.

The pleasant custom may be a hardship if the weather is cold and rainy, as it often is at that time of year. It is so common to eat these meals in a downpour that a saying has grown up about an unlucky event or unsuccessful venture, "Ha, it rains in the sukkah!"

The insignia of Sukkos are the bundles of palm and willow, the *lulav* and the citron, the *esrog,* which should come from Palestine and be a perfect fruit free of all defect. The nogid who can afford to procure one for his own use, wraps it carefully in cotton and keeps it in a handsome silver box, preserving it from any jolt or fall since the slightest defect would make it "possl," unfit. For the common man, the congregation buys a citron and the palms, and each day the shammes carries them from one sukkah to another, so that everyone can perform the required blessing, holding fruit and boughs together, shaking them up and down, to the right and to the left. If a woman is childless, she would do well to secure the citron after the holiday, and bite the tip of it.

The booths for which the holiday is named are part of the home celebration, but the climax of the eight-day holiday is in the shul on Simkhas Torah, when the end of the reading of the Torah is celebrated. The climax is approached gradually. Each day the Holy Scrolls are taken out of the Ark, and carried around the bimah on which the weekly reading is done. The sixth day is Oshanah Rabah, the day of "the Great Help," the day on which the fate that has been inscribed and signed on high is finally sealed. The prayer for help, *Oshanah,* is recited each day during Sukkos, but on Oshanah Rabah it is recited to the accompaniment of "beating the help-me's." The help-me's are bundles of green willow branches, beaten against benches and floors until all the leaves are beaten off and the twigs are bruised and bent. Everyone beats the help-me's, the men at shul, the women often at home.

The end of Oshanah Rabah is the Eve of Simkhas Torah,

when the completion of the annual cycle of readings is celebrated. Gloom changes to gaiety as all the scrolls are taken out of
the Ark, with their gleaming satin covers, silver crowns and
jingling bells. Each scroll must be carried around the bimah at
least seven times, and each adult man must carry one around
once. They are called to "circling" as they are called to the reading of the Torah, by name and in order of status, beginning with
the rabbi. Boys who have not yet been Bar Mitzvah are called in
groups of "all-the-boys," and one prayer shawl is put over the
whole group. These children are not entrusted with carrying a
scroll themselves, but they put their hands under it while it is
carried by an adult. The boy who is newly Bar Mitzvah is proud
to carry a scroll by himself, holding it with anxious care for to
let it fall would be a calamity. To be lumped with a group under
one shawl is childish, and if an adult has no mind of his own
but trails along with others, people say "he goes with all-the-
boys."

The circling process is long and festive. On this one occasion
the girls and women come down from their gallery into the main
section of the shul and watch the "circling." Everyone tries to
"kiss" as many scrolls as possible, and as often as possible—that
is, to touch them with a finger which is then kissed—the same procedure followed in kissing the mezuzah. The cantor leads each
tour, chanting a prayer, over and over. Those who follow him
chant as he does, while the others talk, watch, and dart in to kiss
the Holy Scroll.

Each child carries his Sukkos banner, topped with an apple
into which is thrust a candle that will be lighted the next day.
The apple must be as large, red and shiny as possible, and the
cardboard banner as decorative as the parents' pocket will permit. The decorations include traditional motifs and appropriate
inscriptions. A very lucky child might have two lions of Judah
guarding an Ark with doors that really open, or the ten commandments inscribed on the Tablets of the Law.

The "circling" of the Torah prepares for the next day, the
day of Simkhas Torah, when the last portion is read. It too is a
long process, since each male over thirteen must be called to the
reading, and again "all-the-boys" in clusters covered by one

prayer shawl must come up in turn. The same passage is read over and over again until every male member of the congregation has been called. Then the first sentence of the new portion is read, and the yearly cycle of reading is launched again. All over the world on this day, with the same prayers and the same intonation, the orthodox are finishing the last sentence of the last weekly reading of the Torah, and are starting the cycle for the next year: "In the beginning God created heaven and earth. . . ."

The post-Biblical holidays, like the strictly religious ones, may be sad or glad, home-centered or shul-centered. They are all, however, holidays on which work is permitted, with no special services at shul but merely some additions inserted into the accustomed ritual. They are the holidays most entwined with folk customs and observances, and accordingly most subject to regional and local variation.

The midsummer holiday of Tisheh b'Av, devoted to mourning the destruction of the Temple, has become a symbol of sadness in the shtetl. If a person looks unhappy he will be asked, "What's wrong, is it Tisheh b'Av at your house?" or "Why do you have Tisheh b'Av on your face?" When the atmosphere is gloomy they may say, "Tisheh b'Av is in the air."

The truly pious fast on that day. They go to services very early and stay very late, mourning the destruction of the Temple. In token of mourning the worshipers sit on the floor and wail, chanting Lamentations and Psalms. "By the rivers of Babylon, there sat we down, yea we wept, when we remembered Zion. . . . If I forget thee, Oh Jerusalem, let my right hand forget her cunning, let my tongue cleave to the roof of my mouth. . . ."

They are unkempt, with ashes on their heads, their shoes removed, their garments rent. To add to their discomfort they are also subject to the burrs thrown at them by children as a traditional part of the day's observance. "Tisheh b'Av was the holiday when you remember the destruction of the Temple. It was a sad holiday and a fast day, but we had our fun then too. All the old men used to sit on the ground in shul and say prayers which were very sad and had very haunting and melancholy tunes. We used to gather stickers and throw them at the old men. It used to hurt and it made them cry, but they expected it."°

The reconsecration of the Temple is commemorated by *Hanukah,* the eight-day feast of lights that brightens the cold days of December. Its symbol is the glowing lamp of brass or silver, with eight tiny mouths open to hold an oil-soaked wick. The children watch entranced as each day one more light is added and the "shammes" candle with which they are kindled is returned to its socket at the side of the lamp. But for the children the real feature of this winter holiday is the *"Hanukah gelt,"* the present of money to which each child is entitled from every adult relative. They go the rounds from one to the next, collecting and comparing their spoils. Usually one knows what to expect, which aunt has "a broad hand," which uncle is a "cold lung." The real problem is the poor relative who would "be ashamed" if she could not give enough and would also "be ashamed" if one skipped her house.

All holidays have their special foods, and the chief one for Hanukah is potato pancakes fried in shmalts. During the eight evenings there is time to invite and be invited, so that every balebosteh will have opportunity to display her own talent and to exchange constructive criticisms of her neighbors' recipes with all the other neighbors and relatives.

Each holiday has its special games, and the one associated with Hanukah is cards—frowned on at any other time of the year, at least by the sheyneh layt. The packs are usually home-made, of white cardboard on which the Hebrew letters are drawn in black. There are no pictures and no colors—only the letters, each of which has a numerical value.

Meanwhile the children spin their four-sided lead Hanukah tops. These too are decorated with letters, one on each side of the rectangular top, the initial letters of the sentence, "a great miracle happened there." The miracle was related to the triumph of the Maccabbees, the event commemorated by Hanukah. The lack of color and the intellectual context of the unpainted lead tops make them model toys for the almost toyless shtetl. These are toys with "takhlis."

The favorite historical holiday is *Purim,* and while Pesakh is the grandest of the "glad" ones, this is the gayest of all. On Purim too, the child sees his elders in an unfamiliar light, for that is the one day of the year when frivolity is permitted and even prescribed, and when the law of moderation in all things may be briefly relaxed. Suddenly on Purim the things criticized as "un-Jewish" are "becoming." Drinking, even to excess, practical jokes, masquerading in odd costumes, wearing of women's clothes by men, boisterousness—on Purim, as they say, "es past," it is done. More than that, to drink on Purim is actually a mitsva. This is the day on which it is right to be the way one should never be at any other time. Even the customary rules of respect and deference are relaxed somewhat. The license of Purim is exercised more by the Hassidim than by the rabbinists, and the very sheyneh layt unbend only enough to do honor to the tradition, without violating the decorum that is their second nature.

This moment of mad carnival in the decorous year is preceded by a fast, the fast of Esther who triumphed over the wicked hangman Haman. It is a businesslike fast, observed only by the more pious, and neither that nor Purim itself need interrupt the affairs of daily life.

The Eve of Purim, like any holiday, is the occasion for a feast and for family gatherings. It is preceded both at home and in the shul by the melodious reading of the *megillah,* the story of Esther and how she saved her people from massacre. The children are supplied with "noise-makers" for the occasion and whenever the names of the wicked Haman or his sons are mentioned in the reading, they whirl the rattles with a will. The grownups too beat on benches or tables, adding to the gratifying din.

The whirling fowl of Yom Kippur is a scapegoat for one's own sins. The Haman of Purim is a different sort of scapegoat. Every shtetl has its Haman, and knows edicts not wholly unlike the one against which Esther pitted her beauty and wit. Esther herself served her people as a feminine shtadlan, choosing to risk her life for their safety rather than to accept immunity for herself alone. Her story is paralleled in the shtetl, except that Esther won. Its triumphant repetition flows with the current of the culture, the strong belief in the promise for the future. But the expression of noisy vengeance is as sharp a contrast to the tradition as is the whole mood and license of the carnival.

At the feast which follows the reading of the *megillah*, sweets and wine will be abundant, and before the meal has ended the Purim players will begin to make their house-to-house rounds. Spectacles and plays are "un-Jewish" at other times of the year but they are an important part of Purim. During the rest of the year, occasional entertainers may drift in, alone or in groups, to give street performances for which they will collect donations. "Since it was in the open there was no admission—but it was voluntary. There was something special you wanted to see—you had to pay for it. For example, when they put the horse up to count by shaking his hoof, everybody would want to see it, but they wouldn't begin until people had paid up."°

The status of these performers is extremely low—they are "half beggars" and moreover are known to "eat treyf" and disregard the mitsvos. "If the half beggar didn't earn anything by performing, he started to beg."° He might be an organ grinder, or perhaps an acrobat. "There were two kinds of acrobats. There were the small groups of two or three who performed in the street and there were the larger groups who came with all their apparatus and took up a whole square in the market place . . . they would put up large posters in the shtetl telling the people when the performance would begin and everybody used to gather in the market place to watch."°

To be an actor in the Purim plays is definitely a seasonal occupation, and a professional actor may be a "half beggar" the rest of the year. Often, however, the players are groups of artisans and tradesmen who band together to present the play at house after house, and to be rewarded with "nasheray" and wine, and perhaps some coins.

The chief story acted is the Purim tale of Esther and her wise uncle Mordekhay, who foiled Haman's designs against the Jews through Esther's marriage to the King, Ahasuerus. Most of the characters are likely to stem from the shtetl. The King and Esther are dressed in costumes reminiscent of antiquity, but Esther's long braids and red cheeks are timeless and the king sits back on his throne exactly like the father on his Pesakh pillows. Mordekhay is the model of the learned man, with long caftan, beard, and earlocks. Haman is dressed like a policeman or an army officer, a costume more familiar than popular.

Other plays based on biblical themes may be added to celebrate the one time when it is correct for the shtetl to indulge in theatricals. Among the most popular is the story of Joseph and his brothers, again with an interweaving of the current and the antique, with an announcer to explain each event, and a liberal sprinkling of incidental songs.

On other gift-giving holidays, children are the main recipients of presents. On Purim, the children are also observers of an elaborate interchange of gifts among their elders. The gifts consist chiefly of pastries, presented by one housewife to another, and these *shalakhmones* have come to be more a form of social currency than food. All day long, platters covered with napkins are carried through the streets by servants or boys who welcome the chance to earn a little money in this way. All day long plates full of pastries are being received and sent out. Each carefully covered display is calculated by the intense and painful arithmetic of social obligation, for the amenities require that one must give exactly the equivalent of what one receives.

The computation involves both mathematics and prediction. What will she send this year? If I figure on the basis of last year's shalakhmones and this year she raises it, I shall be "ashamed." If she sends more than I send, she will be insulted. Loud quarrels and long-smouldering feuds have arisen over a miscalculation of shalakhmones.

Even when the level is determined, the figuring of values remains. How many almond-filled tarts equal one orange? How many butter cookies equal one wondrous confection shaped like a tower and filled with honey, nuts and spices?

While the mothers struggle the children watch coveted goodies come and go. These pastries are not for eating, they are for sending. A plate arrives with a ring of nut-powdered stars and crescents, and in the center a horse splendid with sugar and raisins. At once the horse is whisked to an outgoing platter and within a few moments he is on his way. "It shouldn't happen" that he returns to the woman who had first sent him to the woman who

then sent him to the woman who now sends him out again! All
day long the pastries are whisked from one plate to another, all
day they ride the streets under snowy napkins embroidered in
different designs. By the end of the day they have traveled miles.
Perhaps they come to rest somewhere. Perhaps in the end someone eats them. Yet in every home, children are nibbling sweet
crumbs and the plain cookies used to fill spaces on the plates,
and dreaming about those beautiful cakes eaten only with the
eyes.

As on every holiday, there will also be gifts of food and
money to the poor. On Purim, however, the poor feel it correct
to reciprocate. They too will send their humble shalakhmones to
their rich benefactors. "We always got mountains of pastries
from my father's employees—cheap candies and simple cookies."°

When the poor give to the rich, when the pious man drinks
a glass too much, when a "good Jew" plays the rowdy and loudly
bangs a paean of vengeance—then the shtetl is "an upside-down."
But after twenty-four hours out of the usual course, it is again
nokh yontev, and almost far yontev, for Pesakh is only four
weeks ahead. It is time to buy the raisins and prepare the borshtsh,
for sooner than one thinks the next holiday will be "at the door."

Part Five

As the Shtetl Sees the World

AS THE SHTETL SEES THE WORLD

The shtetl views the universe as a planned whole, designed and governed by the Almighty, Who created it from original chaos.* It is a complex whole, but basically it is characterized by order, reason and purpose. Everything has its place, its cause, its function. Apparent contradictions, inconsistencies and irregularities fall into place as complements rather than incongruities. It is not a static universe, for all its parts are interdependent and interacting. The dynamic whole extends in time as well as in space, so that the apparent inconsistencies of the present may be interpreted as parts of a long-term process building toward ultimate integration.

In such a universe, behavior—human or divine—must also be rooted in reason, order and purpose. Any act must be rational, motivated and directed toward some goal. Whether it be the wailing of a baby, the fund collecting of a community leader, or the affliction of Job, any act must have "takhlis."

Being rational, behavior must also be reasonable. God is conceived as a reasonable Being and all the interpretations and modifications of His Law are based on this conception. Humans, if they are really "people," mentshen, are also rational and reasonable. To be beyond the reach of reason is to be dangerous. Yet those who are unreasoning and unreasonable are also part of the divine reason and purpose, working toward an ultimate goal.

The evils that spring from the behavior of the unenlightened are accepted as part of the over-all plan, for every positive not only has but needs a negative. Joy cannot exist without sorrow, Sabbath cannot exist without the weekday world, light would be

*Here, as throughout the book, it is of course the culture and not the theology of the shtetl that is being discussed. Any reference to religious doctrine is not in a theological frame of reference, but is presented as an expression or reflection of the culture.

unimaginable without its counterpart of darkness. Nevertheless, since man is endowed with reason, he is free to expostulate with a reasonable God when things go too far and the negatives threaten to swamp the positive aspects of life.

He is free to argue also because rationality itself has and needs its complement of emotion. A world based on reason, order and purpose must include feeling, and to allow for this element is both rational and realistic. A man is only human—"a mentsh iz nur a mentsh." Like the universe at large, he is made up of complementary forces, good and evil, thought and feeling. God Himself may be appealed to in terms of thought or of feeling. It is assumed that He will be just, but when justice becomes too rigorous, its complement, mercy, is invoked. God is not asked to renounce justice in favor of mercy or mercy in favor of justice, but rather to moderate both elements, striking a balance that will be fair. Fairness is differentiated from justice—it is not always fair to be too just.

Thus, by a logic which views contrasting parts as elements that fit into a complex, dynamic whole, it becomes rational to embrace the irrational as a legitimate part of humanity in an ordered and reasoned universe.

The shtetl believes further that the world brought into being by the Almighty is made for man, not man for the world. Human welfare is paramount and takes precedence over all else. The dietary laws are superseded by health requirements. The major commandments may be modified under stress of mortal danger.

The world is for all men, not only for one kind. It is made up of good and bad, male and female, rich and poor, learned and ignorant, Jew and Gentile. There is no ideal of homogeneity in human beings, for each has his place and all are part of the original design. The ideal is not to make all men into one kind or to convert all to one faith. There is no attempt to change the existing order or to upset the basic design. The shtetl displays no urge to missionary activity, no proselytizing. If one is a Christian, it says, then let him be a good one. Good Gentiles will also find a place in the "real world."

Because the world is for man, the things of this world should be enjoyed. The Covenant specifies enjoyment of Olam Hazeh, this world, as part of human rights. No premium is placed on asceticism and self-denial, "There is no Jewish monastery." On the contrary, enjoyment at the proper time and place is prescribed. On Sabbath one is commanded to put aside all worry and grief; the feast is as much part of religious observance as the fast.

Life itself is to be enjoyed. Inherent in the picture of a rational universe, ruled by a humanitarian God, is the belief that life is desirable, despite its hardships and trials. Two assumptions are implicit in the legend which tells that man is conceived and born against his will, and dies against his will. One is that things are not as we choose to have them, a recognition of human impotence and suffering. The other is that, despite all disadvantages, life offers enough gratifications so that man learns to relish it and clings to it when he is forced to leave. "To a worm in a horseradish, the horseradish seems sweet."

Life on any terms is good, because the state of being alive is good, and life in the shtetl is lived with abounding zest. The "conditional optimism" of the shtetl folk implies not only hope for the future but also relish of the present. Here again the contrasting aspects of the whole are in evidence. Life is hard, man enters it against his will; but life is good, and nobody wants to leave it.

Since it is a system of checks and balances, the world that is "for man" includes elements hostile to man, the inevitable counterparts of the forces that make for his welfare. He is menaced by fire and flood, by bad spirits, by the bad impulses that are part of good people, and by dangers from men who, being without the light, may be as unrestrained and unruly as thunder or drought.

Strict observance of the Law is obviously not complete protection against the hostile powers that swarm the world. The extent to which superstitious practices are employed to supplement religious observance bears witness to intense and unremitting anxiety. A sense of chronic threat is evident, for example, in the frequency of the exclamation, "No evil eye!" and in the rule against categorical commitment: "I may do it, God willing."

The basic assumptions of order, reason and purpose are apparent in any area and at any level of shtetl life, as are the principles and mechanisms which express them: the complementary character, the interdependence, the interaction of the parts which make up any whole. Each element is seen always as part of the whole to which it belongs, yet each is able to retain a vivid and functioning individuality. Any element is incomplete in isolation, and though some parts are considered superior to others, each is regarded as equally indispensable.

The separate parts in turn are not unbroken unities. Each element contains components which interact. The community is made up of families, the families of individuals, each representing a balance of complementary and interacting parts. A similar interaction may be discerned between all of Jewry—the Klal Isroel—and the non-Jewish cultures in which it is embedded.

The structure and process can best be described by borrowing from physics the concept of a "field of forces." The relationships between the parts—their contrast, interdependence and interaction—create a field of reciprocally functioning forces resulting in a dynamic equilibrium.

The shtetl has no monopoly on the mechanisms observed. Like any culture, however, it is unique in its combination of mechanisms and of the features in which they are perceptible. Moreover, the mechanisms are remarkably explicit in this culture. They are not only present but recognized. They permeate the shtetl conception of life, of people, of reality itself, and the formulation of such concepts. The shtetl outlook, its view of the world, is geared to recognize the complementary, the interdependent, the dynamic, so organized as to form an integrated and reasonable whole, animated by and conforming to the principles of justice and mercy—principles in themselves complementary, interdependent and interactive. It recognizes, too, as a complement to reason and order, the element of apparent incongruity, acknowledged in the sense of paradox and irony that forms so conspicuous a part of shtetl humor.

The emphasis on reason and its corollary, law, is linked with an enormous emphasis on words. It takes endless words to rationalize all of life on earth and in heaven, to bring all within a framework of order, reason and purpose conceived in justice and mercy. Words are required not only to explain how past history and present facts conform to divine Law, but also to interpret and apply that Law. Day-by-day existence can be carried on only to the accompaniment of elaborate verbalization.

Every act of daily life is related to the words of the Holy Books and their vast body of commentary. Often it is related in words, through the many daily prayers and blessings. The primary social value, book learning, is expressed and validated through words by the scholars who mediate between the written law and the populace.

The incessant communication indispensable to social well-being is achieved through words, which serve incidentally to communicate far more than their verbal content. Vocabulary, manner of speech, degree of volubility are recognized indices of sex and social status. The paramount role of words is suggested by the popular notion that every human being has assigned to him at birth a definite quota of them. When his quota of words is expended he will die, since obviously to live without talking is impossible. Therefore, the less you waste your words, the longer you live. Women, because of their garrulous nature, are allotted "nine measures to one for the man." Often a disgusted male will exclaim, "So what do you expect of a woman—she has nine measures of talk!"

As a means of communication, the word is supplemented by vocal sounds, grunts or snorts, and also by a rich vocabulary of gesture. Both media are effective only to the extent that they embellish or substitute for words. They may be regarded, accordingly, as an extension of verbalization. The negative power of words is suggested by the strong feeling that silence is unsocial or even antisocial. It is not a passive state, but a notice of withdrawal or exclusion from family, community, or individual relationship.

In this highly verbalized culture, words are more than a medium of communication. The word is a force in itself, a tool. More than that, the word itself embodies substance—the Hebrew root is the same for "word" and for "thing" or "object." Thus the word endows its referent with existence.

The original creation was a verbal act, the world was brought out of chaos by words. "In the beginning God said 'Let there be light,' and there was light." Demands and requests of God or of man carry an element of compulsion. Prayers must be accompanied by one's own effort, but nevertheless they exert a more than verbal power. Rote memorizing of words is the first step toward understanding, and toward the exemplary behavior which understanding of God's command is assumed to produce.

Accordingly, the shtetl sets up no sharp dichotomy between the word and the deed. The word is the threshold to the deed, even the initial phase of it. Or rather, words are deeds of a special order.

Because of their potency, words take on a peculiar danger. The mention of the wrong words is hazardous. A curse is a deep menace, and one would hesitate to express a curse he literally wanted to come true. Words that connote disaster or misfortune call for immediate counteractive phrases—"Not of us be it said!" The baby's name is changed to outwit the Angel of Death.

Words serve also as a safety valve. One discharges his emotions through words and such catharsis is felt to serve also a constructive function. Verbalized worry, like prayer, must be combined with effort to improve the situation; but the verbalization itself somehow furthers the desired end.

Relief through expression is not necessarily verbal. In general, catharsis is an accepted means of alleviating any evil or difficulty. One "cries out" so that his "heart will be lighter." One "worries out." Emotions are made to be expressed, both to achieve communication and to get them out of the system. The ritual of sitting shiveh for the dead is a dramatic application of the principle of catharsis. After mourning intensively and extensively, grief must be put aside. One has "grieved out" and life goes on. In the case of bodily ills also, evil must be eliminated, and the first step for any ailment is an enema or purge.

Tears and outcries, like words, may have a function beyond catharsis and communication. They may be regarded as a positive activity designed to alter the unfavorable situation. Worry is not merely a state of mind, it is also an act. If someone is ill, you go to the synagogue, open the Ark and "weep out recovery." You "worry out parnosseh," "cry out" a dowry for your daughter, always of course coupling this emotional activity with specific moves directed toward your goal. The tears and emotional expressiveness involved are by no means childish. On the contrary, they are correct and expected behavior for adults, under appropriate circumstances.

They are not correct, however, for adults in a senior position. One beseeches with tears a person who is superior in power or learning, but not an inferior. It is appropriate for any Jew to supplicate God with tears and moans, for God is senior to all other beings. A woman or a proster man may weep in pleading with a shtetl superior.

If two contrasting aspects of reality are constantly and explicitly recognized, neither one can be allowed to submerge the other for long at a time. The dualism inherent in all things may be acknowledged either by avoiding extremes or by veering rapidly from one to the other. To some extent the shtetl does both.

The ideal man is supposed to be restrained in behavior and attitude. Excess of any kind is frowned on. More restraint is expected in sheyneh layt than in others, and lack of restraint is associated with un-Jewish behavior. Realistically, it is recognized that women and prosteh men may lapse from the highest ideal of moderation. This is, in fact, one reason why the sheyneh yidn may rate the prosteh as less "Jewish" than themselves.

A different sort of check and balance between extremes is achieved by the rhythmic alternation of fast and feast, sorrow and joy. The great fast days are preceded and followed by feasting, the Sabbath must represent unsullied enjoyment, the joyous climax breaking into the dismal vokh; mourning must be put aside for the glad holidays. When one does mourn, no joy should intrude, but mourning may not be unduly prolonged. Typical Yiddish drama reflects a swift alternation of joy and sorrow.

The condemnation of excess may be regarded as qualitative moderation, the alternating of extremes, as quantitative moderation. The feeling against excess exists side by side with a feeling against diluting one emotion or one occasion with another. Joy must be untainted by sorrow, but qualitatively and quantitatively it must be kept within bounds.

The prescribed alternation of joy and sorrow in many instances sets up a schedule of prescribed emotion. One is gay on

Purim, one weeps on Yom Kippur. A marriage is the most joyful of all events, but at the proper points of the marriage ceremony, one weeps; one weeps at a funeral, but at two points in the ceremony weeping is prohibited. It does not follow that because emotions are prescribed they are perfunctory. Emotions expressed on schedule can be genuinely felt.

To turn a genuine feeling on or off as required demands extreme emotional discipline. A familiar example is the householder who, on the verge of personal bankruptcy or family disgrace, or under threat of pogrom, puts aside all distracting thoughts to plunge into the joy and peace of Sabbath. This is expected shtetl behavior, to be taken for granted in a "real Jew." Just as prescribed emotion need not be perfunctory, so a high degree of emotional expressiveness need not indicate lack of emotional discipline. To express emotions freely and intensely is the way of the shtetl; to govern them at the proper times is also the shtetl way. That the shtetl has its own definition of what constitutes propriety in time and in place goes without saying.

The individual sees himself in the light of shtetl assumptions. He is a field of forces in which contrasting elements exist and interact. Each person has "the bad impulse and the good impulse," just as "every stick has two ends." The constant interaction between the good and the bad need not be viewed as inner strife, any more than the constant discussions in the household are viewed as quarreling. A continuous process of adjustment between two aspects of one personality is assumed to be normal, with neither expected to evict the other and maintain unchallenged dominion.

Nevertheless it is assumed that the good in man should prevail, that if he knows what is right he will do it. The problem is seen, not as a need to persuade man that God's will be done, but rather as a need to acquaint him with the commandments and their complicated application. If he knows, he will obey—providing he is one who has entered into the Covenant, that is, a Jew. If he is not a Jew, he lacks the basic enlightenment that gives him both the will and the obligation to obey. Therefore he moves in a different system and may win his eternal reward under different rules.

The individual is seen as a free agent, even though his fate is foreordained. "Everything is foreseen but the choice is given," says the Talmud. Man's external fate is sealed when he is conceived, but he is always given freedom to choose between right and wrong, which is in theory the only choice that really matters. The coexistence of free will and predestination is recognized as a problem in that it furnishes a topic for endless discussion and dazzling displays of erudition. It does not, however, present a full-fledged paradox for the man in the shtetl street. It is another instance of contrasts accepted as complementary rather than as contradictory.

The combination of the two concepts, free will and predestination, discourages fatalism and fosters anxiety. God has decreed the circumstances of each man's life but the individual alone is responsible for what he does with them. There are so many opportunities for failure in fulfillment of the commandments, in the amount of effort one expends on earning a livelihood, in all one's activities and relationships. Ignorance of circumstances may be an excuse, but ignorance of the Law is not, and there is no excuse for ignorance due to oversight or negligence. Obligations are so many, opposite God, family and fellows, that no matter how much one does it is never really enough. There is always the burden of undischarged duty.

That burden is the ol, the yoke, that weighs on every man, woman and child in the shtetl. There is constant complaint about the ol, and about the difficulty of achieving fulfillment of duty. Yet the gratification of fulfilling one's duty is among the highest pleasures. The "ol of children" is inseparable from the pleasure of children, without which no one can win completion.

To boast of one's yoke is in itself a gratification. The yoke is proof of participation in the life of one's group. There is only scorn for the man who is without obligation—"he has no yoke on him!" Through accepting and fulfilling a complex of duties, status is won. Every value and every pleasure has its yoke, and is referred to in terms of its yoke. The process of maturing is a process of accumulating more and more burdens; the greater one's yoke, the higher one's status; the greater the sum of fulfilled obligations, the greater the complement of gratification, of deference, of honors in heaven and on earth. Ol and nakhes, yoke and gratification increase together; each is the counterpart of the other. The person who complains about his yoke is at the same time boasting about the extent to which he is fulfilling his duties, and himself.

Throughout his life the individual is striving toward completion of two kinds, for the part in itself is always incomplete. One kind of completion is to be accomplished by annexing his complementary parts—wife, children, associates, fellow citizens, fellow Jews; the other is achieved by developing himself, through increase of knowledge, of years, of good works, of worldly wellbeing. The ideal toward which he strives is one of maturity in all respects. In this highly competitive setting, the competition is for superior seniority.

The interplay of complementary elements is most conspicuous in the family, in the balance and interplay both of sex and of age. Despite the recognition of interdependence between the man and the woman, the culture is clearly male-oriented. Even by the women, its features are stated from the male viewpoint, and the inferiority of the female is given at least verbal acceptance. Nevertheless, the woman manages to assert herself, not merely in spite of her subordinate status, but often through manipulating it.

The roles of the parents are completely complementary and completely interactive. The father represents the values of the community, the tradition; he stands for mind and spirit, he is the household spokesman of God's Law. He is timeless. The mother is flesh and blood, the source of warmth, succor, emotional response. Neither one can exist without the other and as a pair they cannot live fully without the children. Opposite the authority and tradition represented by the parents as a twofold unit, the child represents an object of affection, a source of pleasure and gratification. He is subordinate and junior, and in this capacity commands the care and succor of his parents. They in turn are dependent on him, not only for pleasure but also for status on earth and in heaven. Only as parents can they fulfill their whole duty to God. In each case the recipient is also giver, the giver has need of the recipient, and the gift is of a different order than the return.

Within the small area of the family a number of basic contrasts come into sharp focus. The man-woman contrast exists between husband and wife, and also between brother and sister.

The role of the woman in the shtetl is that of the subordinate, with functions different from the man's. Whether she be wife or sister, she is a different kind of human being. Yet this subordinate is the indispensable pivot of the domestic circle. She is rated inferior to the male, but he is dependent on her. At the same time she cedes to him authority in his own realm, and there she is dependent on him. Thus the elements that make for difference at the same time make for interdependence, serving as sources both of tension and of cohesion.

Between man and woman part of the balance can be translated into terms of junior and senior, each being senior in certain areas. The difference between junior and senior becomes central and complex in the relations of parent and child. The child is at the same time pushed toward maturity and kept in junior status by the parents, who in turn depend on him as the validation of their own adulthood. Whereas the balance between man and woman is constant with regard to maturity, the balance between parent and child is continually changing as the child approaches adulthood. Again, the sources of conflict are at the same time bases of interdependence and accordingly sources of cohesion.

The interplay of forces making simultaneously for conflict and for cohesion creates a field of tensions held in balance by their interaction. This equilibrium is covered by the term sholem bayis, peace of the house, the ideal of every shtetl family. Sholem bayis does not mean absence of perceptible tensions, but rather that frictions are assimilated as part of a dynamic whole.

Any event in the family is also a community event. When a baby is born, when a boy is Bar Mitzvah, when a young couple are married, the celebration is by and for the community as well as the family. The individual is always part of a group, a family, a special segment of the community, or part of the community as a whole. His position in the community is defined by his special combination of the three values, learning, money, yikhus. The ideal is a full share of each one and if any is lacking there will be an attempt to supply it—through marriage, through study, or through "buying" a spouse for one's child. One's own lack may be made up in one's child, and this is part of the parent's dependence on the child.

Status is no more fixed and absolute than anything else in the shtetl. The status of any individual may vary radically throughout his life. Moreover, the criteria of status are fluid, and are differently evaluated by different people according to their own position on the social scale. Sometimes also the community judges an individual's status quite differently from the way he himself places it.

However, it may be judged, status is a prime focus of attention in the shtetl. The "chase after koved" is second only to the "chase after a parnosseh." One's claims to status must constantly be on display, and are constantly compared to those of others. A large part of the tremendous expenditure of energy required by shtetl existence goes into the winning and incessant validation of status.

Each social level has its attendant rights and obligations which serve as sources of friction and of cohesion. The community, like the family, is held together by the interdependence and interaction of its parts. The poor and ignorant look to the wealthy and learned for assistance; the latter in turn depend upon their dependents for earthly and heavenly rewards. As in the family, the subordinate is able to profit by his subordinate position.

In the closely knit community, where each is responsible for all and all are responsible for each, privacy is neither known nor desired. Everyone is subject to inspection and criticism, everyone is free to inspect and criticize. The strongest sanction is public opinion, the highest reward is public approval. As a last resort one "calls to people," even against the ostensible authority. And it is the will of the people that implements the ruling of the rabbi in his court. The ones who have least privacy and most criticism are the leaders, and the yoke of leadership is heaviest of all. Yet so great are the attendant satisfactions that leadership with all its burdens is a common goal.

The authority of any leader is not absolute but relative—the shtetl recognizes no absolutes. Almost any category is subject to invasion from another category. Almost any agent is subject to replacement under exceptional circumstances. Any generalization has its exceptions. Any statement has its qualifications. Any authority, even that of God, is subject to check, question and criticism.

The only absolute authority is the spirit of the Torah. Each human authority has his own interpretation of the words through which that spirit is made known, and each buttresses his interpretation by references to what other authorities have said and to the words of the Torah itself. Each new interpreter refers back along the line that flows unbroken through the ages. From Mount Sinai and Moses down to contemporary commentators, the Law of the Torah forms a never-ending continuum, in which the core is immutable while the surface is susceptible to the impact of the latest sage.

The authority of the leader is limited also by the right and duty of each man to try to understand and interpret for himself. True understanding of the Law involves deeper levels, beyond the comprehension of those who are not erudite. Yet the simple and ignorant still have to choose their authorities from among the disputing scholars, and in this choice each man feels bound to use his own judgment. Even the lowliest is incapable of blind acceptance. The zealous Hassid may bow to his Tsaddik up to a point, but if that point is exceeded, the leader will find himself without followers. "Every Jew is his own Shulkhan Arukh."

Because it is accepted with qualifications, authority remains authoritative only as long as it expresses one's own point of view. In any aspect of public activities, people in the shtetl express their point of view either by accepting an acceptable authority or by seceding, refusing participation, and setting up a new group. Nobody is right merely by virtue of being himself. Authority, like yikhus, requires constant validation.

The role of the individual and his relationship to the group show a marked intermingling of the personal and the impersonal, the individualistic and the collective. On the one hand, each person exists only as part of the group. He is defined by his place in the family circle, and in the community as a whole. Conduct toward one's relatives is dictated more by the nature of the relationship than by personal impulse. At the same time, the individual identity is never lost or even blurred. The sense of one's place in the group, one's responsibility to the group, one's dependence on the group is never lost; yet the group never loses a sense of the person as individual.

There is evident a sort of collective identification. The individual is merged but never submerged; rather, he is so strongly identified with the group that it partakes of his own individuality —he *is* the group, and the group is he. Moreover, the group is eternal and the individual passes. Only as part of the group does he achieve immortality in this world. Again it is the structure and mechanism of complementary parts, interdependent, interacting, equally indispensable.

Against the background of strong and affirmative identification with the group, there is room for intense individual activity. Because status must be validated continually and can change in either direction through individual efforts or the lack of them, each individual must strive constantly to maintain and to improve his economic and social level. His standing is measured against his own previous position and against the status of others, an exercise strongly linked with competitiveness and with anxiety, in a world where opportunities are strictly limited and aspiration is infinite. That strong solidarity and intense competition can coexist with no sense of incongruity is the more natural since service to the group is a major source of status.

Like the family, the community is a close-knit unit, made up of interacting parts. The same mechanisms of conflict and cohesion are evident in both. Individual may react against individual within the family, but the unit is solid in facing the community at large. Similarly, the community presents a solid front—not only in appearance but also in feeling—opposite another community. Each town criticizes and ridicules the next. Yet the towns of one region display a common bond and loyalty opposite another region. As the boundaries broaden, all of Eastern European Jewry forgets local rivalries and conflicts in a common scorn of German Jews, who represent distasteful elements of coldness and assimilative tendencies.

The regional groups of Jews, whatever their differences and antagonisms, are all part of Klal Isroel, the whole of Jewry throughout the world. "Whatever else we are, we are," says the song, "but Jews we are." One scorns the Jews whose ways and observances are different. One argues with them, refuses to accept their deviations from one's own usage. Nevertheless they are Jews.

Just as the community is an expanded family, so Klal Isroel, world-wide Jewry, is an expanded and diluted community. Its ties are more tenuous than those of the local community, its areas of estrangement more marked. Despite local variations, however, the tradition of the Torah remains a common bond. And despite friction or disapprobation, that bond entitles members of Klal Isroel to be helped with the essentials of life. Those who are far away would be helped, not as individuals, but only as members of a stricken community.

Membership does not by any means imply mutual understanding or esteem, or the ability to co-operate in sustained action. On the contrary, the only area in which concerted action can be expected is in relief of distress. Like the family and the shtetl, the wider community may be counted on for promoting steps to alleviate hardship and suffering, but not for congeniality or approval. For the people of the shtetl, the Jews in far-off places such as Germany or America are like kinsmen who have wandered from the fold. One may blame, scorn, pity them because they have wandered. If they are in need, however, one would try to help.

Actually, it has been the shtetl that needed help from those who left it, and help has been forthcoming. This, too, is as it should be, according to shtetl tenets. The commandments prescribe it and all the rules of community responsibility dictate it. Those who have are responsible for those who have not, even if the needy ones are separated by miles of land or water. The mutual responsibility does not necessarily include affection. It is not commanded that those who succor should also love those they befriend, any more than "Uncle Froyim" loved the in-laws who enjoyed his bounty. Nor is it written that the recipient must love the hand that feeds him.

Membership in Klal Isroel is elastic and renewable. Anyone born of Jewish parents is a Jew. A Jew who is a stranger has difficulty being accepted as part of the local community, for what does one know of him or of his background? Nevertheless, he is a member of Klal Isroel, just as one's in-laws are never part of one's own family and yet are relatives, mekhutonim.

Even if only one parent is a Jew, there is a tendency to include the person in Klal Isroel. Religious observance is no criterion. Even a man who breaks the commandments is a Jew, even one who eats forbidden food. A person who renounces the faith is repudiated by his family and mourned as if he were dead. Yet he can always repent and return. Moreover, even in his apostasy something of him remains Jewish. The wrong a Jew does is doubly wrong, because he should know better and because it is felt to react against all Jews. Nevertheless, no matter what he does, he is "still a Jew."

He is not a good Jew, however, not an emesser Yid, a true or "real" Jew. There is a vast difference between who is Jewish and what is Jewish. Membership in Klal Isroel is an accident of birth. Claim to being a "real" Jew must be earned and validated, and the criteria are exacting.

A real Jew is known by his heart and by his head. The "Yiddisher kop" is keen and powerful. It must have not only abstract intellect but ability to see all possibilities and to apply them with lightning speed. "He grabs it in the air," they say of such a person. A Yiddisher kop does not make one a real Jew, however, unless it is combined with a Yiddish heart, for "a Jew is known by his pity." The real Jew does not merely sympathize, he acts on his feelings. Nor does he have to be told, he feels the need. He thinks, feels, acts, communicates—for a real Jew is always part of a group. To be withdrawn and isolated is to be disqualified.

The real Jew is a man who never despairs, never stops hoping and trying. And he is a man of peace. Physical violence is abhorrent to him. Verbal and intellectual strife are invigorating exercise and the peace of the household is often enough a strident equilibrium. But a "real" Jew is a pacifist by conviction. His capacity for passive resistance is as great as his capacity to fight on the rare occasions when conviction tells him that he must.

The traits of the "real" Jew are regarded as the highest attributes of man. The greatest compliment the shtetl can pay to a Gentile is to say, "He has a Jewish head," or "Jewish heart."

In describing a "real" Jew the shtetl includes among the qualifications a devout observance of religious precept. The human ideal is inseparable, however—*mentshlikhkayt*. "Be a Jew and be a man," they say. Religious observances are taken for granted, and their neglect will not go uncriticized. Yet the shtadlan who breaks the dietary laws but serves the shtetl well may be revered as a real Jew, and the "beard without a Jew" who obeys the letter of religious laws is certainly not "real."

The shtetl recognizes no physical characteristics as typically Jewish, but Jewish traits can be expressed through the body. "His Jewish heart lies on his face," they will say. Gestures and intonations are recognized as Jewish. The acceptance of the body as a vehicle for Yiddishkayt is in line with the easy acceptance of worldly and physical pleasures as good, the simple absence of asceticism in a culture that lays primary stress on nonmaterial values. Asceticism exalts physical gratifications to the status of major desiderata. By making a virtue of withstanding their appeal, it tacitly rates that appeal extremely high. The shtetl evaluates the appeal not by exalting resistance to it but by placing a higher and more compelling value on nonmaterial joys. By rating the nonmaterial as more desirable it minimizes the appeal of the material. One is not "tempted" by what he values less.

Assumptions about Jewish characteristics are crystallized in countless proverbs and sayings, some of which have been quoted in connection with the positive aspects of Yiddishkayt. The negative side is also caught in word capsules. A large number of proverbs celebrate the misfortunes of the Jew. "There is no Jew without his bundle of troubles." "When a Jew is right he gets a beating." "No misfortune will ever miss a Jew."

The shtetl is as articulate about the faults of the Jew as about his virtues or his misfortunes, and this stern self-criticism is far older than the shtetl. It permeates the entire tradition, beginning with the Bible, extending down through the Talmud, the moral literature of the Middle Ages, and into contemporary journalism. "Ye are a stiff-necked people. . . ."

The shtetl's self-criticism, like its self-praise, can be assessed only as part of a complex whole, a whole in which once more the parts are complementary and interacting. In other settings, especially where assimilation is an accepted goal, the composition of self-attitudes changes. Self-criticism and self-hatred may become exaggerated, self-love correspondingly dwarfed.

Within the shtetl, however, the picture of "the Jew" contains both good and bad, and presents them simultaneously. The Jew, even in abstraction, is "nur a mentsh," having in him "the good impulse and the bad impulse." Neither the good nor the bad will blind the shtetl to the existence of the other, nor will it seem incongruous that they should coexist.

As pleasure and pain are complementary, so self-praise is the companion piece to self-blame. Proverbs of the shtetl accent especially the factionalism of the Jews, their irrepressible individualism. "If Moses couldn't get along with the Jews," they ask, "how could the man in the street?" "A Jew is stubborn," they add, "and he is contrary. If you say 'Sholem Aleykhem' to him, he will answer, 'Aleykhem Sholem.' " If you ask a question, "he will answer with another question." He is insatiable in his "chase after koved." He "likes to poke his nose into everything."

The proverbial criticisms of Jews by Jews do not attack failure to display the paramount qualities, compassion and intelligence. On the contrary, according to the shtetl picture, the Jew's native sympathy prevents him from being brutal or seriously dishonest. "A Jewish robber is not to be found," they say.

The strength of shtetl self-criticism must be understood not only in relation to the contrapuntal self-praise element, but also in relation to shtetl attitudes toward authority, its educational pattern, and the concept of the Chosen People. Each man is privileged and obligated to judge for himself, each is free to criticize all others, and all exercise these rights to the full. They are exercised the more strenuously since the individual is so completely a part of the group and since the group has been a proverbial target for persecution. The sins of any Jew are felt as a menace to the group, in the eyes of God and at the hands of men. Moreover, good behavior in children or adults is taken for granted, as what one expects from any Jew, whereas failures and omissions draw rebuke and punishment. Accordingly, there is great readiness to question and to blame. In addition, since the Jew is a member of the Chosen People, the "bad impulse" in him is more heinous than in others and therefore will be the more bitterly denounced by his fellows.

Just as the sins of the Jew are more blameworthy because of membership in the Chosen People, so their virtues take on luster because of their identity. The virtue of the original choice consecrated in the Covenant descends on every member of Klal Isroel. The values that made this choice right for Israel on Mount Sinai are part of today's virtue.

The joy and pride in this heritage are on the one hand strong enough to stand unscathed against withering self-criticism; and on the other hand, so strong as to breed impatience with the human imperfections that mar the great tradition. The pride of identification gives the shtetl the right to criticize itself, as a luxury inherent in its excellence. The shtetl likes a good sharp joke about itself, feeling so firm in its own worth that it can afford such indulgence. The witty sayings and funny jokes sometimes are even a kind of folk coquetry that yet preserves somewhere, down beneath, the flame of Jeremiah. Accordingly, what may appear paradoxical from outside is no paradox from within. To the shtetl, it is simple, natural and right.

The universe of the shtetl is an unbroken continuum. From early antiquity to the hereafter there is no true break in the tradition and in Klal Isroel. The promise of the Messiah is a nostalgia for the remote future conceived as a replica of the remote past. All the dispersed Jews will be brought together, the Temple will be rebuilt as it was before, God will be worshiped as in the days of Solomon.

There is no true break in space. Over all the world, wherever "real" Jews are found, there the tradition lives unchanged. Nor is there a true break between the individual and the total group. Each merges into the other. The individual is fulfilled only as part of a family and a community, the group is sensed only as a cluster of individuals, each with his conflicts, his tensions, his special traits, his peculiar drives. Injury to one is injury to the other—"What happens to Israel happens also to Mr. Israel."

The shtetl endows the far end of its continuum with attributes of the near. The past is conceived in the image of the present, and the foreign is envisaged as a reflection of the familiar. Yiddish means Jewish and yidn means Jews; the language offers no more generalized words. To Jews in other parts of the world, Yiddish culture means specifically the culture of Eastern European Jews, and the Yiddish language is the language spoken by this group. If there is any "Jewish" language, they would say, it is Hebrew. To the shtetl folk, differences in custom and belief that are forced upon their attention are irritating, deplorable, and subject to resentment. When they think of Klal Isroel, they think of a world-wide shtetl where speech and even thought is in Yiddish.

To the man of the shtetl, "Jewishness" is "my way of life," in which religion, values, social structure, individual behavior are inextricably blended. It means the way life is lived among "us," and "us" means the shtetl. There is no conscious rigidity or purism in this, it is merely taken for granted. We are "the" Jews, our way of life is "the" Jewishness, and the word for it is Yiddishkayt.

That word is charged with the joy and pride that are complementary to "the yoke." "It is hard to be a Jew and it is good to be a Jew." The word Yiddishkayt carries all the associations that make it good. The joy of the Sabbath, brightly cleaving the drab world of the week—candles gleaming over a white cloth, the lordly Sabbath loaf, the clean clothes, the holy peace. The ecstasy of the Passover with its springtime purification, the household made new and beautiful, the soul made new and beautiful. The proud festivity of the boy's Bar Mitzvah, the "pleasure of children" and of family, the warm sense of belonging and participating with one's own—all are blended into the syllables of Yiddishkayt. The "melody of learning," chanted over sacred books whose tattered pages spread back through the centuries and out across the miles, to touch all Jews of all time. The gratification of obeying the myriad commandments, of living out the Law that penetrates every humble act of daily life. The tears of Yom Kippur are also part of Yiddishkayt, the beauty of the "sad holidays," the glad weeping at a daughter's wedding.

The complement of pain is in it, too, "the yoke" that glorifies as it oppresses, the pride of enduring persecution. Bound into the word is also proud pity for those who live without the light and who, in their darkness, fulfill the will of the Most High even as they oppress the children of Israel.

The word Yiddishkayt carries as an aura the veneration of learning, the acceptance of obligations, the inextinguishable hope of ultimate reward. And somewhere between its syllables flickers the wry, ironic acceptance of the price that must be paid for membership in Klal Isroel, a price acknowledged with tears, with groans, and with innumerable quips.

The word olam illustrates the kind of continuum native to shtetl thought and feeling. It suggests too the centering of the world in people, thoughts and feelings rather than in places or things. Olam means world, universe. It also means eternity, eternal. God has promised Olam Hazeh and Olam Habo, this world and the world to come. The same word, olam, means crowd, throng, people. "The whole olam was at shul today," one may say. World, eternity and people are one.

Whatever question may be raised about the genesis and interpretation of the continuum, a continuity has been maintained through long centuries. However the tradition may be defined, however its persistence may be explained, whatever future may be predicted for it, it has survived from biblical antiquity to the shtetl.

Throughout history, nations have had their national, cultural and religious centers located in their capitals. Athens, Rome, Byzantium, flourished and fell. The Jews, however, had their real center in the Torah, the Law. When their capital fell, they took the Law into Exile with them. The stronger the attack against it, the stronger the resistance that rose to meet it.

"God, Torah and Israel are one," says the tradition. That unity is complex and vibrant. Nevertheless, it has held, transcending limits and gaps in time and space. To explain the strength and persistence of the tradition by any single cause would violate the ethos of the shtetl. The cause is made up of many conflicting and interacting parts. Through the centuries, the tradition has been both tested and invigorated by the impact of influences from without. At various times and in various places they have given a stronger slant to one or another of its elements. They have evoked variations and modifications of the core culture. At various times, also, the outside influences have aroused a resistance that has given the culture strength and cohesiveness.

The shtetl is a product of the forces from within and from without. It follows the pattern of Jewish history, which is a history of acculturation. Response to the impact of other cultures is one of the inseparable components of Jewish culture. The resulting flexibility is one of its salient characteristics. The shtetl, with its wide variation of local pattern and its constant core of Yiddish-kayt, is as much in character in its responsiveness to the current environment as in its adherence to the age-old tradition.

BIBLIOGRAPHY

* In Yiddish.   ** In Hebrew.

ABRAHAMS, ISRAEL: *Jewish Life in The Middle Ages.* London, Goldston, 1932.

ABRAMOVITCH, HIRSCH: "Rural Jewish Occupations in Lithuania." *Yivo Annual of Jewish Social Science,* II–III: 205–221. New York, Yiddish Scientific Institute-Yivo, 1947–1948.

AGNON, SAMUEL JOSEPH: *Days of Awe.* New York, Schocken Books, 1948.

AIN, ABRAHAM: "Swislocz. Portrait of a Jewish Community in Eastern Europe." *Yivo Annual of Jewish Social Science,* IV: 86–114. New York, Yiddish Scientific Institute-Yivo, 1949.

AUSUBEL, NATHAN (ed.): *A Treasury of Jewish Folklore.* New York, Crown, 1948.

AYALTI, HANAN J. (ed.): *Yiddish Proverbs,* New York, Schocken Books, 1949.

BARON, SALO WITTMAYER: *A Social and Religious History of the Jews,* 3 vols. New York, Columbia University Press, 1937.

——: *The Jewish Community: Its History and Structure to the American Revolution,* 3 vols. Philadelphia, Jewish Publication Society of America, 1942.

BERNSTEIN, IGNATZ: *Yiddische Sprichwerter.** Warsaw, 1912.

BIBLE, *The Holy Scripture According to the Masoretic Text.* Philadelphia, Jewish Publication Society of America, 1946.

BOGEN, BORIS A.: *Jewish Philanthropy,* New York, Macmillan, 1917.

BRAM, JOSEPH: "The Social Identity of the Jews." *Transactions of the New York Academy of Sciences,* Series II, VI: 194–199, 1944.

BUBER, MARTIN (ed.): *Tales of the Hasidim: The Early Masters.* New York, Schocken Books, 1947.

——: *Tales of the Hassidim: The Later Masters.* New York, Schocken Books, 1948.

COHEN, ABRAHAM: *Everyman's Talmud.* New York, Dutton, 1949.

COHEN, ISRAEL: *Jewish Life in Modern Times.* London, Methuen & Co., 1929.

DUBNOW, SEMEN MARKOWICH: *History of the Jews in Russia and Poland . . . Until the Present Day,* 3 vols. Philadelphia, Jewish Publication Society of America, 1916–20.

DUBNOW, SHYMON: *Geshikhte fun Khasidism* (History of Hassidism),* 2 vols. Vilno, B. Kleckin, 1931–1933.

EISENSTEIN, J. D.: *Ozar Dinim u- Minhagim.* A Digest of Jewish Laws and Customs in Alphabetic Order.** New York, Hebrew Publ. Co., 1938.

EPSTEIN, LOUIS M.: *Sex Laws and Customs in Judaism.* New York, Bloch Publishing Co., 1948.

FELDMAN, W. M.: *The Jewish Child*. London, Baillière, Tindall and Cox, 1917.

FINKELSTEIN, LOUIS (ed.): *The Jews: Their History, Culture and Religion*, 2 vols. New York, Harper, 1949.

FINKIELSTEIN, LEO: *Meguilath Poilin* (Scroll of Poland)*. Buenos Aires, 1947.

FISHBERG, M.: *The Jews: A Study of Race and Environment*. New York, Walter Scott Publ. Co., 1911.

FRIEDLANDER, M.: *The Jewish Religion*. 7th ed., revised and enlarged. London, Shapiro, Valentine & Co., 1937.

GANZFRIED, SALOMON: *Code of Jewish Law* (Kitzur Schulchan Aruch; Hyman E. Goldin, tr.). New York, Hebrew Publishing Co., 1927.

GINZBERG, LOUIS: *The Legends of The Jews,* 7 vols. Philadelphia, Jewish Publication Society, 1909–1938.

GOLDIN, HYMAN E.: *The Jewish Woman and Her Home*. New York, Jewish Culture Publishing Company, 1941.

HERTZ, JOSEPH H.: *The Authorized Daily Prayer Book*. Revised Edition. Hebrew Text, English Translation with Commentary and Notes. New York, Bloch Publishing Co., 1948.

HESCHEL, ABRAHAM JOSHUA: *The Earth Is the Lord's: The Inner World of the Jew in East Europe*. New York, H. Schuman, 1950.

The Jewish People, Past and Present. Jewish Encyclopedic Handbooks, 2 vols. New York, Central Yiddish Culture Organizations (CYCO), 1946–1948.

JIGGETS, J. IDA: *Religion, Diet and Health of Jews*. 2 vols. New York, Bloch Publ. Co., 1949.

JOFFE, NATALIE F.: "The Dynamics of Benefice Among East European Jews." *Social Forces,* XXVII: 238–247, 1949.

KHAYES, KH.: "Beliefs and Customs In Connection With Death."* *Yiddish Scientific Institute, Studies in Philology,* II: 281–328, 1930.

LANDES, RUTH, and ZBOROWSKI, MARK: "Hypotheses Concerning the Eastern European Jewish Family." *Psychiatry,* XIII: 447–464, 1950.

LESTSCHINSKY, JACOB: *Oifn Rand fun Opgrunt* (Al Borde del Abismo).* Buenos Aires, 1947.

LEVITATS, ISAAC: *The Jewish Community in Russia, 1772–1844*. New York, Columbia University Press, 1943.

LILIENTAL, REGINA: "Evil Eye."* *Yiddishe filologye, The Journal of Yiddish Philology,* I: 245–271, 1924.

——: "Das Kind bei den Juden." *Mitteilungen zur Jüdischen Volkskunde,* XXV: 1–24; XXVI: 41–55, 1908.

MAIMON, SALOMON BEN JOSHUA: *An Autobiography;* ed. and with an Epilogue by Moses Hadas (tr. by J. Clark Murray). New York, Schocken Books, 1947.

NEWMAN, LOUIS: *The Hassidic Anthology*. Tales and Teachings of the Hassidim Translated from the Hebrew, Yiddish and German. New York, Bloch Publishing Co., 1934.

NEWMAN, LOUIS I. and FRITZ, SAMUEL (eds.): *The Talmudic Anthology*. New York, Behrman, 1945.

OLSVANGER, IMMANUEL: *Rosinkess Mit Mandlen*. Aus der Volksliteratur der Ostjuden. Schwänke, Erzählungen, Sprichwörter und Rätsel. 2. Auflage, Basel, 1931.

PHILIPSON, DAVID: *Old European Jewries*. Philadelphia, Jewish Publication Society of America, 1894.

RUBINOW, I. M.: "Economic Conditions of the Jews in Russia. Dep. of Commerce and Labor. *Bulletin of the Bureau of Labor*" No. 72. Washington, Government Printing Office, 1907.

RUPPIN, A.: *Die Soziologie der Juden*. 2 vols. Berlin, Jüdischer Verlag, 1930–31.

SAMUEL, MAURICE: *The World of Sholom Aleichem*. New York, Knopf, 1943.

SCHARFSTEIN, ZEVI: *Toldoth Ha-Hinukh Be-Israel Be-Doroth Ha-Hakhronim* (History of Jewish Education in Modern Times),** 2 vols. New York, Histadruth Ivrith of America, 1945–47.

SCHAUSS, CHAIM: "The Birth of a Jewish Child."* *Yivo Bleter*, XVII: 47–63, 1941.

SCHAUSS, HAYYIM: *The Jewish Festivals From Their Beginnings To Our Own Days*. Cincinnati, Union of America Hebrew Congregation, 1938.

——: *The Lifetime of a Jew Throughout the Ages of Jewish History*. Cincinnati, Union of American Hebrew Congregation, 1950.

SHTERN, YEKHIEL: "A Kheyder in Tyszowce (Tishevits)." *Yivo Annual of Jewish Social Science*, V: 85–171. New York, Yiddish Scientific Institute-Yivo, 1950.

STUTCHKOFF, NAHUM: *Der Oytser Fun Der Yiddisher Shprach* (Thesaurus of the Yiddish Language).* Ed. by M. Weinreich, New York, Yiddish Scientific Institute-Yivo, 1950.

TRUNK, J. J.: *Poilen* (Poland),* 4 vols. New York, Unzer Tsait, 1946–1949.

WEINREICH, URIEL: *College Yiddish. An Introduction to the Yiddish Language and to Jewish Life and Culture*. New York, Yiddish Scientific Institute-Yivo, 1949.

WIRTH, LOUIS: *The Ghetto*. Chicago, University of Chicago Press, 1928.

YSANDER, TORSTEN: *Studien zum Bescht'schen Hassidismus*. Upsala, A.-B. Lundequistska Bokhandeln, 1933.

ZBOROWSKI, MARK: "The Place of Book-Learning in Traditional Jewish Culture." *Harvard Educational Review*, XIX: 97–109, 1949.

——: "The Children of the Covenant." *Social Forces*, XXIX: 351–364, 1951.

GLOSSARY

The system of transliteration generally followed is that used by the Yiddish Scientific Institute—Yivo, in New York City. However, the authors have made two major modifications: doubling of the consonant in order to encourage the correct pronunciation of the preceding vowel, and adding an "h" after a final "e" in order to prevent its being interpreted as silent. For a few words which are familiar in English the most common spelling has been retained, and the Yiddish pronunciation is given in parentheses. For certain words known in their Sephardic pronunciation, such as ritual objects or names of holidays, this pronunciation is also given in parentheses, after the abbreviation "Heb.", which indicates that the origin of the word is Hebrew.

The literal translation, often the original meaning of the word, is given in parentheses.

Key to Pronunciation

a—ă as in *palm*		o—ō as in *bold*
ay—ī as in *fine*		oy—oi as in *poise*
e—ĕ as in *end*		u—ōō as in *noon*
ey—ā as in *late*		kh—ch as in German *ach*
i—ĭ as in *pity*		s—s as in *soon*

AFIKOMEN (Heb.)—(Dessert). Pieces of matsos hidden during the seder to be eaten at the end of the seder meal.

AGADA (Heb.)—(Tale, story). Part of Talmud which explains the Torah homiletically through legends and stories.

AGUNA (Heb.)—Deserted wife.

ALIYAH (Heb.)—(Elevation). Calling to the reading of the weekly portion of the Torah.

ALTEH MOYD—Old maid, spinster.

AMKHO (Heb.)—(Thy people). Common people.

AMORETS (Heb. *Am ha-Harez*)—(People of the land, peasants). Ignoramus, boor.

APIKOYRES (Heb. *Apikoros*)—Skeptic; freethinker; heretic.

ARBA KANFOS (Heb.)—(Four corners). A ritual undergarment with fringes at its four corners worn by male Jews.

ASHKENAZ—Hebrew name for Germany.

ASHKENAZI, pl. ASHKENAZIM—Originally German Jews, later all Eastern European Jews.

AZZES PONIM (Heb. *Azuth panim*)—(Insolence, effrontery). A man who is arrogant, brazen-faced.

AVEYREH (Heb.)—Transgression; sin.

BAAL TOYREH (Heb. *Baal Torah*)—(Master of Law). Learned man, scholar.

BAAL TSDOKEH (Heb.)—(Master of righteousness). A charitable person; a person who distributes charity.

BAAL YIKHUS (Heb.)—(Master of pedigree). Man with learned or rich people in his genealogy.

BAAL ZKHUS (Heb.)—(Master of merit). A person who has accumulated heavenly merits through study or good deeds.

BADKHEN (Heb.)—Jester; entertainer at weddings.

BALEBATISHEH YIDN, sing. BALEBATISHER YID—Men of substance and good standing in the community.

BALEBATISHKAYT—Household, property, substance. Respectability.

BALEBOS, pl. BALEBATIM (Heb. *Baal ha-baith*)—(Master of the house). Householder, burgher, man of substance; owner, proprietor; boss.

BALEBOSTEH—Housewife; matron; mistress of the house.

BALEGOLEH (Heb. *Baal Agalah*)—(Master of the wagon). Coachman.

BAR MITZVAH (Heb.)—(Son of the Commandment). A religious ceremony by which a male Jew at the age of thirteen becomes a formal member of the community.

BATLN, pl. BATLONIM (Heb.)—Loafer; idler.

BELFER—Assistant to the melamed, usually in charge of small children.

BEN TOYREH (Heb. *Ben Torah*)—(Son of Torah). A learned man, a scholar.

BEN ZOKHER (Heb.)—(Male child). A celebration on the first Friday night following the birth of a son.

BESDIN (Heb. *Beth Din*)—(House of judgment, of law). Religious court presided over by the rabbi or his assistant.

BESMEDRESH (Heb. *Beth Hamidrash*)—(House of study). Place for religious services and study; synagogue.

BEYGL—Hard ring-shaped roll, first boiled then baked.

BEYGELEH—Small beygl.

BEYS YESOYMIM (Heb.)—(House of orphans). Orphanage. Community organization in charge of the orphanage.

BEYTLER—Beggar, mendicant.

BIKKUR KHOYLIM—(Visiting the sick). The divine commandment to visit the sick; community organization to assist sick paupers.

BIMAH (Heb.)—An elevated platform in the center of the synagogue where the Torah is read.

BITOKHEN (Heb. *Bitakhon*)—Hope, faith.

BLINTSES—Cheese, groats, or berries rolled in dough and fried in fat.

BOBEH—Grandmother; granny.

BRIFSHTELER—Book containing a collection of master forms for letters for various occasions.

BRIS (Heb. *Brith*)—Covenant; the act and ceremony of circumcision.

BRIS MILA—(Covenant by circumcision). The act and ceremony of circumcision.

BUND—Jewish social democratic worker's party.

CHOLENT—Sabbath dish prepared the day before from potatoes, groats and fat.

DARDEKI KHEYDER (Heb.)—Elementary religious school where small children are taught the alphabet, reading and prayers.

DAYAN (Heb.)—Judge. Assistant to the rabbi.

DAYTSH—German; German Jew; a progressive or assimilated Jew.

DEREKH (Heb.)—Way. The special way or system of a Hassidic leader.

DEREKH ERETS (Heb.)—(The way of the land). Respect; good manners.

DER OYBERSHTER IN HIML—(The Highest One in Heaven). God.

DIASPORA—Exile; dispersion of Jews after the conquest of Palestine by the Romans in 70 A.D.

DROSHEH (Heb.)—Address, speech, sermon, interpretation; a scholarly interpretation of a talmudic problem.

DROSHEH GESHANK—Gift given to the married couple at the wedding after the bridegroom delivers his speech; wedding gift.

DYBBUK (Heb.)—A condemned soul which gets hold of a living person and acts or speaks through him.

EMESS (Heb.)—Truth.

EMESSER—True; real.

EREV (Heb.)—(Evening). Eve.

EREV SHABBES—Sabbath eve.

EREV YONTEV—Holiday eve.

ERLIKHER, pl. ERLIKHEH—Pious; honest.

ES PAST NISHT—It is not becoming.

ESROG (Heb.)—Citron used for the ritual of Sukkos.

EYDELER, pl. EYDELEH—Fine, refined.

EXTERNIK—A person who prepares for his secondary school examination and degree without attending courses.

EYRUV (Heb.)—Symbolic act by which a fiction of continuity is established; an act by which the public domain becomes private property for the Sabbath.

EZRAS NOSHIM (Heb.)—Women's section in the synagogue.

FAR YONTEV—Before the holiday.

FARZESSENEH—(One who is left sitting). An unmarried girl, spinster, old maid.

FAYNER, pl. FAYNEH—Fine.

FELTSHER, f. FELTSHERKEH—Medical attendant; doctor's assistant; medical practitioner without a university training.

FINGERNAIL WATER—The first ritual ablution in the morning upon rising.

FLEYSHIK—Pertaining to meat; meat dishes.

GABAI, pl. GABOYIM (Heb.)—Synagogue trustee; synagogue manager; public officer; Tsaddik's attendant.

GALITSIANER—Jewish native of Galicia (province of Poland which before World War I was part of Austrian Empire).

GAN EYDEN (Heb.)—Paradise.

GANEF (Heb.)—Thief.

GANTSER MENTSH—A whole man, a complete man; an adult.

GAON (Heb.)—(Majesty). Genius. Title originally given to the chief of the rabbinical academy in Babylon. Outstanding scholar.

GEBENTSHT MIT KINDER—Blessed with children.

GEHINOM (Heb.)—Hell.

GEMARA (Heb.—Yid. *Gemoreh*)—Part of the Talmud which consists of the interpretation and discussion of the law as presented in the Mishna.

GEMOREH KHEYDER—Higher grade school for children basically devoted to the study of the Talmud.

GESHEFT—Business.

GEYDER (Heb.)—(Fence). Secondary preventive law against violating the original commandment.

GEZUNT—Health.

GMILUS KHEYSED (Heb.)—(Bestowing of loving kindness). Divine commandment of bestowing loving kindness on fellow men; charity; communal loan association; a temporary loan.

GOLUS (Heb. *Galuth*)—Diaspora, Exile. The period of Jewish history after the destruction of the Temple in 70 A.D.

GOTT—God.

GOTT VET SHTROFN—God will punish.

GOY, pl. GOYIM—People; nation. Gentile.

GOYISH—Like Gentiles; un-Jewish.

GRUSHA—Woman divorced from her husband.

GUTE VOKH—Good week! A greeting expressed at the end of Sabbath, the beginning of the week.

GUT SHABBES—Good Sabbath! Sabbath greeting.

GUT YONTEV—Good holiday! Holiday greeting.

HADRAS PONIM (Heb.)—(Adornment of the face). Beard; beauty of the face.

HAFTORAH (Heb.—Yid. *Haftoyreh*)—Selections from the Prophets read after the weekly portion of the Torah.

HAGGADAH (Heb.—Yid. *Hagodeh*)—Historical recitals, prayers and songs read during the evening meals on the first two nights of Passover.

HAKHNOSSES KALEH (Heb.)—(Taking in of the bride). Divine commandment to dower the bride; communal organization to provide poor brides with dowry.

HAKHNOSSES ORKHIM (Heb.)—Sheltering the transient. Commandment to provide poor transients with shelter and food. Hospitality. Communal organization which takes care of transients.

HALAKHA (Heb.—Yid. *Halokheh*)—Legal part of the Talmud.

HALLAH (Heb.—Yid. *Khaleh*)—Sabbath loaf. The commandment to sacrifice by burning a piece of dough from the baked bread.

HAMOYN (Heb.)—Crowd; mob.

HANUKAH—Holiday commemorating the victory of the Maccabbees.

HANUKAH GELT—Money gifts given to children on Hanukah.

HASKALA (Heb.—Yid. *Haskoleh*)—Enlightenment; a philosophical sociocultural trend in the seventeenth century promoting the secularization of Jewish life.

HASSID, pl. HASSIDIM (Heb.—Yid. *Khossid*)—(Pious). Follower or member of the Hassidic movement.

HASSIDISM (Yid. *Khsidus*)—A religious movement founded by Israel Baal Shem Tov in the seventeenth century.

HAVDOLAH (Heb.)—(Separation). Religious ceremony concluding the Sabbath and introducing the week, which marks the separation between the holiness of the Sabbath and the profanity of the week. The benedictions and prayers recited at the exit of the Sabbath over wine, spices and candles.

HEKDESH (Heb.)—(That which is dedicated to a sacred purpose). City hospice for paupers (col. slum).

HOYF—Court, yard. Residence of a Hassidic leader or Rebbeh.

HOYZ—House.

ILUY (Heb.)—(Superior). Genius; an outstanding scholar.

IM EYN KEMAKH EYN TORAH (Heb.)—If there is no bread there is no (study of) Torah.

IVREH—Hebrew text; reading a Hebrew text.

IVREH TAYTSH—Translation of a Hebrew text into Yiddish. The Yiddish language.

KADDISH (Heb.)—The mourner's prayer after the death of a close relative, usually after death of a parent; the son who recites the prayer after the death of his parent.

KAHAL (Heb.)—Congregation, community. Jewish community organization.

KALEH (Heb.)—Bride.

KALEH MOYD—A girl of marriageable age.

KAPTSN (Heb.)—Pauper, a poor man.

KAPTSN IN ZIBN POLESS—(Pauper in seven edges). A very poor man.

KASHRUS (Heb. *Kashruth*)—Religious dietary laws.

KEHILEH (Heb.)—Community, congregation. Community organization.

KEST—Free board and lodging given to the young married couple by the bride's parents for a certain period of time after marriage, as stipulated in the marriage contract.

KEYLEH (Heb.)—Vessel, container. A learned man.

KHABAD—Abbreviation for Khokhma, Bina, Daath—wisdom, understanding, knowledge. A Hassidic system developed in Lithuania.

KHARIF (Heb.)—Sharp, acute, pungent. An outstanding scholar.

KHAY (Heb.)—Living; to be alive.

KHAZOKEH (Heb. *Hazakah*)—Law of possession. Claim based on undisturbed possession during a certain legal time.

KHEVREH, pl. KHEVROS (Heb. *Hevrah*)—Companionship, brotherhood team, association, congregation.

KHEVREH KADISHA—(The holy congregation). Any association devoted to the fulfillment of some divine commandment. The burial society.

KHEVREH MISHNAYES—Association of students of the Mishna.

KHEYDER (Heb. *Heder*)—Elementary religious school.

KHEYREM (Heb. *Herem*)—Excommunication.

KHIDDUSH, pl. KHIDDUSHIM (Heb.)—Novel interpretation, a new idea.

KHOKHMEH (Heb.)—Wisdom, wit, cleverness, intelligence.

KHOMETS (Heb. *Hametz*)—Unleavened. Food and dishes unfit for use on Passover.

KHOSSEN (Heb.)—Bridegroom, fiancé.

KHOSSEN BOKHER—A groom-boy; an adolescent at the marriageable age.

KHUMESH (Heb. *Hamesh*)—(Five). The five books of Moses. Pentateuch.

KHUPA (Heb.)—Canopy. Wedding. Marriage.

KHUTSPEH (Heb.)—Boldness, impudence.

KIDDUSH (Heb.)—Blessing over a cup of wine consecrating the Sabbath or holiday.

KIDDUSH HASHEM (Heb.)—(Holiness of the Name). Death for a holy cause.

KIMPETORN—Woman in labor or immediately after the delivery.

KINDER—Children.

KITTL—White garment worn by the pious at a festive occasion.

KLAL ISROEL—(The all of Israel). The entire Jewish people the world over.

KLAYBN NAKHES—(To gather joy). To enjoy.

KLEY KODESH (Heb.)—(Holy tools). Religious officers of the community: the rabbi, the cantor and the ritual slaughterer.

KNIPPL—Knot in the handkerchief used as a purse.

KOHEN, pl. KOHANIM—Priest. Member of the tribe of priests, which is one of the traditional subdivisions of the Jews.

KOL NIDRE (Heb.)—A solemn prayer which introduces the Day of Atonement.

KOP—Head. Wise man, clever man, bright man.

KOSHER (Heb.)—Ritually fit to use. Food prepared according to the dietary laws.

KOVED (Heb. *Kavod*)—Honor, respect, deference.

KREPLAKH—Dough stuffed with meat and boiled.

KRISHMEH (Heb. *Kriath Shemah*)—(Reading of the Shema). Prayer beginning with the words "Hear oh Israel . . ." Prayer before going to sleep.

KUK—Look.

KVATER, f. KVATERIN—God-father.

KVITL—Note. A written request presented to the Hassidic leader.

LAG BA OMER (Heb.)—(Thirty days in Omer). Mid-spring harvest holiday.

LAMDN (Heb.)—Erudite, scholar.

LAYT—People.

LEHAVDL (Heb.)—(To separate, to differentiate). An expression used when sacred and profane are mentioned together.

LEKHAYIM (Heb.)—To life!

LERNER—A studious person.

LEVI, pl. LEVIYIM—Levite. Member of the tribe of Levi. One of the three traditional subdivisions of Jews.

LILITH—According to the mystical tradition, Adam's first wife, who steals new-born babies. A witch.

LITVAK—Jew from Lithuania.

LUFTMENTSH—(Airman). A man without a steady occupation who makes a living from undefinable sources.

LULAV (Heb.)—Palm branches used for the Sukkos ritual.

MAASSIM TOVIM (Heb.)—Good deeds.

MAFTIR (Heb.)—One who reads the weekly selection of the Prophets after the reading of the Torah.

MAGEYFEH (Heb.)—Plague, epidemic.

MAGGID, pl. MAGGIDIM (Heb.)—Preacher, speaker.

MAKHER—"Fixer."

MAKHN FUN KINDER MENTSHEN—To make people out of children. To make children into people.

MALBISH ARUMIM (Heb.)—(Clothing the naked). Communal association providing clothing to poor people.

MAMMEH—Mother, mommy.

MASKIL, pl. MASKILIM (Heb.)—(The enlightened one). Erudite. Follower of the Haskalah.

MASMID (Heb.)—A studious student.

MATSO, pl. MATSOS (Heb.)—Unleavened bread eaten during Passover.

MAZL (Heb.)—Luck.

MAZLTOV (Heb.)—Good luck!

MEGILLAH (Heb.)—Scroll. Book of Esther read on Purim.

MEKHUTN, pl. MEKHUTONIM (Heb.)—Relatives through marriage.

MELAMED (Heb.)—Teacher. Usually elementary teacher.

MELITS YOYSHER (Heb.)—One who pleads in defense; intercessor.

MENTSH, pl. MENTSHEN, LAYT—Man, human being, person.

MENUKHAS SHABBES (Heb.)—Sabbath rest.

MESHUGGENER, pl. MESHUGGENEH—Crazy, insane.

MESHUMED (Heb.)—Jew converted to Christianity; apostate.

MEYVN (Heb.)—Expert, connoisseur.

MEZUZAH (Heb.)—Portions of the Pentateuch, encased in a small box and attached to the doorpost of a Jewish home.

MIKVA (Heb.)—Pool for ritual purification. Ritual bath.

MILKHIK—Dairy; pertaining to dairy food.

MINYAN (Heb.)—Quorum of ten males for public religious services.

MISHNA (Yid. *Mishnayes*)—Collection of the oral Law which is the basis of the Talmud.

MISHPOKHEH (Heb.)—Family; relatives.

MISNAGED, pl. MISNAGDIM (Heb.)—(Opponent). Anti-Hassid.

MITSVA, pl. MITSVOS (Heb. *Mizvoth*)—Divine commandment; good deed; merit.

MIZRAKH (Heb.)—East; the eastern wall in the synagogue toward which Jews are oriented during the prayers; place of honor in the synagogue; honorable citizens of the community. A symbolic picture or embroidery which designates the eastern wall in the room.

MLAVEH MALKEH (Heb.)—(Escorting the Queen). The last festive meal at the exit of the Sabbath.

MOES KHITTIN (Heb.)—Provisions for Passover distributed among poor members of the community; communal organization to provide for this distribution.

MOHEL (Heb.)—Circumciser.

MOYKHER SFORIM (Heb.)—Book dealer.

MOYSHEV ZKEYNIM—Old people's home.

NAKHES (Heb.)—Comfort, gratification, pleasure, joy.

NASHERAY—Delicacy.

NASHN—To nibble a delicacy.

NIGN (Heb.)—Melody; tune.

NOGID, pl. NEGIDIM (Heb.)—Leader; important member of the community.

NOKH YONTEV—After the holiday.

NSHOMEH YESEYREH (Heb.)—Additional soul which, according to mystical tradition, is added to man on Sabbath.

OKER HORIM (Heb.)—(Uprooter of mountains). Outstanding scholar.

OL (Heb.)—Yoke. Duty. Obligation.

OLAM (Heb.)—Universe; world; eternity; people.

OLAM HABO (Heb.)—World to come.

OLAM HAZEH (Heb.)—This world.

ONEG SHABBES (Heb.)—(Delight of Sabbath). Enjoyment of Sabbath.

OPGEKUMMENER—A formerly rich man who lost his wealth.

OPSHPREKHER—A person who knows how to counteract the effects of the evil eye. Charmer.

OSHANAH RABAH—Seventh day of the Feast of Booths.

OVOS (Heb. *Abboth*)—Fathers; ancestors.

OYFGEKUMMENER—Nouveau riche, parvenu.

OYREKH (Heb.)—Transient; guest.

OYS—Out.

OYZER DALIM—Comforter of the poor; society to help poor members of the community.

PARNOSSEH (Heb.)—Livelihood; earning a living; occupation, trade.

PARVEH—Foods which are neither meat nor dairy, such as fruits, vegetables.

PEKUAKH NEFESH (Heb.)—Saving life from danger. Mortal danger.

PESAKH (Yid. *Peysakh*)—Passover. Spring holiday commemorating the Exodus from Egypt.

PEYOS (Heb.)—Earlocks.

PEYSAKHDIK, pl. PEYSAKHDIKEH—Pertaining to Passover. Chiefly foods and dishes.

PIDYAN (Heb.)—(Redemption). A certain amount of money given to the Tsaddik after consulting him.

PIDYAN HABEN (Heb.)—(Redemption of the son). A sum of money paid by the father of the firstborn son to a Kohen, to redeem the child from services in the Temple. Celebration held four weeks after the birth of the first male child.

PILPUL (Heb.)—(Pepper). A complicated scholarly interpretation of a rabbinical text.

PNEY (Heb.)—(Faces). The most distinguished members of the community.

POLIN (Heb.)—(Here thou shalt rest). Hebrew name for Poland.

PRISBEH—An embankment around the house.

PROST—Simple, common, vulgar.

PROSTAK—An ignorant boor.

PROSTEH YIDN, sing. PROSTER YID—Simple people, common people; vulgar, "low class" people.

PURIM—Holiday commemorating the defeat of Haman described in the Book of Esther.

RAKHMONES (Heb.)—Pity; mercy; commiseration; compassion.

REB (Heb.)—Teacher; title given to a learned and respected man. Used as an equivalent of mister.

REBBEH (Heb.)—Teacher; title given to a learned man. Usual title of a Hassidic leader.

REBBETSN—Wife of a teacher. Wife of a rabbi. Wife of a Hassidic leader.

ROSH HASHANAH (Heb.—Yid. *Roshhashoneh*)—(Beginning of the Year). Fall holiday celebrating the beginning of the Jewish New Year.

ROV (Heb.)—Rabbi.

RUSALKEH—Mermaid.

SANDEK (Heb.)—Syndicus. The person who holds the child during the ceremony of circumcision.

SEDER (Heb.)—(Order.) The festive meal on the two first evenings of Passover.

SEYFER, pl. SFORIM (Heb.)—Book. Books in Hebrew with a religious content.

SEYKHL (Heb.)—Intelligence, wit; good sense.

SEPHARAD—Hebrew name for Spain.

SEPHARDI, pl. SEPHARDIM—Spanish Jews.

SHABBES—Sabbath.

SHABBES GOY (Heb.)—A Christian who on Sabbath does work which is prohibited to Jews. A Jew who desecrates the Sabbath.

SHABBESDIK—Pertaining to Sabbath.

SHADAY (Heb.)—Almighty; Eternal. One of God's names.

SHADKHEN (Heb.)—Matchmaker; marriage broker.

SHALAKHMONES (Heb.)—Gifts exchanged during Purim.

SHAMMES (Heb.)—Servant. Synagogue servant; sexton, beadle.

SHEYN—Beautiful, fine.

SHEYNEH YIDN, sing. SHEYNER YID—(Beautiful Jews.) Upper-class Jews.

SHEYTL—Wig worn by orthodox married women.

SHEPN NAKHES—Enjoy; gather joy; gather pleasure.

SHEVUOS (Heb. *Shavuoth*)—Feast of Weeks. Pentecost. Holiday commemorating the giving of the Torah to Moses.

SHEYDIM (Heb.)—Ghosts, evil spirits; devils.

SHIDDUKH (Heb.)—Match, marriage.

SHIVEH (Heb.)—(Seven). Seven days of intensive mourning after the death of a close relative (parent, wife, child, sibling).

SHKOTSIM, sing. SHEYGETS—Gentile boys.

SHLOSHIM (Heb.)—(Thirty). Thirty days of less intensive mourning following the shiveh.

SHMALTS—Fat. Usually chicken or goose fat.

SHNORER—Beggar.

SHOFAR (Heb.)—Horn which is blown on New Year's Day as part of the ritual.

SHOKHET (Heb.)—Ritual slaughterer.

SHOLEM (Heb. *Shalom*)—Peace. Health.

SHOLEM ALEIKHEM—Peace to you! Usual greeting.

SHOLEM BAYIS (Heb.)—Peace of the house; domestic harmony.

SHOLEM ZOKHER (Heb.)—(Peace of the male). Celebration following the birth of a male child.

SHRAYIM (Heb.)—Leftovers from the Tsaddik's meal, which are distributed to or taken by his followers.

SHTADLAN (Heb.)—Solicitor; interceder. One who uses his influence with the government for the welfare of the community.

SHTETL—Small town, village, townlet.

SHTOT BALEBOS—City boss.

SHTROF—Punishment.

SHUL—Synagogue; school.

SHULKHAN ARUKH—*The Set Table*. Title of the most popular compendium of rabbinical law, by Joseph Caro.

SIMKHAS TORAH—(Rejoicing of the Torah). The eighth day of the Feast of Tabernacles, when the annual cycle of the reading of the Law begins.

SIYUM (Heb.)—Conclusion, completion.

SOYFER (Heb.)—Scribe whose chief occupation is to transcribe the scrolls of the Torah.

SUKKAH (Heb.)—Booth; a wooden construction covered with branches.

SUKKOS (Heb. *Sukkoth*)—Feast of Booths, Feast of Tabernacles, Fall harvest holiday.

SYAG (Heb.)—(Fence). Preventive religious regulations.

TAKHLIS (Heb.)—Goal, purpose, sense.

TALIS (Heb. *Talith*)—Prayer shawl worn by male Jews during prayers.

TALIS KOTON (Heb.)—(Small talis). A ritual fringed undergarment worn by orthodox male Jews.

TALMID KHOKHEM (Heb.)—Wise student. Scholar.

TALMUD—The basic body of Jewish oral law consisting of the interpretation of laws contained in the Torah.

TALMUD TOYREH (Heb. *Talmud Torah*)—The commandment to study the Law. An educational institution for orphans' and poor children, supported by the community.

TATEH—Father.

TATEH-MAMMEH—Parents.

TEFILLIM (Heb.)—Phylacteries. Leather cases containing quotations from the Pentateuch, worn by Jews on the forehead and on the left arm during morning prayers.

TEYGLAKH—Small pellets of dough boiled in honey.

TISHEH B'AV (Heb.)—(Nine Days in Av). Fast commemorating the destruction of the Temple in 70 A.D.

TKHINOS (Heb.)—Devotional literature for women, usually in Yiddish.

TORAH (Yid. *Toyreh*)—The Teachings. The Law. The Old Testament. The entire body of Jewish wisdom.

TOYREH—Teachings of a Hassidic leader.

Treyf (Heb.)—Impure. Unfit for consumption. Contrary to the dietary laws.

Treyf possl (Heb.)—Impure and forbidden. Forbidden literature.

Tsaddik, pl. Tsaddikim. (Heb.)—(The just). The saint. The righteous. A Hassidic leader.

Tsdokeh (Heb.)—Righteousness; justice; charity.

Tsdokeh beseyter (Heb.)—Charity distributed anonymously, secretly.

Tshuva (Heb.)—Repentance.

Tsores (Heb.)—Troubles, miseries.

Vaikro (Heb.)—(And He has called). The title of the third Book of Moses—Leviticus.

Vokh—Week.

Vokhendik—Weekly; opposed to the spirit of Sabbath or holiday.

Vokhendikeh mentshen—People of the week.

Yarmelkeh—Skull cap worn by religious Jews in order to have the head covered at all times.

Yeshiva (Heb.)—Rabbinical academy.

Yeshiva bokher—A student of a rabbinical academy.

Yid, pl. Yidn—Jew.

Yiddish—Jewish. In Jewish language. Vernacular spoken by Eastern European Jews.

Yiddishkayt—Jewishness. Jewish way of life.

Yikhus (Heb.)—Pedigree, lineage. High status based chiefly on scholarship or wealth of ancestors or relatives.

Yikhus atsmo (Heb.)—Status acquired by one's own efforts.

Yikhus ovos (Heb.)—Status based on genealogy.

Yom Kippur (Heb.)—Day of Atonement; Day of Pardon. The most solemn holiday and fast.

Yontev (Heb. *Yom tov*)—Holiday.

Yoysher (Heb.)—Righteousness, justice, fairness.

Zeydeh—Grandfather.

Zivug (Heb.)—Match; couple; marriage.

Zkhus (Heb.)—Merit. The protecting influence of good deeds. Advantage, privilege.

Zkhus ovos (Heb.)—The merits of one's ancestors.

Zmiros (Heb.)—Songs recited after a Sabbath meal.

Znakhor—Charmer.

Zogerkeh—A woman who leads the prayers in the women's section in the synagogue.

INDEX